Integrated Ascension

INTEGRATED ASCENSION

REVELATION FOR THE NEXT MILLENNIUM

Dr. Joshua David Stone
and
Janna Shelley Parker

Writers Club Press
San Jose New York Lincoln Shanghai

Integrated Ascension
Revelation for the Next Millennium

All Rights Reserved © 2001 by Dr. Joshua David Stone

No part of this book may be reproduced or transmitted
in any form or by any means, graphic, electronic, or mechanical,
including photocopying, recording, taping, or by any information
storage retrieval system, without the permission
in writing from the publisher.

Writers Club Press
an imprint of iUniverse.com, Inc.

For information address:
iUniverse.com, Inc.
5220 S 16th, Ste. 200
Lincoln, NE 68512
www.iuniverse.com

ISBN: 0-595-17013-7

Printed in the United States of America

Contents

1. Integrated Ascension 1
2. A Deeper Explanation of the Eight Quotients and How to Use Them 12
3. Integrating the Twelve Levels of Initiation into the Four-Body System 58
4. Integrating the Seven Rays and Ray Types 102
5. An Overview of Non-Integrated Ascension 126
6. The All Important Sub-Quotients 149
7. Transcending Negative Ego Archetypal Dualities 183
8. Integrated Ascension and Developing a Proper Relationship to the Inner Senses 194
9. A More Expansive Look at the Dangers of Non-Integrated Channeling, Clairaudience, and Clairvoyance 231
10. Dr. Lorphan's Healing Academy on Sirius 268
11. A Deeper & More Detailed Look at Some of the Major Healing Tools 287
12. Twilight Masters, Cults, and Non-Integrated Ascension Groups 314
13. How to Develop an Extremely High-Functioning Physical, Psychological & Spiritual Immune System 349
14. Integration of the Mahatma 361

15	The Power of the Spoken Word	394
16	World Service Meditations	399
17	Ascension in the Many Kingdoms of GOD	442
18	My Spiritual Mission and Purpose	491
	by Dr. Joshua David Stone	
About the Author		509

1

Integrated Ascension

This is a book I am incredibly excited to write about. This book may be one of the most important books of the entire series in the easy to read encyclopedias of the spiritual path. There is great interest in the Spiritual Movement, the Ascended Masters, Angels, cosmic beings, Extraterrestrials, other dimensions, passing initiations, building light quotient, channeling, and what I call the esoteric and ethereal aspect of life. The process of achieving one's ascension has a direct link to the experience and knowledge of these areas expertise. These subjects and this aspect of life hold great interest for me as well.

In this phase of Earth's history, characterized by enormously accelerated spiritual growth, there has been a growing concern welling up within me, and within the Cosmic Ascended Masters whom I work with, regarding a great focus among lightworkers on the spiritual aspect that is not properly balanced and integrated with the physical aspect of one's being. And, the truth is, the ascension and esoteric work is often seen as more glamorous and of greater interest. What is happening among lightworkers is that they are becoming a little top-heavy, with their spiritual bodies being far more advanced than their mental, emotional and physical vehicles.

We live in an extraordinary time in Earth's history. In the past what took Masters a whole lifetime to achieve spiritually can literally be attained in six months in some cases now. What lightworkers must understand is that the passing of initiations really has more to do with the amount of light quotient they are holding, and has very little to do with one's over all psycho/spiritual development. The achievement of ascension occurs at the completion of the 6th initiation. Liberation from the wheel of physical rebirth is achieved at the beginning of the 7th initiation. Completion of planetary ascension begins at the taking of the 10th initiation. This also begins the process of cosmic ascension as opposed to planetary ascension. The passing of initiations is extremely important; whether you have to reincarnate again will be determined by these initiations. The process of channeling, communicating with the Ascended Masters, the studying of occult literature, meditating, praying and all esoteric practices are extremely important. The only point I make here is that this work must be balanced with the appropriate psychological and physical earthly work to become a truly self-realized being.

Many lightworkers now are taking their higher initiations and achieving their ascension and liberation from the wheel of rebirth. This is good! Many lightworkers are even moving toward completing planetary ascension and beginning cosmic ascension. This is good as well. What is not good is that the mental, emotional and psychological selves are not evolving as quickly as the spiritual self. In the past, Masters needed a whole lifetime to complete just one initiation and had time for the psychological self to catch up with the spiritual self. With initiations being done now in six months to two years, there is less time for this proper integration to take place.

Spiritual growth, in truth, is very easy. Once you get into the ascension activation work that I have written about in my other books, speeding through your initiations and building light quotient is not that hard to do. In truth, the real core and foundation of the spiritual path is the psychological level.

Integrated Ascension

What is happening in the Spiritual Movement now on a massive scale is that a great many lightworkers are achieving their ascension and/or taking higher initiations and achieving liberation from the physical wheel of rebirth. However, they have not truly realized their ascension yet. To truly realize one's ascension, one must realize this spiritually, mentally, emotionally, etherically, physically, environmentally, socially, financially and/or on all levels and facets of one's being. I am not saying that one has to be perfect, but rather some overall sense of balance and integration needs to be achieved.

What is happening in the Spiritual Movement presently is that lightworkers, spiritual teachers, channels and healers, are taking the higher initiations—let's say even the 7th initiation. I ask you, my friends, what is the value of this—if a person takes their 7th initiation and achieves liberation from the physical wheel of rebirth and is still totally run by the negative ego, lower self, inner child, emotional body, desire body, and is filled with negative thoughts, and is basically not right with self? They may believe they are right with GOD and the Ascended Masters, but they are not right with self. As I wrote about in my book *Soul Psychology*, the single most important relationship in your life is *not* your relationship with GOD and the Ascended Masters, it is your relationship with your *self*. If you are not right with self, this wrong relationship with self will be projected onto every relationship in your life, including your relationship with GOD and the Ascended Masters. My friends and beloved readers, this corruption and contamination is taking place en masse in the spiritual movement at this time.

If a person does not develop a right relationship to self, their channelings will be totally corrupted. I don't care how famous they are, or how many books they have written, they will be channeling their own negative ego and personal agenda, and will not even realize it. All channeling is brought through the information banks, subconscious mind, mental body, emotional body, ray structure, programming, and personal lens of the channel. Lightworkers, with no judgment intended, are incredibly naive about this. Just because a person is clairaudient and says they can hear the Ascended Masters speaking to them, does not change the facts that I have just stated. The corruption I have seen in the spiritual movement on this point is monumental. Lightworkers give their power to external channels overall in a most unhealthy way. They think if it's channeled, it's true, and nothing can be farther from the truth. This point I'm making here is so important and there is such a lack of spiritual discernment on the part of lightworkers in this regard, that the Masters have asked me to write a new book this year entitled *Channeling and the Path of Ascension*, to explore this issue in all its ramifications.

The point I make here about channeling or clairaudience applies equally as well to the process of clairvoyance. The truth of the matter is that people don't see with their eyes, they see with their mind. Every person on planet Earth causes and sees their own reality by how they think. Every person either thinks and sees from the negative ego mind or the Christ mind, or some strange combination of both. The ideal is obviously to interpret life only from the Christ mind. If this is not the case on the psychological level all channeling, clairaudience and clairvoyance will be seen and interpreted through the negative ego filter. As my dear friend Djwhal Khul would say, "…ponder on this."

In my humble opinion, the single biggest problem and challenge in the Spiritual Movement is for lightworkers to learn to die to negative ego thinking and to learn to only interpret life from their Christ thinking. In my opinion, 98% of the lightworkers at this time do not have a firm handle on this lesson. The consequences are monumental. I cannot tell you how many high-level lightworkers I know who have failed at initiations 7, 8, 9, 10, and even 11, because of an inability to control their negative ego. This applies to many of the spiritual leaders in the New Age Movement as well. My beloved readers, I know that you know what I am speaking of here, for I know many of you have shared the same concerns.

What does it matter if one is an Ascended Master and high level initiate if one is on a massive ego trip? Below is a list of a few of the negative ego corruptions that are taking place all too often. Self-aggrandizement, self-centeredness, filled with negative emotion, inability to get along with people, inability to pass the tests of money, fame, sexuality, pride and greed, dishonesty with self and others, full of attack thoughts, and expressing competition, jealousy, envy, divisiveness and judgmentalness. In addition, many are unloving, cannot own their inner stuff, are on a power trip, are seperative, backbiting, uncooperative, philosophically off-kilter, a dictator and an emotional victim. The amazing thing about this process is that most of the time these individuals are 100% completely unaware that this is taking place. If you ask them about their psychological development they will say, "I mastered that level in the Spring of '72, and I'm totally clear on that level." They will often also say, "That is a lower level that I don't have to deal with!"

I know, my beloved readers, you have seen the same things that I speak of here. I do not say these things to be judgmental, but rather to bring the sword of discernment into a very dangerous pattern and trend that the inner plane Ascended Masters are very concerned about.

His Holiness the Lord Sai Baba has said that the definition of GOD is, "GOD equals man minus ego." Notice he did not say, GOD equals 7th initiation. In my work in the Melchizedek Synthesis Ashram I do not care so much about people's initiation level; what I am looking for in the people who work here is egolessness, selflessness, devotion to the Masters, Christ consciousness, purity, unconditional love, and comfort in their own right puzzle piece. I would much rather have a 4th degree initiate working here with these qualities than a 9th degree initiate who is run by the negative ego. I'm sure you, my friends, would agree.

Integrated Ascension

Lightworkers are too often fascinated with ethereal celestial realms and are not paying their rent to GOD on the psychological level. Now, my friends, here comes the cosmic tough love hammer as told to me by the inner plane Cosmic and Planetary Masters I work with. Number One is that even though the 7th initiation is the liberation from the physical wheel of rebirth, if you don't do your psychological self-mastery work equally as well, you will have to reincarnate on the astral or mental plane even if you are a 7th degree initiate or beyond.

Number Two tough love hammer of the Cosmic and Planetary Hierarchy is that all initiates who are not doing the appropriate psychological work on themselves will be held in a state of spiritual stasis of no growth at the end of the 7th initiation indefinitely until this psychological work is addressed properly. The end of the 7th initiation is the "ring pass not." This means that no one will be allowed to complete their planetary ascension or begin their cosmic ascension without this aspect of self being fundamentally mastered. I am not saying here it has to be perfect, however, there has to be fundamental self-mastery on all levels (spiritual, psychological, physical, environmental, etc.).

My beloved readers, in this moment I bring you a new concept and new ideal which the title of this book speaks of. Instead of striving for ascension, I humbly suggest a new ideal and goal, which I now refer to as "Integrated Ascension." In this regard, initiations are not only passed on the spiritual level, they are also passed and integrated in the mental body, the emotional body, the etheric body, the physical body, and the environmental body. This way not only will your spiritual body reflect self-realization, but your mental body will interpret life properly. Your emotional body will be calm, serene, loving, joyous, not contaminated with negative emotions, and able to get along with people well. Your etheric body will be repaired and replaced with the divine monadic blueprint body or Mayavarupa body. You will take good care of your physical body with proper diet, exercise, sleep, fresh air and sunshine, so it will serve as a proper instrument for the Soul and Monad. Your environment will be organized, reasonably clean, aesthetically pleasing, and you will take care of business on the earthly plane so that your earth life reflects Heaven on Earth.

Sexuality will be mastered and used appropriately in service of GOD. Poverty consciousness will be transformed to prosperity consciousness on the financial level. On the social level, right relationships to people will be achieved and mastered with unconditional love and cooperation in service of GOD and Humankind.

Revelation for the Next Millennium

In this revelation for the next millennium called "integrated ascension," the focus will not just be on achieving initiations and building light quotient. The new revelation will now hold the following quotients of equal importance:

Initiations

Light quotient

Love quotient

Psychological wisdom quotient

Christ consciousness quotient

Transcendence of negative ego quotient

Service and spiritual leadership quotient

Integration and balance quotient

To fully realize your planetary ascension you must score reasonably high marks on all these quotients. In a later chapter, there are many more quotients that you will read about that need to be developed; however, in my discussions with the Masters, these eight were of prime significance. Part of the imbalance in the spiritual movement is that the only two quotients that are really talked about are initiations and light quotient. The other six quotients are just as important and can be scored on a one to one hundred percent scale. The Ascended Masters on the inner plane keep careful spiritual records for each initiate. This is basically the job of the Seven Chohans (El Morya, Kuthumi, Serapis Bey, Paul the Venetian, Hilarion, Sananda, St. Germain, and Djwhal Khul). These records of each initiate on planet Earth are stored in their spiritual holographic computers. They decide, based on these criteria, who is ready for initiation, who will be allowed to move on to the cosmic initiation process and who will ultimately have to reincarnate onto the physical, astral or mental plane. These spiritual records and information are passed along to Lord Maitreya, our planetary Christ, and to Lord Buddha, our planetary Logos, for final inspection and confirmation. When it comes to the reincarnation process on any of the three planes, the Karmic Board will also be consulted.

Summation

It is for the reasons mentioned in this chapter that the Masters have guided me to set up the Melchizedek Synthesis Light Academy. It is also the reason I have been guided by the Masters to write my books *Soul Psychology, How to Clear the Negative Ego, Ascension and Romantic Relationships, Manual for Planetary Leadership, Ascension Psychology,* and *Your Ascension Mission: Embracing Your Puzzle Piece*. I cannot emphasize enough the importance of studying and working with this material. The reason lightworkers largely are not developed in this area is that the type of spiritual psychology that is being presented here is a cutting-edge new dispensation in the field of psychology. It is a new paradigm and understanding written from Soul and Monadic levels of consciousness, made easy to understand, practical, and digestible to the reader. The truth of the matter, my friends, is that the world doesn't need more channels or psychics. It needs more spiritual counselors and spiritual psychologists. The world needs more spiritual teachers who not only understand this level of work, but can train others to integrate this material as well. I cannot tell you how many high-level spiritual teachers and leaders are falling by the wayside because of a lack of understanding and proper training in this area. This is not a judgment, this is a wake-up call and a clarion call to lightworkers around the globe to make the needed adjustments within self, and to make the needed adjustments in your service work, to make the needed attitudinal correction on a global level. Lack of training, books, and an absence of teachers and counselors who understand this work are the reason why so many lightworkers and people in general are having problems. Just the concept alone that there are only two ways of thinking (Christ thinking or negative ego thinking) is a completely revolutionary new understanding for humankind and for the field of psychology itself. These are the new wave cutting-edge teachings. It might aptly be called "Soul Psychology" and/or "Monadic Psychology."

On behalf of the Ascended Masters, I now put forth the clarion call to lightworkers around the globe to help correct this growing imbalance in the Spiritual Movement. I ask channels to give channeled readings using this eight-point quotient system so lightworkers hold the proper integrated ideal and just don't strive for spiritual or heavenly growth alone. I put forth the clarion call to all counselors to set forth these ideals and quotients in your counseling sessions. I put forth the clarion call to all lightworkers to speak of these quotients and ideals with your friends, family, and students. Intuitively score yourselves on a 1 to 100 scale as to your development in these quotients. Your Soul and Monad will give you the correct assessment intuitively if you are willing to be honest with yourself. Do not let less than wonderful scores be grounds for self-judgment. Everything in life is just teachings, lessons, challenges, and opportunities to grow.

All is forgiven, and our worth comes from the fact that GOD created us. All that I am speaking of here is attitudinal healing. These lessons can be learned exceedingly quickly if you will read the books I have suggested. It is just a matter of changing your thinking which will revolutionize and integrate your consciousness more completely. Use the tools and techniques I have provided in these various books and they will change your consciousness instantly with the slightest effort on your part.

Strive to be an "Integrated Master" on all levels. Strive to realize GOD on all 352 levels of your Being. Be sure to "pay your rent" to GOD, not only spiritually, but also mentally, emotionally, physically, environmentally, socially, and financially. Always remember that the psychological level is the foundation or "1st floor" of your symbolic psychic home. The "2nd floor" is the spiritual level. If you put all your energies and consciousness on the 2nd floor, and you don't do the proper work on the 1st floor, your psychic house is in danger of collapsing.

The things I speak of in this first chapter are much more common than most people realize. I say this as a loving observation in my leadership capacity in the Melchizedek Synthesis Light Ashram and Academy, and in my capacity as a professional psychotherapist and licensed Marriage, Family and Child Counselor. I have a lot of students under my care, and the things I speak of in this book are widespread across the globe. In my personal humble opinion, there is no single more important issue in the Spiritual Movement than this. If this issue is not addressed even the spiritual level will become ultimately corrupted by the negative ego. The Masters desire that every lightworker on planet Earth be devastatingly honest with themselves and have the courage and egolessness to do their homework in this most important area. It may not be as glamorous as some of the work on the spiritual levels, however, in truth, it is the true test of Godliness, which is what we all indeed seek. The negative ego is incredibly tricky and is filled with self-deception.

Regarding this subject, I close this section with the words of the Master Jesus, from *A Course in Miracles*, where he says, "Deny any thought not of GOD to enter your mind." He also says, "Be vigilant for

GOD and His kingdom." So, my friends, be vigilant against the negative ego's motives, and self-deception. Be forgiving with self, and guiltless in the process of clearing the negative ego from your conscious and subconscious thinking. It is a process and does not happen in a second. It takes a real focus and commitment, however, the fruit which you will receive from doing the real "nuts and bolts" work of the spiritual path will bring "The peace that passeth understanding."

2

A Deeper Explanation of the Eight Quotients and How to Use Them

Initiations

As all of you already know, initiations mark the point of completion of one phase of evolution and the beginning of the next. Until fairly recently, the process was a long and laborious one, involving several rounds of cyclical incarnation, slowly bringing up enough light quotient in order to partake of the ceremony of initiation, and pass on to the next phase of one's development. Although this process was slow in comparison to our present accelerated movement through mass ascension, it allowed for a much more complete integration of all the various bodies as each (physical, etheric, emotional, mental) was deeply worked on and integrated into the process. As initiations are literally sped through during this unique window of opportunity, it is a far less thorough process than what was experienced in the past. This has had the deleterious effect of leaving many out of balance and unintegrated.

The lightening speed at which much of humanity is propelled through the portal of initiation has come with a great price. This price is the lack of integration of all the vehicles and the neglect and/or denial of extremely vital quotients other than simply the light quotient. The light quotient, as you know, is the propelling force that carries one through the various stages and rungs on the ladder of initiation until planetary ascension is reached at the beginning of the sixth initiation and ultimately completed at the fulfillment of the seventh.

As you know, the requirement for ascension is the balancing of 51% of your karma. This will indeed free you from the wheel of rebirth upon the physical realms and open you up to deeper advancements upon the inner realms. This is not the total picture, however, which is why this book is being written. There is, in truth, much to be considered before "Integrated Ascension," involving all the bodies, is complete. "Integrated Ascension" is what we are ultimately after, for in order to fully ascend, all of the bodies and many other quotients must be lifted up to GOD. In a similar vein, the GOD force must also be brought down by what is called the process of "decension," or anchoring spirit into the body (matter). Initiation, leading to ascension, must therefore be seen and embraced through a full spectrum lens.

Light Quotient

Light quotient is an aspect of initiation that almost every lightworker is familiar with. At 80% light quotient you are able to take the sixth initiation, this is the beginning of actual ascension. In order to ascend and/or complete the sixth initiation, the required amount of light quotient that must be reached is 92%. As previously stated, initiation, and ultimately ascension, is achieved through the meeting of certain standards of light quotient. That is why so much emphasis has been placed on the building of the light quotient when striving to reach the glorious state of ascension.

However, the difficulty in focusing on this quotient to the exclusion of all others is becoming more and more obvious. I would like very much to bring two very important points to your attention before proceeding further. The first point is that, viewed from a certain lens, the Cosmos itself is Light, and therefore I fully honor and embrace the vital importance of the light quotient. We could not progress without it. As beloved Master Jesus/Sananda so eloquently states, "By their light ye shall know them." This is indeed pure truth.

Sananda, however, likewise stresses the quality or quotient, if you will, of Love and the achieving of Christ consciousness, or the Christ consciousness quotient. In fact, the quality of Love is one that is stressed by Masters and leaders of all the many varied paths and religions. So is the quality of wisdom, which is another aspect of light, but one that likewise has its own definite properties. Wisdom is involved in the Psychological Wisdom Quotient, the Transcendence of Negative Ego Quotient, Service and Spiritual Leader Quotient, and Integration and Balance Quotient, all of which will subsequently be explored as this chapter unfolds.

We begin by taking a brief look at the Light Quotient, since that is the one we are most familiar with, and the model by which the various other quotients shall be explored. The building of the light quotient actually involves raising the frequency of light within the four-body system to higher and higher vibrational resonances. Very simply put, it would be as if our four lower bodies were darkened chambers or rooms, and by the inverse use of a dimmer switch, slowly, increment by increment bringing the light to brighter and brighter radiance. This is literally what happens as we purify and draw ourselves through various meditations, activations, initiations, and invocations closer and closer to Source. The light quality of our bodies becomes brighter and brighter, more and more rarefied. The atomic frequencies are raised within all twelve bodies and we become reflective of the Light of GOD Itself! This is absolutely necessary, and no progress could be made upon the path of initiation without this transformation and divine alchemy. The point where misunderstanding or misinterpretation of the process comes into play is where we mistakenly operate from a belief system that tells us that this is **all** that is involved in the process of ascension. This simply is not true!

Light quotient building is an extremely vital part of the process, but so are the other quotients that we shall now look into. We will, however, use some of the basic patterning within the light quotient system with which to help us discover and work with the building of the various other six quotients. As each of the quotients is unique unto itself, however, we will likewise explore them within the specific parameters of their own domain. When this is done we will be exploring them as unique entities, qualities, or aspects, and will not therefore use the light quotient system at all.

There will be times when our investigation of these other quotients will parallel that of the light quotient and times when they will stand in their own right as totally specialized functions of the Cosmos with specialized and definite functions and expressions within our own four-body systems. For detailed information on light quotient building please see my books *The Complete Ascension Manual* and *Beyond Ascension*. So much information is imparted in these two works with regard to this subject that I do not want to repeat it here. In fact, much of New Age material focuses upon this particular quotient, which is why I have, with the guidance of the Masters, decided to focus upon the other quotients which are equally necessary but often overlooked in the achieving of "Integrated Ascension"!

Love Quotient

We have probably heard the familiar quote, "GOD is Love," more times than anyone of us can recollect. The sad truth remains, however, that for one reason or another, the focus upon love has been very much missing from the Ascension movement. Love has retained its stronghold in the more traditional religions and spiritual paths, including Christianity, Bhakti or devotional Yoga and certainly within the grace of the teachings of His Holiness the Lord Sai Baba. The New Age Movement, however, has confined much of its research, meditations, and focus in general, solely upon light. This, beloved readers is but part of the full journey home to Source.

In truth, light and love are two halves of the same coin. When the element of 'wisdom' is brought into it, we are adding that fact of light, which along with love comprises the very structure of our solar system. When we add the use of 'will' into the equation, we then embrace the trinity of GOD, which we are meant to manifest within our lives. For the purpose of this section, we will explore love. We ask that you join in this process, not simply with your minds, but with your hearts, which are the receptacles as well as the distributors of the love that GOD is.

If we were first to take a quick look at love quotient with our mental bodies for measuring it in a similar fashion to the way that we do with light quotient, what we would find is that they are exactly equal. You are required to reach a minimum of 80% love quotient in order to begin your sixth initiation and 92% in order to reach your seventh initiation. The difference between love and light quotient is that with regard to the light quotient, these levels must be stabilized before the initiation occurs.

With regards to the love quotient, the same criteria must be met, however, it becomes the individual's job, so to speak, to see that it is maintained and demonstrated in action even after the initiations of ascension are completed. There has been far too much inconsistency in this regard due to the fact that love is related as much to the mental and feeling (astral body) as it is to the spiritual essence of the universe. For this reason many often get these facets of love confused, and inappropriately bring it down into uncontrolled aspects of the mental and astral body. This causes the pure essence of Love Itself to be diluted, contaminated, and sometimes ultimately relinquished in the process.

The true intent is that the emotional or feeling body acts as a transmitter of the high and glorious frequencies of divine love. This does not mean that love is not experienced emotionally, but rather that the feeling body be upraised by the frequencies of divine love and not the inverse. Divine spiritual love can be filtered through the emotional body in a manner that elevates it, while at the same time honoring the emotional vehicle. Where many often go astray, is when they do not work upon elevating their mental and emotional bodies in order that this may occur. In cases such as this, the mental or astral elemental holds sway, and the pure essence of love is distorted, degraded, or denied expression altogether.

What is truly sought after is that divine balance wherein the mental and emotional bodies are sufficiently purified so that the purest divine love frequencies may radiate through them in order to both enrich an individual's life, and to express the highest aspect of the sacred and holy essence of love upon the outer plane of manifestation. This later type of love would be demonstrated in acts of selfless service to humanity and all life upon the planet, to the planet itself, and beyond to the vast starry reaches of the heavens.

One point that demands further exploration is that Love is meant to be free flowing within all 12 bodies, which obviously includes the four lower bodies. It does not mean that one should give up personal expression of love by any means. This is a false concept propelled forward from earlier epochs where the astral elemental was in such complete control that it was deemed wise by certain religious leaders to divert humanity away from any expression of human or personal love whatsoever. This was, in some cases, good advice, but in the majority of cases, it was detrimental, as it caused a great schism between the feeling body and all other bodies. It also promoted a great deal of unnecessary guilt, of which a vast majority is still suffering the ramifications. In addition, it promoted unhealthy denial of an essential aspect of our culture.

The feeling body, as stated, is capable, and in fact, has been created to express love both on a personal basis and as a means by which to selflessly express GOD through acts of service. Where service is not made a

Integrated Ascension

part of one's ultimate spiritual program; one will be cut off from their integrated ascension!

Building the love quotient is extremely vital to making real progress upon the spiritual path. As all in this solar system must ultimately wear the cloak of love/wisdom since Earth's solar system is a second ray solar system, those who want to truly proceed forward must develop the quality of love to the highest capacity. This is law. This is also one of GOD's greatest gifts to humanity. Anyone who has been in the presence of a Being who radiates pure love knows the incredible joy, peace, and oneness that this energy conveys. That is why so many people gathered around Sananda in His incarnation as Jesus 2000 years ago. It is why so many gather around Sai Baba today, to bathe in, drink in, and melt within the essence of Love in its purest form! Love can be expressed on several different levels. The closer one is to Source, the greater is the capacity to love. Source, however, containing both the quality of light and love, requires one to climb the golden pink stairway of love Itself in order to fully embrace and demonstrate one's essential nature. Love, in essence, breeds love. It is the path and the destination. You get closer to the source of love as you open to your own unique energy flow and field of love, which is already inside of you.

Love must ultimately find its expression upon the outer world of form. The key to demonstrating love is to become a living example of "love in action." If we speak love but neglect to demonstrate it within our lives then we are uttering empty words devoid of one of the primary substances that comprise our being and the cosmos itself. Many fall into this trap. We know GOD is love, but we know it as a sentiment, platitude, or even as a basic truth; however, we fail to be living examples of that truth. In order to build love quotient, in order to be GOD upon Earth, we must each seek to be love, experience love, live love, and be the gentle hands and very embodiment of this great divine truth!

The specific way in which each individual will feel called to serve and to express the divine quality of love, will of course, vary tremendously.

Integrated Ascension

We each have our own puzzle pieces and ascension mission, and we each have our own particular way in which we have been encoded to serve. There are certain contracts that we have made with our soul, monad, and the Masters between embodiments, which many have yet to discover. When we open to our higher selves, pray, meditate and request that our unique plan of loving service be revealed, the Masters and our own Mighty I Am Presence will joyously do so.

It is vital that we all take the responsibility to do this. More important, we need to realize how essential a component love is within the equation of our lives. If we ask for the unfoldment of our mission within this understanding, we will open to the splendor of the plan as it is meant to be brought forth, and not to some dry blueprint that is devoid of this most blessed and essential nectar that flows from the heart of GOD Itself into our heart.

We must all realize that the integration of love into our lives, into our service work and daily interactions is of paramount importance. For example, even if we get in touch with the fact that it is our mission to be "the healer," if we attempt to do this without first invoking and incorporating the energies of love into our work, and ourselves then we will be fulfilling half our mission at best. The mechanics of our work may stand revealed before us, yet without the radiance of love we shall get partial results at best. The best that one can achieve if healing would take place without love, is to effectuate a physical result, which is a wonderful thing, but quite incomplete from the point of view of divine purpose and that which the Masters seek to achieve through the lightworkers of this planet. In order for a full healing to take place one must unveil or help to unveil the cause of the disease. In order to do that one must be coming from a place of core essence of Being. This core essence is Source, is GOD, and is therefore Love!

It is the same with all service work, no matter what the outer expression of that work is. If love is not radiating within your actions, then there will be hollowness to them. They will be incomplete, half-baked, and may even ultimately be a disservice. The quality, attitude, attribute, and energy of love is so important, that to truly be a lightworker, you must also be a "love worker"! There is no way around this essential fact. Light and love are two intermingling streams radiating out from the Great Central Sun. Beloved readers, if you truly want GOD and find that you are deficient in love, then I tell you to seek this love from within yourself and from Source. Love must be fully, totally and completely integrated, activated and expressed by any and all who seeks to demonstrate GOD both in their inner and outer life. This is Law!

It must also be understood very clearly that light quotient is a quality that has less to do with demonstration and more to do with calling it forth from the Celestial Realms and sustaining it. Love quotient, however, is exactly the opposite. Love quotient building has more to do with demonstrating and less to do with having the Masters build it into your field, for example. For this reason, love quotient is more of a psychological development process. Without learning to master the mind, the emotional body, the negative ego, the subconscious mind, lower self desire and properly parent the inner child, you won't be able to raise your love quotient. So in this regard we can see that building light quotient is much easier than building love quotient. It also must be understood that all light quotient building will be stopped completely at the end of the seventh initiation if it is being done in a fragmented way that does not include a proper balance of love quotient building. The proper integration of the spiritual, psychological and physical earthly levels is not just a good idea or new concept for the next millennium, but, in truth, a requirement for true GOD Realization, not jut passing initiations or achieving the first stage of ascension.

Some may be dealing with the very difficult issue of self-love. If you find that you are a sufferer of low self-esteem, unworthiness, guilt, and so forth, please do check out my books specifically addressing these issues: *Soul Psychology* and *How to Clear the Negative Ego*. There are other wonderful books and tapes that deal with these issues, including directly working with a qualified spiritual counselor. Whatever method you choose, whatever tools you find most beneficial, please stick with them until the desired result is achieved and these issues are banished from your lives. By no means judge yourself if you find that this is a stumbling block for you. It is an area that all must confront and deal with until mastered. The important thing is that you learn to love and nurture yourself as a Son or Daughter of GOD. When you can do this for yourself, the gateway of nurturing others in the same GOD-like fashion will swing wide open.

Love is to GOD what breathing is to sustaining the life of the physical body. In truth, it is greater! Certain yogis and Masters can bypass the breath by various forms of meditation and the specific use of prana. Love can never be bypassed, for it is the very essence of GOD, even as is Light. Therefore, remember this most glorious energy always, for it is essential to your ascension progress and your ascension work. It is also essential to your life, for love is that which you are even as it is that which is GOD. The two are one and "That thou Art"!

Psychological Wisdom Quotient

As the path of initiation is traversed, unfortunately the Psychological Wisdom Quotient is often not even considered by lightworkers. The consequence of this is that progress is brought to a screeching halt as one or several areas of imbalance kick in, throwing the initiate off their course and straight into confusion and fragmentation. This is what so many are suffering from at this unique juncture of mass acceleration. The development of psychological wisdom must absolutely keep pace with the other divine qualities. When this is not done, as is so often the case, then one must take the necessary time out to set things in proper balance by the light of this wisdom. Although this is more easily done while climbing the ladder of ascension, be assured that it will have to be

Integrated Ascension

done at some point. This is something that every one should be acutely aware of.

Here is an area that many lightworkers actually try to avoid as they hold to the false belief system that this facet of life is beneath them or one that has been previously mastered. In truth, all need to keep careful watch over this area, and most lightworkers have not done the fundamental and necessary work. Beloved readers, this is an aspect of ourselves through which we interact, serve, communicate, and, in fact, approach GOD. We must be clear about this. Psychological wisdom is not beneath any, but is, rather, crucial to all!

As with the measurement of both light and love quotient, one should strive to be within the 80% range at minimum and work upwards from there on this quotient as well. The difficulty in integrating this aspect of self with those previously discussed is that a certain standard of light and love quotient are absolutely mandatory before one achieves ascension. The Psychological Wisdom Quotient does not hold such a requirement in the actual achievement of ascension; however, it does hold this strict requirement in maintaining the standard of Mastership, and in achieving initiations beyond the seventh initiation. This is where most lightworkers find their weakest link and consequently are "called on the carpet" by their Higher Self and Monad and forced to make major and often drastic adjustments before proceeding further.

This is also one of the quotients that most lightworkers are resistant to working with, for their faulty thinking tells them that this is a lower fact of their being or one that is not as interesting as the spiritual level. In truth, this trait comprises who we are during any given incarnation and what we bring with us in our auras when we cross over. The Psychological Wisdom Quotient therefore extends over many subsequent incarnations and remains a full and potent part of ourselves requiring balancing and integration. This quotient, in truth, is the foundation of our entire spiritual life; all spiritual work will ultimately be corrupted and contaminated if this quotient is not integrated properly and raised to a high enough standard. The reason this is true is that one cannot be right with GOD, the Masters, and other people if one is not right with self. Developing right relationships with self, GOD, the Masters, and other people is the core essence of the Psychological Wisdom Quotient. A person can have a great deal of intellectual wisdom or concrete knowledge or even occult knowledge and still be extremely deficient in the psychological wisdom quotient. In truth, one cannot even develop their love quotient if they are undeveloped in their Psychological Wisdom Quotient.

It must be remembered, however, that we are dealing with this particular quotient within the specific time frame of exceedingly rapid mass acceleration. This factor plays a great role in contributing to the severity and widespread nature of misalignment within this particular area of development. During earlier phases of Earth's evolution when initiations occurred at a much slower pace, it was much easier to keep pace with all the various levels needing integration. It was a very precise step by step process of unfoldment, development and maintenance of certain basic frequencies and requirements of the 12-body system.

During these earlier periods in history, the psychological intricacies of modern day society were not as developed and complex as they now are. The quotient that had to be mastered and maintained was comparably simpler. The requirements to master the mind, emotions, negative ego, and so forth were always prevalent, however, the overall development of the consciousness of humanity is much higher now. Current civilization being so much more complex requires a more sophisticated Psychological Wisdom Quotient than was required 2000 to 5000 years ago. The core essence lessons are the same. Because of accelerated evolution, each one is bombarded with accelerated input consequently making the Psychological Wisdom Quotient increasingly more involved. Know that it has always, however, been the cornerstone and foundation of all spiritual growth.

Integrated Ascension

What we must also bring to your attention is the fact that the requirements of any given age must be fully met by those who have chosen to reincarnate during that particular cycle. This obviously includes all those who are truly working through their path of ascension for the very first time. It might surprise you to learn that this likewise includes those ascended Masters who have reincarnated through the natural process of birth in order to reenact the initiatory steps so that others may be inspired and uplifted by both their example and frequency. This would include most all of the star seeds, but also extends to others that have passed through several portals of initiation in previous historical periods of Earth's evolution.

The complexities of the mind, the subtle weavings of the psychological fabric must be delicately unraveled so that you may proceed unencumbered upon your journey. This quotient is vital, and to disregard it is to set yourself up for a fall.

Bearing all this is mind, we then request that you face your psychological self with as much joy and fearlessness that you face your Divine Self. Tune into your Psychological Wisdom Quotient and see what your score is. Are you tapped into the wonderful wisdom inherent within the conscious mind that can help program and free the psychology from any and all blockages that have been put there by faulty negative programming? Are you awake, alert, vigilant and conscious, or are you operating on automatic pilot too much? Are you in control of the negative ego? Are you in control of your subconscious mind? Are you thinking with your Christ/Buddha mind? Are you properly parenting your inner child? Are you free from attachments? Do you own your personal power at all times inwardly and outwardly? Have you developed unconditional self-love and self worth? Are you a cause of your reality or an effect? Have you properly integrated your archetypes? Have you properly integrated the seven rays? Have you properly balanced your four bodies? Have you properly integrated your four minds (subconscious, conscious, Higher Self and Monad)? Have you mastered lower-self desire? Are you properly directing and integrating your subpersonalities? Have you found your proper selfish/selfless balance? Have you found the proper integration and balance of your spiritual life, psychological life, and physical/earthly life? These questions, my beloved readers, are the nuts and bolts of developing a high level of Psychological Wisdom Quotient. These are questions that only you alone can answer. Your outer world, however, can serve as a great mirror in this regard. Take a look, see what is being reflected back to you, and note where you want to make the necessary and needed adjustments. Never doubt that it lies within your power to do this, for it most certainly does!

The Psychological Wisdom Quotient deals primarily with the understanding of your own personal psychology. The higher the wisdom is functioning, the less evidence there will be of greed, fear, lust, competition, sabotage (self or others), attachments to fame, power, money, to name a few. There will be a sense of completeness within self and GOD. Where the wisdom of your psychology is weak, negative attributes will surface and run the gamut. If indulged in to a disproportionate and exaggerated degree, they have the power to throw you completely off track and thwart your divine intent and mission until you set things straight. Because of this very real and pertinent danger, it is imperative that you work diligently in building up your Psychological Wisdom Quotient, aligning it with the requirements of the present era, and freeing yourself from any and every subtle form of manipulation and trickery that is a byproduct of unclarity within this realm.

Allot some time each and every day to take inventory of this most vital aspect of self and to request help from your Higher Self and from GOD and the Masters so that any and every thread of disharmony abiding within this field is brought into the light of day. Logging and journaling are wonderful processes in regard to this most elusive and intricate quotient. Don't be afraid to disclose your secrets to yourself and to GOD and the Masters. There will be no judgment, unless you

Integrated Ascension

generate it, and if you do then you will know that that is a psychological area in dire need of purification. I suggest that in using this logging and journaling process you rate yourself on a 1 to 100% scale, the same as you do when observing light quotient. Remember that any form of self-judgment does you a great disservice and reveals an area that sorely needs your attention. GOD does not judge you and neither do the Masters. This is a personal log to be used to catapult your Psychological Wisdom Quotient and hence your psychology clarity. Above all, state the truth as you see it. By revealing what is hidden all can and will be healed! You have the power to provide that which is hidden, and bring it forth into the light of purification.

Again realize, my beloved readers, what does it matter if a person has achieved their ascension or a high level of initiation and yet are psychologically unclear? When I personally look for people to serve in the Melchizedek Synthesis Light Academy & Ashram, what I look for is a high level of Psychological Wisdom Quotient and a high level of Love Quotient. These quotients are a thousand times more important to me then their initiation level or light quotient. The best co-workers are those who are more psychologically clear and are selfless, egoless, right with self, comfortable in their puzzle piece, harmonious with others, possessive of honor and integrity, are hard workers, devoted to GOD, cooperative rather than competitive, unconditionally loving, and striving to develop a flawless character. Often I find these types of people are not necessarily at as high a level of initiation as others, yet ultimately these are lightworkers who will make the greatest progress. I would rather have a third degree initiate work in the Academy & Ashram than a seventh degree initiate who is run by their negative ego and is very power hungry and emotionally reactive in a negative sense. I think you, my beloved readers, feel the same way. One's initiation level is not indicative in the slightest of their overall spiritual development and this point cannot be emphasized enough. For this reason, lightworkers should focus less on initiations and light quotient, and more on overall psychological, physical and spiritual development. If you truly wish to realize GOD and achieve Integrated Ascension.

Our psychological make-ups are quite complex; there is much to diligently and systematically work with. Remember that we are referring to a deeper facet of wisdom, a greater understanding and purification of and by the light. It is therefore a process conceived in joy with the intent to bring one into as much freedom and balance as possible. It also serves to put one on close guard against any potential weakness. Adding the Psychological Wisdom Quotient to your path of ascension will accelerate your full ascension process and bring you cleansed and purified to the altar of your own GOD Self!

Christ Consciousness Quotient

The concept of Christ Consciousness is truly an exquisite one. In essence, it means to see the world through the heart/mind of GOD, to refrain from all judgments whatsoever, remaining in a perpetual state of unconditional love and always choosing love over fear. In truth, however, there are many subtle nuances contained within this simply stated explanation. There is also the fact, that although almost every single lightworker would like to be operating out of Christ consciousness, one must be extremely "vigilant for GOD and His Kingdom" as Sananda/Jesus so perfectly puts in *A Course in Miracles*. The subtleties within this glorious "ideal" direct all of us seeking to operate from this elevated vantage point to truly keep vigilant over all that we put forth. We likewise need to observe how we process what comes into us via the four minds (Monad, Higher Self, Conscious mind, and Subconscious mind) and the four-body system, as well as through the senses.

The core principle of the Christ Consciousness Quotient is that there are two philosophies or thought systems. These are the Christ/Buddha thought system and the negative ego thought system. Every person on Earth, or in the infinite universe for that matter, falls into one, the other, or a combination of both. The key to building up your Christ Consciousness Quotient is to deny all negative ego thoughts from entering your conscious mind from self or others and to keep your mind thinking, affirming and visualizing only Christ thoughts and Christ images at all times. It only takes twenty-one days to cement a habit into the subconscious mind, so the more you practice this, the more habitual, in a positive sense, it will become. As the Bible says, "Let this mind be in you that was in Christ Jesus." Christ consciousness is an attitude and philosophy of life that creates unconditional love, oneness, joy, inner peace, equanimity, non-judgmentalness, forgiveness, and compassion in all moments and situations of life. It is a choice! So, in each moment and situation in life ask yourself, "Do I choose GOD and Christ consciousness in this situation or do I choose negative ego consciousness, glamour, illusion and maya?" To build your Christ Consciousness Quotient, keep choosing GOD, unconditional love, positivity and oneness in your thinking and interpretations of life which will lead to the creation of only positive, loving, spiritualized feelings and emotions. It is our thoughts that create our feelings and emotions and the question you must continually ask yourself in every moment of your life is whether your thoughts, interpretations and motives are coming from the negative ego or the Christ consciousness, Higher Self, Monad, Ascended Masters and GOD. It is that simple. For a deeper explanation of how the Christ Mind and Negative Ego Mind think, please read my books *How to Clear the Negative Ego* and *Soul Psychology*. For this reason Christ Consciousness becomes one of the eight primary quotients that is deserving of our constant attention.

The ideal for all lightworkers in regard to this particular quotient is to operate from the Christ Consciousness at a minimum of the 80th percentile at all times. This would mean that this mode of consciousness is so integrated within your system that even when you fall into automatic pilot, all thoughts, words, emotions and deeds will flow from the inner Christ. There will, of course, be specific situations or tests that challenge this mode of consciousness. It is during these particular crises that we have the opportunity to learn and grow. It is also estimated by the Masters that since we will be put within these situations in order to make the needed adjustments of consciousness those who are sincerely working at this quotient will at first fall out of Christ consciousness 20 percent of the time. That is why 20% is given as the basic standard. As we practice the application of this mode of spiritual consciousness within our lives, the goal is that we then come as close to the 100% quotient as possible. This is the ideal and the way in which humanity will achieve GOD consciousness. It is important to understand that minor mistakes and adjustments will always come up. The key is to make these attitudinal adjustments as quickly as possible, so what threw you off for a whole day or week in the past can be resolved in a moment or two once you get the hang of it and really see how you cause your own reality by how you think.

Let us take a look at how some of the intricacies within this mode of consciousness are meant to potentially function. One of the key choices that we all have is to choose love over fear. Yet for many fear has become instinctive. The body reacts, the emotions react, and the mind takes off in a thousand different directions, literally scattering and fragmenting one's consciousness. In situations like this, one needs to turn to love, for "Perfect love casteth out fear." One must, however, make this turn with gentleness and ease, which boils down to essentially meaning, without judgment of any sort.

This is one of the trickier aspects of maintaining Christ consciousness. The force of judgment is very powerful. For some, the judgment turns outward and gets thrown in another's direction. For many upon the spiritual path, the judgment is turned inward. When this occurs, one is shaken out of their peace through self-judgment of one's own fear; instead of turning to love, self-judgment calls in guilt or shame. These are obviously not attributes of Christ consciousness nor can love blossom within a field of judgment of any sort. What I am in essence saying, is that in order to turn fear into love, one must first be willing to cast aside the judgment of the fear itself!

Fear prompting one to judgments operates on very subtle levels, such as fear of dishonor in the eyes of humanity, fear of not being seen as you see yourself, fear of intimacy and so forth. It is a fact that people do not like to be judged. Looking at us as a race as a whole I would not hesitate to say that we live in constant fear of judgment. The fear of being judged inferior to someone else, has played itself out in the third dimensional world through guises too numerous to even begin to name here. I will, however, guide you to consider the world of business, politics, or the arts, in order to see how this is manifesting in those arenas. Socially it can be seen in the continuing desire to keep up with the Jones's. The most cursory look, beloved readers, will reveal this in operation everywhere and at all levels.

Unfortunately, this all-pervasive fear permeates much of the spiritual movement as well. The fear of being judged "less than perfect," actually has no basis in reality as we are all already perfect because we are Sons and Daughters of GOD, yet this fear often prompts us into the mode of judging either others or ourselves. This judgment and fear falls like a shadow across the faces of many wonderful workers of the light, and creates a divisive barrier between them and their true goal, which is Christ consciousness! This type of fear and judgment, however, falls upon the lightworker in a subtle and almost undetectable manner, which is why I have stressed the point that it takes great vigilance to maintain Christ consciousness.

The higher one travels upon the ladder of evolution, the more subtler and subtler things become. The overt war between two businesses can become the silent struggle for power between two lightworkers. If the core of this struggle is explored it would reveal the two key elements, fear and judgment. If these can be eradicated, then the consciousness can be raised up to the realm of Christ, Buddha, Melchizedek and GOD!

Integrated Ascension

If you truly want to operate out of the Christ consciousness, which I hope you do, as it is one of the primary keys to integrated ascension, you certainly can! To do this, however, your utmost attention is demanded in any and every situation along with absolute honesty. There is no shame in noting where your weaknesses are; in fact, just the opposite is true. The light that reveals the muddiest spots within self is the same light that cleanses and purifies them. Courage to face self and willingness to change join with our lesser attributes when we offer them up at GOD's alter. When this is done, then that which is a block from Christ consciousness, namely fear in its many guises and judgment in its many forms will be transcended and transmuted into divine love and light. One will then be upraised to the point where one operates from out of the Christ consciousness 99% to 100% of the time.

So, in truth, there are only two emotions. All negative emotions, no matter what the quality, stem from fear. All positive emotions, no matter what the quality, stem from love. Any negative emotion you may have, if you trace its roots back to its source, will come from the illusionary premise of fear, which you unconsciously allowed to infiltrate your mind. This is not a judgment, but rather a keen insight to understanding the causative nature of how feelings and emotions are created. The same, of course, is also true with all the positive emotions, with the difference here being that love will be the root cause and foundation.

Creating the atmosphere that is nurturing to the Christ consciousness and then keeping vigilant watch to hold to that precious and sacred space is one of the most important pieces of integration work that one can do. The Christ consciousness quotient should be built to its highest capacity and once established within the 90 to 100 percent range, all efforts should be given to maintaining these levels. Actually Christ consciousness is more than just a quotient; it is a way to manifest GOD upon the Earth. It is life at its most glorious capacity, a place of pure connection with our brothers and sisters, with self and GOD.

Integrated Ascension

Just because a person achieves their ascension or seven levels of initiation and are now considered a Master doesn't mean they can let down their vigilance. This is a very big mistake that many advanced lightworkers are making. The ultimate result of this is summoned up in the Biblical statement, "After pride cometh the fall." One has to work with the same self-discipline and single focus and commitment after ascension as one did before. It does not become easier just because you have achieved your ascension. Ascension and initiations are really just percentages of light quotients that serve as markers on an infinite journey. There are always more initiations and more light quotient as one transfers over to the Cosmic Light Quotient scale. If one really gets off track, one can lose initiatory status and can greatly fall in all the quotients mentioned in this chapter. So never take anything for granted. Even when one becomes a Master in name, one must continue to demonstrate this mastery to truly be considered a Master in the eyes of GOD and the Spiritual Hierarchy of inner plane Ascended Masters. It is not so much what you've done in the past that is so important (although this does hold some weight), it is what you are doing in the present moment that is most important. Again, you may have been an incredible spiritual teacher, prophet, channel, or leader in a past life, however, this does not mean in the slightest that the negative ego is not running you in this life. The key here is to be devastatingly honest with self and to strive for the purity of GOD every moment of your life regardless of your initiatory status, past lives or present fame. This is the true test of a lightworker. When positions of power are achieved, the lightworker needs to embody the greatest vigilance so the negative ego does not take over.

Take time, beloved readers, to cultivate this quotient and radiate these glorious and beautiful frequencies within you and around you. In this way, both you and the planet will accelerate in love and harmony. There is truly no greater way to uplift both self and humanity than to become a vortex of Christ consciousness. The wonderful thing is that this divine state of grace is ours just for the asking, seeking, cultivating, and claiming. When we remain vigilant within this area, we will know beyond the shadow of a doubt that we are emissaries and embodiments of Christ on Earth!

Transcendence of Negative Ego Quotient

The sister quotient to the Christ Consciousness Quotient, so to speak, is the Transcendence of Negative Ego Quotient. Whereas the Christ Consciousness Quotient exemplifies GOD or spiritual consciousness in its highest capacity, the negative ego exemplifies lower consciousness, with all its attendant difficulties. For this reason, the transcendence of the negative ego is one of the eight major quotients.

When dealing with the Transcendence of Negative Ego Quotient, what we are rating is our success in *not* operating out of the negative ego. In order to do this, however, one must first be aware of the negative ego itself. This is that part of ourselves which operates solely out of selfishness, isolation, fear, and fragmentation, as well as embracing the entire gamut of lower impulses, tendencies and expressions. It is often the place from which the inner child is operating without proper parenting. It basically functions from the level of the subconscious.

This is not always the case, as many times, where people are third-dimensionally focused, it will openly operate and consciously choose negativity. This can be seen in the conscious choices made that clearly lead to pain, destruction, hurt, harmfulness, and so forth. In fact, in the third-dimensional world the ability to function selfishly is often deemed as an asset, even if that takes the form of consciously harming another being. The entertainment industry is notorious for using people as stepping stones and the political arenas generally function shamelessly in the mode of the negative ego. These are but two very generalized examples. The truth is that the planet, viewed from a higher perspective, functions almost exclusively from this negative vantage point.

Integrated Ascension

In the case of lightworkers, 99% to almost 100% of the time the negative ego is functioning at a subconscious level. We all have consciously chosen to be workers of the light and many spend the greater part of waking hours trying to be of service to humanity and moving into deeper stages of the initiation and ascension process. Often one doesn't understand what is holding progress back or causing negativity. This is because one is not aware that the negative ego still reigns supreme within the deep recesses of the subconscious mind! Destructive thoughtforms and emotions of the negative ego block us and prevent our service work from fully taking hold. That is the crucial reason for including the Transcendence of Negative Ego Quotient as one of the most significant and important quotients of all. It is also one of the more elusive ones. It is elusive because the negative ego thought system is as brilliant as the Christ thought system only in reverse to GOD's Divine plan of Creation. To master the negative ego one must understand how the negative ego thinks and operates for it is incredibly seductive and manipulative. There are not that many books on the planet that truly understand the psychological mechanics of the negative ego and Christ thinking. Most lightworkers have not been trained in this work. The entire field of traditional psychology is completely void of understanding of this most basic principle of spiritual psychology.

Traditional religion, as we know, has been contaminated and corrupted by the negative ego. Most counselors operate out of a personality level understanding of psychology, which has great value but lacks true understanding of how the negative ego operates. This work is not taught in traditional school, it is not taught in higher education (Master degree programs and Ph.D. programs). Very few books really explain this work in a way that people can understand and practically apply it. This is why lightworkers have not been trained in the work and why humanity is basically unconscious of what is, in my opinion, the single most important understanding a person needs to have to function effectively, be successful and to realize GOD. No matter how much work you do in other areas spiritually or on any other level, if you don't learn to master and subjugate the negative ego, it will corrupt and contaminate every aspect of your life with its need for power over others, negative selfishness, fame, greed, self-aggrandizement, vanity, separateness, negative manipulation, attachment, materialism, and lower-self desire. As Sai Baba has so eloquently stated, "GOD is hidden by the mountain range of negative ego."

The negative ego will also use the inner child if the opportunity is given it. In fact, the negative ego will seek to surface through any holes within the auric structure which one is usually not even consciously aware of. Working with the Transcendence of Negative Ego Quotient takes much training, self-inquiry, introspection, self-examination, vigilance, and self-honesty. It is a lifelong work; even the Ascended Masters on the inner plane are still working to clear remnants of its elusive nature on subtle levels.

The most vital aspect of working with the negative ego is that of self-intimacy. "Know thyself" is stated over and over again. These two words strung together are two of the most important words and keys to integrated ascension. By knowing yourself you can free yourself from the machinations of the negative ego and strip it of its power over your life. You then begin the process of building up the Transcendence of Negative Ego Quotient within you. The greater advance you make in this regard, the more control you have over your life, the faster you accelerate your process of initiation and the more integrated your ascension actually is!

For those who have already achieved ascension, let me take this time to point out that it is never too late to work on the building of this quotient. Unless the transcendence of the negative ego is mastered, all face the prospect of being held back upon our path of freedom until the negativity that we have given expression to is resolved upon the astral or mental realm. It is therefore of paramount importance to work on this quotient and to become full-fledged masters of every aspect of self, including the subconscious realm, where the negative ego lies in wait till an opportunity is given it to express itself. No one is beyond influence of the negative ego until they have mastered the Transcendence of Negative Ego Quotient and brought it up to at least 80% to 90%. The higher the quotient, the higher the clarity. The pure radiance of GOD will be able to be brought through unimpeded and unsabotaged. The goal to strive for is a solid 92% with movement towards the 99% range.

Some very definite signs indicate that the negative ego is controlling self rather than the Christ consciousness. In order to build up the Transcendence of Negative Ego Quotient, familiarity with these signs and indications is essential. These signs or manifestations will become apparent when one first questions their motivations. It is the motivation behind any given response or action that will reveal and expose the negative ego in operation. The signs, therefore, are actually inward motivations that will become apparent when you take the time to look inside and see what is prompting you to act, think, or feel in a given way.

As said before, the negative ego is very tricky and sneaky, and is quite well adept at covering its own tracks. The way it does this is to try and disguise inappropriately selfish and often even cruel motivations under the guise of pure motivations. For instance, it might try and convince someone that their attempts at exercising control over another individual are really for that other person's own good. The negative ego can be quite persuasive at this. If you don't think so, I ask you to simply recall Nazi Germany and Hitler. All that Hitler did, he did in the name of serving his country and cleaning up the world for the ultimate betterment of the human race. He was the epitome of the negative ego at its worst, and simultaneously at its best. From the point of view of the negative ego it did one incredibly wonderful job of convincing a great many German people and their allies that what Hitler stood for was indeed for humanity's highest good. It's hard to believe, and yet there it stands, the negative ego in its awful corrupted glory!

Integrated Ascension

This is an extreme example to be sure, but it serves to demonstrate the basic way that the negative ego asserts itself. It can put us on guard against the deviousness of our own negative ego and those of others. Whenever someone tries to enforce any sort of inappropriate control over you, sticking their noses into business that is truly not their own, I guarantee you that if you take but a moment to look, you will see the face, hands and feet of negative ego at work. I am, of course, not speaking here of the appropriate guidance that parents need to exert over their children. Neither am I speaking of adhering to certain codes of conduct, such as wearing appropriate business attire, obeying the basic laws of our nations, cities, and so forth. There are basic codes of conduct within any given societal structure that simply form the foundations upon which we do our daily 'thing', so to speak. This is not what I am talking about here, however. These situations reveal themselves to be benign in nature, and simply serve as a nuclear base from which we function.

What I specifically seek to address are those situations where someone oversteps their appropriate boundaries within these harmless structures for the express purpose of controlling another. For example, due to certain climactic conditions, there are different dress codes in different parts of the world. This would be an example of the nuclear foundations within which any set group of individuals is functioning. If, however, one person's negative ego desires to hurt or control another person, they can do it by denigrating their intended victim's mode of dress "within" that structure. They can do this by telling them that they should or should not dress in a certain fashion, that they have bad taste, that they look too fat or too thin in an outfit and so on.

This might seem harmless enough, perhaps even too petty to mention, but I assure you it is not. It is upon such little things as these—picking on someone's dress style, telling him or her what food they should or should not eat when they never asked in the first place—that the negative ego builds its foundation and then expands it. I am, again, not talking here about the giving or the sharing of helpful advice or suggestions when sought after, but the invasion of another person's private and sacred space. What the negative ego seeks to do by such acts of invasion is to gain control, for where there is control the negative ego is free to then launch an all out offensive of its corrupted power. Remember, the negative ego does this while all the while outwardly protesting that it is acting in the best interest of the person, or as in the case of Hitler, the world's "best interest."

All lightworkers must be on the lookout for this type of invasion that the negative ego will launch if given the free reign to do so. All must be ever mindful that it may even come from our seemingly well-intentioned friends and family and spiritual teachers and gurus, no matter how famous they are and no matter what level of initiation they claim to be at and what past life personages they claim to be, which may even be true. This, however, does not protect them in the slightest from being run by their own negative ego. We must be even more mindful that it does not come from the hidden recesses within our selves trying to control our divine souls and goad us into following the wrong direction on the pretense that it is for 'our own good'.

The negative ego is subtle and very powerful until it is revealed by the Christ light and tamed by the Christ mind. We all have the power to do this, it is just a matter of claiming it and continually working on it every moment of our lives. In order to truly get where our conscious minds, heart, soul, and spiritual aspirations want to take us, it is we who must rise above the influence of the negative ego. The sooner we do this, the more integrated we become, and the swifter we rise upon our paths of ascension.

The examples given of Hitler and clothes in a foreign country are great examples, however, the real crux of the lesson lies within how the negative ego seduces advanced lightworkers. The negative ego will tell you as you read this section, "You have mastered this." This may even be true, however, I'm also here to tell you that 100% of the people who are

Integrated Ascension

run by the negative ego who are advanced lightworkers are hearing the exact same statement from their negative ego.

The negative ego is so sly, seductive, tricky, conniving, and subtly manipulative that it is unbelievable. It will tell you that it is doing things in the name of the Masters or GOD when this is complete illusion. It will make up and formulate all kinds of spiritual fantasies of past lives, superior missions, grandiose spiritual leadership or specialness that is complete illusion and the negative ego will tell you that it is channeled information.

The negative ego will buy into any information from a psychic or channel as long as it builds up the ego, even though this has been a manipulation by the channel or psychic to build up their own ego. In high level spiritual initiates, the negative ego will often bring forth all sorts of psychological and emotional poison in a false sugar coated manner, thinking that they are being spiritual when nothing could be farther from the truth.

The negative ego in spiritual leaders will often criticize other spiritual leaders even in public and the negative ego will claim that they are doing a service, when in truth they are doing nothing more than being judgmental and being run by self aggrandizement. The negative ego will act in a tyrannical, dictatorial manner while giving a spiritual counseling session and the negative ego will tell the person that they are being a Master.

The negative ego will have you give channelings for people and use that as an opportunity to boss other people around and the negative ego will have you go into a self righteous, angry rage and will tell you that this is righteous anger and spiritually appropriate when in truth, there is no such thing. Inversely, the negative ego will tell you that you are being victimized and direct you away from you true personal power and into a mode of fear and self pity.

The negative ego will have advanced lightworkers communicate in tones of seeming unconditional love, sweetness and syrupy Pollyanna spirituality, when in truth they are running through negative ego agenda clothed in white robes, so to speak. My beloved readers, you all know what I'm talking about here.

The negative ego will have some advanced lightworkers bring forth words of concern for another, while all the time having as their agenda total control and self-interest as their true concern. The negative ego will have some advanced lightworkers manipulate words and writings in a very subtle way that makes them think that they are being spiritual when in truth the motivations are still purely of the seperative self. This is where lightworkers need to be incredibly spiritually discerning. Did not the Bible say that the antichrist would appear in the beginning as the Christ? The antichrist is just the negative ego.

The negative ego will hide its true motives in a veil of vast esoteric and spiritual knowledge and/or channeling and psychic abilities when in truth they are stealing like a common criminal except on more subtle realms. The motivation is the same. The negative ego will make you gossip and judge other people and tell you that you are just practicing spiritual discernment. Do you see, my beloved readers, the subtleties of the negative ego? I am just touching the very tiptop of the iceberg. I could literally go on for an entire book. There was a book written by an author whose name escapes me called *Spiritual Materialism*. I never read the book, but the title speaks to the issue I am speaking of here. It is the science of how the negative ego has infiltrated and contaminated the New Age Movement, the Consciousness Movement, and the entire Spiritual Movement. My beloved readers, it is not just traditional religion where this has taken place.

The negative ego will tell advanced lightworkers that they are the highest being on the planet and create elaborate spiritual charts to prove it. The negative ego will tell you that you are the wife of one of the Ascended Masters or the counterpart of one of the female Ascended Masters. The negative ego will tell people they are the actual physical embodiment of certain famous Ascended Masters on Earth. The negative ego will use psychic and channeling abilities to create Earth change prophecies to create power over others who are left in fear with no place to turn but to the channeler bringing forth this information.

The negative ego will create elite and separate spiritual groups, thus creating division rather than unity. Then negative ego will have you compete with other spiritual lightworkers and leaders, which is the manifestation of the exact opposite of true spirituality. The negative ego will create a feeling of false pride, rather than humbleness, within the arena of the true spiritual work you are engaged in!

The negative ego will tell you that you are serving for pure motives, when in truth what is going on is an unquenchable desire for fame, money, power or any combination of the above. The negative ego will often keep lightworkers tied to past teachings in written form and not allow them to integrate these teachings and then move forward with the continuing revelation of GOD. The negative ego will have you adopt false philosophies and spiritual ideals and then tell you that you are being spiritual when in truth, for example, you may be taking your emotions and/or attack thoughts out on others. The negative ego will have you seek spiritual and global leadership and have you attach, judge, and psychically destroy anyone and everyone who gets in the way of your lofty spiritual goal.

My beloved readers, I have tried to give you a few examples of how the negative ego has infiltrated the Consciousness Movement. Some of the things it does are almost comical. "Do not underestimate the power of the dark side of the Force!" In repeating this quote of Master Yoda, I am being both humorous and serious. As a spiritual teacher, spiritual psychotherapist and spiritual leader, it is unbelievable what I see, the inner plane Ascended Masters see and I'm sure what you, my beloved readers see going on in the Spiritual movement. I know you, my beloved readers, share these thoughts, feelings, observations, and concerns with me. For this reason, let us all focus on building our Negative Ego Transcendence Quotient to its highest possible level as our top priority, along with building our Christ Consciousness Quotient to its maximum potential. The achievement of this goal is the key to developing the "Midas Touch" in life along with insuring full, Integrated Ascension, rather than fragmented or Non-integrated Ascension.

Service and Spiritual Leadership Quotient

When the preceding quotients are being maintained at a high level, it will almost be inevitable that the Service and Spiritual Leadership Quotient will likewise be activated to a high degree. This is because the energies of light and love, combined with the act of keeping the negative ego at bay or inoperative altogether, and demonstrating a high Christ consciousness quotient, will propel one into the field of world service by virtue of the state of being that they have attained. This is fact. Yet despite the truth of all this, there are indeed many phases and specificities to the higher manifestation of service, and certainly to that of embracing the mantle of leadership!

The Service and Spiritual Leadership Quotient has its own criteria and calls forth its own need for vigilance, as well as cultivation. To be sure, the impulse to serve will be there, but the means of service is something to be cultivated. For instance, it is assumed that all of us with high quotients in other areas will serve humanity in basic and fundamental ways, but, in truth, there is more to this than meets the eye.

Our preceding victories will bring us up to about a 75 to 80% service quotient, with about a 70% spiritual leadership quotient. There is indeed an art to this quotient, and it is this art which is not to be taken lightly. Being of service and accepting the mantle of leadership is, in fact, a most delicate undertaking. It brings one into other peoples auras and areas of need and vulnerabilities. One becomes, in a sense, a divine or spiritual physician, and must exercise the utmost of care. By the same token, this particular quotient's ideal is around 100%. At least that is what one should be striving for. One, of course, will not start out there,

Integrated Ascension

but the more awakened one becomes and the further along the path of integrated ascension one travels, the more one is required to master this particular quotient.

Has not Sai Baba said, "Hands that help are holier than lips that pray"? As one moves into higher and higher initiatory status much has been given to the initiate by GOD and the Masters, and much is now expected. Although one is considered to have entered the portal of being a Master at the beginning of the sixth initiation, full-fledged mastery in GOD's eyes does not occur until Integrated Ascension is achieved.

An interesting point in regard to this quotient that many lightworkers often overlook is that the attitude of service and leadership is primarily thought of solely as being directed towards humanity, the planet and all life forms that one encounters, yet it equally applies to the individual initiate themselves. This, beloved readers, means you. It applies to your own level of appropriate and healthy service and leadership to your self! One is obviously not directing this to the lower egotistical self, but to the precious Son or Daughter of GOD that you are! The balance within this quotient is therefore twofold. It most certainly extends outward into the arena of world service. In this arena it has much to do with finding and embracing your appropriate puzzle piece, as was explored in detail in my book *Your Ascension Mission— Embracing Your Puzzle Piece*. I will explore it a bit further in relation to this particular quotient, shortly. You must, however, be equally aware that it simultaneously applies to the honoring of your own Divine being and attending to your individual needs. Service begins first with Self-actualizing self.

Many begin serving before achieving wholeness or being right with self and right with GOD, which leads to improper outward service ultimately and/or depletion of one's energies. Let one's first service be achieving integration on the path of ascension. True service can begin after one takes the third initiation if the psychological self is properly integrated. Spiritual leadership can begin in the same sequence. It must be understood, however, that one cannot become a spiritual leader for others until one has attained leadership over self. This is called self-leadership. One must become the captain of one's own ship, so to speak. For a more in depth look at the subject of spiritual leadership, please refer to *Manual for Planetary Leadership* in my series of books called "The Easy to Read Encyclopedia of the Spiritual Path."

Spiritual leadership can begin by helping one person and will slowly grow to working with clients, then groups, classes, seminars, and workshops. It may begin focused in the city you live in, and if it is your puzzle piece, may expand to a whole state, country, and/or become global. How one serves and leads does not matter as long as it is in tune with the dictates of one's own Higher Self, Monad or Mighty I Am Presence. One should not compare or compete with others, but rather follow the beat of one's own drum. There should be no glamour in this process. Some are meant to serve and lead quietly behind the scenes and others have a destiny to be in the public eye. Listen to your soul in this regard, not your negative ego.

This applies to embracing your puzzle piece, whatever it may be, and taking your rightful position within the world arena. Perhaps your particular mission is to lead by quiet example from the sidelines, within household or community. Perhaps it will mean that your particular divine destiny will place you upon the world stage where from a large podium and via the means of telecommunication you will make speeches that go out to the entire world. As long as it is your appropriate puzzle piece, it will unfold in divine order. This, however, does not at all preclude the leadership responsibility you have within the arena of your own personal life and those around you.

If you are truly to build this particular quotient, as indeed you are called upon to do, this cannot be done if first it is not done within self. It is up to each person to hold the reigns of leadership over their own personal lives, beginning with their own inner selves. The first mantle of leadership that must be honored is that which abides unseen by any but one's own inner vision. One must first embrace the leadership of one's own personal being, which involves holding to the highest level of all the quotients that have been under discussion thus far. This would mean holding the mind and heart steady in the light in both an impersonal or universal way and a personal way. There is the familiar saying that "charity begins at home." Well, beloved friends, true leadership likewise begins at home. It beings within the home of one's very self. When it is actualized there, expansion then becomes a relatively simple task.

A great many lightworkers are getting misaligned in their missions, service work and puzzle pieces because of negative ego contamination and interference. For example, a person might be meant to serve and lead behind the scenes, however the negative ego, power, fame and glamour tell the person that they should be in the limelight. While out of harmony with their soul and monad they do it anyway creating misalignment, comparison, competition, and fragmentation. It appears they are doing spiritual leadership and world service work, when, in truth, they are following the dictates of the negative ego. One must be devastatingly honest with self on this issue, for the negative ego wants power, fame, glamour, and money, at all costs.

The negative ego might tell you to write a spiritual book when this is not your destiny or true ability. The negative ego may tell you that you need to be a clairaudient voice channel when this is not GOD's true destiny for you. Your destiny, however, might be to voice channel for yourself and friends. Lightworkers often think that spiritual leadership and world service means channeling or teaching on stage in front of a thousand people or a million people on television, or traveling the world doing workshops. I'm here to tell you that this is not most people's destiny or puzzle piece and is not what GOD or the Masters want you to do. Spiritual leadership and world service means serving and leading only in the way your Higher Self and Monad want you to serve and lead. For some lightworkers, this may be doing mostly inner plane work. For others, it may mean involvement in politics. For others, raising a family and serving friends and people you meet. Do not compare. There is no one way of serving and leading that is better than another. What is best is finding your right puzzle piece in GOD's Divine plan.

You can therefore see that this quotient of service and spiritual leadership is the natural outpouring of the radiance of the higher quotients and demands care and attention that is quite detailed and most assuredly quite specific! It is not what it seems at first consideration.

As mentioned earlier, service to others is indeed a very delicate matter. One wants to support the needs of humanity and one's brothers and sisters upon all levels possible. Yet, as was discussed in the section dealing with the negative ego quotient, one does not want to be invasive. One wants to serve the highest good of all kingdoms upon the planet, and yet one does not want to invade another's free will or circumvent valuable lessons. What one must therefore seek to achieve can best be described as helping to meet the essential needs of all whenever possible, and being there in a gentle manner, much like that of a guardian angel who acts when called upon but is otherwise completely respective of a person's own free will.

Now this does not exclude us from offering our suggestions in a most respectful manner, for those with greater vision can help their brothers and sisters learn much from grace rather than from karma. Yet, if one is too heavy handed in this regard one will be inadvertently creating more karma, which must then eventually be overcome. The balance, beloved readers and fellow servers, is indeed a delicate one. The best way to know how to proceed is to consult with your own oversoul and Monad, and to communicate with GOD and the Masters.

As you can see, spiritual leadership is intricately interwoven with service. Because they are so intertwined, they fall under the same category of quotient building. The best way to lead is by example. That is why it has been stressed so adamantly that each must first learn to both serve and lead within one's self. This is also the reason that it is imperative that one ultimately finds their ascension mission and truly embraces their own unique puzzle piece. One cannot build their quotient is this area or be effective servers or leaders if one is coming from a place of dishonesty within oneself.

One whose divine calling is to be a statesperson would fall flat on their face if they tried to be an effective artist. The same would work vice versa. This actually holds true for all puzzle pieces, including the subtle variances and nuances within a seemingly similar puzzle piece. For example, a watercolor painter would not get their message across if they tried to do it in the medium of oils. It gets that subtle, my friends.

Remember that there is absolutely no judgment of one's puzzle piece when viewed via the lens of GOD, and that is the only appropriate lens in which to approach both your puzzle piece and your Service and Spiritual Leadership Quotient. Anything less is totally off base, and will only serve to veer you from your best and most well meaning intentions. If you faint at the sight of blood, you are obviously not meant to be a surgeon. You might, however, be an incredible healer upon the etheric. Don't rush in and say I am going to heal, or I am going to paint. Tune in to the nuances of the call of your own puzzle piece in order to find out how best you may serve it.

It is vital that you remember that the person who is fully embracing their puzzle piece as an introvert, researcher, or a homemaker will be infinitely more effective than one who seeks public notoriety in their work if that is not their calling. Again, GOD does not judge. What is looked for in the building of this quotient is total sincerity, honesty, and devotion to one's true calling. Whether the mantle of leadership is the crown of a king or the torn jeans of the funky musician is of no matter to GOD, nor does it reflect the level at which one has achieved and maintained the quotient under discussion. What does reflect this is one's ability to be of true spiritual service and leadership wherever destiny and free choice have placed you! It is there that you can reach your maximum capacity in this regard and hold a steady 97 to 100% Service and Spiritual Leadership Quotient.

Integrated Ascension

Your Spiritual Leadership and Service Quotient will actually decline if you try to do a puzzle piece that is not your destiny, even if the negative ego has placed you on stage in front of 5000 people. It may appear that your quotient would be going up, but really it is going down for doing that kind of work, for you are misaligned with your soul. Another example might be a person who is trying to be a visionary when their true mission is to be a manifester or vice versa. Another example of this is how lightworkers in the vein of enthusiasm for spiritual leadership, growth, and service will sometimes inappropriately divorce spouses, abandon children, and leave friends and jobs. Sometimes the lesson is to stay in the marriage, be a guru to the children, and spiritualize your present job by adopting the attitude of being of service and radiating spiritual energies, maintaining friendships and spiritualizing those friendships. The idea is to begin serving and leading exactly where you are and not necessarily moving to a spiritual community. Sometimes it is appropriate to leave certain situations; however, the key is to make sure this is the soul's guidance and not the negative ego's guidance. There is an ancient spiritual axiom that states, "One should never leave a situation until they have learned the lessons of that situation, otherwise it is likely to repeat itself in even a stronger form."

Another example of the negative ego contamination and interference in this quotient in the New Age Movement is when a person acts from a place of self-righteousness and/or being a know-it-all. They think because they have achieved their ascension that they are a Master which gives them a right to order people around and tell them what to do. They perceive themselves as speaking as the voice of the Master, which in truth is the voice of the negative ego and a massive power trip, that is most often unconscious, which actually is the exact opposite of what true spiritual leadership is. Another example is a woman who is more feminine and soft in nature who is not an informational channel trying to be an informational channel, when their true destiny might be to lead through the example of love and more lady Master energetic meditations. A woman may be trying to bring through her spirituality and service work in a more masculine paradigm, when her true spiritual mission is to bring it through the Goddess paradigm. Another similar but different example might be a man or a woman who brings through wonderful channelings, however, when they try to teach from their conscious mind, or maybe write from their conscious mind rather than the channeled state it just doesn't work. It is important for every lightworker to know their puzzle piece and not try to move into a puzzle piece that is not their destiny or forte. In reverse, a person could be an excellent spiritual teacher and try to force clairaudient voice channeling when their true purpose is to be more of an integrated channel or a telepathic channel, or just speak from their own inner wisdom and not think about channeling at all.

Other examples in the New Age Movement are mystics who are forcing themselves to be occultists and occultists who are trying to force themselves to be mystics when this is not their true destiny. This may manifest in a person wanting to serve in the capacity of being a voice channel when their true channeling ability might be in the form of being a writer or channeling poetry and/or music. To many lightworkers, being a channel, psychic, spiritual teacher, author, and healer may seem glamorous, when, in truth, it is not. It is not glamour that should be sought but rather divine right spiritual mission. The most effective way to accelerate your ascension is to find your right puzzle piece and to serve and lead in that capacity. A person who is supposed to be a housewife or househusband will move through their initiation process as quickly as a person who is meant to be world famous as a channel, spiritual teacher or governmental leader. In GOD's eyes, there is no difference as long as each person is doing their appropriate part in the Divine Plan.

A person who is trying to be an informational channel without that being their true destiny could end up channeling inaccurately even though they mean well. They would be better off channeling healing

Integrated Ascension

energies, love, and light, thereby serving instead to help uplift their client to a place of divine attunement via these means.

My beloved readers, what is essential to understand is that no one person is meant to have all abilities or fulfill all puzzle pieces. The negative ego with its need for self-aggrandizement will try to push many lightworkers to try to accomplish this. The inner plane Ascended Masters wish me to tell you that this will just create misalignment and cause you to disperse your true light and true ability to shine in the way your Higher Self and Monad would have it be. GOD is so infinite and vast that it takes all of us working together, which includes the inner plane Ascended Masters, to fill all the lenses in the prism of GOD's Divine Plan. Pick out the thing that you are best suited to do and focus on that. Let other people and lightworkers who have other puzzle pieces and destinies support you in those areas where you could use help or support. It is only by all of us working together in cooperation and divine alignment that GOD's Divine Plan can be fulfilled. Some are meant to be channels, some spiritual teachers, authors, psychics, psychologists, counselors, social workers, healers, dancers, poets, artists, politicians, comedians, nurses, doctors, business people, religious leaders, secretaries, scientists, musicians, lawyers, actors, housewives, househusbands, pilots, diplomats, car mechanics, computer technicians, gardeners and on and on. GOD needs lightworkers to serve and spiritually lead in every single area of Earth life. It is not what you do that is important, it is to bring the attitude of spiritual service into whatever you do, whether you are doing a professional job or are away from a professional job. Who cares if one is a world famous channel or spiritual teacher if the negative ego is the guiding force behind their motives? On the other hand, if you are called by your soul or Monad to the forefront of spiritual leadership, then by all means follow that calling; however, do so from a place of total purity and total egolessness.

GOD could be likened to the Sun, which shines down upon the forest and creates beams of sunlight upon the forest floor. We each are a beam or ray of GOD's infinite Light. Let us not try to be a beam of light that is in truth not what GOD created us to be. Let us instead see all the beams of light stemming from the same source, all being of equal value and importance. GOD's Divine Plan cannot be completed unless each and every single person on planet Earth fulfills his or her puzzle piece, as GOD would have it be!

These Spiritual Leadership Service Quotients, beloved readers, cannot be faked nor can they be forced. They must open like the bud, and grow like the flower. The only way that this can happen is by being utterly honest with self and equally vigilant in holding to the higher vision and intent. It is truly hoped that the profundity of this particular quotient will not be overlooked in its seeming simplicity or in the ego's faulty belief that propels one in the direction of spiritual leadership only in the public arena rather than in the place that is in resonant harmony with the frequency of the entire twelve-body system. This is a most serious quotient. It is one that the world needs each of us to express for the sake of helping to establish the kingdom of GOD upon the Earth. It is likewise a quotient that GOD seeks us to express inward for the manifestation of the kingdom of GOD within self.

Do not take this quotient lightly, for its importance on a personal and planetary level cannot be overestimated. At the same time walk lightly upon your path, for this quotient is the natural expression of who we are as GOD beings, and as such, cannot be forced in any way. Enjoy the path of this quotient and the fruits of manifestation will ring forth of their own accord. Be vigilant, yet joyful, and do seek out and embrace your ascension calling and mission. In this way will you become one of the great world servers and spiritual leaders, and you will do it in the way that is 100% right for you and you alone!

Integration and Balance Quotient

This is the last of the eight main quotients that we seek to explore. This quotient is the summation of all the other quotients plus all the subquotients that you will be reading about in a later chapter, and needs to be operating at the highest level possible. This quotient is itself the subject of this book, for as odd as it may seem, a great many lightworkers have high readings on many of the other quotients but have not brought them into alignment, integration and balance with this most important quotient of all. This quotient, beloved readers, is the one that will lead you through the portal of fully integrated ascension. It is the quotient that has revealed itself as the requirement for the next millennium and must therefore be treated with the respect it deserves!

We need to aspire to be functioning within the 92 to 98% range of this quotient. Although 100% would be the ultimate ideal, the Masters seek to be realistic, as this is the hardest and most undeveloped quotient at this present time. One of the reasons this has been the hardest quotient to even get a handle on is that so many lightworkers have paid little heed to some of the other quotients which have been explored, and most are not even aware that these other quotients need to be mastered to any degree at all.

As stated previously, the basic requirement for initiation and ascension lies within the realm of the light quotient, and so it has followed that almost all lightworkers have focused their development almost exclusively on light quotient. It is interesting to me that we do not call ourselves "Love Workers" which embraces the Heart of GOD, which, in truth, we are. Love is such an integral part of our being and evolution that it can no longer be ignored. Most lightworkers do embrace this quotient to one degree or another, for it is part of the Light energy itself. The fact that it deserves specific focus, however, has been sadly overlooked.

Another contributing factor as to why the Integration and Balance Quotient is so out of balance and unintegrated, is that many do not

Integrated Ascension

have the faintest notion that the negative ego has so great a hold over so many. In fact, the term 'negative ego' is itself unheard of in most circles, in terms of its true meaning and because of this, one of the biggest factors to achieving integrated ascension is often overlooked entirely. That is why I have written so much about it, and even devoted an entire book on the subject entitled *How to Clear the Negative Ego*.

When you consider all this, you must then realize that, along with the understanding and the raising of these eight most important quotients, or, in actuality, the seven ones previously discussed, they must then be fully integrated and balanced within the whole. The fulfilling of this process brings forth this eighth most significant quotient. This requires two distinct levels of mastery to be developed. The first is the mastery and quickening of these quotients until one has stabilized them each within themselves to a very high frequency. Second, one must then master and integrate them within all levels of one's being, so that all eight quotients are aligned and functioning at the highest possible frequency, not only in relation to each specific quotient, but also in relation to one's entire being. In this way, one becomes fully integrated, balanced, and whole. If one does not learn how to do this then there will always be a chasm between various aspects of self and true and holistic ascension will not be able to be achieved. One may indeed gain freedom from the round of earthly rebirth, however, one will be forced to bring the unbalanced and unintegrated parts of one's self into alignment upon the astral and/or mental planes. This then would delay one's ultimate complete and total liberation, which I am sure, none would like to see occur.

In actuality, if one is totally honest with one's self, I am sure all would equally agree that when one is not balanced at these various levels, one feels the uncomfortable sense of being out of harmony with self and GOD. One likewise feels cutoff from the fulfillment of one's highest potential. For example, great light will activate much love. Love will seek to express itself in service. If, however, one is totally unfamiliar with the leadership aspect of service, one may find that one does not

Integrated Ascension

have the backbone or will that is necessary in order to make vision a reality. This then leads to personal frustration as well as to the fact that one's appropriate field of service will not be fulfilled. You can see by this quick example, just how interdependent and intertwined all these various quotients truly are!

As we have just spent an entire chapter exploring each of the aforementioned quotients individually, I ask you to join with me now in the exploration of the Integration and Balance Quotient itself. The way this quotient works is that focus is placed upon the particular aspect of alignment and integration of the various other quotients with each other. One point I would again emphasize is that we are each totally unique in the manifestation of our individualities, and, therefore, each of us has our own unique point of balance.

For example, someone with a second ray monad, sixth ray soul and fourth ray personality would certainly be constituted to balance differently than someone who is a first ray monad, fifth ray soul and third ray personality. The point of balance that each are looking for is, consequently, unique. This does not alter the fact that everyone does indeed have a point of optimum balance and that balance needs to be integrated fully and completely within the totality of our beings.

Irrespective of how and where each person reaches their point of optimum balance, all quotients then must function synchronistically and harmoniously. A sixth ray soul, second ray monad may manifest their lives in expression of the heart center, whereas a first ray monad and soul will manifest their lives in areas more associated with "will." This does not alter the fact that each must exhibit the highest possible frequency range within all the various quotients, despite the fact that one person's puzzle piece is bound to be significantly different than another's. All of these quotients under discussion must function in joint rhythm and harmony, pulsating in a unified energy field that is self-contained and self aligned. They must ultimately form a cylindrical passageway and flow easily back and forth between the various frequency ranges and centers of operation, much like the chakras eventually do.

It may help you to visualize this cylinder between each of the eight major quotients. Begin by seeing the initiation quotient as a circle which then extends into a cylinder which connects this particular quotient with the Light Quotient, the Love Quotient, the Psychological Wisdom Quotient, the Christ Consciousness Quotient, the Transcendence of Negative Ego Quotient, the Service and Spiritual Leadership Quotient, all the way through the Integration and Balance Quotient itself. When the above seven quotients are perfectly aligned and attuned, the Integration and Balance Quotient will be operating at a range of 92% at its lowest point and 100% at its maximum potential. The median would be between 97% and 98%, which would be exceedingly high in comparison to what is happening now, and would definitely enable you to gently walk through the sanctified doorway of integrated ascension.

I adamantly ask you, my beloved readers, to take these quotients to heart and to strive to bring each of them up to the heightened level of frequency that they so well deserve. As spiritual beings, we each deserve to be functioning at the highest, most activated and actualized level as possible. This, in truth, is what we have set out to do when we began our path of initiation in the first place. Our own enthusiasm along with the great increase of light and opportunity for mass ascension has pushed us forward in a way that necessitates, for the majority of us at least, a reevaluation and readjustment of all the eight primary quotients simultaneously. When you do this for yourself you will not be sorry, for the level of wholeness and well being that you will feel within yourself will only be surpassed by the knowledge that you are at last totally free to demonstrate your particular puzzle piece and ascension mission in full accordance with the Divine Plan!

You will also have the true peace of mind that comes from the knowledge that you have indeed left no stone unturned, nor any of the eight major quotients unfulfilled. Your pathway of integrated ascension will be complete! You will stand forth fully liberated from all the lower worlds, while simultaneously honoring them as part of the whole and as incredible realms within which to demonstrate your Godliness and service! Remember what I have said earlier, the ladder of evolution is, in truth, circular or cylindrical in shape. It is an ever widening more inclusive spiral that encompasses vaster and vaster aspects of the all pervading *Whole* within its sphere. This is the glory that awaits each one of us that follows the divine path of integrated ascension and this, my beloved readers, is your true and glorious destiny!

My beloved readers, when you read the chapter called "The All Important Sub-Quotients," do be sure to add all that material into the concept of the Integration and Balance Quotient. This will ensure that your path of Integrated Ascension will be manifested from the widest possible full spectrum lens of Planetary and Cosmic Ascension that is available to us at this time.

Summary

I end this chapter with one final suggestion and prayer that each one of you, my beloved readers, makes use of the eight major quotients that we have examined in this chapter and raises them to the highest possible level you can without the negative ego getting involved in the process. Ultimately all levels must be fully integrated and balanced so that the full glory of our own unique and individualized Mighty I Am Presence can be made manifest upon every single level of our existence.

We touch the heart of GOD that we may radiate that love essence outward to a needy world. We fill ourselves with the Light of GOD that we may serve in helping to enlighten the planet. We leave behind the negative ego so that "the mind may be in us that was in Christ Jesus." We learn how to attain psychological balance that we may demonstrate it in love and service and appropriate leadership. We do all this from our own specific place of balance and integration. Integrating these quotients within ourselves allows us to stand forth strong and steady, as the fully Self-Actualized, Self-Realized and GOD Realized beings that it is our divine birthright to be!

This path, obviously, should not allow any room for comparisons, competing, or judgments. If you find you are getting caught up in any of this, know that it is simply the misguided voice of the negative ego! There is no judgment involved, no guilt, and no race to win. It is simply The Path itself that we each are called to walk in order to achieve and demonstrate the wonders of Integrated Ascension. I therefore ask you again, to proceed vigilantly, yet joyously, upon this expanded pathway towards and within the Infinite and Eternal.

This is a path of both grace and work, my beloved readers, and these quotients are meant to serve as lighted lamps and signposts along the way. Remember always to have joy in the building of these quotients, even as you would want to have joy in the building of any Earthly structure or the manifestation of any strictly Earthly dream or vision. These quotients are given forth to aid you upon your journey, and so are given forth from the Heart of the Great Central Sun, and given forth in Love. Tread your path of love and light lightly, and with love in your hearts. Do make use of these quotients, as they are of utmost importance, but do so with no stress or strain. They are simply a gift to help you on your journey, and a further Revelation of GOD upon Earth as we enter the glorious world of the New Millennium!

3

Integrating the Twelve Levels of Initiation into the Four-Body System

Dispelling the Illusion

One of the great difficulties and misperceptions that has infiltrated the consciousness and belief system of many high degree initiates and light-workers is that each level of initiation supersedes the one preceding it. While there is truth to this when viewed from one perspective, greater exploration and more extended perception will reveal that, in truth, each level of initiation 'incorporates' and 'integrates' the preceding level. What actually occurs, or more aptly, what ideally occurs, is that each subsequent level integrates all the energies, frequencies, love, light, cleansings, clearings, and accelerations of the initiation most recently passed through. When done via this holistic approach, each initiation both builds and refines upon each initiation, with a total and complete integrated Ascension being the inevitable outcome.

As a great many of us have not fully utilized this process, this time of awareness is the time to see what, as yet, remains unintegrated and unassimilated. No matter what level initiate you currently are, begin to explore the gaps that may yet remain unattended within your initiatory process. If you are at a so-called lower rung of the ladder, this expanded understanding of Integrated Ascension will help facilitate a more rounded out approach to your path. You are, in one sense, fortunate to come upon this understanding at an earlier stage in your process, so that you can proceed upon your path holistically at the outset. In truth, however, it does not matter where you currently stand upon the ladder of evolution, for we are each equally enjoined to fully integrate the entire process within the four-body system, in order to be totally balanced and liberated from the chains that bind or the illusions that encapsulate us in the deepest sense possible.

The First Initiation

The first initiation has to do with control over the physical vehicle, or more aptly stated, over the physical elemental. It does not, as so many inaccurately think, mean that we live separate and apart from our physical bodies. There is a certain aspect of this, of course, as we become abundantly aware and awake to the fact that our essential selves are not the temporary form within which we dwell. This is of course essential to our basic understanding that we are soul/spirit dwelling within the form. While in embodiment, however, our job is to purify the physical/etheric vehicle and bring our higher self into it. This is vastly different from detaching ourselves from it altogether. This type of wrenching detachment is the antithesis of integration and ultimately does not serve our true purpose.

What is expected of us is to control the physical/etheric to the highest degree possible. At this stage of evolution, this excludes any forms of mutilation, denial, separation or lack of proper nourishment. The physical elemental needs to be brought under control—which entails the process of self discipline whereby the lower base self and animalistic tendencies of lust, overindulgence, lack of self discipline and so forth are subjugated to the conscious mind which is learning to become totally subservient to the oversoul.

This process also requires proper nourishment, which is seldom given it. As an extraordinary spiritual and physical healer once told me on the subject of nutrition, the root of the word nutrition comes from the word nurture. In order to nurture the body, we must follow the guidelines of a diet that is healthy and suited to our individual needs. Obviously, we do not want to saturate ourselves with junk food or other toxins. Expanding upon the concept of true nurturing, we also want to nurture and love our physical/etheric vehicles. A great many lightworkers do not do this at all, as they are far too busy disassociating from the physical altogether. The energies of the cycle in which we live will not tolerate this, we must integrate the proper feeding of the physical vehicle on every level. This of course does not mean indulging. It does, beloved readers, mean nurturing!

For ages upon ages, as long as there have been disciples treading the path of initiation, the control of the physical body has been well known and generally, although not always, attended to properly. Many of us still have unresolved issues regarding proper diet, exercise, and control over the lower appetites. We are here to now reveal to you that this is not enough. Proper nurturing is as vital as proper control. We must embrace and love ourselves within our forms! This is absolutely essential. If we do not do this a barrier will be set up between soul/spirit, the Mighty I Am Presence and the physical form, and we will not be doing the job that we came into embodiment to do in this millennium, which is to fully anchor Spirit into the physical!

Do consider the holistic approach to what is generally considered as the basic requirement of the first initiation. Remember what I have previously stated regarding the fact that we must incorporate or integrate all of your will that the specific age or cycle in which we live seeks to outpicture. This is the age of anchoring the Divine on Earth, which must therefore include our physical selves.

Integrated Ascension

For any of you who are struggling with basic control over the lower appetites and desires of the physical elemental, or diet, or exercise, give that the required attention. Most of you know the work you need to do. There are also countless books, physical/etheric healers, nutritionists, and the like to help you in this process. If you need help, please do not feel any shame in this. Most all of us need to recapitulate and refine our process in this regard, which is one of the reasons so many healers and helpers have been guided to assist in this direction. Never forget that the Masters themselves can be contacted at anytime and will give abundantly just for the asking. We therefore have the inner plane Ascended Masters and Angels, and the outer plane healers—whose puzzle piece is to help nurture us through this integration and help us refine our process to meet the standards of this new millennium, and a library of books, both of ancient and modern teaching to which we can refer. Remember, he goal is to honor and purify the physical that it may shine with the light and love of GOD upon Earth.

If you find any area, which most all of us do, that requires some work in this regard, do pursue it. Keep in mind, that even amidst the most stringent disciplining of the physical vehicle, we must also nurture it with our love. Proper diet, exercise, supplements and self-control will get us just so far. We must also bring in proper love, nurturing, and an attitude of gratitude for being in physical embodiment. We must love who we are in form and allow others to love and honor our embodiments. This, beloved readers, is the larger scope of requirements and the full fleshing out, so to speak, of the first level of initiation. All this then needs to be brought forward, to blend and integrate with the second initiation.

It must be understood that you do not have to have total mastery of the physical vehicle to pass this initiation. There are seventh degree initiates who are totally run by their physical appetites. Although it is not required to have total balanced control to pass the initiation, if you ever want to achieve integrated ascension and full GOD Realization this is required. In truth, initiations are much easier to pass than they once were. They are so easy to pass that a book like this has to be written to remind advanced lightworkers to do the homework that is required to fully integrate these initiations properly. Lightworkers are passing these initiations on the spiritual level but not in the mental, emotional, etheric and physical level of each of these initiations. GOD has made it easy in this current period of history which we should all be grateful for. All GOD requires is that we pass them on a spiritual level. By the time we reach the seventh initiation GOD then has set up a ring-pass-not which says if you want to go farther you must integrate each initiation in all four bodies, not just the spiritual body. So just because you or someone you know has passed initiations doesn't mean in the slightest that you or they have really passed them in the mental, emotional or physical bodies. In the past, this was required; in this current dispensation of history, it is not. Although GOD does not require a very high standard to pass these initiations He would prefer if you would. If you do the homework now you won't have to go back and do it as a seventh degree initiate later.

The Second Initiation

Most of you will have already passed through the portals of the second initiation, which is control of the astral or lower desire body. What I am now asking you to do is to be open and willing to further refine this so that the feeling body may demonstrate more accurately the frequencies of this new millennium. This would, of course, incorporate and integrate all the refinements and requirements of the first, or preceding initiation. Remember that we are aiming at full and total integration of all levels, such as never before demonstrated upon this hallowed Earth.

The control of the emotional body and astral elemental is not the simplest aspect of self to work with. Much in our present society is

Integrated Ascension

geared towards its stimulation rather than its control, and we are like salmon swimming upstream in this regard. Do be aware that almost all of you reading this have achieved enough mastery to have passed this initiation in preceding lives and this life. What is being asked of you again is to refine and to integrate this process to bring it to the standards that seek expression in this current world cycle.

This being the case, know that you already have a firm foundation upon which to do the necessary work. Take comfort in the fact that you have made an inner plane contract to do this before taking embodiment within this cycle. The "Force" is truly with you, dear friends, and all is aligned to assist you. With that in mind, let us proceed.

First let us understand, as we did regarding the First initiation and the physical and etheric bodies, that what is sought is both proper and total control of the emotional vehicle along with the proper nurturing of it. To nurture does not mean to indulge. It means to feed it with love. It means to share love, consideration and caring among each other, thus honoring the feeling body of humanity in general. To do this while implementing the highest degree of control is, in truth, the call of this New Age, as well as the challenge. If you take a moment to stop and think about this, however, you will clearly see how this is reflective of total integration. self-discipline over the emotional body, along with the proper nurturing through love, brings this body into an integrated alignment that is indeed new.

Too often initiates have passed through the sacred portal of the second initiation utterly cutoff from the emotional self. This was appropriate in the past, for it was basically the supplication of the astral elemental that was sought in order to bring this body under the control of the higher self. Today it is not enough. On the one hand, a greater control is being called for so that this body reflects the highest aspects of feeling, which is that of feeling and sharing pure and unconditional love. On the other hand, an anchoring of this love within the feeling world is being called forward. It is therefore essential that we put forth the highest level of control over this vehicle while simultaneously allowing the feeling body to anchor love upon Earth.

The intricate subtleties through which the emotional body can assume inappropriate control are numerous. As they are addressed elsewhere in this book, they will not be focused upon here. Much of its subterfuge comes via the subconscious mind, discussed elsewhere, which is why it is imperative that we do all that we possibly can upon a conscious level to reprogram and refine that aspect of ourselves into a place of total positivity. The best food we can possibly feed the subconscious inner child and/or unconscious part of self, are positive energies. We, therefore, should do that with 100% of focused intent while functioning on a conscious level.

In conclusion, with regard to the Second initiation, the best tact to take in order to effectuate the fullest integration of every aspect of the feeling world is the demonstration of control of the lower self by the conscious mind and will that is subservient to the ideals of the Higher Self. The next step then is to train the mental and emotional vehicle to express only unconditional love. It should likewise incorporate, embrace, and demonstrate care and nourishment for the feeling bodies of all sentient life. This may be demonstrated as the love between mates, the love of family, the love of the Animal Kingdom, and the love of the devic/nature kingdom. The emotional body is meant to be used as a vehicle for expression upon the physical plane, be it in a broad sense or an extremely intimate sense. It is not meant to be stifled or suffocated, only under absolute control of the conscious mind, Higher Self and Mighty I Am Presence. In this way, the feeling self will assume its rightful place. As this is done, remember to incorporate the highest, most balanced of the first initiation described above. Likewise, remember to bring the integrated qualities of the Second initiation into the subsequent levels. In this manner will Ascension itself be embraced and manifested in the most balanced and integrated manner as possible.

Integrated Ascension

The Third Initiation

As you know, the third initiation deals with control over the mental body. As there are the three minds that we are dealing with, this is in truth an intricate process. For our specific purpose in this section we will deal primarily, if not exclusively, with the conscious mind. We will also bear in mind that we are not doing this in an isolated fashion, but in an integrated fashion. This means that everything that has been previously discussed regarding the first and second initiations must be fully integrated within that which we will discuss with regard to the third initiation. It likewise means that everything that is refined, manifested, and demonstrated within the third initiation must be fully incorporated and integrated within all following initiations. Our object remains to integrate all seven levels of initiation. To bring them to their highest most balanced and integrated state singularly, and then to see them as one functioning whole.

In truth, if only the minimum level of mastery is achieved within the first and second initiation, it will not allow the full potential of the third level to be anchored, activated and actualized. All levels must be maximized and then blended one into the other. The clearer you are, the more direct and on the mark you are. Consequently, in dealing with the vehicles of one level of initiation, the smoother the transition to the next level and the easier it will be to achieve the desired result. All bodies, chakras, and initiations are interconnected and ultimately function as a singular unit and whole. This precious truth should not be forgotten, lest fragmentation lead you from your true goal, creating unnecessary lessons that must then be attended to later.

As the third initiation deals with mind, there is no better way to express what is necessary in dealing with this aspect of self than to quote beloved Sai Baba, "The mind creates bondage or the mind creates liberation." Within these words are the very key to this initiation. The *key* to Integrated Ascension, however, is to fully and totally claim the

Integrated Ascension

mastery of the mind. It is one thing to grasp the concept of the 'monkey mind' as it is so often referred to, and another thing entirely to manifest the total control of this vehicle within the dimensions in which we play out our life's intent!

So many lightworkers use only one facet of the mind to understand and implement the refined level of mind control necessary to bring into manifestation the higher frequencies. Intellectually, we all understand the need to make the mind subservient to the Oversoul and Monad or Mighty I Am Presence. This is not at all the complete picture, but rather only a fragment of what requires our utmost attention and diligent work. What we must inevitably do, beloved readers, is to bring the "monkey mind" under the control of the consciousness and frequencies of Spirit itself. We must anchor all energies, guidance, key codes, and sacred geometries, into the concrete mind itself. So many lightworkers do not do this. They meet the minimum requirements of mental control and then allow distortions from the feeling and etheric/physical to play upon the mind. This happens as a result of having met only the minimum requirements of the first and second level of initiation, and that in an unintegrated fashion. The result of all this is imbalance within these three vehicles, and a fragmentation that allows the negative ego to still extend its power over the initiate.

By now I hope you are seeing the interconnectedness of this whole process and how utterly vital it is to achieve the highest standards of integration and refinement on each successive level or rung of the spiritual ladder. This next millennium calls out for the full and complete anchoring of the Spiritual upon the Earth. This cannot be done upon the Earth unless it is first done within each of us individually. This is law. When a certain rate of frequency and heightened development and integration is developed and held within each of us, the microcosm, it cannot help but to expand and be upheld collectively within the macrocosm of humanity itself!

Integrated Ascension

It is also quite fitting here to remind you that the current cycle in which we are presently engaged is one that involves subtle intricacies of psychology. All of this must be taken into full account as we move forward towards making Integrated Ascension a fact within our selves and within the world.

The Fourth Initiation

As you are all well aware at the fourth initiation the individual soul body is burnt up and the initiate is then in direct rapport with the conscious-ness of the Monad or Mighty I Am Presence. This occurrence marks the point wherein your four lower bodies—when integrated, balanced and aligned—would receive direct impressions from the Monad itself. The disruption to this process occurs when initiation and ascension is not done holistically, but rather in a fragmented and unbalanced fashion. When the high standards of the preceding initiations are not upheld, the negative ego and personal agenda comes into play. Rather than the hoped for attitude of selfless service and love, the initiate remains run by the negative ego.

The Fifth Initiation

Taking the fifth initiation elevates one's frequency to the Atmic plane. This is a very high initiation and is, obviously, the one preceding the sixth initiation, or that of passing through the Sacred Portal of Ascension itself. It is at this initiation where the being proclaims, "I and the Father are One." The challenge which this book addresses, is namely to integrate in full force the highest qualities of the preceding initiation.

The Sixth Initiation

The taking of the sixth initiation brings you into the full light of Ascension. I lovingly refer to taking the first phase, or sub-level of this initiation as becoming a full-fledged "Kindergarten" Ascended Master. At this point the term Master is given to you, as you have obviously earned it by the building of your light quotient and the meeting of certain necessary requirements regarding the preceding initiation. The completion of this initiation occurs at the seventh sub-level of the seventh initiation.

An extremely vital point to note here is that in regards to Karma, we are required to balance a mere 51% of it before taking the 6th initiation of Ascension. This obviously leaves much that can still bubble up to confront us and provide us with many a lesson. This does not necessarily have to happen for it is literally within our power, our light, love and wisdom, to circumvent much of this and to learn all we need to know by Grace rather than Karma. This is at issue here, however, since so many lightworkers are not even upholding the earlier initiations and the negative ego has claimed the power that the individual should have. This must ultimately be corrected!

The Seventh Initiation

As was just stated, completing the seventh sub-level of the seventh initiation brings you into the status of a full-fledged Ascended Master in the context of light quotient only. You have graduated "Kindergarten" and stand as a Master, as one who has fully gained access to the higher levels, from a planetary perspective, of the great Order of Melchizedek. Wonderful cosmic energies flow through your Being as you take your hard-earned place as a Master among the other Masters of Hierarchy. This is all quite wonderful, and you are to be congratulated.

By passing the seventh initiation, you have achieved liberation from the wheel of physical rebirth and this is a fantastic accomplishment. However, it must be understood that just because you passed the seventh initiation doesn't mean you have mastered your negative ego, lower self desire, your emotional body, your inner child, your subconscious mind, the mental body, your physical appetites or the spiritual tests of power, fame, money, sexuality, pride, and vanity, to name just a few. What you have achieved is from 92 to 98% light quotient. That is all this initiation means. Also understand that 98 or 99% light quotient is the planetary scale and when you switch to the cosmic scale what you really have is 10% light quotient in the whole scheme of things. As I said in the first chapter, if you haven't integrated each of the initiations in all four bodies, although you have passed the seventh initiation, you will still have to reincarnate on the astral or mental plane if this hasn't been done. You will also not be allowed to take any higher initiations until this psychological work is done. I actually know one lightworker who I would consider to be a full-fledged schizophrenic and megalomaniac, and he is a seventh degree initiate. Talk about a paradox. This particular schizophrenic happens to channel and do psychic work. So, do you see, my beloved readers, that the seventh initiation isn't what it used to be! It meant a lot more in the days of Jesus, Lord Maitreya, St. Germain, El Morya, Kuthumi, and Djwhal Khul. When they passed initiations, it meant business. Because of the great acceleration that Earth itself is going through, we have been allowed to literally slip through the sacred portals of initiation in order to help facilitate this by virtue of our bringing in the higher light frequencies. This has served its purpose and we are now being asked once again to purify and cleanse ourselves at every level in order to be the full-fledged integrated Master. To help serve this new dispensation, this book has come into being, my beloved readers.

The Ring Passeth Not

The vital thing to be aware of here is that there is and ever has been a "ring-pass-not" at the seventh sub-level of the seventh initiation. This "ring-pass-not" is in actuality a point of accountability. As the energies flow in at incredible speeds propelling so many of us through our seven

Integrated Ascension

levels of initiation, so very much is obviously gained, not only for ourselves, but also for the planet as a whole. By increasing our light frequencies enough to become Ascended Masters in our own right, we serve to anchor these energies upon our planet. This is all in accordance with the Divine Plan.

What needs to be understood, however, is that until there is applied integration of all the preceding initiations, you are withheld from taking any of the higher initiations and are basically kept in stasis at the seventh level. The "ring pass not" and the law of accountability are actually two different ways of expressing the same truth. You can get so far but no further. You can gain total liberation from the rounds of birth and death upon the physical, but you will have to make the appropriate adjustments upon the astral and mental planes before continuing onward upon the path of higher evolution.

There are also cases that are somewhat less common, but prevalent within the heightened frequency of this current cycle, where a being does take the higher initiations and then falls out of harmony with the laws of the physical/etheric, astral and mental planes. This is quite serious, for as the saying goes, "The higher one is, the farther one falls." One of the areas of utmost concern in reference to these cases is that the person that this happens to is usually totally unaware of what is occurring. This is due to the fact that the negative ego has taken hold and they therefore assume they are operating at the same level of integrity as they had before they veered off the true path.

They become, in essence, a victim of their own faulty belief systems. In most cases, they are not aware that the Masters have cutoff their energy flow so that the given individual may learn the needed lesson. Instead, the person is so inflated and driven by their own power, that they keep themselves in delusion. This leads one into the area of the "Twilight" Master, which I have devoted an entire chapter to and so will not be explored here. Suffice it to say that when an initiate makes the choice to veer from their path of Godliness, a "ring-pass-not" is placed around them, and they are held in stasis, no matter how high a degree initiate they are. If this occurs at the eighth, ninth, tenth, eleventh, twelfth initiation equivalent, or even beyond, the "ring-pass-not" will be installed and they will be stuck at that level until every "jot and title" of the law be answered for. They will be held accountable for their misdeeds the same as anyone else and will be continually placed in the best possible situation to learn their needed lesson. When the lesson is learned and all actions are accounted for, the "ring-pass-not" will be removed and they will continue onward upon their path of evolution.

In order to avoid this from occurring at any point upon your journey, I stress the dire need for an integrated and balanced approach to Ascension. I also remind you that you must ever remain vigilant in your intent and in the constant monitoring of your basic motivations. This monitoring process need not at all be tedious or consuming. All it really requires is to be aware of your intent. Are you serving self or are you serving GOD, the Masters, humanity, and the planet? Are you integrating and implementing the lessons and teachings of all your prior initiations? If that is indeed the case, then you are in harmony with Divine Will and operating within the perfect Tao. It really is as simple as this. You must, however, be willing to be vigilant upon these points.

So, it cannot be emphasized more emphatically that initiations have to do with the amount of light quotient you are holding and nothing more. Just because a person has achieved their ascension and passed their seven levels of initiation doesn't really mean they're a Master in the true sense of the word. They may have freed themselves from the wheel of rebirth, however, what does that mean, in truth, if they are totally power hungry, fame hungry, egotistically ambitious, filled with self-aggrandizement, self-centered, competitive, run by the emotional body, run by the inner child, run by lower-self desire, filled with impure motives, philosophically and psychologically totally misaligned, and filled with negative emotions and negative thoughts. My beloved readers, I personally know hundreds if not thousands of high level initiates who fall into this category. I do not say this to be judgmental; I am just sharing a simple, loving, observational fact. It is for this reason the Masters have guided me to write this book.

Integrating Into the Physical

At this point, it is sincerely hoped that the reason why this integration is so vitally necessary to the process of Ascension is felt by the very core level of your being. Without this process, beloved readers, Ascension is at best incomplete, and at worst, can be undermined by fragmentation and imbalances that lead the individual away from their pure path and purpose within Source. As all this has just been explained in detail, we will now explore the means by which we can practically implement true integration within our four-body system.

The above is a critical and crucial subject, for it deals with Ascension as Decension, the bringing in and anchoring of Spirit on Earth. It also deals with each initiates' responsibility to 'the Path' and the puzzle piece that they hold within Hierarchy. In essence, it is monadic in scope, for at the levels of the higher initiation it is the Monad itself that is expressing within the four lower bodies and likewise endeavoring to pursue ever higher initiations. It also holds true that by neglecting to fully balance, actualize, and integrate all levels of initiations simultaneously within the four-body system, the initiates endanger themselves and humanity if they fall prey to the negative ego. In essence, there is much at stake on every single level, both personally, planetary, monadically and even cosmically, if the initiate is advanced enough. This subject, therefore, is of paramount importance to every single person upon planet Earth.

To begin with, as was stated at the start of this chapter, the goal regarding the physical body is to fully integrate all the succeeding activations, heightened frequency levels, the installment of the higher chakras, sacred geometries, key codes and love/wisdom of the higher initiations right into the physical vehicle. This cannot be accomplished

Integrated Ascension

if we engage in the process of disassociating ourselves from the physical vehicle, as so many lightworkers tend to do. It can only be accomplished by anchoring into the physical vehicle all that has been obtained from the levels beyond it. We must therefore embrace, rather than detach ourselves from the physical vehicle, as it is the means by which we are to express our GOD Selves upon this Earth, for it is indeed the temple of our Spirit.

Many people still adhere to the outmoded and outdated belief system that if we allow ourselves to experience joy or pleasure by means of the physical vehicle, then we are somehow moving out of alignment with GOD. I assure you this is not the case. It can be the case, however, if the physical elemental is allowed to exercise its power over the true Self, the inner Spirit, our divine monadic essence. This is the reason that control of the lower tendencies is stressed so strongly. There is, however, a vast difference between holding the appropriate control over the lower aspects of this vehicle and denying any bond with it whatsoever. Beloved readers, while in embodiment there is an undeniable unity between spirit and form. This is expressed within our physical and etheric selves. It is likewise expressed within the physical/etheric self of the planet as a whole. It is the call of this new millennium to honor this bond and not to falsely deny it!

The divine intent is to anchor and physicalize Spirit smack into the very heart, or core, of the material world in order to make the golden age a "fact" upon the densest levels of the planet. The best place to start with is within our own physical structure. I am aware that this appears to be the antithesis of some of the more familiar concepts and precepts set forth in other ages and in more ancient traditions, such as that of Yoga, to name but one out of many. I assure you, however, that it is not truly antithetical in nature, but only appears to be, as certain aspects dealing with the physical vehicle were more appropriately stressed during other ages and cycles.

Integrated Ascension

The strong injunction to control the physical vehicle was absolutely appropriate, and still is. I am by no means guiding you away from this aspect of the first initiation, for without having that in proper perspective the physical vehicle will control you! The conscious mind, subservient to the Soul and Monad, must absolutely hold the reigns over the lower appetites and inclinations of the physical self. This point has, hopefully, been made abundantly clear by now. What I am adding to this most vital teaching is the call of the New Age to cease from turning away from this vehicle but rather to actualize within it all that has been brought forth by achieving the higher initiations, including that of ascension, and beyond.

One expression of this would be the expression of the opened heart chakra. The heart holds the quality and nature of love. Love seeks to be expressed in the physical. This is not to imply by any means that one should have a mate or even an intimate relationship. That is entirely up to the individual's personal choice, as well as the basic blueprint for any given lifetime. It does however, mean that we as lightworkers reach out to one another and make the appropriate physical contact and connections. Many lightworkers are so withdrawn they pull away from even giving a good hug to some of their closest friends and colleagues. They do not touch. Instead, they stay within their higher energy centers and do not relate at all on the physical level. This, in truth, is not healthy.

It is a proven scientific fact that every human being needs touch. Infants in orphanages are known to die due to the lack of touch. One of the more esoteric reasons for this is that the individual heart chakra, which in reality is a focal point for the Heart of GOD itself, seeks to touch the parts of itself that have taken form in various human bodies. The only means that the heart has to anchor and express itself physically is via touch and the various other senses.

When two high level initiates touch there is a vast and dynamic explosion of Love itself that shoots from out the Heart of GOD, travels through the heart chakra of the two individuals involved and radiates a great healing love light through the multitude of subatomic mini chakras residing within the contact points of the physical vehicle. The touching, therefore, is truly not one of flesh to flesh, although that is what seems to be enacted. It is rather the touching of the fire heart of GOD Source through the activated heart, etheric and physical structure of a human being!

If we do not honor the physical body, we are in reality not honoring the fullness that is GOD, is Source. We are fragmenting one part of GOD from other parts of GOD and creating a chasm where none in truth exists. One of the best ways that I can think of to drive this point home comes from guidance given to me by the Mahatma, the Avatar of Synthesis. Time and time again, "He" has told me that in order to fully embrace him and the height, depth, and breadth of what he represents, He must be fully embraced upon every level of His Beingness. In order to do this He must be incorporated into every single aspect of existence, as He is indeed the great synthesizer of the Cosmos. What this, in essence, means is that if one truly seeks to know Him and then merge with Him at the 352nd level of the Godhead, one must know and embrace Him at every single rung upon the ladder of evolution. The first level must be as fully and completely embraced as the 352nd level! It becomes apparent, therefore, that the physical level must be embraced as fully and completely as the spiritual.

Now, beloved readers, I must tell you that I myself have the tendency to seek Him at his higher octaves. This seemed to me the most obvious place to seek Him, as it has always been Source that I have been heaven-bent to merge with, and nothing less. Then along comes the Mahatma, who more than once has told me that if I want to merge utterly and completely with Source I must likewise merge with every level that Source contains! What I have discovered is that the so-called 'ladder' upward is actually cylindrical in shape. There are levels, to be sure, but they are not in actuality stacked one above the other. What they are is what the Mahatma Himself calls, "Levels of Inclusiveness." Within this

Integrated Ascension

statement of undeniable truth, which the Mahatma has been kind enough to bless us with, is much, much more to ponder upon!

Most lightworkers have all the necessary knowledge they need in order to get plenty of exercise, rest, good nutrition and so forth. What is often missing is the will to just do these things. It is not necessary to be fanatical in any of these areas, however we should all honor the messages that our bodies themselves are giving to us. We do not need to be psychic to know if we are getting enough rest or exercise. We simply need to pay attention to what we already know, what the body itself is saying, and then to take the appropriate course of action in order to promote optimum care for our physical selves. The Mahatma abides within these vehicles, even as we do, even as GOD does. The process of integration involves every level of self, and there is no way around this.

Part of integrating the Mahatma on all levels is not just taking care of the physical body. It is also honoring the entire third dimensional reality. Integration of the Mahatma involves making sure the third dimensional needs of family, friends, neighbors and clients are met. For example, if they come to visit, make sure they are not thirsty or hungry. Make sure the air conditioner, fan or heater is not too high or low. Integrating the Mahatma, which is the highest frequency of energy on Earth, is complimenting on their clothing or their new haircut. Integrating the Mahatma is helping your neighbor even if it is a sacrifice. Integrating the Mahatma is being sensitive to the third dimensional needs, wants and desires of family members even though you do not have those needs, wants and desires yourself. Integrating the Mahatma is remembering birthdays, names, and writing thank you notes. Integrating the Mahatma is serving a meal to a friend or family member that you may not even eat yourself, but you know that this is the kind of food or drink that they like. Do not just seek the Mahatma at the 352nd level of the Godhead. If you truly want to know Him and to merge with Him, which is just about the same thing as merging with

GOD, then seek Him in all 352 levels which include earthly, physical, emotional, mental and all spiritual levels.

The Mahatma tells me to express and suppress, not repress. Implicit in that statement is, of course, the necessary discipline and control of the physical elemental that was spoken of earlier on. Remember, however, that it is only until very recently that the Mahatma Himself has anchored fully upon our physical sphere. This is a momentous occurrence, and also hails the coming Golden Age where we'll see the Kingdom of GOD fully anchored and expressed upon the Earth. We need to begin to facilitate the birth of this Golden Era first within ourselves. We then need to extend it outward towards humanity as a whole, to the animal, plant, and mineral kingdoms, as well as to the kingdom and evolutionary line of the devas and angels. The entire physical Earth must be embraced and empowered by the Love of the Divine Heart and the shinning Light, flowing from Source through us into the very core foundation all that finds expression with physical manifestation!

Integrating Into the Etheric

The etheric, as you know, forms the subtle aspect of our physical selves. It likewise has a function specific unto itself. For example, frequency of the chakras are expressed via the physical glands, such as the thyroid, reflecting either over stimulation or under stimulation depending upon the spinning of the chakra. One must be careful in assuming the position of diagnostician in this process, however, for it takes a highly trained initiate to discern the cause of any physical discomfort. What may on the surface appear to be a disease, may from a clearer perspective reveal itself to be a cleansing or a reconfiguration and adjustment to higher frequencies. The truth, however, is that the developing process of the etheric chakra system will be felt in the physical vehicle, and more specifically upon the associated glands.

Integrated Ascension

The etheric body in general, although directly connected to and interwoven with the physical body, has a range of frequencies specific to itself. It functions both jointly and independently from any given physical body, as can be easily seen when one detaches from the physical to journey within their etheric body. Much information regarding the well being and health status of a given individual can be accessed and worked with by coming into contact with their etheric body. It is really quite an interesting system, involving many subtleties and intricacies that are indeed indicative of a life of its own. Although it is most often seen as a facet of the physical vehicle, it serves us well to broaden our horizons a bit and to see it as a vehicle unto itself. Once we have done this, we can expand upon the various ways in which this body can be more fully integrated into the full spectrum of initiation, so that it is accurately known to be both an extension of the physical body of humanity, yet a body deserving of specific focused attention.

An interesting point to note is for those whose evolution is upon the devic and angelic line, they enter the physical through embodiment upon the etheric. For these beings, the etheric vehicle functions as their so-called physical vehicle as they vibrate to a somewhat heightened frequency than that of humanity at present. The worlds between them and us are moving into closer alignment, however, and the veils between the two evolutions are lifting. This is being indicated by the rapid increase of those among our race that can see and communicate with their world. It needs to be noted that in conjunction with all that has been previously stated, the etheric is, after all, but a heightened expression of physical embodiment. This does not, however, exclude the fact that it likewise functions as a unit, or vehicle unique unto itself.

As we proceed upon our path of initiation, the chakras automatically reflect the frequency of each initiation that we take. The petals within each chakra open and the speed at which the chakras spin are all indicative of the level of initiation. As the higher initiations are taking place, there is an anchoring of the higher chakras within the etheric spaces. All

Integrated Ascension

of this outpictures upon the physical level and upon the etheric level. It becomes our job to oversee the level of purity within these systems, to keep them free and clear from any negative psychic debris. One of the primary ways this is done is by approaching our initiations and ascensions in an integrated and balanced way. Likewise, we must keep vigilant watch over the etheric space around us, disallowing other people's negative energy from entering into our sacred etheric sphere.

We do this by invoking a protective bubble of golden white light around our auric field, and calling upon the pure white light of the Christ. We can also invoke the aid and assistance of any Master or Angel whom we feel a direct attunement to to assist us in this process. We watch our motivations at all times and upon all levels, so that only the purest energies of intent are called forth. In this manner, we will set in motion the healthy expression of the best that we have garnered via our path of initiation. We will therefore be running only the highest energy through our etheric system, and this will keep us balanced upon the etheric and dense physical planes alike.

As the chakra system outpictures some of the more subtle energies that are being circulated through our system, there are definitely occasions where a chakra cleansing, clearing and balancing are in order. There are certain specific initiates who are specifically trained in this subtle art of healing with whom we can work to balance and unclog our etheric mechanism. Some of these initiates are more attuned to this subtle system via their intuition. Others can actually read the bands of frequency being emitted through each of the chakras. It is a good idea to occasionally consult a healer in this specific field, for they can be of tremendous help in keeping our etheric system free from all negativity, whether it be of a psychic nature, due to implants and/or negative elementals, or simply due to our own misalignment which has caused us to run unbalanced negative energies through this vehicle. There is also a certain amount of debris that we are apt to pick up by simply functioning within the etheric emanations of the planet itself. I would be most happy to reference one of these healers to you if you contact me at the phone number listed at the back of this book. Also, feel free to call on the inner plane Ascended Masters and Galactic Healers for they are happy to help and are but awaiting your request.

The main point that we are trying to make here is that it is up to you to guard and nurture this body in the same basic manner that you have been guided to do in regard to the physical. This means, first, by honoring it through your full acknowledgment of it. Once we have done this then it is up to each of us individually to bring the purest and highest expression of our GOD or Soul/Monadic Beingness through it. It is essential that we view our four lower bodies as one singular unit for the express purpose of anchoring GOD within them. In this sense the etheric/physical, astral and mental bodies are to be respected, loved, nurtured, honored, and cared for. We integrate the spiritual body within these vehicles, while knowing them to be a collaborative expression of the Soul/Monad. We likewise deal with each of these four bodies in the specific manner that they require. Under no circumstance, however, do we want to ignore them or see them as lesser than the Spirit body or bodies. The ideal is to integrate them fully with the body of Spirit and to allow them to do what they were created to do, namely to be the expression of the Most High upon the specific plane in which they abide. This, beloved readers, will help establish the Golden Age and finally anchor GOD fully and completely within all these precious realms. The work of Integrated Ascension is therefore a work that we should all be attending to in a diligent yet joyful manner. This is the work that will ultimately reveal the face of GOD upon this hallowed Earth!

Integrating the Astral

The astral or emotional vehicle is one of the more difficult bodies to actually integrate within one's ascension process. This again, is due to the extremely accelerated rate at which many lightworkers are speeding through their initiation/ascension process by virtue of a high light quotient, without the benefit of fully gaining the necessary control over the astral elemental. Even if we assume that the second initiation was taken and therefore mastered in a life preceding this one, it is imperative that the lessons learned then be reactivated and applied to the conditions of this current world cycle. This is not being done, beloved readers, and this is cause for much concern on the part of the inner plane Hierarchy of Ascended Planetary and Cosmic Masters, and cause for much distress within the life of the non-integrated initiate and those to whom they extend their influence.

As long as the astral or feeling body has not integrated the frequencies and energies inherent in the higher initiations or is running the initiate's program in any way, it is absolutely imperative that this be corrected. Remember that it is the Monad whose place it is to run the higher energies through each of us and not the place of any of the four lower bodies to dictate the frequency, programs, or agendas of the personal self. In the area presently under discussion, this would directly apply to the astral body and astral elemental.

It must be clearly understood that there is a very large degree of reenactment that must take place of the initiations that one has undergone in previous incarnations. The chakras, however, that were opened in previous lives remain opened, the cellular reconfiguration, the heightened frequencies all remain intact. It therefore follows that much of these higher attributes will demonstrate within the initiate's life. The conscious mind, however, must attune to all the work that has been done and reacquaint itself with the level of mastery that it is responsible to demonstrate. This takes some work and a great deal of attention. If you factor in that the initiate must likewise acclimate to an entirely different world cycle and deal with any remaining karma that surfaces for cleansing and healing, you will realize that this can be a most difficult process indeed.

Integrated Ascension

Just because you have passed a certain initiation in past lives doesn't mean in the slightest that you are going to be in control of your negative ego, subconscious mind, lower self desire, inner child, astral body, physical appetites, and mental vehicle in this life. You may have been an incredibly famous spiritual being a past life, however that will not stop you in the slightest from being totally run by your negative ego and psychological unclarity in this life if you don't do your homework. For this reason, you must assume total mastery and control of the negative ego and astral body in this life every moment. Passing past life initiations or having famous past lives will not help you in the slightest. It is what you are doing each moment of your life, not necessarily what you have done in the past. Everyone basically must go through the entire initiation process again. If that weren't the case, you would not have reincarnated. The only exception is someone like Sai Baba, who is a Universal Avatar.

As a general rule, the feeling body is one of the more sensitive bodies that we have to contend with. It's needs are not often obvious even to the eye of the trained initiate, and much of what it wants or thinks it wants arises from the sub-conscious level of awareness. These feelings and desires, often interpreted as 'needs' will dominate the unwary pilgrim, and sabotage the best of intentions and spiritual aspirations if not carefully watched and guarded against. Much of the confusion among lightworkers today is arising out of the fact that the feeling body is in control and subtly operating beneath the level of any awareness on the part of the initiate. This allows the astral elemental to grow in power, when it should rightly be subjugated to the will of the conscious mind, personal power, Oversoul and Monad. A lot of lightworkers have consciousness; however, they do not have personal power. This is why some people say ignorance is bliss. It isn't really, however, if you have consciousness without personal power it is. To have consciousness without personal power and mastery is to be hyper-aware that you're a victim without having the personal power to do anything about it.

Integrated Ascension

I must remind you that the extremely heightened frequencies of ascension occurring during this time frame are likewise pushing many a new initiate quickly through the seven levels of initiation by virtue of the incredible light quotient now available upon our planet. This is wonderful in every regard, but for the fact that the period of acclimation that was given for each level of initiation in the past is no longer available. A great number of individuals are passing through their ascension at lightning speed, and then are ultimately forced to deal with integrating their ascension into the four lower bodies while concurrently running an incredible light quotient. Many do not want to have to deal with the four lower bodies when they know the bliss of standing in their body of light. The truth remains, however, that no matter at what rung upon the ladder of evolution we were at, at the start of this lifetime, each of the four lower bodies must fully and completely be brought under the control of the conscious mind, Higher Self and Spirit. Each of the initiations must be completely anchored into each of the vehicles.

Since we are at present discussing integrating the astral body, we will resume to concentrate upon this particular vehicle. I hope my little diversion helped to clarify why both those who are new to the second initiation and those who are reawakening to it from higher spheres have basically the same dilemma. This holds true for every level of initiation we may have undergone. Each new cycle and each new incarnation must see the complete integration of all that came before. What was learned in the past must be demonstrated in the present. Many are not doing this, particularly with regard to the feeling body. Beloved readers, unless this is done and done at maximum potential you will be trapped at a level that you should be far beyond.

The truth is, there is much the feeling body has to offer. In order to do this, however, we must first be the masters over it and demonstrate that fact in the interactions that comprise our daily lives!

Integrated Ascension

One of the primary areas where the astral or feeling body is diverting lightworkers from following their highest path, is in the desire for fame, recognition, power, greed, control and money. These 'tests', so to speak, arise upon every rung of the ladder of evolution, but nowhere near the intensity that they do when approaching the initiation of ascension, except perhaps following it! This may at first strike you as odd and perhaps inverted to what you might think would be the case, but I assure you it is not. The reason for this is because those of us who have passed through these sacred portals must be put to the test of upholding that which we represent. It is critical and crucial that we walk as living examples of integrated ascension and demonstrate the heights we have achieved and the grace we have been gifted at every level of our being.

Those of us who hold leadership positions of any kind within the New Age movement must be in absolute integrity at all times. This is the reason that the tests which were mentioned above are being given to us fast and furiously, for we cannot afford to fall or be found wanting. We are leaders, and therefore our sphere of influence is great and affects many lifestreams. If we are caught off balance, if we allow the negative ego emotions such as greed, lust for power, fame, and personal recognition to run us, it is not simply ourselves, but great numbers of lightworkers who will be veered off course. If we allow pride to interfere and to try and deceive us into believing that we have passed these emotional tests and have gone far beyond them, then we are entering dangerous waters!

Someone who has recently passed the second initiation or the third initiation is generally more comfortable working with the "stuff" of unresolved emotional karma then those who are at the ascension levels or beyond. The younger initiate expects to be tested and is generally more willing and often eager to look at life's challenges as "tests" to work at overcoming. For those who have traveled far upon the journey, there is a most dangerous tendency to think ourselves way too advanced for such trivial concerns. Beloved readers, there is nothing further from the truth. If a second-degree initiate gets caught in the astral realm, they will have to pay the consequences for the glamours and emotional havoc that they have wrought upon themselves and those who comprise their small circle. This is not the case for the ascended being. If we allow our emotions to consume us and fall prey to negative ego glamours and illusion, not only will we be called on the carpet for the harm we have done to ourselves and those within our immediate sphere, but for the ripples of disturbance that we have sent out through our vastly extended auras and sphere of influence. Trust me when I tell you this is something to be avoided at all costs. It is both in your own best interest and in the interest of those to whom you have pledged service that you are vigilant about controlling the emotional body. You must truly understand that you are not beyond the tests of this part of self, but rather more subject to them than most of humanity.

Dear brothers and sisters of the light, it is imperative that we each integrate all the levels of our initiations within our emotional selves, that these bodies radiate the light and love of Spirit and nothing less! We must stringently uphold the love and light that we have accessed via our Monad and radiate that outward with every breath we take and within each of our individual missions and divine calling. Once this is achieved, we are then free to use the feeling body as the wonderful tool of communication that it is meant to be. The feeling body has the power to anchor in the joy of the heavens. It has the capacity to appreciate the work of great art, to rejoice to soul stirring music and to demonstrate love in action. This body is not meant to be denied, even as the physical body is not meant to be denied or disengaged from. There is much service and divine, loving exchange of energies that are within the capacity of the feeling body to demonstrate and celebrate. We do not, therefore, want to cut ourselves off from it. What we do need to effectuate is the proper control over it, so that we are its master and not vice versa. When this is fully actualized, it is divine intent that the emotional vehicle be one of the most powerful conduits of GOD's love and devotional energy as well as the energy of pure joy!

The artists of the world are called to serve specifically within the emotional sphere, to elevate and uplift. In a like fashion so are any and all who serve upon the Ray of devotion. The Angelic line of evolution works primarily with the feeling frequencies. Anyone who has been graced by the touch of his or her guardian angel or blessed with the presence of beloved Mother Mary can easily attest to this fact.

We therefore urge you all to face any storms or tests that are given you with regard to this sensitive vehicle. Be vigilant and pass them with flying colors. Do not let the negative ego deceive you into 'faulty feelings', if you will. Stay ever true to your Divine intent. When you continue to demonstrate this in every thought, word, deed and action that plows through the promptings of your feeling body, your feeling world will be uplifted to the glorious heights of Spirit. The blessings that will be forthcoming defy description. To say that your soul will be filled with the music of the spheres, the song of the Angels, and the love of the Divine Mother, is simply an attempt to feed the feeling body with ideas; which are food for the mental body and not the heart. The individual heart alone can feast upon the love that flows from the Source of all love. This treasure of beatitude awaits all of us who exercise vigilant control over the astral elemental and yet are fearless and trusting enough to open our hearts to the Heart of GOD! This is my humble prayer for us all!

There are a lot of lightworkers who run their life by their feelings. My beloved readers, please understand that one's feelings can be trusted only when the negative ego is no longer the programmer of the emotional body. Your feeling body in a given situation may want to strike out and attack someone psychologically or physically, for example. This is not of GOD. The ideal is not to be over identified with one's feelings, but to rather find the proper integration of intuition, the mind, and the feelings. When these three aspects of self are integrated properly and the

Higher Self, Monad and Christ mind are the programmer of the emotional body rather than the negative ego, then and only then can your feelings be trusted to come from the proper center.

Integrating the Mind

Integrating the seven levels of initiation into the mental vehicle is quite a complex endeavor. It brings into play the subconscious, conscious and superconscious minds. It touches into the needs of the inner child and interweaves with the emotional body. In truth, the mental body actually functions in conjunction with the emotional body, to produce the unique entity called the psychological self. For the purposes of this chapter, I will try to confine my discussion to the mental body itself, as I will explore the psychological self in greater detail elsewhere. Let me alert you in advance, however, that there will inevitably be some overlapping here, as the psychological self plays such a vital role in the integration process and therefore cannot help but reveal itself during a discussion of the mental vehicle.

The mind is unique also in that it functions as the receptacle of Divine wisdom. It is through the full opening and flowering of the crown chakra that we receive what is commonly called "illumination." The higher mind has a direct link to the monadic level of Beingness and light. This then flows downward into what is known as the concrete mind, and into the actual physical brain itself. The Ascension chakra is likewise located in the head area, as is the third eye that is the eye of inner seeing and inner illumination. Is it any wonder that the saints and Masters of the world are depicted in art as having a shimmering halo about their heads! It is now already obvious how vital it is to integrate the mental body with all that has been garnered throughout our initial ascension process. I hope it is, for it is the mind through which we ultimately gain control over the physical, etheric and astral vehicles, and the mind that serves as the very doorway into the light of ascension!

Integrated Ascension

The key area that all lightworkers must watch with regards to the mind and all of its multifaceted processes is that we do **not** let the mind deceive us into believing is faulty thinking or the negative ego. It is indeed essential that we are the masters of our minds and of our thoughts, but even more so that we keep ever vigilant over the many ways in which the mental vehicle will try to "tell us," so to speak, that the messages that it is sending forth are of the highest order.

The mind may try to deceive us by telling us that we **should** be hurt, angry, or jealous. It may tell us that because we have come far along the spiritual path we have the right to sit in judgment of others, or to know what is for another's highest good, and therefore possess the right to exercise control over others. Many lightworkers are on massive ego trips because they buy into the mind's own inflated opinion of itself! By the deception of the negative ego many are being led astray from their own best intentions. They do this by acting upon the false belief system that they are better than other lightworkers or have authority over them because they have achieved a higher level of initiation. As explained before, if the initiation process is not integrated within the totality of your being, including the mind, then you still have a great deal to learn. The above mentioned deceptions of the negative ego are just a few examples of a mind that is not integrated with the higher frequencies and levels of initiations. These very thoughts are proof enough that you need to diligently work upon your process of Integrated Ascension!

The ultimate goal within the realm of mind is to function from Christ consciousness. The Christ consciousness is the flip side of negative ego consciousness. Within its sanctified field thoughts are brought into resonant harmony with unconditional love. Perfect love not only "casteth out all fear," but it also casts out negative ego perceptions, reactions, justifications and emotions. It is really quite simple to discern for yourself whether or not you are functioning out of this highest caliber of Christ mind, or out of the negative ego. If you are able to maintain an attitude of unconditional love, if you are able to see life's challenges as 'tests' rather than "bummers," if you are able to see Oneness rather than separation, faith rather than doubt, choose selflessness rather than negative selfishness, forgive rather than hold grudges, cooperate rather than compete, have preferences rather than attachments, humbleness rather than false pride, and if you honor yourself for who you are and equally honor every other living being for who they are (experiencing each encounter as the "holy encounter" of which *A Course in Miracles* speaks), then you are on your way to achieving Christ/Buddhic/GOD consciousness. Anything less then this is the program of the negative ego's faulty belief system and indicative of the fact that you still have much work to do in this area.

The mind is tricky, and in truth, hard to control. In order to extricate yourself from the dominance of the negative ego and uplift yourself into the Christ consciousness mode of thinking, you must be ever on your guard as to what your true motivations are, where they are coming from, and ever vigilant in your process of Integrated Ascension. When you are able to so integrate all the wonderful spiritual frequencies and revelations within the mental body itself, you will then be able to hold your mind within the Christ consciousness, and be fully integrated within the mental vehicle. The road to this most simple and pure state of Beingness can often be quite complex, with much to unravel within one's self, and much to be discerning about.

For one thing, the subconscious mind will have to be reprogrammed from the many and varied aspects of faulty thinking that have been programmed into it, often while still within our mother's womb, and most certainly by society. The bottom line, however, is that faulty thinking, or positive thinking for that matter, that has been programmed into the subconscious vehicle or mind, will bubble forth and appear to us as basic truths by which to live our lives. Beloved readers, these in most cases are definitely not truths, but just the opposite. They are the spewing forth of all the negative ego programming that has been fed into it from this life and past lives, and a confused society. It is up to us to erase

Integrated Ascension

this disjointed and deceptive computer disc and replace it with the light frequencies of GOD!

There is also the inner child that requires proper parenting in order to function joyfully and peacefully within us. The basic point to be clear on here is that the mind is functioning upon all these levels simultaneously, and in order to integrate Ascension frequencies, Monadic consciousness and our oversoul or higher mind within the concrete or physical mind and brain, these aspects of the mind must all be adequately and appropriately dealt with.

The superconscious mind is a wonderful tool by which to access the love/wisdom and Will of our GOD Self in order to anchor and integrate our ascension into our entire mental sphere. The superconscious mind is, by virtue of its very nature, in attunement with the higher spiritual energies. When we learn to access this aspect of mind and pull vibrational energies into the other facets of our mind, then the process of integration will be enormously facilitated. By the same token, when we align with the superconscious mind, the other aspects of mind will be drawn upward into it's sphere. As the subconscious and conscious mind drifts upward and the superconscious mind flows downward to anchor its higher frequency, all the aspects of mind begin to align and resonate to the Monadic blueprint. In the aligning and intermingling of the higher and lower aspects of mind, it is the higher that will inevitably elevate the lower and a greater outpicturing of mental integration will be the ultimate outcome.

The bottom line concerning mental integration is keeping vigilant watch over every thought, as well as being utterly honest as to the source of origination of your thoughts. Do not let the negative ego try to deceive and seduce you through its manipulations and justifications. If you are absolutely honest with yourself, and have done all the clearing, cleansing and purifying work, you will know whether it is the Christ mind or the negative ego that is talking to you. If it is indeed the negative ego, you will have the awareness and the good sense to say to it in so

Integrated Ascension

many words, "Get thee behind me, Satan!" Then simply invoke the Christ mind. If it is the Christ mind that is speaking within you, you will recognize it as such and joyfully allow it to be. When you fully assume responsibility for this process, you will have integrated all the levels of initiation into your mental vehicle. Joy, peace, love, and lightness will be your constant reward and delight!

The mind, as every other aspect of the four lower bodies, has its own specialized requirements concerning its nourishment. One of the basic nutrients for the mind is positive and peaceful thoughts. The more positivity you fill your mind with the more positivity it will give back to you. By feeding the subconscious, inner child and conscious mind a diet of positive thoughts, images, visualizations and expectations, this programming of the mind will fill your entire being with the same thoughts and images of upliftment.

Another nutrient that is vital to the mind is that of silence itself. If you recall, early on in this chapter I discussed how the word "nutrition" stems from the root word "nourish." There are elements contained within the deep silence that nourish the mind in ways that supersede anything that can be conveyed through spoken or written language. A diet of proper nutrition will always include adequate rest, and this is found when the mind enters the still and silent resting-place of "pure Beingness." The calm that is encountered there is vital to not only the mind, but actually floods the entire four lower bodies with its calm and gentle graces.

Beloved readers, you can hopefully see by now how essential it is to integrate and balance the four lower bodies. The Divine intent is that each of us manifests our ascension within the realms of every single level of our personal being and then, from the point of inner balance, radiates it outward and into the world.

Integrated Ascension

Integrating the Spiritual

There is a myriad of spiritual bodies and it is not our intent to examine them individually at this point. What we are seeking to establish in this chapter, and in this book as a whole is the importance of embracing your ascension in a fully rounded and integrated fashion. This essentially means having all the bodies functioning at maximum potential and reflecting of the highest spiritual energies that are available to you. This also infers that the bodies would be in total and complete alignment with one another and that we would know ourselves as the Monad, the Mighty I Am Presence, and seek to demonstrate that level of Beingness within the vehicles that are anchored upon Earth, as well as the vehicles which we have chosen not to discuss at this point that are located upon the higher spiritual planes.

I ask you to bear in mind that we are multidimensional, and what was said concerning the four lower bodies is equally, although differently, applicable to the bodies that we inhabit upon the higher spiritual planes. Each of our multidimensional bodies needs to be aligned with Divine intent. We must recognize our connection to our own oversoul and likewise to our individual Monad, which is that part of us that is an individualized flame of the great fire of GOD and Mighty I Am Presence. This spiritual essence must be welcome within every vehicle within which we dwell and expressed appropriately in each vehicle respectively.

For the purpose of the last section in this chapter, we will confine our discussion primarily to our own Monad or Mighty I Am Presence. That is, after all, our essential Selves. What occurs automatically upon taking your full ascension, having worked through the areas of non-integration so that you are now a totally liberated being, is that all that comprises the vital essence of your lifetimes of experience is absorbed within your Monad. There is nothing then to tie you to the four lower bodies except the desire to serve upon one of the four lower planes. You return from whence you came into the sphere of birth and death, back to your monadic source. I again remind you, as I have done many times throughout my books, that your individuality remains. You do not disappear into the nothingness. Rather you integrate back within your individual I Am Presence to continue upon your greater solar and cosmic adventure!

The above point is vital to understand. Many lightworkers have called or written to express concern that they would disappear and lose all sense of individuality. This is not the case. In fact, nothing could be further from the truth. Merging with your Monad, or Mighty I Am Presence, is actually a merger into a vaster more inclusive self, which is at one with GOD, yet unique and individual. This pure essence of self then continues to evolve into ever-greater vistas within the many mansions of the Godhead! I have explained this process quite intricately in my book *Cosmic Ascension*. Integrating back into the Monad is integrating back to our own individual Source. Beloved readers, you are not lost in this process. More than you have ever dreamed of spiritually is gained!

In order to help facilitate this glorious experience what you need to concentrate on is integrating your monadic essence into your four lower bodies. The spiritual body then becomes one with the physical body during incarnation, and perfection, relatively speaking, is expressed. This is why we put so much emphasis upon the balancing, mastery, and integration of the four lower bodies, and ultimately of the spiritual bodies. This allows the Monadic self and the highest light body to find expression upon all planes of existence. It is in this manner that true and complete liberation and ascension is known to be an indisputable fact.

Meditation is another vital element in anchoring the monadic or Mighty I Am Presence into the vehicles. This may or may not take the shape of what we commonly think of as formal meditation. It will, however, invariably take the shape of holding a meditative attitude while involved in any and all of your endeavors. This is the true understanding of the words spoken by beloved Master Jesus which tell us to "be ye in the world, but not of it." That is to say, we ultimately reach a point of constant meditation and monadic alignment in all our daily activities. We live a life of service, expressing love and light because that is simply who and what we are at the level of oneness with Spirit.

In terms of nourishment, which we have spoken of in regards to Spirit, little needs to be said, as Spirit is nourishment unto itself. Yet, from another perspective we do indeed contribute to the nourishment of the Mighty I Am Presence, as well as to our other spiritual vehicles by contributing to the expression and manifestation of higher intent! When we serve our brothers and sisters, when we radiate light to the world, when we feed those who are hungry whether physically or spiritually, when we exhibit tenderness to the Animal Kingdom and compassion to the entire planet, when we rejoice with the Angels, when we give that which we are called to give for the upliftment of the planet, not only do we bring nourishment to our individual Monad and other spiritual vehicles, but we actually help to nourish that which is Source itself!

All that we do and express of a holy and sanctified nature expands upon wings of divinity that carries it upward to the 352nd level of the Godhead Itself. This may sound exaggerated, but I assure you it is not. When Jesus/Sananda said, "eat of this bread for it is my body and drink of this wine for it is my blood," he was not speaking as even his exalted Self, but as an embodiment of the Divine Father/Mother GOD. He was, of course, doing this as a stepped down channel in this process. On another note, do not let the fact that he spoke in the masculine throw you off track on this one. It was incumbent upon him to speak in the language of the cycle in which he manifested. Although stepped down through many levels of Beingness, and despite the fact that it played out in the drama of his crucifixion, when he spoke those words he was actually channeling from Source. So, my beloved readers, from this full spectrum lens it can be seen that although Spirit is indeed sufficient

Integrated Ascension

unto itself, we likewise bring it nourishment. This is possible, my brothers and sisters, because since before the worlds were even breathed forth, never was there a time that we were not one with Source, nor shall that time ever come. It is therefore true that Spirit *is* sufficient unto itself, for we are part of it, and from this point of view when we nourish it by our light and love and Will-to-good, we are nourishing our selves upon the highest possible level!

The task then that primarily stands before us lies not upon the realm of Spirit or within the spiritual bodies, but rather in the integration and anchoring of those higher levels within the four lower bodies. It is not enough to simply take our initiations and ride on the high of our personal light quotient, but to make all possible energy fields that we have contacted and activated fully alive and properly functioning within our physical/etheric, emotional and mental selves and bodies. There is no one who can do this for us, as this is a responsibility that we each must assume individually and for ourselves. I do promise you this, however, that when you even just begin to make the effort all the forces in the Universe will rise up to aid you. The greater your commitment to this process of integration, the more powerfully you will draw forth the assistance of the inner plane Planetary and Cosmic Ascended Masters, and the Angels and Archangels. The inner plane Planetary and Cosmic Hierarchy is standing by awaiting your call for assistance in this regard, for they want nothing greater than to be of service to us!

Within the Oneness wherein these Great Ones abide, Unity alone exists. They know "as fact," that by serving one another we are ultimately serving ourselves! If you do not believe me then I ask you to test this truth for yourselves. Begin now, at this very moment to work upon your process of Integrated Ascension, and see if you are not immediately filled with a Divine upliftment that signals the activity of these most blessed beings within your life. Take the attitude of integrating all the levels of initiations that you have achieved into your four-body system and into the four-body system of the planet. Accept this now as your personal responsibility and we guarantee that you will find that you are most assuredly not alone in your endeavor, but that you are immediately blessed and graced by those who serve the plan that emanates from the Heart of Light and Love of GOD Itself!

Integrating Initiations 8—12

Before I bring this chapter to its conclusion, I feel compelled to address the subject of integrating the levels of initiation 8—12. It has been previously mentioned that a ring-pass-not is placed around the initiate that prevents them from expanding beyond the seventh sublevel of the seventh initiation if the basic requirements of proper psychological integration are not met. It was also made clear that there are a number of individuals who succumb to their negative ego after taking the higher initiations. This must be fully considered, my beloved readers, for I trust that you yourself do not want to fall into this category.

To begin with, one of the primary reasons that this is occurring is that only the very basic requirements of mastery are being exhibited in the passing of the earlier initiations. We have a planet with ever increasing numbers of Ascended Masters who are not fully integrated and rounded out. I go into eight main quotients in the preceding chapter, which I encourage all of you to study in depth and take to heart. The higher the standard that you achieve at the outset, the easier it will be to maintain that standard of mastery. Light quotient alone has been the great propelling force for so many lightworkers, and it has already been established that a high light quotient in and of itself is "not sufficient to becoming a fully integrated Ascended Master."

Once initiations 8–12 have been taken, it becomes of paramount importance that these initiations are integrated within the four lower bodies in as complete a way as the seven preceding initiations. The higher the initiation level, the more power, force and intensity we have, and also the more influence we have over the planet in general. This is due to the fact that we have embraced our unity to such an extended level that our influence permeates the very field of the oneness we have embraced. Our auric emanations grow enormously and hold vast numbers of beings within their circle. If we are not properly integrated the harm that we can do at this level both to self and others is so vast that our path will be brought to an immediate halt. As we do not want this to happen, we must be sure to build upon a firm foundation of integration!

Beloved readers, all the energies of even the highest initiations must be fully integrated within the four lower bodies. Some of these energies will of necessity be stepped down so that they can adequately express upon the world of matter without causing any harm or disturbance to the delicate fabric of the lower ethers. Other energies will be allowed to fully flow through the well-integrated initiate, thus facilitating a great healing and stimulating influence. Divine order and the fulfilling of one's appropriate puzzle piece will determine exactly how the energies flow. The bottom line is, however, that we must see ourselves as one whole and integrate all levels of our being within the forms that we inhabit at any given time.

What it all boils down to is this: The higher you go, the more vigilant you must be over every single aspect and facet of self. You may be operating out of a belief system that is telling you just the opposite. If that is so I am here to tell you that no person is beyond falling from grace, even grace that they have earned by virtue of hard work and spiritual commitment. The commitment to Spirit and service must remain ever uppermost in your heart, mind, soul, and monad, and find its appropriate place of service upon the planet. Vigilance over the four lower bodies and the maintaining of high levels in all the quotients discussed in the following chapter are of utmost importance. Balance must be strictly upheld at each and every level of spiritual achievement.

There are, of course, certain areas where we are freed from our labors once these higher levels of initiation are reached. These arenas would be

Integrated Ascension

those such as having to do very specific types of meditation in order to get in attunement with Spirit, working at cultivating telepathic rapport with the Masters, and struggling to achieve ascension or liberation. The truth remains, however, that while we may relax within these types of arenas, we cannot at any point allow ourselves to become lazy or spiritually, mentally, emotionally, etherically or physically lethargic. Keep attuned to your I Am Presence, to GOD and the Masters at all times. Above all, do not neglect to keep integrating all your bodies into your process of initiations.

Never allow yourself to drift into automatic pilot and forget that you are incarnated within the four lower bodies. These bodies must ever be kept in their place, so that they can serve as the best possible vehicles in which to express the Divine Will and plan of GOD. While in embodiment they are an essential part of GOD. We are, and we must always remember that. We can enjoy the world through these vehicles, and in fact are encouraged to do so. Yet we must ever remain masters of these vehicles and keep them cleansed and purified, clear of all debris so that they may be the finest channels of our GOD Self as possible.

Beloved readers, allow each of your bodies to raise its frequency to match that of Spirit itself, and to anchor in the energies of your ever-expanding initiations. Don't stop at the seven, but keep on anchoring and anchoring every single level of initiation that you reach within each of the bodies you inhabit. Yes, there is a certain amount of discipline involved, in fact, often a great deal of discipline. Yet, the reward is equally as great. The ecstasy of resonating to the tones and radiations of the higher realms and initiations far exceeds words. All I can suggest most adamantly is that you integrate all of these levels within all of your bodies. Then you will know for a fact what I am talking about here. The joy you will experience will so far surpass any sacrifice of discipline, that I guarantee you, you will know for a fact what is meant by the sacred Hindu chant, "Sat Chit Ananda," or Existence, Consciousness, Bliss, within each and every cell of your Being!

Integrated Ascension

I have two last points I would like to make here in closing. Although I stated in my first book *The Complete Ascension Manual* that you cannot take initiations higher than the seventh, I was speaking here of the actual physical rod of initiation. Although one cannot physically take the higher initiations, one can spiritually and inwardly take all those initiations. In essence, one is doing all the work, activations and integrations to achieve those initiations, however one does not receive the actual physical/etheric rod of initiation for those initiations until one leaves or physically ascends the body. So, higher initiations can be taken well beyond even the twelfth. There is no limit to spiritual growth.

The second point I just wanted to make has to do with the belief that many lightworkers have that they are going to physically disappear at their ascension. This is an advanced Ascended Master ability that in this current dispensation of ascension will not take place. Melchizedek told me that one should realistically not even begin thinking about such Ascended Master abilities until they complete the seventh sub-level of their twelfth initiation. When I say twelfth initiation, again I am speaking of the twelve major initiations, not the twelve initiations spoken of as being equivalent of the seven levels of initiation completion that a great many New Age groups are working with. For example, to complete the twelve levels of initiation you must have fully anchored and activated your solar, galactic and universal bodies, anchored and activated your 200th chakra into your crown, integrated and cleansed over one million of your soul extensions in your monadic group, cleansed 98% of your karma, built up 40% light quotient on the Cosmic Light Quotient scale, fully anchored and activated your Anointed Christ Overself Body and Zohar Body of light.

I should mention here that the initiation system that Brian Grattan was using in his books is not the initiation system I'm speaking of here. The twelve levels of initiation in his system are equivalent to completing the seven sub-levels of the seventh initiation. When I am speaking of initiations, I am speaking of the major initiations, not sub-levels. The

Integrated Ascension

confusion stems here from certain other systems dividing each of the seven levels of initiation into three parts beginning with the sixth. They are calling each of these three sub-levels in the sixth and seventh initiation a full initiation. If you would like to know your level of initiation and you have not as yet received it inwardly or you just need a confirmation, please give me a call and I will set you up with a channeled reading with a high level initiate that I have trained to give you some accurate feedback on this point and any other personal questions you might have.

The negative ego will try to tell you that you are at a higher level of initiation than you are, or it will tell you that you are at a lower initiation than you really are. GOD will tell you exactly where you are, no more and no less. Do not fall into this glamour or trap. Do not fall into the glamour or trap of comparing or competing with friends, associates, or your ascension group. My personal recommendation, if you are graced to know your level of initiation, is to not talk about it with anyone except in rare circumstances where there is a particular spiritual purpose and service mission in doing so. I have seen spiritual groups so contaminated with negative ego on this point that it is almost comical. Initiations are important, but Godliness is more important. I don't care what level of initiation a person is at, if they are run by the negative ego they are not demonstrating Godliness. As was earlier stated, a person can fall at any level of initiation, even beyond the twelfth. Lightworkers, in my opinion, should be less interested in initiations, less interested in past lives, less interested in psychic phenomena, and less interested in developing spiritual powers (dematerialization, materializing things, becoming clairvoyant and clairaudient), and should be more interested in practicing the presence of GOD every moment of their life, being unconditionally loving at all times, Christ/Buddha consciousness, egolessness, balancing the four bodies, spiritual leadership, spiritual service work and Integrated Ascension. If you follow these more positive spiritual ideals and dedicate your life to GOD and the Cosmic and Planetary Masters, your initiations will take care of themselves and the spiritual gifts or powers will come if GOD wants you to have them. My beloved readers, never forget for even an instant that the greatest spiritual gift and power of all, bar none, is Love!

4

Integrating the Seven Rays and Ray Types

The Importance of the Rays

In regard to a discussion of the seven rays comprising our solar system, I remind you here, that the five higher rays have only been recently activated in relationship to humanity's evolution. The three major rays are the first, second and third, the third being the major ray department which overlights rays four, five, six and seven. In my books, *The Complete Ascension Manual, Cosmic Ascension,* and *Your Ascension Mission: Embracing Your Puzzle Piece,* I have gone into great detail explaining these rays and therefore will not repeat myself here. Very specific charts have been drawn up which are easily accessible and easy to follow in these books. In fact, several other of my books make definite references to these various charts, exploring their various facets in great detail. I therefore refer you to these sources for any specific or detailed breakdown of the rays that you might be seeking. These charts are purposely omitted from this book and section in order to refrain from repeating what has already been explained.

Integrated Ascension

I am therefore writing with the assumption that you, my beloved readers, are quite familiar with the basic ray structure and tendencies. If this subject is very new to you, then I highly recommend that you do make use of the extensive charts drawn up in the aforementioned books. For the beginner, *The Complete Ascension Manual* might be the best choice for this resource, as the rays are explained from the point of view of basic introduction and understanding. Any serious student of the occult should certainly familiarize themselves with the rays and the Ray Masters, as they form an intrinsic part of our development, growth, evolutionary process, process of initiation and ascension, and ultimately our Planetary and Cosmic destiny.

Looking at the Rays through the Lens of Integration

As you are aware, we cycle through the various rays in order to develop specific qualities, attributes, and aspects of the rays within ourselves. Our monad, or Mighty I Am Presence, stays constant upon one ray throughout our cycles and rounds of birth and death of the physical form. The ray of the oversoul or Higher Self is fairly consistent, but it too makes cyclical changes when it is deemed appropriate by the Hierarchy of Masters and our own Higher Selves. The ray of the personality is in constant flux and cycles through the various rays, much as it cycles through the various signs of the zodiac.

Each successive birth that the personality takes upon a ray that it has cycled through before is designed so that the personality will manifest higher and higher attributes and facets of that particular ray. An astrological corollary to this would be a person being born under the Sun Sign of Leo at various cycles of their evolution. This would be very much like being born as a first ray personality. Both of these represent fiery will. The goal is that each successive time within that particular influence the individual demonstrates higher, clearer, purer, more spiritualized facets of that ray or that sign. The same is obviously true for all the various signs and all the various rays.

What simultaneously occurs is that various aspects of the personality likewise cycle through various rays. For example, the emotional and mental bodies are each found upon a very specific ray, as is the dense physical body itself. This is continuously changing, even as do the various governing planets change from life to life. All of this is for the purpose of learning the lessons of each particular ray, developing the higher frequencies and attunements to each particular ray, as well as raising our point of focus so that it ultimately expresses the highest qualities that any given ray carries within its core matrix light structure.

Due to the fact that this is an ongoing process, what we are essentially doing is integrating the seven major rays and later the five higher rays within our four-body system. Ultimately we ascend upon the ray of our monad, which forms part of the energy field of the Master of that ray, a fact not generally considered. When we do this, however, what is hoped for is that we have integrated the various other rays within our monadic essence as well. The fact that we ultimately ascend upon one of the rays does not discount the fact that one of our essential goals is to ascend with each of the various rays brought to a point of integration within each of us. This serves to round out our own individualized essence.

Nothing Is Ever Lost

One of the most important concepts to grasp is that, in truth, nothing that exists is ever lost. This is a concept that is commonly bantered about, yet seldom contemplated or understood. Within the essence of this basic truth is the fact that all we have ever been, done, or experienced is incorporated within our monadic essence at the time of our full ascension. The specifics are obviously let go of, but the essence of all that has transpired within the rounds and cycles of our many births upon the many planes and various worlds that we have traveled upon is

Integrated Ascension

absorbed within the Mighty I Am Presence. It's colors, tones, qualities, and frequencies all contribute to the regeneration of our Beingness itself.

This is not to say that our negative ego, fragmented, divisive, manipulative, non-integrated acts go with us, for they do not. When dealing with any of the negative energies they will ultimately be transcended or transmuted before the time of our actual ascension. They certainly will not come with us "…unto the High Places." At some point they will be worked through and cleaned out. Their negative energy vortex will be transmuted and changed into a higher frequency. This is known as "alchemical transmutation." So, even in the case of the lower frequencies, nothing indeed is ever lost.

Basically, however, what we were in fact designed to do was to cultivate the highest aspects of each of the rays so that we may enrich the whole by carrying within our unique monadic essence the integrated best of all of the rays. This is quite a different lens than those used by various lightworkers who blatantly say things such as, "I am a 1st, 2nd, 3rd, etc., etc., etc., ray person and therefore do not really care about the other rays within my life." Beloved readers, you must care, for although you are indeed a specific ray type in regards to your monad, your soul, and the various personality aspects, you are also a compilation of all that you have cycled through before.

The intent should not be to disregard any of the rays. The only true intent should be to work on overcoming the lower aspects of all of the rays in order that you are free to manifest each ray's highest potential within your Being. I trust that you now have a pretty good sense regarding the facts about the integrated various ray expressions and their relationship to the "whole." What we do at the soul level we will ultimately do at the monadic level. This process of assimilating the essence of our many and varied ray experiences is then directly absorbed into the core matrix of He whom is the Lord of our particular Monadic Ray. This is then repeated on a Planetary level, a Galactic,

Universal, Multiuniversal, and ultimately Cosmic level. Therefore, beloved readers, nothing of our basic experience is truly ever lost, but expands and expands enriching and adding various qualities to the Eternal Whole of which we are a part.

Integrating the Rays within a Given Lifetime

Let us now move our thoughts from the cosmic scope of things and bring them down into the particular life in which each of us presently finds ourselves. The practical question then arises as to exactly how to proceed with proper ray integration. We shall therefore consider certain specific possibilities, and how we can use the atmosphere, frequencies, tendencies, and motivations of a given lifetime to integrate the various rays.

To begin with, we must first realize that depending upon the ray structure of our monad, soul, and personality, we will definitely have certain very specific ray tendencies and inclinations. These are not meant to be denied in any way, but rather to be raised to the highest level possible. The main point to be aware of is that when we consider the integration of all the various rays we are not meant to do this by trying to escape the specific ray configuration with which we are born. We come into each incarnation stamped with a certain ray structure in order to explore and cultivate the potentiality within that particular ray patterning.

When I talk about integrating the various rays into each incarnation, I am specifically referring to the incorporation of the rays into who and what we each essentially are. The truth is, the more we get in touch with our particular ray configuration and the qualities and tendencies of that structure, the more we will be able to add the various other ray aspects into our Being and expression. I do not, therefore, suggest avoiding your "ray reality" by any means! Rather, I suggest exploring it to the fullest, which includes finding out what your specific ray patterning is,

Integrated Ascension

and then and only then, working at the integration of the other rays into your core ray structure!

If you are a person who is very much first ray, i.e. first ray overall personality and first ray monad, you will be very strong within the will. Personal power, which I emphasize so often, will most likely not be one of your major concerns, as that would come to a person dominated by first ray qualities quite naturally. You could easily find yourself within the arena of politics, a firm and powerful leader of nations. In essence, you may be doing quite well in the honoring, manifesting and expressing of the first ray. If this is done from a spiritual vantage point, and we will assume for the sake of discussion that you are acting from that vantage point, it can serve as a great transformative force of politics and of civilization itself!

Upon the Cosmic planes, and more directly in relationship to our planetary expression, the Head of the First Ray is the Manu Allah Gobi. His function, although shrouded in mystery, is clearly related to planetary government as a whole. Under His Divine auspices works beloved El Morya, Chohan of the ray itself. The individual whom I am using as an example would be holding a similar position within the ring-pass-not of the four lower worlds. In a sense they would be representative of both the Manu and El Morya's frequencies and purpose.

Having taken human birth, however, they would have some of their own personal refining that yet remains to be done. True to the title of this book, they would most likely be faced with the task of integrating their eight major quotients, as well as integrating the other rays that are not functioning as prominently in their life as is the first ray. This integration of the rays is what we shall confine our focus to in this section, as that is what we are presently exploring.

Our wonderfully first ray centered political leader may have some very definite issues with regard to the proper and required integration of the love aspect of the second ray, as well as integration of the sixth ray of devotion. He may have the ability to be devoted to an ideal, an

Integrated Ascension

abstract political concept, but when it comes to the appropriate devotion and loyalty to those with whom he lives and works, he is at a total loss. His heart center, through which love and devotion flow, is shut down. We then have a being who has fully actualized his monadic ray and expressed it through his personality ray, both of which are first ray, but who is completely unintegrated with two highly vital rays.

There is always the hovering danger that his staff will desert him, for they do not trust that he will remain in support of them. That is because they rightly sense that he is entirely cut off from his emotional nature. Although he can be devoted to an ideal, as was earlier stated, they know he cannot demonstrate personal devotion, or even personal love for that matter, to anyone. All who know him therefore "walk on eggshells" around his most powerful first ray. They are not wrong in assuming that love, tenderness, devotion, or caring in any sort of personal way will not stay the wrath of his first ray unintegrated personality if it is crossed.

The people with whom he shares his life mourn for his heart center. They see before them a being who is quite adept and capable but who drastically and dramatically needs to integrate the love of the second ray and the devotion of the sixth into his life and into his work. Without that, they see him heading for a fall, as he is too unbalanced a personality to deal with. He himself feels an uncomfortable hardness within himself, but does not know how to deal with it.

One simple solution, when looked at through the lens of ray integration, would be to invoke the second and sixth ray into his life. He could call upon Kuthumi the Lord of the Second Ray, and Sananda, Lord of the Sixth Ray, to help stimulate and activate the qualities of those rays within his very Being.

The Masters of each ray are extremely eager to help anyone who requests assistance in whatever way he or she needs it most. All of you, my friends, should be aware that any ray imbalance that you feel can be activated simply by either calling upon the Master, Lord or Chohan of that ray or upon the ray itself. If you are familiar with the colors of the rays you can help activate any particular ray simply by sounding the frequency of its color!

The person in our example might very well consult with a ray-reader or someone who does ray clearing. In this way he could find out exactly what his total ray structure is. The channel could tell him which ray his soul is on, as well as break down the personality ray into its component parts. More than likely, the ray of love/wisdom comprises either his soul body or a particular aspect of his personality, such as the mental body. This could equally be true with regards to the sixth ray, or perhaps the fourth ray of harmony and art. He would then be able to work directly with that aspect of himself that these rays are anchored upon and begin the process of integrating them fully into his life.

If he chooses a path such as those suggested, it would work wonders for him. It would also work wonders for those with whom he shares his life both personally and professionally, as well as to help add balance to his career. This type of healing is specifically called "healing through ray integration." It is even possible to do this by accessing rays that are dormant in your present life, but are nevertheless part of your essential make-up because they were active in a previous life. The possibilities for this type of healing integration are exponential. I do hope that you take this idea and run with it. Use it and apply it to your own life.

The fact is that most of us are unbalanced within our rays. We generally focus upon one ray to the exclusion of others. The successful artist, demonstrating a highly developed fourth ray personality and having a fourth ray monad may be in exactly the same position as our first ray politician. He would, however, be at the opposite spectrum of things. He would be immersed in love, beauty, poetry, and harmony with the likelihood of having no backbone, no "will" to speak of whatsoever. "Healing through ray integration" would work just as well on him as it would on the first ray individual. In fact, it does not matter what the particular scenario is; the cure is always within the proper integration of the rays. This is a most effective tool for healing, balancing, and integration work in general, and as I have stated, it is my sincere hope that you make as much use of it as possible.

Individual Points of Balance

Another important consideration is that based upon ray configuration, each person will hold his or her own unique balance within any given incarnation. Ray integration and ray balancing will therefore be a unique and individualized process.

Each of us has come into incarnation with a specific Divine blueprint. We each are encoded for the fulfillment of a specific ascension mission and we each have our own puzzle piece within that mission. Because of this, we will each be configured differently with regards to the rays. This is again a parallel situation to that of astrological configuration. Our specific patterns have been given us with Divine intent. We therefore must tend to the best cultivation of them, for this is literally what we were born to do.

In doing this, however, the ultimate goal is to do so with as much integration on all levels as possible. We therefore strive to reach the heights of our Divine blueprint and particular ray configuration while simultaneously calling forth for the full integration of all of the various rays to play their perfect part within our given puzzle piece and design. This must obviously take various shapes, as each person finds their own particular point of balance within their own unique destiny.

For example, an individual who is a strong second ray being, with perhaps both soul and monad upon the second ray of love/wisdom, would obviously be very dominant within those areas. If their overall personality ray is upon the fourth ray, they will probably teach the spiritual principles of love and wisdom through one of the arts. When this person seeks to integrate and balance the other rays within themselves, they may prove to be extraordinarily successful at it. If we were to compare that person with the earlier example of our first ray politician, and assume that both of these individuals were equally successful at healing through ray integration, we would find two distinct results, and rightfully so.

The point of maximum balance for the predominantly fourth ray person would necessarily be different from the point of maximum balance for the predominantly first ray person. This would not be the earmark of imbalance, but of balance and success! As each and every one of us does indeed have our own unique mission and calling, we were, in a sense, breathed forth from the Heart of GOD differently. In other words, we each have a different blueprint for each specific lifetime and even for the life of the monad itself. That higher blueprint is called the Monadic Blueprint, which replaces the Soul's Blueprint as we continue to evolve.

The basic point, however, is that no two of us were created or configured exactly alike. By Divine design, we were each designed to hold a specific energy matrix. This basic fact is the reason why no two of us will ever achieve the same exact point of balance. The mistake that many lightworkers make is in thinking that we should!

All too often, the vision of what is right for one person is foisted upon another person. While it is true that we all can be mirrors for one another, and that it is often easier to perceive a situation from outside of it rather than from the inside of it, it is also true that no one is better qualified to know what you "need" than your own GOD Self! That, my beloved readers, is fact pure and simple.

The wisest of us knows when to speak and knows when to keep silent. In this moment, I am speaking on the behalf of your own uniqueness and individuality. I am telling you that the balancing of the rays is a wondrous opportunity for healing and coming to center within yourself. I am *not*, however, presuming to tell you what your own point of balance is, for there is no way in which I could know that.

There are sometimes insights that can be revealed by consulting with a qualified channeler in regard to this. As previously mentioned, they are able to see into your basic ray configurations and can offer some guidance and assistance. What neither they nor anyone else can do is to tell you **how** to best manifest your point of balance, or exactly where your point of maximum balance lies. That is between you and GOD.

A complete understanding of this process would take into account not just this one life, but your many lifetimes. It would also take into account the specific point of balance that you are not only meant to hold within yourself, but to hold within the complex of the world. During the Victorian era, for instance, any soul in male embodiment who demonstrated a great tendency at dreaminess or fancifulness or even beauty in a certain sense was greatly criticized and thought weak, although these qualities in women were expected. The truth is that things were so "proper" then that any male who held a strong fourth ray energy would have appeared unbalanced to the casual onlooker. In actuality, they were holding a point of balance that was sorely needed for the planet as a whole. A woman who was assertive and demonstrating her free expression would also serve to hold a planetary balance.

This type of planetary balancing is still going on, beloved readers. In countries that are extremely first ray, a person apparently out of balance because they are overly emotional, overly sentimental; or artistic may in fact be holding their very civilization together! While it is true that for their own integration they would probably do well in seeking a point of greater balance, I would be very much surprised to find that their personal point of maximum balance would not still have them somewhat sentimental, dreamy, and artistic. GOD, the Karmic Board, and the Masters deliberately look for individuals that are predominately structured in just such a capacity in order that they provide the greater function of helping to balance a community, city, state, and even an entire nation!

We must, therefore, be extremely careful not to ever judge any situation, particularly one regarding the delicate balancing of anyone's ray configurations. Each individual has their Divine work to do; part of which is deliberately governed by the total structure of all the active rays with which they came into embodiment. While it is their ultimate destiny and for their greatest good to find balance and integration within that ray structure, it is also extremely vital that they properly honor the specific ray configuration with which they were born. There is then the greater work of helping to balance our community, nation, and planet as a whole. We can do this best by first being who we are and living our ray to its highest potentiality and possibility of expression and simultaneously having the courage to find our own unique optimum point of balance within that structural patterning.

As you can see, the subject of ray balancing is vast and extremely intricate. It is one that most assuredly involves each of us individually, but equally involves the part we have to play within the greater scheme of things. Our planet is itself a fourth ray planet, and so we must realize that all of us in incarnation upon Earth are balancing within a sphere that has its own particular hue, frequency and point of balance. The greater solar system of which we likewise form a part is upon the Ray of Love/Wisdom. All of us involved in the evolution of this particular solar system are therefore going to be balanced a bit in the "favor" of Love/Wisdom! When we tune into Melchizedek, our Universal Logos, we find that our entire universe is build upon courage. This influences all within our universal sphere and is so vast that we can only pretend to fathom the true significance of this. However, there is a corresponding point of balance within the Universal and Multiuniversal levels which affects all initiates at the appropriate time in their cosmic evolution.

It behooves us all to be humble within our approach towards balancing the rays, and to not presume we know what is best for any of our brother and sisters upon this planet anymore than we would dare presume to know what is best for a species evolving in another galaxy or universe all together. We, therefore, must simply work with what is revealed to us in the moment.

Integrated Ascension

Beloved readers, we are all smart enough to know when we are out of balance in regard to the rays, as well as in regard to anything else. If we can summon the courage, which is the keynote of our universe, then we will be well on our way to balancing ourselves through the process of ray integration. In doing this we will *not* under any circumstances compare ourselves to anyone else! The point of balance for one person may very well be the point of imbalance of another, and that other person may be you. If you try to fit into someone else's conception of what balance looks like to them, you may indeed end up walking a path that is not yours!

Trust yourself and your own inner senses. Seek your own point of maximum balance, and do avail yourself of the Master's help in doing so. Do not, however, ever try to be who or what you are not. If you do, you are endangering the balance of the greater whole in which you live and move and have your Being, and in which you have a specific and deliberate part to play, as well as doing a great injustice to yourself. Ray integration and balance is the key, however, it must be your rays and your personal point of balance. Just as does the Kingdom of GOD, balance lies within! It is never to be measured against anyone else's, but to be aligned and integrated within your own individualized being, in the fulfillment of your own ascension mission!

Integrating the Rays within Various Bodies

Earlier in this chapter, I have explained to you that each of the four lower bodies are upon their own individual ray. In brief review, there is the overall ray of the personality, and then there are the specific rays of the physical body, the feeling or astral body, and the mental body. There is, of course, the ray of the monad, which is the dominating source for the higher initiate, as well as the ray of the soul, which is highly active from the third initiation onwards. These various rays must all be brought into alignment and balance in order to function at your maximum capacity. In this regard, the proper integration of the rays of the four lower vehicles within themselves, as well as within soul and monad, is vital!

Getting a ray reading from a qualified and trusted professional can be helpful in this regard. This is a service we provide at the Melchizedek Synthesis Light Academy. For those of you who can directly access the Masters and Inner Plane Guides, I suggest that you ask them to enlighten as to which ray each of your various bodies is on. With this greater knowledge available, you will be able to work more clearly, directly, and specifically on the process of integration and balance.

This can be one of the most valuable tools towards working on your own integration process. For example, to know that one of the prime reasons that you are overly sensitive and prone to mood swings or outbursts of intense emotion is due to the fact that your emotional body is upon the sixth ray, and you are therefore extremely devotional and highly emotional, offers you a deep understanding of self. If your astral body is on the fourth ray while your overall personality ray is upon the second ray, the feelings within you will be quite intense, and the heart space, if not properly balanced, open to the point where it knows no boundaries and feels too much. I am not talking about the higher aspect of "heart" here, but specifically that which is focused upon the four lower planes and susceptible to the emotions of humanity en masse, as well as and especially to those who you associate with closely.

Now, if your ray reading reveals that you have a mental body that is upon the third ray and a soul that is upon the Scientific, or fifth ray, then you have conscious knowledge of your basic make-up, as well as a clear understanding of where you need to work. If further investigation reveals your monad to be upon the second ray of Love/Wisdom, you can likewise access the higher aspect of love and the greater scope of wisdom that comprises your Mighty I Am Presence itself. The adjustments that you can make with this type of information are enormous.

Integrated Ascension

To begin with, you can immediately start to bring your mental body, which is well-endowed with intelligence, mental illumination, and clearmindedness, into the picture. Integrate the more feeling or emotional rays within the four lower bodies with that of the mental body. Ask to see with the clearmindedness and active intelligence that is the primary qualities of this ray. Before you go into emotional overload by allowing the two lower vehicles, as well as the overall personality vehicle and their attendant rays to completely dominate you, consciously bring in the energy and lens of the mind. This will be extremely transformative in and of itself.

Realize that your over emotional nature has most probably cut you off from the energetic frequencies of your soul and monad, and attune to these higher aspects of self at once! If the ray of your oversoul is that of the fifth, it is structured quite scientifically and rationally. Invoke it, meditate upon it, call beloved Master Hilarion who is the Chohan of that ray, even envision the color of that ray, which is a pure and clear orange, as a stream of light surrounding and penetrating all your four lower bodies. Each and every one of us who are lightworkers, and I am certain that if you are reading this book you fall into this category dear friends, certainly have access to the ray of our own soul. Call upon its great, potent overlighting power to help you integrate all of these facets of your Being within one whole. Also, call upon the Higher Self or soul to help you raise the frequency at which each of the four lower bodies is functioning.

If you recall, very early on in this book we addressed the varied vibratory rates of frequency that each of the four lower bodies can function at. If you have not done the work of fully integrating, balancing, and clearing these vehicles completely so that your true self, the Mighty I Am Presence is the one and only guiding force of your ship, then you can be certain that these bodies could use a bit of a raise in frequency. Both calling upon the Higher Self, regardless of what ray it is upon, and asking that the ray structure of all of your bodies be

Integrated Ascension

brought into balance and harmony will most definitely raise the frequency and vibrational tone of each and every one of these bodies.

In order to have full and complete personal integration, and to help raise the vibrational qualities of all of your many bodies, it is imperative that the ray of the monad, or Mighty I Am Presence, be fully anchored and integrated within the whole. Remember that the fifth initiation is that of monadic merger, wherein the monad begins to take an ever increasingly active role upon the life of the initiate, which is, in truth, an incarnated aspect of itself! Almost all, if not all of you who were drawn to this book, have taken at least the fifth initiation. For the very few of you who have not, the Masters tell me that it is right around the corner.

The monad and the monadic ray, therefore, have quite an influence upon each and every one of you who are reading about it in this moment. For most of you it is literally what you know yourself to be, as the majority of readers have already passed through the gateway of ascension. The remainder of you simply needs a bit of time to catch up with the full realization that you are yourself the monad. Therefore, for all of you, my beloved readers, the ray of the monad is of utmost importance.

The ray of the monad itself has, in truth, the greatest impact and influence upon each of our lives. It is that which can bring to balance and fully integrate each and every aspect of self. It holds the greatest power for it is upon the highest level of GOD-attunement, knowing itself to be a spark of the ever-burning flame of GOD!

What is needed in the example that is being used, as well in all possible ray configurations, is that you attune to the frequency and level of Beingness of the monad itself. In dealing with the rays, you would specifically invoke the ray energy of the monad, which in the above example would be the second ray of Love/Wisdom. Request that your monad, or Mighty I Am Presence, completely overlight and integrate all the rays of all your various bodies within the sphere of its own Divine radiance. Ask that all other ray frequencies present within you adjust,

Integrated Ascension

harmonize, and balance themselves within the total infusion of the monadic ray.

Until the lower bodies are totally and completely balanced and integrated on all possible levels, there will always be some degree of fragmentation within your system. One of the ways that this fragmentation often manifests is in the non-integration of the various rays that are active within you. By invoking the intervention of the monadic ray, you are immediately putting yourself in alignment with the highest resonance of your Divine configuration. As was previously stated, the monad truly holds the point of maximum influence within the initiate. When you specifically ask for the intervention of the monadic ray frequency, it is guaranteed to call all the rays comprising its lower vehicles into alignment with its radiant purpose.

If the ray of the monad is indeed that of Love/Wisdom, it will impart this quality into all other aspects of itself. Being the primary ray, it will help each of the bodies function in Divine attunement to itself. The over-emotional, over-devotional aspects that have gotten out of alignment will become infused with the light and love of the Heart of GOD, flowing from The Great Central Sun through the monad and into every cell of your multidimensional bodies. The lower aspects of each of the rays that have taken hold of the personality will vanish within the Divine fire, leaving in their place only the highest aspects of each of the rays that jointly govern each of the bodies. The soul or Higher Self will serve as a direct channel through which the Mighty I Am Presence radiates, and the process of ray integration will be brought to levels of unity and harmony that would not be possible without the direct intervention of the monad in this specific manner.

In truth, it does not matter at all what ray your monad is on. The ray of Love/Wisdom simply serves to complete the given example. If your monad is upon the first ray, that of Will, it would likewise provide the same function in the process of harmonization, upliftment, and Divinely transforming all of the other rays so that they become totally aligned with its Divine intent. The only difference is that the signature of the first ray is obviously different than that of the second, or any other ray. A first ray monad would overlight all the various bodies with a keen sense of personal power and will.

You must, however, bear in mind that the "will" I am speaking of here is the Will of GOD Itself! No matter what the particular ray anyone's monad is upon, it is focused within the light, love and power(Will) of that which is GOD, and therefore brings rays of all the lower bodies into the same attunement with the GOD-Self as does any other monadic ray. The fact that each monad has its own distinct frequencies is obviously by Divine design, and is one of the primary components of individuality. There is no distinction, however, in the fact that attunement to the monadic ray is attunement to the ray of one's own Mighty I Am Presence, and ultimately to GOD Itself.

When dealing with the rays, beloved readers, I cannot urge you strongly enough to seek to fully integrate the rays that you are composed of into one beautifully functioning, interdependent "whole." This "whole" will be established and maintained throughout any given incarnation when brought under the direction and guidance of the ray of the monad, Mighty I Am Presence, or GOD-Self! Within the many tools I am sharing with you in regard to becoming fully integrated Ascended Masters, the integration of one's personal ray structure is a little known gem.

Integrating Rays that are NOT Part of Your Basic Configuration

Sometimes we are configured in such a way that a particular ray or group of rays is not built into our basic ray structure. This again, is by Divine design, as our puzzle piece and ascension mission would obviously require a specific type of vehicle. This does not mean, however, that we cannot call upon those rays, or the Masters of those rays, in order to help us and perhaps add a bit of balance to our overall configuration.

We may be structured according to certain rays in a manner that would present us with a particular destiny in a particular line of work. As I have said, we are working at helping to balance the planet, even as we work to balance ourselves, and if there is a certain gap that needs filling and the Lords of Karma and our Mighty I Am Presence see that we can easily fill that gap, we will come under the ray structure that will most quickly and efficiently see that we proceed along our chosen path.

Chances are that this particular ray structure will leave us somewhat at a disadvantage in other areas. This may all be well and good, as this is not our purpose, and cultivating our own personal point of balance within that given incarnation requires very little in regard to these other rays and their properties. More often than not, however, at some point down the line we will find that in order to proceed upon our given path, and even to be at maximum harmony within our personal life, we do require the qualities of certain other rays than those upon which the monad itself has built its other vehicles upon. In fact, it is almost a 100% certainty that we will.

What I suggest in this case is to simply invoke the activation of that ray in the area or vehicle where you feel in most need of it. For example, if you are definitely serving the purpose of a visionary artist and channel, you may possibly be constructed without any first ray. At least for this example, suppose then that your work is flowing perfectly, all your personal ray configurations are aligned and in harmony with the Divine plan and purpose of the monad. Out of the seeming blue, a specific situation arises that requires you to hike up a very high mountain in order to participate in a global visionary art and channeling conclave. You look within, but find that the physical vehicle has little if anything to draw upon to make this arduous and seemingly physically dangerous trek.

Integrated Ascension

This, my beloved readers, is the time to invoke the aid of El Morya and the power and Will energy of the first ray over which he presides. You would invoke it specifically into your physical vehicle, as the task you will be undertaking requires the use of "will" within the physical body. Most likely, you would also want to invoke it into your emotional body, as I imagine there would be some fear present. You could, however, be experiencing the lack of the first ray specifically in the physical vehicle, as you have never had to "will" it to exceed a certain limit. It therefore has grown a bit tender, lazy, weak, and mistrusting of its own abilities. Perhaps it is a most delicate second ray body, and cannot fathom even putting on hiking boots and knapsack, much less taking the journey!

The advantage that the study of the rays and the study and integration of the various ray structures that we each have provides us in this instance is with the understanding of what to ask for and where it needs to be directed or applied. In a situation such as this, I would definitely encourage you to call upon both El Morya and Archangel Michael. Lord Michael is, as you know, the Archangel of the first ray, and is focused upon protection of all kinds. His energy, in combination with that of El Morya's, would serve to both stimulate your own will power and to provide you with the needed protection.

As you know exactly what area, or what body you need strength of will and protection in, you would specifically put this request forward. This would engender a dramatically quick response, as your invocation would be direct and to the point. You would not be vaguely asking for willpower in general, but for the power of will to directly pierce into your physical vehicle!

You could also help hasten this process by invoking the color red into the etheric structure surrounding your physical vehicle. I would definitely suggest the actual wearing of the color red, as the color of the ray is itself a stimulant of the specific ray that you are calling upon. Since hiking would be your major challenge, I would definitely advise wearing red about the feet or leg area. Red socks would be perfect, or a red ankle band. Anything red upon the physical body would greatly aid in the facilitating of this process and send direct signals to the physical vehicle, which would serve to stimulate and infuse it with the power of Divine Will.

If there is more of an emotional need, then what I have said regarding the physical body would be applied, only directed toward the emotional body instead. For example, if a similar situation was occurring, except that in this instance you had to fly for 18 hours to get to the conclave, and you had a great deal of fear concerning flying, then it would be the emotional vehicle that would need to feel the strength of will to proceed upon the journey.

The same Masters would be called forth, but their help would be requested within the emotional vehicle. Wearing the color red could still prove quite helpful, as it is a visual and energetic reminder of what ray frequency you wish to stimulate. More importantly, however, would be to do a specific meditation wherein you clothe your emotional body itself within the frequency tone of red, or Will. Wearing a medallion or amulet, or a gemstone such as a ruby or garnet that touched the heart area, would be quite helpful. The red amulet or stone should be placed at stated intervals upon the solar plexus area, for in truth that is where the energies would be the most helpful.

This situation has countless permutations; however, the above examples provide enough basic information upon which to build. Whatever ray structure you may be in need of is available for the asking. It does not matter if you are configured in a certain way that allows you to fulfill 98% of your life's mission and purpose without the direct activation of a specific ray energy. If there ever comes a time when you find yourself in need of that energy, and you most likely will, simply apply all the techniques that I have given you in the previous examples to your particular circumstance. Remember to call upon the particular Ray Master whose assistance you desire, as well as to activate the color of that ray within the body where it is most needed. It is always beneficial to wear at least a little bit of that color, preferably around the area that needs the stimulation, as the color itself emits the tone and frequency of the ray you are invoking.

There is one other point that I would like to add here. It is also quite helpful to get help from another ray that works in harmony with the particular ray that you are invoking. Using the previous example, you might also benefit greatly by calling upon a ray that already exists within your personal ray structure which can help facilitate the needed results in its own way. If your physical body is lacking in the necessary trust of itself to take the required hike up the mountain, definitely do what I have suggested in regard to invoking the first ray of Will directly into the physical body. Concurrently, if your emotional body is upon the sixth ray of devotion, you can also access that ray from within your own ray configuration to help motivate the physical body to take the journey. Your devotion to service within the sphere of your ascension mission would engender this activation and response.

In truth, it does not matter whether the ray is active within your four-body system or not, as Devotion works complementary with Will to motivate and stimulate a particular vehicle to fulfill its calling. I do want you to know, however, that you can absolutely access a ray that is active in one of your bodies in order that it can help stimulate another of your bodies. I have already explained how this can be done with the Higher Self and monad, or Mighty I Am Presence, however, I want you to know that it is equally as valid in regard to the lower vehicles as well.

Conclusion

It is always a good idea to call upon the Master, Lord or Chohan of whatever ray it is that you seek stimulation from and also extremely beneficial to ask them for specific help in the body where you require it. In this case, suppose you want to bring in the devotional energies that exist within the emotional body in order to motivate the physical body to take the trek to the conclave in the high mountainous terrain. Call upon beloved Master Sananda to help you radiate the sixth ray frequencies from your emotional body directly into the physical body. Remember that the Lords of the Rays are here to assist us in any way they can and what better way is there than in dealing with the direct application of a particular ray frequency?

If you feel that the Devotional ray energies would benefit you, then by all means do not limit yourself to accessing it only from within your own personal ray configuration. This can and is most beneficial, however, why not ask Sananda to directly infuse you with the frequency and currents of the sixth ray? This will help to facilitate the work that you are already doing when you are accessing the ray from within your own field.

Beloved readers, do not place any limitations on this process whatsoever. The rays hold one of the great keys to Integrated Ascension. The Masters, Lords, or Chohans of each ray are eagerly waiting to assist you and to help facilitate your process of Integrated Ascension. Call upon them, even if you simply think that there is some possibility of a certain ray's frequency assisting you. Once they come within your auric field, if they do not deem it appropriate to help you in that way, they will certainly help you simply by virtue of their Divine radiance.

I personally invoke each one of them at the start of every day. I ask for what I feel I require and then I turn it over to them. If I am in need of a certain outpouring of a specific ray, then I know I shall get that. If I am in need of healing in any way, I am certain they will provide that. The Chohans of the Rays are benedictions in and of themselves. I cannot emphasize the benefits of calling upon them in any and every regard, and certainly when dealing with the energies of the rays and their influence in our lives!

The subject of the rays is so vast that it could comprise the length of a book in itself. I have chosen instead to write about this subject

Integrated Ascension

throughout my many books in order that they can be explored through many various lenses and looked at through various perspectives.

What I do encourage you to do is to continue to explore the subject of the rays through the many and varied lenses that I have presented them in. Learn how they can best be integrated within your personal life. Explore as well, my friends, how they can best serve you within your unique field of service.

As I have alluded to throughout this chapter, the integration of the rays plays a most vital part in the total process of Integrated Ascension. This chapter demonstrates through example how the rays can best be used to help facilitate the process of integration as a whole. It offers as well very definite tools and examples of how the rays can be integrated in and of themselves. It is my earnest prayer that you make use of these tools and find the place of maximum balance within your own personal ray configuration.

5

An Overview of Non-Integrated Ascension

As I have mentioned earlier, the achievement of one's ascension and the passing of one's seven levels of initiation have more to do with spiritual development and the building of light quotient rather than a concept of overall development in one's spiritual, mental, emotional, etheric and physical vehicles. Ascension and initiation does not also necessarily include development in areas such as leadership, world service, prosperity consciousness, relationship skills, family skills, and Earth plane mastery. This is why the revelation for the next millennium is not ascension, it is "Integrated Ascension." Another term I have used is full Self-Realization. Self-Realization or GOD Realization being a more full realization of Godliness on every level; not just the spiritual level or in terms of the amount of light one holds.

 I would like to begin this discussion of what Non-integrated Ascension is by going over some of the archetypal potentials or patterns of how it can manifest. The key to achieving Integrated Ascension is to understand these archetypal ideals and to then monitor one's self constantly to make sure one is staying within the parameter of these ideals and precepts. Some of these will initially seem very basic, however, in my humble opinion it is some of these most basic ideals and Christed

Integrated Ascension

archetypes that give a great many lightworkers the most problems. Let me explain what I mean here.

Let's begin first with the ideal of balancing the masculine and feminine aspects within one's self. Just because one is ascended or has passed the seven levels of initiation, or even twelve levels of initiation for that matter, does it mean these aspects of self are balanced? Do you have the proper balance between the yin and the yang? Do you have the proper balance between the mind and your feelings and emotions? Are you the cause of your feelings and emotions by how you think or do you let your emotions victimize you rather than being the master of your mind and emotions? Is the negative ego the programmer of your emotional body or is the Christ/Buddha attitude the programmer of your emotional body? Do you properly integrate your emotional body, or is it not allowed to have its proper Christed expression? Have you spiritualized your emotional body, or is your emotional body filled with negative emotions caused by negative ego thinking? Are you the cause of your emotions by how you think, or are you letting outside situations and other people be the cause of your feelings and emotions? Are you the Master of your mind, or do you let your mind master you? Have you achieved the balance of doing versus being? Have you achieved the balance of joy and the need for serious focus at times? Do you have the proper balance of work and play? Can you quiet your mind or are you constantly at its mercy? Have you struck the perfect balance of giving and receiving? Have you integrated the mystic and the occultist aspects within self? Have you found the proper integration with the mind and the heart? These are a few of the questions and/or ideals one needs to examine to determine if one is truly integrated in their ascension development. If you are not, this is not a judgment it is rather a gift from GOD and grace pointing out to you an area where you need to focus your consciousness and where you need to make some attitudinal adjustments. It is not my purpose in this book to get heavily into explaining how to do this for I have already done this in my books *Soul*

Integrated Ascension

Psychology and *How to Clear the Negative Ego*. This chapter is meant to give you more of an overview of the process.

Balancing Heaven & Earth

Another Christed archetypal ideal is the need to balance and integrate the Heavenly and Earthly aspects of self. Many lightworkers on the spiritual path are too heavenly and celestially focused. It must always be understood that there are three distinct levels of GOD that must be mastered to achieve Integrated Ascension. These levels are the heavenly (spiritual), the psychological, and the physical earthly. In my experience as a spiritual teacher and spiritual psychotherapist, most lightworkers are more developed in their spiritual body than they are in their psychological body. A great many spiritual teachers and channels are brilliant at what they do, however they often have not addressed some very basic personality level issues which often serve as a great stumbling block to the full Godly expression of their mission. Other lightworkers are often not physically grounded or may not take care of their physical health in terms of proper diet, physical fitness, proper sleep, and such. The improper physical earthly integration can also manifest in not keeping their Earth life as together with the same effort that they keep maybe some of these other levels together. Some example might be not being on top of finances, running errands, lack of mastery and control of sexuality in service of the soul and monad. Other examples might be hygiene habits, proper aesthetic clothing, decorating one's home, dharmic employment, and not finding one's earthly service and right earthly puzzle piece in the Divine plan. Also maybe not stepping into one's earthly leadership that is one's potential to manifest within the Divine plan.

The ideal is to bring Heaven to Earth of course as all of you, my beloved readers, know. The material plane is one of GOD's heavens and the ideal is not to leave it but rather to make it mirror a fifth dimensional

Integrated Ascension

reality or higher. Many lightworkers try to solve these three distinct levels of GOD using the wrong methods and tools. For example, if your lesson is lack of self love, you can chant from here to kingdom come and it's not going to solve that issue. Chanting is wonderful and will help the overall Integrated Ascension itself, however, to really solve the self-love issue you have to go into the psychological realm. So, the key question is, "Are you paying your 'rent' to GOD on each of these levels?" (Heavenly, psychological, and physical earthly). Balance and integration is the ideal. Many lightworkers lump the spiritual and psychological level together, not seeing the unique level of mastery that is needed distinctly at each level. This causes Non-integrated Ascension. In more extreme cases, I call this fragmented ascension.

Balancing the Four Bodies

This next Christed archetypal ideal is similar to what was discussed in the last section, except a little more specific. Do you have the proper balance and integration of your spiritual body, mental body, emotional body, etheric, and physical body? Which body do you spend the most time cultivating? Do you feel that one body is more important than the other bodies? If you do this it's faulty thinking. These are the four faces of GOD, so to speak, and all are equally important. Are you paying your "rent" to all of them equally? Take a moment to consider how much time you spend each day focusing on each body. This little exercise may surprise you. A common belief I have come across in high level lightworkers is that they look at the emotional or psychological level as a lower level and something that they mastered in the "Spring of '72." Nothing could be farther from the truth. This is a sure-fire sign of fragmented ascension.

Integrated Ascension

Love, Wisdom, Power

Another Christed ideal to be very aware of is the balance of love, wisdom, and power in your life. A big weak spot in my opinion among many lightworkers is that they don't own their personal power, and when they do own it, it is not surrendered to GOD's power and Will. Their personal power is not owned and hence becomes given away to other people and to their own non-reasoning subconscious mind, emotional body, lower self desire, inner child and negative ego. The other side of the coin in Non-integrated Ascension is that they own their power and it is used egotistically in a dictatorial and aggressive manner.

Other lightworkers may be not unconditionally loving enough to self or others. Other lightworkers may love too much in a possessive, attached manner. Wisdom must balance these first and second ray energies. Many have occult wisdom but do not have psychological wisdom. Others may have wisdom intellectually but do not demonstrate it in their daily lives and interactions with others. My beloved readers, I think you are quite familiar with these issues and ideals and it takes constant vigilance in the proper balance and integration. The psychological level is a level that needs to be constantly monitored. Since it is our thoughts that create our reality then going on automatic pilot even for the shortest amount of time can throw us off balance. Life is a constant process of making adjustments to keep oneself in balance and spiritually attuned.

Integrating the Three Minds

This next Christed archetypal ideal is extremely important. Its lack of understanding in lightworkers is one of the causes of enormous non-integrated fragmentation. The ideal is that it is our job as the conscious mind to retain absolute mastery over the subconscious mind at all times. This is because the subconscious mind has no reasoning. This is why you must own your personal power at all times. If you do not own your

Integrated Ascension

power, in essence you are allowing your subconscious mind to run your life. Contrary to popular opinion or understanding, your Higher Self, Oversoul, Monad, Mighty I Am Presence and the Ascended Masters and Angels cannot and will not control your mind and/or your emotions for you. You can pray for this from here to kingdom come and it will not happen. Each mind has its part to play in an integrated ascended being. The subconscious mind has wonderful abilities within it, however, it needs a "computer programmer." That is the conscious mind.

Just as the conscious mind needs to make the subconscious mind subservient to it, the conscious mind must become subservient to the Higher Self, Oversoul, and Monad. The Monad being the fourth level mind. One's Higher Self or Oversoul is their teacher up to the fourth initiation. At the fourth initiation, one begins receiving guidance from the Monad as opposed to the Higher Self or Oversoul. This understanding is the key to properly integrating the three minds. When this is understood and applied the three minds like connecting rings merge and function as one mind. The seventh initiation is when this fourth ring merges as well and this is Integrated Ascension.

In the process of Integrated Ascension, affirmations and/or visualizations program the subconscious mind. Prayer is a request to the superconscious level. For the superconscious and Ascended Masters to help, you must ask. To the subconscious level, you must command with love. It will listen to you to the degree that you own your personal power.

Lightworkers get disintegrated often when they pray to the spiritual level and then forget to simultaneously remain in their personal power and remain vigilant over their subconscious mind and negative ego. The other place where fragmented ascension is the most rampant in lightworkers is that they believe they have mastery in a great many areas of their life, but the truth of the matter is that they only have mastery on a conscious level because the subconscious mind is not under their control. In other words the conscious mind is doing one thing, and the subconscious mind is doing another. My beloved readers, I cannot tell you how pervasive this is. Lightworkers very often have enormous spiritual information, however, they do not know that the subconscious mind is running renegade. There are millions of examples of how this can manifest. For example, a situation arises of a negative nature and the lightworker says, "I'm not angry." This may be true on a conscious level in terms of what they're showing. On a subconscious level however, they are having a fit. Another example of this inconsistency between the subconscious and conscious mind is someone who thinks they have forgiven but on a subconscious level is still holding a grudge. Another example might be someone who thinks they are out of their negative ego when in truth their negative ego is creating havoc all over the place. Another example may be someone who thinks they are totally clear psychologically and holding the Ascended Master ideal and their negative emotions are constantly taking over their consciousness and they are not even aware they are doing it, and are not aware that they are out of harmony with the superconscious ideal. Another example is someone who thinks they are out of their ego when, in truth, they are manifesting massive self-aggrandizement in all their interactions, and don't even realize it. The key principle here is that one must develop an "efficient perception of reality." An efficient perception of what their subconscious is manifesting. An efficient perception of the ideals, the conscious mind is holding, and how these ideals relate to the full spectrum prism ideal of Integrated Ascension. Lastly, one must develop an efficient perspective of reality, of what the ideals of the Soul and Monad are and how the conscious mind's ideals and demonstrations are exemplifying the desires of the Soul and Monad. The spiritual axiom "Know Thy Self" sums up the key to this lesson. Most lightworkers are more interested in the celestial realms, the Ascended Masters, esoteric information, and this is fine as long as they have done and are doing their homework on a conscious level and subconscious level. Hear this, my beloved readers, "all higher level spiritual work will ultimately become corrupted and contaminated with negative ego if the conscious/subconscious relationship isn't kept totally clear." Every belief and program in the subconscious mind must follow the dictates of the spiritual ideals the conscious mind holds. Every belief and program within the conscious mind must follow the dictates and ideals of the Higher Self and Monad. This is the proper integration of the three minds. To totally master the subconscious mind, emotional body, mental body, lower self, negative ego, desire body, and inner child takes an enormous amount of focused work on one's self and continuing vigilance and work through the 12 levels of initiation and beyond.

Another common pattern within lightworkers is that they work really hard and finally are told they have achieved their ascension and seven levels of initiation and they get cocky, prideful or over confident. As the Bible says, "After pride cometh the fall." I cannot tell you how many times I've seen this happen in high level lightworkers. They think, "Oh, I've ascended, I'm a Master." The truth is, they are a Master on a spiritual level in terms of light quotient, but that is all. You are only truly a Master if you continually demonstrate your mastery every moment. In some way mastery is even harder to maintain after taking higher levels of initiation because the higher one goes, the more responsibility and leadership one is given, which means a lot more lessons.

The process does get easier, however, in the sense that as these lessons are learned it becomes a habit in the subconscious mind and conscious mind to operate in an integrated way. Although this is the case, one must always maintain vigilance and not go on automatic pilot. Also the higher you go the more available the Masters are to help and assist you.

In terms of manifesting, most lightworkers do not own the power of their three minds, which is why they have problems manifesting. They are doing what I call non-integrated manifesting. Manifesting must always be done from all three minds simultaneously. Personal power and proper action is manifesting from a conscious mind. Prayer is proper manifesting on a super-conscious or spiritual level. Affirmations, visualizations, and positive thinking which program the subconscious mind to emanate a magnetic and attractive radiance is the key to manifesting on a subconscious level. Most lightworkers focus on just one type of manifestation and this is why they are not often as effective as they could be. It must be understood that each of these minds are an aspect of GOD and need to be used. Personal power without prayer or personal radiance is not effective. Prayer without proper subconscious radiance sabotages the prayer process by putting out conflicting energy. Prayer and subconscious radiance without personal power and right action will cause enormous amounts of missed opportunities.

Do you see how pivotal it is to properly integrate one's three minds? Many lightworkers don't have a full and complete understanding of how the three minds really work together which is the cause for much of Non-integrated Ascension. This is not a judgment and the true responsibility and reason for this is that these principles are not being taught in church, school, or by spiritual or psychological counselors. This form of psychology is the new wave. In one sense it is very simple when it is explained, but on another level very complicated. To truly get one's self truly together psychologically takes enormous understanding, the ideal which is like a map. If one comes into this world and is not given counselors and often even spiritual teachers, how is anyone supposed to learn? It is your job for those who understand these things and are reading this material to bring it out to the world. I went through traditional school and I was never exposed to this kind of psychology. To be honest it was something I figured out myself in my own journey attempting to heal myself and help my clients and students. I would get fragments of help and understanding from certain books and workshops, but nowhere did I find someone who put it all together in an easy, understandable, practical way. This, my beloved readers, has been my humble mission and it is my heartfelt hope and prayer that you find this synthesized approach and information useful.

Integrated Ascension

The types of teachings coming from a great many books, lectures, workshops, ministers, professional schooling, spiritual teachers, counselors, psychologists, social workers, family counselors, and hypnotherapists, are good and excellent, but don't include the whole picture. They are often half-truths, slivers of truths, partial truths. Then we have to go to a new book, counselor, or teaching to get another sliver. In essence, we have all been in the position to invent the wheel. All these different teachings are excellent teachings, but not fully integrated teaching from the full prism spectrum into the ideal of Integrated Ascension. In essence, people are often following maps that can't' often get them to the goal they seek. This is not a judgment, just an observation and insight; it is important to take a closer look at the map or ideal you have been following. This is why I, and I'm sure many of you, have chosen the path of synthesis, which is to take the best of all teachings and make it into your own philosophy, so to speak.

In summation I would just empathize again the importance of learning to master the subconscious mind and intensively examining the contents of the subconscious mind to make sure it is consistent with your conscious mind ideals. Also, make sure that there is no hypocrisy going on or inconsistency between these two minds and ultimately that these two minds are totally consistent with the ideals of the Higher Self and the Mighty I Am Presence. This is the new wave of psychology in the future. This might aptly be called Soul psychology, Spiritual psychology, Transpersonal psychology, and/or Ascended Master psychology. One of the key points I've been attempting to make this last half of this section is that you need to follow a map or philosophy or paradigm that embodies the full scope of what Integrated Ascension is, otherwise how could you possibly integrate this ideal? All these different teachings and paths can be extremely helpful as long as this is kept in perspective and one doesn't get locked into a partial truth or sliver of truth. This is often what happens when people get locked into a certain path or teaching and think it is the whole picture or the ultimate truth. Again, it is only one lens or maybe a number of lenses in a prism. The ideal is to ultimately be able to see through all of the lenses of the prism simultaneously which would be the full GOD consciousness and Mahatma consciousness perspective. This is where the path of ascension and being eclectic can be very helpful and is why I have attempted to write this easy to read encyclopedia of the spiritual path.

For some lightworkers, it is appropriate to follow one path. Let's say, for example, the Self Realization Fellowship of Paramahansa Yogananda or the Siddha Yoga of Swami Muktananda. Everyone has to tune into this for themselves. I, for one, have chosen the path of synthesis and look at the integration and synthesis of all paths as one path. I have also studied all forms of traditional psychology and spiritual psychology, have taken the best of each, and have combined this with teachings that I have developed and channeled over time. I hope this brief and humble explanation on this most important subject has been helpful to you, my beloved readers.

Parenting the Inner Child

One of the most common ways that Non-integrated Ascension takes place in lightworkers is in terms of improper parenting and improper relationships to one's inner child. Again lightworkers often are more interested in celestial realms and Ascended Masters and they don't realize how real the inner child is within each person's psychological reality. The most common form of non-integration is to ignore the inner child completely and give it no psychic reality within one's conscious mind. This fragmentation leads to the person being either totally run by the inner child or the inner child being so repressed that the inner child is in a chronic state of depression, unfulfillment and lack of joy. Lightworkers don't often realize that there's an inner parent that needs to be trained and educated as well. In the case of non-integrated or fragmented ascension the inner parent is either too critical or too permissive, or both. This creates an inner child that is lacking in both self-worth and self-love, and is also spoiled and overindulged in lower-self desires.

An interesting observation I have made about many channels and/or psychics is that they often have great mastery when doing their professional work or on stage, however when they return to their personal life they are back to the inner child being in control. So, what you have here is the spiritual self being developed and the subconscious psychic senses being developed, but the conscious mind is not developed which allows the inner child to control one's personal life. This is a pattern I feel that psychics and channels need to watch out for. The conscious mind is very connected to the parenting principle.

It is very essential for all lightworkers to properly program their parent and properly honor and integrate their inner child. The inner child is just as important as the Higher Self. Again, the Higher Self in the Hawaiian Huna teachings is called the Aumakua. This translates into English to "the utterly trustworthy parental self." We as conscious minds must train our inner parent to also be the utterly trustworthy parental selves for our inner child. No matter how old you are chronologically, you will always have an inner child. The proper ideal for raising your inner child is to do so with firmness and love. What lightworkers must realize is that if this relationship between the Higher Self, conscious mind and inner child is not in proper alignment, the entire foundation of your psychological house will become off kilter. This will distort and even possibly corrupt all psychic, clairvoyant and channeled work over time if not corrected and adjusted.

The Seven Rays

This topic has been addressed in a previous chapter, but what I want to say here is that even though your Soul and Monad may be on a given Ray, it still is essential that one synthesize and integrate all the Rays.

Integrated Ascension

This relates to the proper synthesis and integration of the principles of power, love, wisdom, active intelligence, harmony, concrete science, devotion, and ceremonial order & magic. The danger here, in Non-integrated Ascension, is that one can focus all of their energies on one of these principles and would not be a well-rounded, integrated person. It is essential that I develop my active intelligence, my devotion, harmony, and so on. The 2nd ray deals with spiritual education. If I only focused on this ray this might be the only thing I focus on and I would miss the cultivation of the Arts, which is 4th ray. I would miss the political aspect, which is 1st ray. I would miss the economics aspect of life, which is 3rd ray. I would miss the religious aspect of life, which is the 6th ray. I would miss the New Age science of life, which is the 5th ray. I would miss the business aspect of life, which is the 7th ray. These are all aspects of myself that I greatly cherish, honor, and respect, and focus a great deal of energy upon within myself and within my service work.

The same applies to astrology. Just because you may be a Sagittarius or Aries, don't get locked into your horoscope. Use that information just like you would use your ray structure, but develop yourself in all houses, planets, and aspects. The same applies to numerology or any system your are working with. As everyone obviously knows, each ray, sign or number is not better than another. GOD is in all of them and to truly become GOD-realized one must develop all aspects of self while still honoring the unique way each one of us were built by GOD.

Non-Integrated Ascension and the Chakras

Another way that Non-integrated Ascension can take place is in regard to a certain over identification or under identification with one or more of the chakras. The ideal is obviously for the seven major chakras and all the higher chakras that eventually merge with these third dimensional chakras to be balanced and integrated. It is, however, understandable and appropriate for lightworkers to be stronger in

Integrated Ascension

certain chakras than others because of their unique ray structure, astrological configuration, puzzle piece mission and purpose. Although this is the case, balance and integration is ever the ideal.

One of the common things that takes place within the chakras because of certain psychological programming is a certain identification with certain chakras. For example, some people may be very focused on survival and material concerns. Other lightworkers may be more focused at a given time in their lives on sexuality. Other lightworkers might be focused more on their emotional body. As we move up the chakras, other lightworkers might be focused primarily on unconditional love. Other lightworkers might be focused on communication and expression. Other lightworkers, more on the sixth chakra, which is more inner vision, concentration and GOD-centeredness. Lastly, other lightworkers are focused on a more transcended GOD consciousness in its fullest manifestation.

The ideal is to balance all these aspects within self and it would be a helpful exercise to survey these aspects within self to see if the full Integrated Ascension of GOD is taking place within you. If it is not, this is no judgment, all that is needed is an attitudinal adjustment to place more energy and focus in that area where that chakra is a little under active. On the other side of the coin, it also might be necessary to remove some focus of your consciousness out of that quality or chakra because it may be a little over active or over developed. Everything has to do with conservation of energy and proper use of one's energies in the most integrated, synthesized and efficient way possible.

One of the common misunderstandings and schisms that often occur within lightworkers is they sometimes embrace teachings that may be too heavenly focused which then shows up as there being no energy or very little energy in the lower chakras. Some teachings actually promote the disowning of the three lower chakras. This is an improper teaching for all chakras have their integrated purpose in Divine manifestation. In the ideal state all seven chakras are still

Integrated Ascension

functioning in a balanced, integrated state, however, in an integrated ascended being the chakras function totally under the will of the Monad or Mighty I Am Presence and not under the will of the lower self, negative ego, astral elemental and/or inner child. Also in the ascended state the seven chakras function as one chakra, a stream of light-energy which can be seen clairvoyantly. All the different sections of this chapter, in terms of how Non-integrated Ascension can take place, will show up in the chakras if one looks at them clairvoyantly or even just intuitively.

One of the main ways non-integration takes place within the chakras has to do with a person's psychology and philosophy on a conscious and subconscious level. When the mental body is not philosophically aligned with the philosophy and psychology of the oversoul and Monad, this will manifest in a partial imbalance within the chakras. The same is true of the emotional body. When it is not fully aligned and attuned to the will of the oversoul and Monad this will show up in the chakras. We all know that it is our thoughts that create our reality and our belief systems. Any negative ego thoughts or beliefs will cause corresponding negative emotions which will all show up as slight chakra imbalance. The importance of getting one's mental body totally aligned with Source every moment of one's life, if possible, cannot be over emphasized. Many Eastern paths teach that the mind is a negative thing or is bad and should be gotten rid of. Nothing could be farther from the truth. All aspects of self (intuitive, thinking, feeling, and sensation function five senses) must be properly honored and integrated. Carl Jung, the famous Swiss psychologist, taught that many people identify with one or more of these aspects of self to the neglect of other ones and this is true. This will also show up in the chakras. The key again is to constantly survey and monitor oneself as to one's overall balance. At times it is appropriate to focus on one chakra or one quality, however, one must then step back and see the full prism perspective, so to speak, before entering a single lens focus again. Sometimes

Integrated Ascension

lightworkers can get too focused and not see the forest through the trees and other lightworkers being too expansively focused are not able to see the tree through the forest, so to speak, or being unable to focus their energies to fulfill the spiritual assignments they have been given. The need for vigilance over one's consciousness cannot be over estimated and this overall reviewing process, His Holiness the Lord Sai Baba has called, "self inquiry." As the Master Jesus said in *A Course in Miracles*, "There are no neutral thoughts." This is why it must be understood that every thought is either of the Christ mind or the negative ego mind and why vigilance and a continual process of self-inquiry must be constantly maintained. Even the slightest bit of mis-thinking and going on automatic pilot for one second will show up in the chakras.

The other key thing that must be very carefully examined for a full spectrum prism consciousness is the books and teachings that you are using to govern your life. I mean this as no judgment but most are not full spectrum prism teachings. All the different forms of psychology are focusing on a different sliver of truth, and hence a different chakra or chakras. The same principle applies to spiritual teachings. For example *A Course In Miracles*, which is one of my favorite books in the whole world, if followed exactly as written will make you too heavenly and too much in your upper chakras to the exclusion of the lower ones. This book was purposely written that way to serve a certain purpose. Not all books are meant to synthesize everything, and this is appropriate. For this reason, *A Course in Miracles* needs to be integrated rather than overidentified with. It is the light at the end of the tunnel, but until one gets to that place a more integrated approach is needed.

The problem that some lightworkers have is they read a certain book or work with a certain spiritual teacher who helps them develop certain chakras or aspects within self that they need, but the book or spiritual teacher is focusing on a certain aspect of truth and not the whole Integrated Ascension full prism picture. The problem arises when the lightworker, because of negative ego infiltration and maybe just youth,

Integrated Ascension

thinks that this sliver and/or partial truth is the whole truth and enthusiastically promotes it as such. This will show up in the chakras as being over developed in one or more chakras and under developed in others. Many Eastern teachings, for example, are much more focused on the spiritual level and not on the psychological level. They also may reject the social level, or sexuality. There is a need for lightworkers to be very discerning about such matters. There are very few teachings on the planet on a psychological or spiritual level that promote a full spectrum teaching. This is not a judgment, just a truthful observation. Understanding this, the different forms of psychology and spiritual teachings can rightly be seen as tools and aspects of self to be integrated. Some teachings being more integrated than others. The only danger comes in embracing books, teachings, spiritual teachers, counselors, or psychologists, as the ultimate total truth when it is not.

Often you will be intuitively guided to a partial truth that you need to correct a certain imbalance in your whole program. This would be then the perfect thing to do, however if embraced too long will cause an imbalance in the opposite direction. For example, a man who is too intellectual and cut off from his emotions may get involved with humanistic psychology and encounter groups. This may be the ideal thing for him in truth. After two years of being absorbed in this work he has now become very emotionally opened and there is a danger of becoming too over-identified with the emotional body, and maybe what is needed now is a more spiritual approach. If that person thinks this is the ultimate truth, he will remain stuck in his third chakra. Someone embracing Freudian psychology will get stuck in their second chakra. If they follow the psychology of Carl Rodgers, the Humanistic psychologist, they would get stuck in their heart chakra. If they follow the yogic path as it is taught in many places, sexuality is seen as something to be cutoff and there will be little energy in the second chakra and much guilt if the path of celibacy is not chosen from a clear space.

Integrated Ascension

So, my beloved readers, it is an interesting science to study the different forms of psychology and spirituality to see how much of a full spectrum prism, philosophy and chakra system balance they are involved with. When looked at from the greatest full spectrum perspective, all forms of psychology and all forms of spiritual teachings when combined form all the infinite numbers of lenses and facets of the prism of truth. This encyclopedia I have written has been my attempt again to honor each of these lenses and synthesize them all together with my truth as I have received it and conceived it under the touchstone of ascension, and with a foundational theme that underlies all my books which is the teachings of the Ascended Masters. Each aspect and lens which are like the chapters in each of my sixteen books so far, is an attempt to bring more light and understanding to the process of GOD-realization which we are all striving to achieve at different levels of initiation and integration.

Non-Integration and the Twelve Archetypes

Another very interesting aspect of achieving Integrated Ascension has to do with integrating all the major archetypes. One of the ways Non-integrated Ascension often occurs is when lightworkers over-identify with one archetype and under-identify with other archetypes. Since I've spoken of this subject in other books I am not going to get too heavy into this subject here, however, as a reminder or for those of you who may have not have read certain of my books, the twelve major archetypes are: the destroyer, the fool, the innocent, the magician, the martyr, the patriarch, the ruler, the seducer, the seeker, the servant, the warrior, the wise one. Just as with the twelve signs of the zodiac and the seven rays, all archetypes must be integrated to fully achieve Integrated Ascension at its highest potential. Now in certain past lives you may have chosen to live out one or more of these archetypes and this is good and appropriate. For all of you, my beloved readers, I'm sure this will be your final lifetimes upon Earth. Since I am sure you will all achieve liberation in this lifetime, it becomes vital for you to integrate all of the archetypes. For those who would like more information on this subject, I would guide you to read *The Complete Ascension Manual, How to Clear the Negative Ego* and the revised edition of *Soul Psychology* published by Ballantine Books.

Non-Integration and Christ Thinking vs. Negative Ego Thinking

I have saved the biggest place that Non-integrated Ascension takes place for last. The very core of all spiritual work comes down to whether you are interpreting life from your Christ mind or the negative ego mind. There are no other choices. There are only two philosophies of life and every person on planet Earth is in one or the other or a combination of the two. Every thought you think is either the negative ego mind or Christ mind inwardly talking to you. As the Master Jesus said in *A Course in Miracles*, "Deny any thought not of GOD to enter your mind." His Holiness the Lord Sai Baba calls this "the process of self inquiry" and says that it is 75% of the spiritual path.

My beloved readers, it's absolutely astounding in the field of psychology, spirituality, religion, and life itself how little understood this core understanding is! It is your job, my friends, to practice this within self, to demonstrate it to the best of your ability every moment of your life, and to teach it to others where and when appropriate. This is what the world needs most of all. If the negative ego is allowed to enter it will create negative emotions, fear, negative selfishness, separation, and ultimately isolation. It will throw your entire program on every level off kilter. Everything you think, say, and do will be colored by it. It will color your perception of every situation. It will contaminate your channeling, psychic abilities, intuition, clairvoyance, and clairaudience. It will poison your relationships and business endeavors. Keeping the negative ego out of your mind and replacing it with Christ thinking is the only way to achieve inner peace, happiness, and joy. It is fundamental to having a right relationship to self.

Your relationship to yourself is the most important relationship in your life. If you are not right with self it will become projected onto every relationship and situation of your life, including your relationship to GOD! The need to be vigilant over one's consciousness from within and without, all day and all night long cannot be stated emphatically enough. In the beginning this can be very difficult for lightworkers, however, over time the subconscious gets reprogrammed and one trains oneself not to go into automatic pilot. One trains oneself to remain in their personal power and attunement to oversoul, Monad, the Ascended Masters, and GOD, and to not give this power to the subconscious mind, emotional body, inner child, lower-self desire, physical appetites, and mental body. Some of these aspects are important to integrate, except for the negative ego ones, in their proper holistic and synergistic perspective, however the conscious mind remains the captain of the ship, so to speak, in total service of the oversoul, Monad, inner plane Ascended Masters, and GOD.

When the negative ego can be kept out of your mind and Christ thinking always at the forefront, you develop the Midas Touch, where everything you do in life turns to gold. I like to call this having your head screwed on straight. Since your thoughts create your reality, you can see how important this is. When the negative ego is in control power, fame and money become your false gods and idols. Do not underestimate the seductiveness of the negative ego. It is as brilliant as the Christ mind is in its guise and deceit. One must examine their true motivation every moment of their life to see who is really running the show. Your level of initiation means nothing in regard to vulnerability of being taken over by the negative ego, if not careful. One must examine every aspect and corner of one's conscious thinking and subconscious thinking to cleanse it from your Being. Just because you have been in control of it at one phase of your life doesn't mean you can't be taken over at a later phase. Ninety nine percent of the time it takes over you will not be consciously aware of it. Learning to control the negative ego is the single most important lesson in my opinion of the spiritual path, and the most difficult.

When you move into positions of leadership, you will find that fame, money, and power will be your greatest tests. This is where a great many spiritual leaders and lightworkers lose it. They are more humble getting to their goal, but once they achieve it then watch out. Never forget, as the Bible says, "After pride commeth the fall." The negative ego is incredibly devious in the way it operates, so lightworkers need to be on guard for this both within themselves and within others. Just because one is a great spiritual teacher, channel, clairvoyant, healer, or psychic, doesn't mean for one moment that they have control of their negative ego. In fact, some of the worst cases of negative ego corruption and contamination are taking place within this group. Ninety-nine percent of the time they have no idea this is happening, and if you ask them to their face if they are in control of their negative ego they would say "yes."

The highest achievement, in my opinion, of Integrated Ascension is to live in a state of total "egolessness" in this regard in terms of everything you do while still owning your personal power and functioning as a fully integrated Master on Earth in service of GOD and the inner plane Ascended Masters. Motivation is a real key. Examine the motivation of everything you think, say and do to see if self-motivation and self-interest is the source of what you are doing. One must be devastatingly honest with self. When this state is achieved to a very high degree, I call this living in a state of purity. There are very few beings on this planet who really are pure in this regard. Strive to be one of them.

There are spiritual tests at every turn. In truth, every thought you think is a spiritual test. How you respond or react to every situation is a spiritual test. Remember above all else that every moment of your life

Integrated Ascension

you are choosing GOD or you are choosing the negative ego. Every time you choose the negative ego you do not truly separate yourself from GOD and your brothers and sisters, however, you are creating this reality within your realization of GOD. The negative ego will tell you that you are gaining by following its dictate, however you are losing. What would you rather have, petty gains of the negative ego or the bliss of GOD-realization? Would you rather be right in every conflict with another person or do you want love? There are only two emotions love and fear. Do you have only preferences in life or do you have attachments? All suffering comes from attachment. Do you look at things as teaching and lessons and spiritual tests, or do you look at things as bummers and problems and respond in upset and anger? Do you practice unconditional love in your attitude to self and others or conditional love? Are you the cause of your reality or an effect? Are you a Master of yourself and life or a victim? Do you worship false gods and practice idol worship in the form of putting power, fame, money, sex, material concerns, vanity, false pride and even people before GOD? Are you run by lower-self desire or by higher-self desire? Do you put your relationship to self and your relationship to GOD before all other relationships? Do you have self-love or does the negative ego abuse you with programming of being too critical and/or too permissive with self? Do you choose to love your enemies or do you choose to give into your attack thoughts? Do you choose automatic pilot or are you vigilant for GOD and His kingdom?

These, my beloved readers, are the attitudes and questions that will determine most of all whether Integrated Ascension will be achieved. Letting the negative ego program your reality will knock your whole psychological and spiritual symbolic house off-kilter. Spend the appropriate amount of time in your life doing your meditations, spiritual studies, ascension activation work, praying, chanting the names of GOD and so on. However, never forget the real core of the work and the true test of Integrated Ascension and the achievement of

Integrated Ascension

Christ consciousness is involved in the lessons I speak of in this section. For more information on this subject please read *Soul Psychology, How to Clear the Negative Ego, Ascension and Romantic Relationships, Your Ascension Mission: Embracing Your Puzzle Piece*.

My beloved readers, I realize in this section I have been very firm and direct. What I want to say is that this firmness and directness is given with great and profound unconditional love. This section in a sense is a wake-up call for it is very easy to get overwhelmed with the vast amount of spiritual and esoteric knowledge and wisdom that is available to all of us in the world today. This section has been an attempt to keep this whole process in proper perspective. For proper perspective is the key to Integrated Ascension and inner peace. This section is my attempt out of total unconditional love to you, my beloved readers, to distill this entire book down to its quintessential essence. I have stated this next quote many times in my previous books and I will repeat it again here, for this is the bottom line. His Holiness the Lord Sai Baba has stated that the definition of GOD is, "GOD equals man minus ego." Let us all never forget and always keep in perspective and priority this quintessential truth! Learning to control your negative ego will bring you unconditional love, joy, happiness, bliss, and an inner peace that passeth understanding. It is for this reason I speak so passionately and firmly on this subject, for I want all of you, my beloved readers, to have this level of love, joy and peace. It cannot be obtained or achieved if the negative ego is not subjugated. This takes great mastery and commitment, however the fruit gained is worth the tilling of the soil! I am passionate and firm in my writing so you may have the full potential of unconditional love, joy, happiness, bliss and inner peace that is your birthright as Sons and Daughters of GOD!

6

The All Important Sub-Quotients

The Importance of the "Sub" or Minor Quotients

We have, at the beginning of this book, explored the eight major quotients and the importance that they play in the achieving of Integrated Ascension. To quickly refresh your minds, these eight major quotients are: the initiation quotient, the light quotient, the love quotient, the psychological wisdom quotient, the Christ consciousness quotient, the transcendence of the negative ego quotient, the service and spiritual leadership quotient and the integration and balance quotient. These eight quotients form both the foundation of this book and the foundation for your process of integrated ascension.

There are, however, minor quotients that are extremely useful upon your path of initiation and therefore must not go unmentioned. While they do not form the foundation of your process, they do in truth facilitate your process making it both easier and more enjoyable to ascend the circular ladder into and beyond the seventh initiation of ascension. They likewise serve to help make daily living flow in greater harmony and balance with self, others and GOD. I therefore will explore these minor quotients with you, in no particular order. Each of you will find one or other grouping of them to be of greater importance to your life and overall being than are others. Pay attention to your own inner voice, and allow yourself to raise your standard to the highest level possible. You will see that by doing so you will find the missing link to your ascension practice and be helped enormously on a personal, planetary and spiritual level.

Each quotient will be highlighted and commented upon in a manner most befitting that particular quotient. Some may be longer in length and some shorter. You may even want to add some of your own thoughts in journal form that may help you to more fully personalize and understand that particular quotient in relationship to yourself. They will be divided into three basic categories: The Physical Earthly Quotients, The Psychological Quotients, and The Spiritual Quotients.

The Physical Earthly Quotients

1. Integrating Spiritual and Earthly Energies Quotient

This seems most appropriate to begin with, as this is the core foundation of all that has been presented here. Without the proper balance of the physical (including etheric, astral, and emotional) with the spiritual, you will always be out of balance with yourself. That is not to say that at certain times one is not focused more in one body than another, or that one's mission may require a generalized or predominant focus in one or other of the bodies. However, the key is for you to find the appropriate point of balance and integration. Whatever your unique point of balance and integration is, you should strive to maintain it at its highest possible level at all times. When this is done, it will maximize your efficiency in whatever area and arena you are both guided to and choose to work in.

2. Environmental Consciousness Quotient

The more integrated within self and GOD we become, the more aware we become that we are integrated within the planet in which we live. Take a look at how you are honoring and caring for this planet by the way you treat it in your immediate environment. If there is trash in your own home, I am certain that you would not hesitate to pick it up. What about your extended home, that of planet Earth! Let us all be aware enough not to contribute to the mess of garbage and pollutants that already deface our world. We need not become fanatical and pick up trash that litters our street. By the same token, we can be sure to not contribute any further to it either. We can make it easier and healthier for those that do dispose of our trash by making sure all food-stuff is tied within a trash bag and not spilling out all over. We can recycle. We can carefully remove a broken piece of glass that a neighbor or fellow traveler might step on or trip over. See where you own level of awareness and contribution to environmental problems lie. If we all do just a little bit here, together we can accomplish much!

3. *Political and Social Consciousness Quotient*

It is obviously that some of us are just more politically minded than others and that is okay, and actually a product of Divine design. Since we are all part of this world, however, it is up to all of us to have some awareness in this area. In order to direct our light, love, and healing efforts, we must know where they need to be directed. This is a very personal quotient, as some of you will be very first ray and actually work within the political and/or social arenas, while others of you are pulled away from this particular area. Even if this is of little concern to you, give it that little bit of concern and attention by somehow keeping apprised of worldly matters. First get in touch with how much your own puzzle piece and interest pulls you to this area, and then create for yourself the appropriate exposure to these matters. It may require a minimum of attention for you to have fulfilled a 99% quotient based upon your particular mission and puzzle piece. I do, however, encourage you to honor that minimum level so that there is some exchange going on between yourself and your sociological and political world. For those of you on the political track, do give it your full 100%.

4. *Staying Grounded Quotient*

Doing the vast amount of spiritual work that all of you, my beloved readers, are doing these days, staying grounded is not always the easiest thing. Many have the tendency to become top-heavy, filled with spiritual ideas, ideals, and out of the body adventure. It is essential that we are grounded as well. This new millennium is asking us to both ascend to Heaven and have Heaven descend to Earth through us. Remember your grounding cord and your place upon this planet. Take stock of your ability to be grounded quotient. I will tell you this, beloved readers, the more integrated that you are between the spiritual and the physical, the heavens and the Earth, the happier and more balanced you will be.

5. *Physical Rest and Sleep Quotient*

Many have the tendency to get so caught up in our mission and work that we, in fact, forget to give the body the physical rest that it requires. Look at this for yourself, this very moment. Please do not forget to give the body its due. Let it rest, kick back, and relax. Get the amount of sleep that you personally require. That amount may vary. When you are ill, take the time to give your physical vehicle the total rest it needs. That is not giving in to the body, my friends, it is honoring the body. Remember that this book is about integrating and honoring all the levels of our being. Driving the physical vehicle to excess will not get you to the Kingdom of GOD any quicker. Don't coddle your physical self, but don't ignore your need for physical rest either. This is most important as the body is the temple of the spirit and does require adequate rest!

6. *Enjoyment, Fun, and Recreation Quotient*

There is an old saying that indicates that the more complex a person's work is, the more fun and recreation they need. The intensity of the work of lightworkers is great, and therefore the need for recreation, fun and simple enjoyment is equally great. Many lightworkers function under the misconception that any time that is taken in this regard is wasted time. In reality, nothing can be further from the truth. We all need to take the time for some simple pleasures. These can and will vary according to your basic personality structure and may run the gamut from cooking, going to see movies, to hiking and camping out. Whatever your enjoyment and recreation is, I encourage you to give it adequate attention. See where you feel your quotient lies in this regard and aim higher. Trust me, you deserve to fulfill this quotient to its maximum potential!

7. *Spiritualizing Sexuality Quotient*

Sexuality is a delicate subject for lightworkers in particular. Many of us have had a run of past incarnations as monks, nuns, hermits and other forms of celibate lifestyles. In consequence, many of us mistakenly think we must deny our sexuality altogether. This can lead to a type of sexual rebellion, where indiscriminate and non-heartfelt sex takes hold. What we need to do is to find the right balance for us, where our sexuality and our spirituality are "integrated." This is not impossible, in fact, as a collective group, this is our next step. To connect both sexually, through the heart chakra and also through all chakras, which brings forth a total appreciation for the spiritual beings in form that we each are is the highest ideal. Take a good look at this for yourself and then jointly with your partner. This particular quotient works best when you deal with it both individually and with your mate or partner. See if you can both align with each other to manifest this quotient to its highest potential. In order to do this you must first be willing to take a good look at where you are currently at. I highly recommend you do this, for increasing this quotient to its highest level will increase your pleasure, joy, and ultimately Divine ecstasy on all levels as well.

8. *Taking Care of Business & Non-procrastination Quotient*

Beloved readers, take a deep breath and then take an honest read at where you think your quotient is operating in this regard. So many lightworkers are so busy in the higher realms that the little things are never attended to. This has a chain effect of non-efficiency and wastes time. It also contributes to making you an unreliable person. Please take a good look at this quotient so that you may begin to take care of the business of your everyday life.

Where we are most prone to procrastination in this regard is in matters that pertain to the little unpleasantries of life such as going to the dentist, keeping good tax records, car maintenance and so forth. Let's face it, none of us particularly enjoy these aspects of life, yet they are there. The sooner they are appropriately dealt with, the sooner they will be 'off our heads' so to speak. See where your quotient lies in this regard and upgrade it accordingly.

9. *Business Integrity Quotient*

While you are taking care of your personal and worldly business, take a read on the level of integrity that you are upholding. This particular quotient is extremely important on both a personal and professional level. As they say, you are as good as your work. If we as lightworkers are not operating out of the highest integrity, then we are dishonoring our own inner connection to GOD as well as setting a poor example for humanity. This quotient requires daily monitoring, as it is that important both to ourselves and the higher work that we came here to do.

10. *Proper Vitamin and Mineral Supplementation Quotient*

Maintaining the physical bodies to maximum potential involves taking your personal quota of vitamins and minerals. Do you know what these are but get too distracted or too lazy to stick with your own program? Lack of proper vitamins and minerals can really throw our bodies out of balance. If you are unsure what to take I highly recommend consulting with an expert in the field. If you know what you need to help you promote the healthiest physical body you can, but space this out, please do look at this. Try to build your quotient up to its peak level. We often tend to pay the least attention to our physical vehicles. We must shift this thinking into one that sees this vehicle as part of the whole and then treat it accordingly. This along with good diet, proper exercise and relaxation and drinking plenty of water will help the overall build-up of your physical immune system. This ties in with the following quotients.

11. *Drinking of Sufficient Water Quotient*

As lightworkers we should all try to drink as much water as possible. This is essential to our overall physical well being and helps to keep the system balanced and flushed clean of toxins. It is easy to forget this, particularly during the cooler weather. Some climates experience extreme cold spells and this makes it even less appealing. While it is true that the hotter and dryer the climate the more water is necessary for the prevention of dehydration, no matter what climate we live in the body still requires a good amount of water. Take a look at how you rate on this quotient, beloved readers. Some of us are not very good at remembering the importance of pure water. This quotient is put in as a friendly reminder to get out your favorite bottled water and start drinking away.

12. *Healthy Diet Quotient*

This is a tricky one. This is an easy quotient to have down 100% in the mental body, not necessarily in the physical body where good diet is needed to manifest. My friends, I ask you to take an inventory of your personal overall diet and see if your actual physical diet is even in the same ballpark as to where you mentally understand that it ideally should be. Once you have done this, do not get judgmental if you find that, indeed, your mental understanding far exceeds your physical doing. Just decide that you will raise this quotient day by day until you are functioning at least around the 90% range. This allows for a few of the less harmful addictions to find their appropriate substitute, such as honey in place of sugar, fresh fruit in place of desserts, an occasional light dessert in place of an overly rich heavy dessert and so forth. Do, however, try to implement physically all that you know about nutrition and diet into your actual daily life and physical vehicle. All the study and knowledge in the world will not serve you if you do not apply it.

You might find writing down what you are eating to be of enormous benefit, particularly at the beginning stages of seriously implementing a healthy and nutritious diet. You might even include how much organically grown food you eat as opposed to non-organic, how much processed as opposed to fresh. This will show you just where you actually are in this issue and indicate the progress that you are making as you continue to log this quotient. Diet plays an important role in our physical/etheric, emotional and even mental well being. Ultimately it helps to create a calm and peaceful inner environment, which in turn effects the spiritual level as well. Therefore, with absolutely no judgment whatsoever, do begin to take a serious look at how you can most quickly and easily upgrade your healthy diet quotient!

13. *Physical Fitness Quotient*

Physical fitness or proper exercise goes hand and hand with a healthy diet. Some people love formal exercise while others have an aversion towards it. Following a specific exercise routine is not, in truth, what is important. Getting enough physical exercise in a way that is harmonious with your own personal taste is! If you are an individual whose work involves physical activity then you are actually quite fortunate. Most of the jobs of the day are quite sedentary which necessitates that one set aside a specific time to get exercise in one form or another. You do not have to join a gym or build one in your home in order to do this! If you like such a routine, then that is fine for you. If not, be creative. Dance, walk, be involved in sports, jog, let your dog take you on a nice long walk every day, ride a bike or a horse. The physical body can be moved in many ways. Seek those that are most appealing to your make-up and temperament. It is a good idea to do some basic stretches or take a yoga class to keep flexible. You might, however, incorporate stretching into your chores at home. The point is that there is not one way but many, many ways to keep the body strong, supple and exercised. See where you are in your physical fitness quotient and work on building that quotient to a good and healthy range.

14. *Personal Hygiene Quotient*

This is one of the more basic quotients but one that bears mentioning. Although it is a simple matter to maintain good personal hygiene, many people don't. Lightworkers who are low in this quotient are probably so because they are focused outside the body most of the time. As this book is dedicated to the integration of all levels of Beingness, I ask you to realize that your physical body is in fact interacting with the world in a very concrete way. Your personal hygiene is going to have an influence and effect upon your spiritual work in a less than desired fashion if you just space it out. Beloved readers, please do incorporate this quotient into your lives it you are not already doing so. All of the bodies are interconnected within the whole of each of us. Let us all bring this basic quotient to its highest standard.

15. *Home Environment, Earthly Order, and Harmony Quotient*

If our bodies are the temples of our Soul and Spirit, our homes are the temple of our incarnated form. It is easy to forget this fact and let the home become a simple crash pad or a "den of clutter." I suggest that you strive instead to make your home as much like a temple as possible. Begin with basic cleanliness. Whoever first said "cleanliness was next to

Godliness," was quite on the mark. A clean environment is reflective of divine order and purity. Then proceed to create a temple atmosphere. You should, of course, do this to taste.

If you are not allergic to incense or flowers, both are a great addition. Plants serve well in both manifesting beauty and in sharing of love and nurturing. However you chose to do this, make your environment as clean as possible and as reflective of your own personal vision and taste as well. You should feel like you are walking into embracing arms welcoming you home every time you walk through your door. Your guests will feel the same. This is a fun quotient to work with and I encourage you all to do so. It need not be an expensive endeavor by any means. More often than not, it involves the elimination of unnecessary clutter that no longer serves. Have fun with this. You will, I guarantee, feel all the better the higher up on the quotient scale you go.

16. *Earthly Aesthetic Quotient*
The above discourse covers most of what I would say in this regard. The only other aspect I would add is that this can be used in the area of the physical body as well by incorporating it into the way you dress and carry yourself. Often we get lazy or simply pay no attention to the clothes we wear, the way we move, the way we speak and in fact, our own personal physical aesthetics. See how you feel with regards to yourself and this quotient. My guess is that you will enjoy taking this quotient up a few digits as well. It is very centering when this is done, and serves to physically convey what is spiritually felt.

17. *Tithing or Seed Money Quotient*
Once you have made sure that you have taken care of your immediate family and personal needs, it is a good idea to do some sort of tithing. This helps to create a flow of abundance from you out into the universe and back to you a thousand fold. It likewise serves to cultivate the spirit of giving and does indeed do much good to your

chosen service area. This does not need to be much money at all. You don't literally have to give 10% of your earnings to the church or charity of your choice. Whatever you do give, if it comes from the heart, will be of great benefit to yourself and to the receiver of your energy in the form of financial aid. Most lightworkers are pretty involved in one cause or another. I would suggest aligning yourself with the cause most dear to your heart. If you do not have the money to give, you might just as well give a bit of your time. It is the flow of energy, the exchange of love and aid in whatever form you choose or are able to give that is truly of import. Check this quotient out and see if you are in touch with it at all. If not, you may want to start small and see how it feels. This is a wonderful way to move the energies of the universe and be of service to others and self at the same time.

18. *Financial Responsibility Quotient*

This quotient again, refers to the importance of attending to your own affairs and making sure that you are being responsible towards them. It is easy as lightworkers to get a bit floaty in the light and to forget practical matters altogether. The wave of energies of this next millennium seeks to bring forth balance within all areas of our lives. Take stock of this area and set yourself the goal of reaching and maintaining a high quotient in your financial world in the same way that you seek to establish and maintain a high quotient in the more esoteric areas of being.

19. *Your Ascension Mission Quotient*

The more in touch with your own ascension mission, the more easily you will be enabled to pursue it on all possible levels. Try and get a good read at exactly where you are at in regards to this. It is very important that you get as clear and concise as possible, so that you can freely follow your true life's mission and calling. If you are running low on this quotient, I would recommend reading my book *Your Ascension Mission:*

Embracing Your Puzzle Piece. It will serve to stimulate ideas and catalyze further action in this area. You might then consider journaling and experimenting with certain areas that you feel particularly drawn to. Rate how you feel about these areas. Journal in detail about them. I assure you that a light of recognition will come on when you hit upon that particular area that is your true divine destiny. When that happens, you will be able to rate yourself high in regards to this quotient, as you will have uncovered your true spiritual work. This will bring with it a great sense of peace and focus of being.

20. *Prosperity Quotient*

Many lightworkers have a hard time letting go of poverty consciousness, which stems from many incarnations as monks, nuns, hermits, and ascetics. As Ecclesiasticus tells us, "To everything turn, turn, turn, there is a season…and a time for every purpose under heaven." Where once it served well to wander the wilderness with nothing but the clothes upon your back, this new millennium seeks to merge Heaven and Earth. This is a time, beloved readers, for abundance rather than poverty. It is a time where we are called to demonstrate and manifest the abundance of Heaven upon the soil of Earth. How are you doing in this regard? Does poverty consciousness still rule supreme in your life? If it does, set yourself little goals that step by step and stage by stage you can learn to change your way of thinking to that which allows for prosperity on every level of your being, physical as well as spiritual. I am not here saying that each of us has the same puzzle piece and must therefore manifest a certain amount of money in order to score high with this quotient. What I am saying is that all of our thinking should shift from that of poverty to that of abundance, and there should indeed be an openness and acceptance of abundance upon the physical plane as well as the spiritual. The way I would guide you in reading this quotient for yourselves however, is not by the amount of money you earn, but by the amount of prosperity consciousness you contain within your mind and heart. As form follows energy, if you hold to the thought of prosperity then you will inevitably attract the prosperity you need on the levels that you need it most. I do however ask that you don't try and limit the realms upon which your abundance will manifest on. It may be physical or it may be of a more spiritual nature. The consciousness of abundance must, however, be open to the flow of abundance on every possible level.

21. *Gardening and Plant Kingdom Consciousness Quotient*
In exploring this quotient, are you taking into account your awareness of the beloved kingdom of nature spirits as well as the plant kingdom itself? These two kingdoms operate as one, and care and respect must be shown to both the nature spirits and elementals that tend to the plant kingdoms as well as to this precious kingdom itself. This is a most vital quotient, for it is in the joining of the lines of evolution, the elemental, angelic and human that the new millennium will be established. It is also in our mutual cooperation with these beings that a healing can take place upon Mother Earth and the entire plant and plant kingdom in general. Do take a look at where you are at in regard to this. Strive to bring this quotient to as high a standard as possible, for much depends upon humanity's joint effort in this regard.

22. *Tender Handling of the Animal Kingdom Quotient*
It is a spiritual fact that the Animal Kingdom is literally our younger brothers and sisters. They feel to a great extent, with the more domesticated animals demonstrating a high level of emotionalism along with the seed of mind. How are you treating this most precious kingdom? We must all become aware that from the highly evolved dog or cat to the lion in the wilderness, every single animal is worthy of our respect and harmlessness. We all can participate right where we are at by ourselves acting in accordance with the virtues of harmlessness, by supporting those who are playing a more active role in this issue and by

prayer and affirmations for the tender handling of the Animal Kingdom. We can all be aware of the sensitivities of our animals and treat them more as the family members that they are and less than pets or an amusement. Look at your awareness on this issue and do strive to reach as high a quotient as possible. It is we, humanity, who serve as the voice of the Animal Kingdom. Let us use that voice to express their beauty and to encourage love and gentleness when dealing with them in any and every possible way.

23. *Community Activism and Participation Quotient*

This quotient really does not require very much in order to score high on. We all can show an awareness and concern for the community in which we live. We can do this simply by holding the door open for a neighbor, or offering help to someone struggling with heavy packages. The possibilities for this quotient run the gamut from smiling at an elderly person walking down the street to helping establish a community center for troubled teenagers. We must each determine what our appropriate puzzle piece is in this regard and then, and only then, determine how well we are doing in fulfilling our personal responsibility. This again is one of those very personal quotients. When you know what your work within this given area is, then strive to do that work to the best of your ability. If you are doing your particular puzzle piece to its highest standard then you score a 100% in this and any given quotient.

The Psychological and Spiritual Quotients

24. *Meditation Quotient*

Meditation continues to play as important a role as it ever did in the path of the lightworker. Where the shift is actually occurring is that more and more initiates and embodied Ascended Masters are learning how to hold a meditative attitude throughout the day. The more formal standard periods of mediation are giving way to a more continuous flow of inner connectedness and a daily state of meditation. I would like to point out something I have noticed in this regard. For some, it is actually better to hold an attitude of meditation on a moment to moment basis rather than to set aside specific periods of meditation.

However, there are a great many lightworkers who are attempting this type of attunement for whom it is not effective and therefore their meditation quotient is suffering. There is absolutely no judgment involved in this; it is simply a matter of which method one is best suited for. For some, the period of formal meditation is most crucial. Many of these people are themselves Masters in their own right and are capable of personally staying within their own monadic sphere or Mighty I Am Presence regardless of whether or not they follow a set meditation pattern. Their specific personality is constructed, however, in ways that crave the type of silent communion that formal mediation offers, and to see them try to bypass this is to see them not honor who they truly are in this incarnation. I therefore ask you, beloved readers, to be totally honest with yourself when you gauge your Meditation Quotient. If you are the type that really requires set periods of meditation and are not giving that to yourself, then score yourself at a lower percentage in order to remind yourself of what you need to do. If, on the other hand, you find that you are forcing yourself to sit in meditation just because you think you are supposed to, then be honest with that. Score yourself at a lesser percentage level in order to remind yourself how you best need to function. When you are meditating in accordance with your own personal Tao, then you can feel free to give yourself 100%, provided, of course, that you are adhering to your Tao to the maximum degree possible!

25. *Prayer Quotient*

"Why worry when you can pray," Edgar Cayce said in his trance channelings of the Universal Mind. The only thing I would add to that is, why not pray when you can! I believe prayer to be one of humanity's most powerful tools in moving both the Earth and the heavens. Prayer calls into action the divine Hierarchy of Masters and Angelic Beings who but await our call to leap into action. Prayer is an energy mover, and we ourselves can effectuate change by the heart, will and determination of our prayers. Prayer calls forth our own Mighty I Am Presence and helps to anchor it within the core of our twelve-body system.

Beloved readers, the world of people is always in need of prayer, and in truth we could not engage in this practice too much. I am not talking about whining or working out bargains with GOD here, but in using prayer as divine invocation and also as a request for divine intervention. Take a look at how great or small a role prayer plays in your own life. How much do you pray for self, how much for others and how much for the world? Consider all these things as a whole and then come up with your personal prayer quotient. Note where you can add your energies of prayer and then set about to do so. Watch as your prayer quotient grows higher and higher. Prayer, my beloved readers and friends, is truly one of the best tools for world service that GOD has given to us and it is one that is readily available at any hour of the day or night, whether alone or in a crowd, whether in a temple, ashram or in the supermarket. Please make use of this most precious gift and set your quotient standard at the 100% mark. There can never be too much prayer!

26. *Ascension Activation Quotient*

Working on your ascension activations is a job unto itself! While it is most certainly true that by simply attuning to your own Mighty I Am Presence you will be activating your body of light, there are likewise specific activation meditations or exercises geared to accelerate this process. I suggest that you make use of some of these that I have put on tape or written into my books. You may of course use other ones specifically designed for the express purpose of activation of the light body and the love centers. You can create your own through the use of your own invocations to the light. You may also use your service work

Integrated Ascension

to activate the light body. In truth, there is no greater way in which to bring through the highest quotients of light and love then when we are channeling it through ourselves in order to be of service to others. The question is, are you doing this work or aren't you? If you are doing it, to what degree? Be honest and then rate yourself on this quotient. See how you can improve your quotient rating. Do realize that you have enormous control over your own acceleration and activation, and you are capable of moving as slow or as fast as you like. Never try to push the river or go at a faster speed than you are comfortable with, for that would only defeat your intent. Do, however, take stock of where you are at with this and set your intent at moving at the swiftest speed possible without causing any discomfort or stress to any of your vehicles. Beloved readers, this quotient is at your command. Go with Godspeed but remain in the Tao!

27. *Chanting the Name of GOD Quotient*

There is incredible power in chanting the name of GOD. As you are well aware, there are in the Kabbalistic tradition alone 72 sacred names of GOD. Add to that the countless names of GOD in the Hindu, Buddhist, Christian, Egyptian, Muslim, Native American and Tibetan traditions, just to name a few, and you will find an ample selection of sacred names of Spirit from which to choose. This is an incredibly wonderful practice to add to your spiritual path. In fact, there are a couple of spiritual paths that are predicated solely on chanting the name of GOD and nothing else. Whenever you feel the mind wandering in search of something constructive to do, I highly recommend filling head, heart and voice with the chanting of some of these most sacred names of GOD. If you are inclined to rate yourself on this quotient, I would recommend that you do not rate your percentage level in a vacuum, but instead, give yourself a rating that is based upon your conscious choice to replace a mind that is either drifting about aimlessly or indulging in negative ego thinking, with the chanting of the sacred names of GOD!

28. *Silence Quotient*

The silence quotient is not based upon periods of formal meditation. It is not unusual to find that one is attempting mediation, but the mind is chattering on anyway. The way in which I am referring to "Silence" here is actually twofold. First, it is the ability to still the concrete mind, whether in or out of meditation, that the inner voice, sound of GOD, or "sound of silence" can be heard. Secondly, it has to do with your ability to keep your tongue from wagging away in gossip, criticism, negativity, or chitchat. We all experience moments in which it would be easy to indulge in gossip or negative judgments concerning others and it is a challenge to stay silent when the voices of friends and/or associates are carrying on in such a fashion. This, my beloved readers, is the test of a true Master. The Master has the ability to remain silent in such situations, and exercises that ability. When you check out how you are doing on this quotient, first rate yourself in regard to the hearing of the sound of silence within and then see how you are doing in regard to the ability to remain silent when many voices around you are engaged in the ceaseless chatter of gossip. Combine both quotients and see where you stand. Work to bring your silence quotient to a very high level. This will provide you with a wonderful sensation of peace, as well as help to create a peaceful and calm atmosphere around you.

29. *Devotion to GOD Quotient*

Devotion to GOD is one of the most glorious ways to direct your energy. Devotion is, in essence, a great motivation for action. A devoted heart will seek to express that feeling in the activities that one is engaged in. As this is the millennium in which the Kingdom of GOD seeks to manifest Itself upon the Earth, devotion serves a vital function. In the previous era, or the Age of Pisces out of which we are emerging, devotion was more or less to a single representative of GOD. A perfect example for this can be seen in the great devotion to Jesus Christ. Now we are being asked to be devoted to the GOD within ALL, to the Christ within all selves, to the Divine Plan and Divine Purpose of the seventh Golden Age. Devotion is a very key element in our evolution and in the evolution of humanity as a whole. If you can feel devotion to GOD first, then you can certainly feel devotion to the Masters and Angels who stand forth as representatives of GOD. You will also have the ability to feel devotion toward your fellow lightworkers and to humanity and all the kingdoms upon the Earth. This is a very important quotient to have highly developed, for it indicates an open heart. One of the dangers encountered in this New Age is that there is so much information coming through at such lightening speed, people run the risk of closing their hearts and becoming overly mentally focused. Devotion is the absolute cure-all for that. I therefore ask you, beloved friends, to try to raise that level within you as high as you possibly can based upon your particular ray configuration and to keep the heart open to love!

30. *Love & Service of Humanity Quotient*

This brings us to the love of humanity. The love of GOD is ultimately demonstrated in our love and service of humanity. If this is not demonstrated then what we have is an abstraction of love rather than a manifestation and demonstration of love through service. See where you are at in actually manifesting your love for GOD within the arena of humanity. This quotient, beloved readers, is one of the most important of the so-called minor quotients. If the love of GOD is not demonstrated within the field of active service to the Sons and Daughters of GOD, and ultimately to all that dwell upon the planet, then the Golden Age will not be enabled to manifest. Love must demonstrated through service, that the face of GOD be seen shining in every man, woman and child upon the Earth!!!

31. *Constant GOD Attunement Quotient*

The way that the above quotients, and in fact all of the spiritual quotients can best be activated, is through constant attunement to GOD.

Integrated Ascension

Just how attuned you keep yourself to GOD can only be known to you through the silent recesses of your heart and through taking an honest look at where you are focusing your energies. This is another extremely important quotient. It is actually a key quotient, for it is in our attunement and alignment with GOD that we both evolve and serve. Take a good, hard and honest look at where you are with this quotient and do set your intent on the 100% mark. It is of paramount importance that all lightworkers stay in attunement with their own Mighty I Am Presence, the inner plane Hierarchy of Ascended Masters, the Angelic and Elohim Kingdoms and our space brothers and sisters who have come from afar to champion our cause of ascension into the light. None of this is possible, beloved readers, if you are not first attuned to GOD!

32. *Spiritual Affirmation Quotient*

Spiritual affirmations are another tool that has a double function and therefore is best to look at singularly first, and then in a combined manner in order to determine which area you feel you need to do the most work and which area you may be excelling in. The first way I suggest that you look at this quotient is with regard to using positive spiritual affirmations to reprogram negative ego belief patterns or to move any aspect of your life forward in a positive direction. See whether or not you are using this most valuable tool on a regular basis. When you become adept at using spiritual affirmations on a consistent basis you actually change the lens or window through which the mind looks at any given situation. Be completely honest with yourself when doing your evaluation as this is an extremely vital quotient, and one that deserves as clear and accurate a reading as you can give it. The power of positive spiritual affirmations can literally transform a situation from despair to joy, from darkness to light, from that of the negative ego to that of the Christ/Buddhic mind itself! Therefore, be very diligent when examining this aspect of the quotient.

Secondly, the spiritual affirmation quotient can be used as a tool for meditation or just simply for quieting the mind and helping you keep focused on the positive aspect of things in general. See if you use this quotient in this way as well, for it is healing in and of itself and very useful in providing positive points of focus and providing positive "seed thought" for meditation.

After you have fully explored each of these areas and found a quotient for each of them separately, then combine the quotients to see what your overall score is. As this is such a key and vital quotient I sincerely hope that you will all try to bring the rating of this quotient to the 100% mark.

33. *Spiritual Visualization Quotient*

The spiritual visualization quotient is very similar to the spiritual affirmation quotient. The person who primarily relates to the world through the visual sense will most likely be drawn to using this type of imagery, than one who is a more mental or auditory type. The value of this particular quotient is that it actually places the person who is practicing it within the visualized moment of positive imagery. There is an immediacy that is involved in the visualizing process that is not quite available in the same way through other means. If you find yourself inclined to work with this tool then I suggest that you cultivate it to maximum potential, for it is very powerful. Work at increasing your rating until it is so high that the mind will automatically move into positive imagery when it is confronted with challenging circumstances. If you are not that drawn to this particular technique, I still do encourage you to use it from time to time as it has great healing and manifesting potential.

34. *Spiritual Book Reading Quotient*

This is a tricky quotient to work with, as reading spiritual literature will vary depending upon what one is working with at the moment.

Integrated Ascension

There are definite phases that cyclically occur when one finds one's self all consumed with reading spiritual books. There are other cycles in which one is guided to spend more time in meditation and/or service work than in the reading of spiritual books. When working with this quotient you must first decipher which cycle you are personally on at the moment and then rate yourself based upon the appropriate cycle you are focused upon. Do, however, realize that it is a good idea to keep some sort of spiritual, motivational or educational reading up, as a support of whatever you are doing on your own spiritual path. The one exception to this would be if you receive clear inner guidance suggesting that you do not read for a given amount of time or at all! If this comes to you then of course follow it. Do make sure, however, that this is not the voice of laziness. Setting a percentage rating on this particular quotient is however, impossible, as you might be at a phase of your practice where you are devouring one spiritual book per week, or at a phase where you are reading just one spiritual thought for the day. I therefore suggest that you stay in the Tao with yourself, and if you are at a reading phase, make sure that you take the time for yourself to do the reading that your Higher Self or Monad is urging you to do!

35. *Spiritual Journal Writing*

Some of you may be inclined to make detailed logs of your spiritual journeys, marking your progress in a multitude of areas and detailing your entire initiation process in a most specific manner. Others of you may reserve your spiritual journaling for key issues that you find yourself confronting upon the spiritual path that you are on. Whatever your preference, I do highly suggest that you use writing in some form or another, as it helps to concretize many of the abstractions or ideas with which you are working. Find a way of journaling, logging, or writing that is comfortable for you personally. Then set about rating yourself in relation to your own personal standards. The purpose of monitoring this and other quotients is simply to keep you in touch with what for you is your "personal best." It also helps to keep you alert and aware of what your intentions are so that you follow through with them rather than go on automatic pilot and just space them out.

36. *Spiritual Leadership Quotient*

It often takes a certain degree of courage to step forward and go public with your spiritual work. If this is your puzzle piece, then this is an area that you need to work with until you grow confident and comfortable with it. If you feel that there is something that you are specifically supposed to do in regards to your spiritual work but are holding back from doing it, then I suggest that you seriously get to work on building this quotient way up. Use whatever tools that work best for you in order to do this and concentrate on building up the quotients that can help you in this specific regard. Also, call upon the assistance of the inner plane Hierarchy of Masters, and your own Higher Self and Monad to help facilitate this process. The birth of this new millennium is likewise birthing many new and needed spiritual teachers and forerunners. If you feel you are one of them, then again, do any and everything that you have to do in order to fulfill your divine calling. Those who have taken the sixth initiation and above should begin to seriously focus on this quotient. Once ascension is achieved spiritual leadership and world service should be your main focus.

37. *Spiritual Interaction and Fellowship Quotient*

Much of the spiritual path is of a very personal nature, as we each are responsible for self-purifying, cleansing, facing our "stuff," clearing our negative ego, and connecting with our own Higher Self, Monad, the Masters and GOD. The path of the Spirit, however, is also one that is shared by all of us, as it is the journey that every soul will ultimately take. Interaction and fellowship with other lightworkers on the path is as vital a part of our spiritual pilgrimage as is the periods of meditation where we commune with GOD in the silent recesses of our heart, or in periods where we study, read, journal and so forth. There is a danger that we face if we allow ourselves to get too isolated and cut off from one another as we forge ahead upon our individual paths. There really is a proper balance that needs to be struck between the time that we spend in personal communion with GOD and the time that we spend interacting with fellow lightworkers. If we do not allow ourselves to interact with others on the path, our lives can grow very narrow and self absorbed. We will not even notice this occurring, as we will not have the people we need around us to mirror this back to us. This puts us in danger of becoming overly introverted and narrow in our thinking.

Remember, beloved readers, that spirituality is ultimately about oneness. In spiritual fellowship, ideas are exchanged, as well as feelings. Oneness with one's brothers and sisters on the path are experienced as "fact" rather than as mere ideas. We are able to run the spiritual energies and currents that we each are receiving through us in love, allowing them to freely flow outward to one another. By the same token, we will receive the unique spiritual energies as they manifest through our brothers and sisters on both a vibrational level and through the exchange of ideas, work, insights, and vision.

Much of the work of bringing in the new millennium is to be done in group formation. This obviously applies to groups that exist on the inner planes, but applies equally to groups that we are connected with on the outer planes. See where you are at with this quotient. If you are scoring very low, realize that you are isolating yourself from your outer plane spiritual family and most likely from the work that you are destined to do as a part of the New Group of World Servers. Allow yourself to begin experimenting with various spiritual gatherings. Allow yourself to be guardedly open. If you feel particularly attuned to a specific group of initiates or to a specific work then experiment in letting your guard down. Do however, always keep up your personal bubble of protection. This semi-permeable bubble of light should be part of your psychological and spiritual attire no matter what your environment or circumstance. This has been discussed elsewhere and also relates to your personal immune system. This is a habit you should form regardless whether you are in the middle of a city or a wilderness, for it operates as basic protection anywhere and everywhere. I simply restate it here for emphasis of its inherent importance.

When you feel you have found spiritual colleagues, friends, or co-workers, then allow yourself to join in work and fellowship with them. From time immemorial, people have gathered in groups to pray and to celebrate. They have gathered to chant or sing the name of GOD and to enjoy each other's company on spiritual festivals, or simply just to share in friendship. The road traveled is always a bit easier when it is not walked alone. The Age of Aquarius is definitely not the age of isolation. I therefore call your attention to this most important quotient and ask you to work with expanding it to the point of proper balance within your lives. This is more important than you perhaps realize. Let us join together in enjoying one another's company and friendship as we seek to co-create the Golden Age upon our world!

38. Spiritual Communion Quotient

Practicing the Presence of GOD, or taking the time to commune with Spirit should seem like the most obvious thing to every lightworker on the spiritual path. In truth, however, many lightworkers often get so engrossed in their service work and personal path that they actually forget why they have begun that path in the first place! If you find yourself so immersed in working the path that you are forgetting to commune with GOD, then this quotient should serve to remind you of why you are doing what you are doing in the first place. Beloved readers, it is imperative that we each maintain that blissful, joy filled, wondrous, love and light filled connection with Spirit on a daily, hourly, and moment to moment basis. This quotient is not, in truth, simply a minor or sub-quotient, but the very truth and joy of our existence. I put it in here to help remind you to make it a point to stay within Holy Communion even while working your path or doing your service work. Make sure that you work with this particular quotient until it reaches the 100% level. "What does it matter if we gain the whole world, yet lose our own soul (or Mighty I Am Presence)?" While we walk the path of GOD, let us be sure to remember GOD in the process!

39. *Seeing GOD in Everything and Everyone Quotient: "The Holy Encounter"*

As you go about your daily life, are you remembering to see GOD in every person, place, and material expression? Are you remembering that when you encounter another Son or Daughter of GOD you have the ability to acknowledge that as the "Holy Encounter" that it truly is? If you are doing this on a consistent basis, then you would be living this quotient to its highest capacity. If you forget that all of life is but GOD in various forms and all people are Sons and Daughters of GOD, then you need to be honest with yourself and make a conscious effort to stay within that state of Realization at all times. I promise you that the joy that you will experience when doing so will be worth all your efforts! Each and every moment is an opportunity to experience GOD both within self and within everything and everyone.

40. *Higher Body Anchoring Quotients*

When doing your activation meditations it is important that you set your intent on anchoring the higher bodies. This would obviously not be the core of your meditation, nor does it need to be done on a regular basis. If, however, you are not asking for this on a semi-regular basis and incorporating this into your practice, then I highly suggest that you do so. The same should be done in regard to the higher chakras and the twelve strands of DNA. As Jesus says, "Ask and ye shall receive." These, my beloved readers, are things that you should be asking for in order to facilitate the process of receiving them. The inner plane Hierarchy of Ascended Masters can be of far, far greater service to you in this and every area when you ask them for their help. I suggest that you invoke the aid of the Divine Hierarchy of Inner Plane Ascended Masters in your process of anchoring your higher bodies, higher chakras, and twelve strands of DNA. If you make this part of your meditations and/or activations on a semi-regular basis, you will help to speed up this glorious process and move much more quickly and easily into the higher aspects of self!

41. *Soul Extension Integration and Clearing*

I have written about the importance of helping to clear and integrate your soul extension in many of my other books. I am putting it here as a reminder to you that this is something you should be working with in your process of integrated ascension and to consider it as one of the quotients with which you are working. The idea is to do this in a balanced manner so as to not overwhelm yourself with the cleansing that your soul extensions are processing, yet at the same time to be sure to assist in the cleansing, clearing and integrating of this most important soul group or family to which all belong. I suggest that when you make the request for integration and clearing of your soul extensions, you likewise add to that request that you want to do this in as easy and gentle a manner as possible, yet as quickly as possible. In this way you will be moving both yourself and your soul extensions through the path of integrated ascension in the best possible way.

42. *Antakarana Development Quotient*

Our personal antakarana, as you know, is the bridge that fully connects us with our Monad. On a higher turn of the spiral there is a Planetary antakarana and even a Cosmic antakarana, which when constructed will put us in rapport with the Planetary Purpose and Whole, and ultimately the Cosmic Purpose and Whole. Between these various stages are the Solar, Galactic, Universal, and Multiuniversal Antakarana. It is up to each of us to individually work upon the building

Integrated Ascension

of our personal antakarana. The building of your personal antakaranas up through the various levels back to the GODHEAD helps to build the group antakarana for the whole planet as well up through the various levels. Therefore, as we each construct, for example, our own planetary antakarana we are actually helping the planet as a whole in its evolution. We are serving as bridge builders for all of humanity when we contribute to this process.

Likewise do we gain the advantage of experiencing our own personal connection with the intent of the Planetary Logos. Each of us would be wise to work on all the various antakaranas simultaneously. First, of course, is the building of the personal antakarana. See how you are doing quotient wise in regard to that. Seek to bring that quotient to its greatest limit. While you are doing that, you are likewise encouraged to ask to participate in the building of the Planetary antakarana. The same is true through all the graded expansions. In this way, you will be accessing and connecting with aspects of greater and greater Wholes even while building the firmest and strongest bridge between your incarnated self and your Monad. Do consider this a quotient you can work with and then do work with it at the highest level that you feel comfortable with.

43. *Seven Ray Integration Quotient*

The need to integrate each of the seven rays has been dealt with in great detail within this book. I ask you now to realize that the integration of the rays is itself a quotient and to run a daily check to see how well you are doing with this process. Remember that you will always exhibit more of your dominant ray characteristics and that is how it should be. The point is to also make sure the other rays are fully integrated within your being as well. They will not be your primary focus in most likelihood, yet neither should they be absent or missing from your auric sphere of functioning. Be as honest as possible and work hard at integrating all of the rays into your field. Try to bring this quotient up to maximum potential, so that whatever situation presents itself to you, you will immediately have the energy and support of whichever ray can serve you and your work most.

44. *Hierarchy Integration Quotient*

This quotient, beloved readers, is one that I am sure you all want functioning at the highest possible level. It deals with actually integrating your work with that of the Hierarchy of Inner Plane Ascended Planetary and Cosmic Masters. As this is the path that we have all consciously chosen, then this is something that we certainly want to integrate within our lives in as direct and potent a manner as possible. The deeper our integration with the beloved Celestial Hierarchy, the more they will be able to help us in our personal work upon the Earth plane, as well as in our service work. By the same token, the more available we will be to be of service to them in their divine work and missions. The energy exchange will bring proportionate joy, protection, divine love, divine light, and divine purpose. Our vision will grow ever clearer and we will see the path laid out before us and know that we are being guarded and guided every single step of the way. As I previously stated, the Hierarchy of inner plane Ascended Planetary and Cosmic Masters, the Angels, Archangels, and Elohim will be ever more present within our lives and we will be conscious of them there. Our service exchange will be mutual and the greater plan of GOD will be served. I encourage you from the bottom of my heart and the depth of my soul to make this a priority in your lives. I tell you here and now that there is nothing of personal self or individuality lost in this sanctified process. There is only expansion into ever widening vistas of beatitude and a joining with our elder Brothers and Sisters in GOD! Work with this quotient on a moment to moment basis, while at the same time know that it is through the center of your own Mighty I Am Presence, your own unique individuality that you stand in service, love, light, power and joy with the most resplendent and wondrous Hierarchy of inner plane Ascended Masters whose glory it is to be One with GOD and to serve GOD eternally.

45. *Pursuit of Excellence Quotient*

Every single endeavor that we become engaged with should ideally be approached from the attitude of the pursuit of excellence. Doing this will certainly help us to produce the highest quality work that we are capable of. It will also create the mindset of excellence, so that the manner in which we approach even minor endeavors will automatically carry forward into major endeavors. It will help us approach everything from the small to the great with excellence, as do the Masters, which will assure our maintaining the highest standard possible at all times. As stated by Thoth/Hermes, "As above, so below." All that we demonstrate with excellence in smaller matters will then easily set the stage for our basic approach in more vital and inclusive spiritual matters. This quotient is one of the more powerful and vital of all the minor quotients.

46. *Courtesy & Neighborly Quotient*

This quotient is quite obvious and one which all of us need to pay attention to. Remember, it is often by the little acts of kindness and love that we demonstrate GOD upon Earth. Please take stock of how you are doing in this most important area.

47. *Being vs. Doing Quotient*

Check yourselves to make sure that you allow yourself to just "be." You do not always have to be "doing" or accomplishing something outwardly or even inwardly. It is often in the hours of pure being where we make our most progress. We all need to just "be," for, in truth, it is from this center that all action proceeds anyway. See how well you are doing in this regard, as it is vital that you establish this ability to maximum potential. When doing and being become as one, you will never leave you eternal home in GOD again!

48. Social Integration Quotient

Be honest and see whether or not you are allowing yourself to integrate on a social level with your fellow human beings, or if you hold yourself separate and apart, as a 'special divine emissary' of sorts. My beloved readers, the ultimate truth is that the more we embrace, embody and manifest our own Divine and spiritual connection with GOD and the Masters, the more we see the equality and not the differences among ourselves and the mass of humanity. I am not saying here to disregard the level of initiation or Divine union you have achieved, but merely to demonstrate it where it is needed most, which is right where you are in your personal and social world. If others see you as a bit odd or strange, then simply smile and take it as a compliment. You, however, need to see yourself as one with humanity, for that is how service will actualize and demonstrate. Take a good inventory to see if you are walking around with a 'better than' attitude. If you are, know that it is the voice of the negative ego that is telling you this and disregard it. Oneness and unity is an attribute of every dimension, including the social. Remember, everyone and everything is part of that which is GOD!

49. Time for Self Quotient

Taking time for one's self is extremely important. This would be special time "just for you." It would involve some sort of relaxation or simple pleasure. It could run the gamut from shopping to taking a long hot bath to spiritual reading, etc. It does not matter what this special time is, as long as it is something that brings you personal joy, peace, and relaxation. It could just as well be mediating alone or going to the movies with friends. The main ingredient is that it is something that you want for your self! Many lightworkers do not even consider this option, much less realize that it is an important quotient that needs to be integrated into their lives. I lovingly ask each of you to see if you are including this most essential facet of being into your path. If not, begin to do so immediately. We all need personal time just for ourselves. See how high you allow yourself to go in regard to this quotient. You may have to release some old belief patterns in order to move this quotient into an enjoyable range for yourself. If you need the time, then by all means take it. I do suggest, however, that you begin to implement this quotient within your lives immediately. I promise you that when faulty thinking is let go of in this regard and you allow yourselves the joy and utter freedom of taking this time for self, you will be extremely glad that you did!

50. *Earthly Family Responsibility Quotient*
If you have chosen to co-create your own earthly family, then you are well advised to pay attention to your earthly family quotient. You are part of a group that is dependent upon you in many regards, and you need to honor the obligations that you have agreed to assume. Evaluate yourself as to how you are doing in that area and in what range your quotient lies. Be honest. This is one of those delicate quotients that you want to keep in balance. Honoring your earthly family responsibility is of utmost importance, yet so is creating and maintaining your own boundaries within that group body. What the appropriate balance is only you can decide. Be careful however, not to overemphasize one to the exclusion of the other. The proper balance is essential in every area of one's life. Be aware also that there is a certain amount of earthly responsibility that flows towards our parents, siblings, cousins and so forth. In this instance, there are many variations. Sometimes it may be appropriate to be much less involved in this regard than in others. This is an extremely personal arena. I therefore suggest that you create your quotient in respect to this aspect of family life based upon your individual circumstance, and proceed from there.

51. Educational Development Quotient

What all of us in general should be aware of is that the world is developing at a very rapid and expansive state itself. In order to be qualified to do our spiritual work we may need to learn certain fundamentals that are necessary to our particular area of expertise. We each should at least keep up with the language of our particular area of service work so that if we do not, for instance, become proficient at the computer, we know enough to communicate with those who have chosen to pursue this field.

Another aspect of this has to do with more esoteric work, such as channeling. The more we fill our personal computers, our minds, our data banks with information, the more we are providing the Hierarchy with well filled information banks to work with. It is far easier for them to communicate with a scientist when dealing with scientific issues than with an artist. Our education should be as inclusive as possible along our own particular area of interest and work. This way, when the Masters come to us in order to transmit certain knowledge to us, they will find pre-activated brain cells and data banks with which to more easily convey their intent. It also allows ourselves to communicate more knowledgeably with friends, family, clients, students, colleagues and our world.

52. Romantic Relationship Quotient

If you are involved in a romantic relationship then I suggest you look at the level of physical consideration that you are giving to your partner. I mean this on all possible levels. Are you helping them with the daily chores, taking time to consider the needs of their physical, emotional and mental aspects, as well as their spiritual needs? Are they spending too much time alone or are you perhaps demanding too much of them? When you are involved in a romantic relationship then it is important to take into consideration all aspects of that relationship. I have devoted an entire book to this subject and would suggest that you take a look at

Integrated Ascension

it in order to get an in-depth picture of all the many aspects that such a relationship entails. What I would also suggest is that you do a quotient reading just by yourself and then do one with your mate or partner. You can then be in a better position to work together in order to achieve the highest joint-quotient possible in regard to romantic relationships.

I wish you well with these quotients, my beloved brothers and sisters. I trust that they will serve you with Godspeed upon your path of Integrated Ascension.

7

Transcending Negative Ego Archetypal Dualities

In my work as a spiritual psychotherapist and spiritual teacher I have developed certain models and paradigms for understanding spiritual and soul psychology. One revolutionary model that has come to me from Spirit for understanding the difference between negative ego thinking and Christ thinking that I feel is one of the clearest ways of understanding how the negative ego works, has to do with the understanding that the negative ego has an upper and lower side to it. They are like two sides of a coin. If you get caught in one side of the coin, you will also unavoidably get caught in the other side of the coin. The only way to achieve true Christ consciousness and inner peace is to transcend the whole system. In esoteric and Eastern thought this might be aptly called transcending duality. Let me begin here by listing some of the archetypal negative ego dualities that every lightworker must learn to ultimately transcend. Again, remember the first quality listed will be the upper side of the negative ego. Under it will be the lower side of the negative ego and horizontally across from both of them will be the Christ Consciousness attitude, antidote and cure. So, on this note, let us begin with the first negative ego archetypal duality and its Christ Consciousness antidote.

Integrated Ascension

Negative Ego Archetypal Dualities with Their Christ Consciousness Counterpoint

Negative Ego Duality or Christ Consciousness Attitude
Attack/Fear or Unconditional Love

Anger/Depression or Bubble of Protection, Preferences, Looking at things as lessons, Never giving up

Win/Lose or Win-Win

Rejecter/Rejected or Not meant to be, Not GOD's Will, "I'm O.K., you're O.K."

False Pride/Low Self-esteem or Self-confidence, Unconditional Self-love and Self-worth

Manipulator/Victim or Own personal power through Love and Non-attachment

Attachment/Non-attachment or Preference attitudes

Self-righteous/Self-doubt or Knowingness while still allowing others to have beliefs

Needing no one/Loneliness or Ability to be alone but still interrelate with others

Aggressive/Passive or Assertive

Worry/Uncaring or Concern

Integrated Ascension

Too Self-centered/Too Other-directed or Proper Selfish-Selfless balance

Sociopathic tendencies/Guilt-ridden or Properly balanced conscience and Self-forgiveness

Pollyannaish/Pessimistic or Optimistic

Manic High/Manic Low or Evenmindedness, Equanimity, Unceasing Joy

Arrogant/Insecure or Self-confident tempered with Unconditional Love

Holding a grudge/Being a doormat or Forgiveness

Overindulgence/Underindulgence or The Middle Path, Moderation in all things

Fear of failure/Fear of success or Pursuit of excellence, Mistakes are O.K.

Judgmental/Embarrassment or Non-judgmentalness

Impatient/Too laissez faire or Patient

Blame/Shame or Self-responsibility, Bubble of protection

Hate/Possessive conditional love or Unconditional Love & Forgiveness

Too controlling/Out of control or Self-control, Not controlling over others

Betrayer/Betrayed or Utterly secure within self & not attached to situation

Abandoner/Abandoned or Complete, full, whole within self & bonding in relationship from that place

Jealousy/Open relationships or Commitment without co-dependence

Too independent/Dependent or Independent, interdependent and group consciousness

Sadistic/Masochistic or Doesn't believe in giving or experiencing suffering

Overly responsible/Irresponsible or Responsible

Too closed/Too open or Proper boundaries

Mean/Hurt or Invulnerable, Bubble of protection, Cause own reality

Too selfish/Too selfless or Selfish/Selfless balance

Overly confident/Insecure or Quiet confidence

Attack/Defense or Defenselessness, Harmlessness

Accepts no feedback/Approval seeking or Seeks feedback from appropriate people

Too Impulsive/Indecisive or Appropriately decisive

Dictator/Herd consciousness or Uses & owns personal power in loving manner only

Insensitive/Overly sensitive or Sensitive, Divine detachment

Workaholic/Hedonist or Work-Play balance

Obsessive-Compulsive/Disorderly or Organized without being overly perfectionistic

Driven/Lazy or Hard worker within reason

The Pusher/Procrastinator or Strives for completion without being obsessive

Immobilized/Reactive or Respond

False sense of security/Vulnerable or Faith, Invulnerability, Confidence, yet practical & realistic

Too affectatious/Too repressed or Integrated and balanced expression

Emotionless/Moodiness or Mastery of emotions in service of Oversoul and Monad, Joy

Overly giving/Overly taking or Giving/Receiving balance

Intimidate/Too shy or Own power in a Christed manner

Too future focused/Too past focused or Live in the "now," with appropriate past/future thinking only

Integrated Ascension

Overly deserving/Undeserving or Deserving because GOD created us

Greed consciousness/Poverty consciousness or Prosperity consciousness

Too serious/Too lighthearted or Serious-Lighthearted balance

Fault-finder/Undiscerning or Love-finder, Spiritually discerning

Rebel/Conformist or "Above all else, to thine own self be true."

Overly organized/Disorganized or Organized

Felix Unger(Obsessively clean)/Oscar Madison(Slob) or Clean, but not neurotically clean

Overly jubilant/Sad or Evenminded, Unceasing joy from positive thinking

Can't admit mistakes/Everything's my fault or Admit mistakes when they happen

Too trusting/Too distrustful or Trusting with spiritual discernment

Too focused/Too scattered or Ability to see through full prism & single lens as moment requires

Too brazen/Too cautious or Assertive with spiritual discernment

Too critical inner parent/Too permissive inner parent or Firm and loving parent

Integrated Ascension

Too goal-oriented/Too process-oriented or Goal & Process balance

Too loquacious/Too silent or Appropriate talking-silence balance

Too rigid/Too flexible or Firm-Flexible balance

Too disciplined/Out of control or Discipline-Flowing balance

Too structured/Too flowing or Structure-Fluidity balance

Too willful/Too allowing or Willful-Allowing balance

Too impersonal/Too personal or Impersonal-Personal balance

Good luck/Bad luck or No such thing as "luck," cause own reality, past life karma

Too vertical(spiritually inward)/Too horizontal(relationship focus) or Vertical-Horizontal balance

Too expansive/Too contracted or Appropriate Expansion-Contraction balance

Uptight/Too laid back or Own personal power & surrender to GOD simultaneously

Too tough/Too coddling or Strong, but respectful of laws of nature

Sins of commission/Sins of omission or Responding appropriately as GOD would have it be

Integrated Ascension

Summation

In summary what I would like to say to you, my beloved readers, is that what I would recommend is that you get out a piece of paper and pen and go through very carefully each one of these negative ego dualities and the Christ Consciousness attitudinal antidote. Intuitively determine for yourself if there is any upper or lower negative ego aspects influencing your personality and/or character development. Do this from a totally unconditionally loving, non-judgmental attitude towards self. Remember mistakes are O.K. and the true lesson here for highest integrated ascension potential is to be devastatingly honest with self. Make a list on your paper where attitudinal adjustments need to be made. I would then suggest making a log for yourself and listing those qualities and their antidote and every day maybe twice each day giving yourself a percentage score in how you are doing controlling the negative ego attributes and demonstrating the Christ attitudes and qualities. You also might consider writing up some affirmations for those negative ego dualities that need the most work in clearing. Also, pray to GOD, the Ascended Masters, your Angels, and your own Higher Self and Monad for help in attitudinally changing those qualities. Also, write out on a piece of paper a spiritual vow to GOD and yourself about your commitment to create a flawless character. Also, ask the Ascended Masters of your choice to perform the core fear matrix removal program on those specific negative ego dualities that you intuitively feel are still present. The Ascended Masters will actually pull these dark weeds out of your four-body system. This work in combination with your logging, affirmations, prayer work, spiritual vows and overall conscious commitment to Christ thinking at all times will do the trick. Also, call to the Holy Spirit for help in undoing all past programming. The Holy Spirit has a specialty in this area of undoing negative ego programming and mistakes.

Integrated Ascension

This multifaceted program I am suggesting is worth its weight in gold. No time spent working on self is more valuable than proper character development. It may not be as glamorous as communing with celestial realms or other esoteric studies; however, I am here to tell you, my beloved readers, that this is the real key to making integrated ascension work. Without proper character development, all other aspects of your spiritual life will become poisoned by the contagion of negative ego. In truth, it is just illusion or faulty thinking and is nothing to be feared, however since our thoughts create our reality on every level it is essential that you make your number one spiritual goal to remove it from your consciousness. For added information and support read my books *Soul Psychology*, *How to Clear the Negative Ego*, *Ascension Psychology*, *Your Ascension Mission: Embracing Your Puzzle Piece*, and *Ascension and Romantic Relationships*. The first two books listed being the most important in this regard.

It is well worth your time and energies to meditate upon the upper and lower sides of the negative ego to get as clear a sense as possible as to how the negative ego operates. To transcend negative ego thinking you again must transcend both sides of the negative ego both upper and lower. As the Bible says, "After pride cometh the fall." You must learn to laugh both sides off the stage. This is called transcendence. Most people on planet Earth remain stuck in the washing machine cycle of negative ego thinking. The only reason they are not able to get out of it is that no one ever taught them how the negative ego thinks and how the Christ mind thinks. It is really that simple. If it was taught in school and church everyone would be doing it. It really is not that hard to do. It is just a matter of changing your thinking. Your emotions come from how you think as does your behavior and what you attract and magnetize into your life. Change your thinking and you change your life. As the Bible says, "Be ye transformed by the renewal of your mind."

The process is really very simple. Every time a negative ego thought or emotion comes up in your consciousness push it out of your mind

Integrated Ascension

and replace it with the Christ consciousness attitude and antidote. By not giving energy or water, so to speak, to that weed it will die within three weeks time. That is how long it takes to cement in a new habit into the subconscious mind. By not giving water to negative ego thinking and emotions and watering Christ consciousness attitudes and feelings they expand and grow. Pretty soon you have a habit of Christed thinking and feeling and a habit of being in inner peace and joyous all the time. The happiness you seek is an attitude and perspective that is attached to nothing outside of self, and nothing having to do with another person. "Let this mind be in you that was in Christ Jesus," the Bible tells us. So my recommendation, my beloved readers, is to do the program I have suggested for at least 21 days. I give you my solemn oath it will be the best energetic time investment you have ever made. When your mental and emotional body are properly integrated your spiritual growth will accelerate a thousand-fold. You will develop the Midas touch. Your channeling will become a thousand times better in whatever form you do it. Basically every aspect of your life will become a thousand times better. Your relationship to yourself is the foundation of your life. Take the time to build a Christed foundation and only Godliness will then be built upon this spiritually integrated structure.

I have purposely made this chapter as easy to understand as possible. I have strived here to bring the whole process down to its very bare, quintessential essence. If more support and/or understanding is needed read the first two books I have listed with the *Ascension Psychology* being the third I would recommend the most. With the understanding and the tools I have provided, this work can be easily done as long as you are willing to take the time to commit yourself to the process and as long as you are pure in your intent to achieve true integrated ascension and GOD Realization.

My beloved readers, the Force is with you, so be about the Father's business and take advantage of the profundity, clarity, and simple practicality of this information. This is the new wave of psychology of the future that is being made available to you *now*. As the Bible says, "The truth will set you free." It is time to wake up from the nightmarish illusory dream of the negative ego and to realize that the negative ego and all its hallucinations doesn't really exist, we just think it does. The law of the mind is what you think is the reality you live in. It is time, my beloved readers, to wake up from this negative dream and to instead think and live in GOD's dream of total unconditional love, forgiveness, inner peace, equanimity, joy and bliss!

8

Integrated Ascension and Developing a Proper Relationship to the Inner Senses

Generally, when someone thinks of the subject of the inner senses the first thing that comes to one's mind is the five outer senses of smell, taste, touch, sight and hearing. When one thinks of the inner senses or extra sensory perception lightworkers might think of intuition, clairvoyance, clairaudience, and clairsentience. What many lightworkers don't realize is that we actually have thirty-eight overall planetary Ascended Master inner senses and this doesn't even begin to explore our cosmic Ascended Master inner senses. Let me begin first by discussing the planetary Ascended Master senses.

Just as we have five outer senses, we have five inner senses in our subconscious mind that corresponds to our five outer senses. This might be correlated "…as within so without, as above so below."

Outer sight—Clairvoyance
Outer hearing—Clairaudience
Outer touch—Clairsentience (inner touch)
Outer smell—Inner sense of smell
Outer taste—Inner taste

Integrated Ascension

We all experience these five inner senses every night when we dream. In our dreams we can see, hear, touch, smell, and taste although our physical bodies are asleep and our outer senses are shut down. We often wake-up blown away at how real the dreams seemed. A lot of times they are actual real experiences on the inner plane. Many times these real inner plane experiences will translate symbolically to the brain for teaching an insight. This type of symbolic transference to an easily comprehensible dream occurs most often when the inner plane experience is of an exceedingly high nature and needs to be stepped down for brain assimilation. What is very important to understand is that these inner senses exist within the subconscious mind. This is a very important point because often people and/or psychics who have developed these inner senses consciously during waking life (psychics) do not necessarily even believe in GOD. This may be hard to believe but it is true. This is also why there are groups of people who are very much caught in what I call lower psychism, rather than what I might call higher psychism. Higher psychism relates to these five senses when they are used in service to the Monad, Oversoul, and Ascended Masters. Just because someone has these inner senses doesn't mean that they are developed spiritually or psychologically in the slightest. I must remind you that children often see and hear "imaginary" playmates or people. Also, schizophrenics often hear voices and see beings on the inner plane. In these cases, of course, the negative ego has taken over to such a degree that all they are attracting is lower astral energy and entities.

It is my purpose is this chapter to give my beloved readers a more in-depth understanding of the whole subject of extra sensory perception in the full scope of how the Cosmic and Planetary Ascended Masters see it. It is also my purpose to share with my beloved readers the unbelievably enormous effect one's psychological development plays in filtering our inner senses. Let us begin with the introduction of a chart that I first presented in my first book *The Complete Ascension Manual*. This chart was channeled by Djwhal Khul through Alice Bailey in her wonderful series of books called the Alice Bailey material which contains approximately twenty volumes of Ascended Master teachings. These books were the second dispensation of Ascended Master teachings after the first dispensation of Ascended Master teachings brought forth by Madame Blavatsky. Djwhal Khul prophesied that there would be a third dispensation of Ascended Master teachings at the turn of the century which he and the other Ascended Masters would help bring forth. My sixteen volume series of books on ascension and the Ascended Master teachings is the prophecy he spoke of. It has been my great and humble honor to serve the Spiritual Hierarchy and the Ascended hosts in this capacity. There are currently sixteen volumes that have been completed, and over the next five years I plan to complete all thirty volumes. I am speaking here specifically of the Theosophical lineage, however, there is another Ascended Master lineage that is connected with the Theosophical lineage of Ascended Master teachings, which is, of course, the I Am Discourses and Dispensations of St. Germain written through Godfre Ray King, which I also highly recommend studying. I would also like to recognize the work of Janet McClure in her channelings of Djwhal Khul and Vywamus. Janet wrote some wonderful spiritual books of Hierarchical teachings before passing on to the spirit world.

Anyway, getting back to the subject at hand, the following chart delineates each person's thirty-eight inner senses. I have also added to the chart our senses on the monadic and logoic planes of consciousness, which were not included in my book *The Complete Ascension Manual*.

The Planetary Senses and Supersenses

Logoic senses
Logoic Plane
Synthesis

Seeing with the eye of GOD
Divine plan comprehension
Full attunement with Planetary Logos
Logoic comprehension

Monadic senses
Monadic Plane
Synthesis
Monadic group consciousness
Full monadic merger
Monadic comprehension
Monadic vision
Monadic realization

Atmic senses
Atmic Plane
All knowledge
Perfection
Realization
Active service
Beatitude

Buddhic senses
Buddhic Plane
Idealism
Intuition
Divine vision
Healing
Comprehension

Higher mental senses
Higher Mental Plane

Spiritual telepathy
Response to group vibration
Spiritual discernment

Lower mental senses
Lower Mental Plane
Discrimination
Higher clairvoyance
Planetary psychometry
Higher clairaudience

Astral senses
Physical-Etheric Plane
Emotional idealism
Imagination
Clairvoyance
Psychometry
Clairaudience

Physical senses
Physical Plane
Smell
Taste
Sight
Touch, feeling
Hearing

Physical Senses

This chart shows the inner senses that each person potentially contains within them and shows the plane of consciousness where those senses reside. So, let us begin our discussion here at the very bottom of the chart on the physical plane level. There we see, as I've already discussed, the five outer senses that we are all familiar with. Even on that level some people are more developed in certain outer senses than others. Some people have a more refined hearing than others. Some people have a more refined sense of smell than others. Some have a more refined sense of taste than others. The same is true with the inner senses, but to an even greater degree.

Astral Senses

In terms of the astral senses we see emotional idealism, imagination, clairvoyance, psychometry, clairaudience. Now what is important to understand here as we begin to get into extrasensory perception is that the clairvoyance or inner sight with this sense is restricted to the astral plane. The same applies here to the clairaudience and psychometry. Psychometry is the ability to pick up an object and receive information about the person who owns it by following the psychic or metaphysical threads so to speak.

It must be understood that there is clairvoyance on each of the seven planes of existence and beyond into the cosmic dimensions of GOD. This also applies to clairaudience, clairsentience, inner smell, and inner taste. This is an extremely important point because many people who are giving clairvoyant readings, and clairaudient voice channelings are only doing so from an astral sensory perception. An Ascended Master does not even operate on this plane of reality. Lightworkers are often way too spiritually undiscerning about the level that the psychic or channel is operating out of. In many cases, the person coming for the reading is more evolved than the psychic and the entity being channeled. So just because someone is clairvoyant or clairaudient one should not give their power away and should not be so enamored with such abilities as lightworkers often are. Lightworkers often become fascinated with this psychic realm and completely lose their spiritual path. Lightworkers also often give enormous power to the process of channeling. If someone tells them something from one conscious mind to another, they don't believe it. If you tell them it's channeled or you bring it through in a channeled way, they think it's automatically true. My beloved readers, I know you know what I'm talking about here. There are many channeled books on the market that are so filled with inaccuracies and untruth it is unbelievable. I see lightworkers buying into this material, hook, line and sinker, with absolutely no spiritual discernment because the author says it's channeled from some spirit or Extraterrestrial. I'm going to get into this whole subject in great detail later in this chapter, however, for now I wanted to begin planting this seed thought to you.

One other interesting thought to consider on this subject is that children are often very clairvoyant or clairaudient. Given their chronological age and emotional and mental development this is obviously very filtered through an astral level, however sometimes children can access a higher level as well. What is interesting is that children are often much clearer than adults in this regard. The older one gets the more contamination from the conscious mind and personality begins to ensue as the emotional and mental vehicles begin to develop. This is why most adults lose a great deal of their inner sensory perception that they had as children. Children have a certain innocence which adults lose most often through life experience and the difficulty of this particular mystery school. So, my beloved readers, please be more spiritually discerning in dealing with this whole subject of psychic development and channeling. What I've shared with you so far is in truth just the tip of the iceberg in regards to the need for spiritual discernment in this area. I am most definitely not putting down these abilities for they are wonderful spiritual senses. However one must look at the level one is coming from and one must see very clearly how one's psychological development and spiritual development filters and, in most cases, contaminates the process.

Integrated Ascension

Often the people who have developed these particular type of inner senses are the ones who are more right brain, more subconsciously run, more fourth ray, more artistic types, more mystic in nature, more emotional in nature. What I'm trying to explain here is that these psychic senses don't necessarily indicate any high degree of psychological or spiritual development. They may hear inner voices, however they may be doing this from a state of consciousness of being completely undeveloped in their left brain, totally run and victimized by the subconscious mind and being totally victimized by the emotional body and lower self desire. Although all this is going on, they can still channel and they can still see things on the inner plane. The key question is what effect does all this psychological unclarity and spiritual immaturity do to the channeling process and clairvoyance. The answer is that it contaminates it and what you think is true clairaudience and true clairvoyance is not. All clairvoyance and clairaudience, regardless of what level it's coming from or what level of initiation you are, is brought through the filters of your personality, your subconscious mind, your mental body, your emotional body, and your belief system to name just a few of the hundreds of filters all channeling and clairvoyance must come through. It is essential that all lightworkers understand this. Again, I will get into the subject of all the other factors affecting and filtering this process later in this chapter, however, for now, this lays the initial groundwork. I must add here that some fourth ray artistic people are, in fact, some of the best channels available. With them, as with everyone, it all depends on the level of psychological clarity, spiritual maturity, balance, and integration that they are working with.

Emotional idealism deals with the concept of being able to formulate ideals, however what I'm speaking of here is when this particular sense is coming from an astral level. For example, a teenage girl who dreams about getting married and having kids would demonstrate such emotional idealism. She might also use her other astral sense imagination to daydream about what her life would be like. This is imagination very connected with the emotional body and desire body. The ideal here would be to utilize these inner senses from the point of view of higher-self desire rather than lower-self desire.

The Lower Mental Senses

The lower mental senses are discrimination, higher clairvoyance, planetary psychometry, and higher clairaudience. Discrimination is a sense I think we all understand, however, it is important to understand here that this would refer to discrimination more on the concrete mind level and not at the level of spiritual discernment that I was speaking of in this last section. An example of this might be a scientist who has discrimination in his scientific work but has not opened to the realities of his own soul.

The higher clairvoyance is again just clairvoyance on the lower mental plane and no higher. A person with this type of clairvoyance can see beings who exist on this plane of reality and no higher.

Planetary psychometry would again apply to the ability to use this sense on a planetary level on the lower mental plane. The higher clairaudience uses inner hearing on the lower mental plane and no higher. This type of person could channel entities from the lower mental plane.

The Higher Mental Senses

The senses on the higher mental plane are spiritual telepathy, response to group vibration, spiritual discernment, and higher clairvoyance. Spiritual telepathy is the inner sense of being able to give and receive thought transference. All lightworkers do this from one degree to another. Mystics are often more developed in clairaudience and those who are more occultist in nature do this more through spiritual telepathy. We all experience this when we think of someone and then they call, or we bump into them. This ability can obviously be developed to a very high degree and automatic writing would be an example of this. Again, one has to be careful what level it is coming from. This is why the Masters recommend that people do not fool around with Ouiji boards.

Response to group vibration deals with the sense of tuning into one's group affiliation on Earth and/or even the group vibration of the Spiritual Hierarchy as a whole. The keynote, and/or touchstone, for the New Age is group consciousness. The ideal is to maintain one's individual identity, however, to also simultaneously remain in touch with one's group identity as well. An example of this would be one's group identity as sons and daughters of GOD. Another example might be one's group identity as part of the hierarchy or representing a certain ashram within the hierarchy.

Spiritual discernment in this case is a higher level of discernment than in the previous category. The clairvoyance and/or clairaudience at this level is again higher than in pervious categories, however it's still restricted to the higher mental plane.

The Buddhic Senses

The senses on the Buddhic plane are idealism, intuition, Divine vision, healing and comprehension. This level of idealism is a much higher level of idealism than we spoke of earlier when I spoke of emotional idealism. This is an idealism in the realm of pure thought on the Buddhic plane. This type of idealism involves the ability to conceptualize and understand the plan of GOD on the Buddhic plane. This is the plane that intuition comes from which might be aptly described as a pure knowingness beyond rational thought. Divine vision has to do with having a higher sense of the plan. It involves a clear seeing, intuiting, and knowing of the Ascended Master's intent and of the Divine plan as they conceive it on the Buddhic plane. It also involves the holding of the vision of the New Age or the next step fully

Integrated Ascension

within one's consciousness. Divine vision also includes a more refined state of vision, seeing and communicating with the Masters.

The inner sense of healing involves the ability to heal with light in an inner plane sense or in a type of laying on of hands using the pure radiance of GOD. This inner sense of comprehension lightworkers usually don't think of as a inner sense, however, it is a wonderful inner sense indeed. For example, someone might channel some information, however, they have absolutely no ability to comprehend that which they are channeling. Another example might be the reading of a spiritual book. One lightworker can't make heads or tails of it and another person is able to comprehend it. I think what you are beginning to see, my beloved readers, is that there are many inner senses that in truth are more advanced senses than just clairvoyance or clairaudience. Many lightworkers are filled with self-doubts because they are not clairvoyant or they cannot clairaudiently channel, when the truth is it is not your destiny to do this kind of work and the truth is you are accessing a much higher level than a great many clairvoyants and clairaudient channels.

I know of one case of a friend of mine who was married to a woman who was a voice channel for the Ascended Masters for twelve years. This friend of mine couldn't clairaudiently voice channel but was very telepathic and highly developed in his higher senses. On checking into this situation, I found out that this person was operating on the master A grid while his wife was operating out of the B grid. This is not meant as a judgment or negative ego comparison, but rather just as an extremely important spiritual discernment and illustration that things are not always as they seem. Clairvoyance and clairaudient voice channels are often not highly developed in their higher spiritual senses on the Buddhic, atmic, monadic, and logoic planes. Some of the higher senses which I'm beginning to speak of here are actually much higher extrasensory apparatus than the common ESP abilities we are used to thinking of.

Integrated Ascension

One of the biggest factors that affect this process is the person's psychological clarity level. If the person's psychological clarity is not developed all channeling and clairvoyance will be extremely corrupted and contaminated. My beloved readers, please imprint this last statement indelibly into your mind. It is so important I will repeat it again. If a person's psychological clarity is not developed all channeling and clairvoyance will be extremely corrupted and contaminated. This is not even getting to the issue of whether they have developed their higher senses which is another major factor in the whole discussion.

So do you see, my beloved readers, why it is so ridiculous to give your power to external clairvoyants and channels and to think less of yourself for not having those abilities which only about 5% of lightworkers have. Again if you have developed psychological clarity and your higher senses, fifteen of which I haven't even talked about yet, you are operating at a thousand times higher level than the people who are doing the channeling and clairvoyant work. Again, I do not mean to be critical to clairvoyants or channels. I am rather just bringing the sword of spiritual discernment to this most important subject which lightworkers tend to be very naive about.

I also bring up this subject to encourage all clairvoyants and channels to develop themselves psychologically and to develop all their inner senses and not overly focus on just a few of these senses. Moreover, for clairvoyants and channels to fully see and comprehend the extent to which one's relationship to one's self filters and colors this process. Often channels and psychics do not realize this themselves and this is another one of the reason's I am writing this book.

Clairvoyance and clairaudient voice channeling is a wonderful thing and I encourage all my readers to develop these abilities and/or senses if it is their destiny to do so. I am not criticizing channeling for I think it is one of the most important abilities for lightworkers to develop in some form. Some will do it clairaudiently as a voice channel, some telepathically, some through automatic writing, some through music, poetry, art, dance, energetically through healing and some through love. Find the form of channeling that is your true puzzle piece as GOD would have it be and do not try to live out someone else's puzzle piece.

So, channeling and clairvoyance are wonderful, wonderful abilities as are all thirty-eight of our inner senses. As is the case with all the inner senses, they are channeled through our psychological and spiritual development. The biggest reason I'm writing this chapter is to help make lightworkers aware of all the filters that the channeling process, clairvoyance and inner senses must go through before it is given forth. I am very passionate on this point because I have seen so much corruption and lack of understanding in regards to these points in the New Age movement. Channels and psychics often become very self-righteous in their guidance not realizing the extent to which all channeling and psychic abilities are colored by the personality and other factors. Even the finest channels and psychics on the planet are still having to bring their information through an enormous number of filters. Because this is such an important point I am going to pause from our discussion of our inner senses, going up the chart, and instead talk about some of these other filters that affect the channeling and psychic reading process.

Filters in the Channeling and Psychic Reading Process

The number of filters affecting this process is so enormous that you, my beloved readers, are going to be blown away by this amazing discussion. The discussion I'm about to have with you on this subject is the number one reason that I initially had to write this book in the first place. I saw the lack of proper integration in the ascension process and I saw the enormous corruption it was causing in the New Age movement. It was from these spiritual observations made in love that the Masters guided me to write this book. So on this note let me begin.

Integrated Ascension

The first example I would like to give is that, let's say a person who does channeling has power issues and is a little bossy in their personality. Then what will happen when they channel is that although they may be channeling the Ascended Masters the channeling will come through in a bossy, dictatorial manner. This may be hard for lightworkers to fathom, however, I absolutely guarantee you this is exactly what will take place. The person receiving the reading will think that the Ascended Masters are overly tough when in truth it is just the channeling coming through the particular channel's psychological programming.

If the person who is giving the channeling is very shy and meek then the channelings will come through from the Ascended Masters in a very meek, overly gentle manner.

Channelings will also totally take on the belief system of the person doing the channeling. The person doing the channeling believes they are getting confirmation from their beliefs, when, in truth, it is just coming through their belief structure. For example, if a channel for the Ascended Masters believes that there are going to be massive earth changes that are going to destroy the planet even though this may not be the case, they are fully capable of channeling information from the Ascended Masters (that is not really the Ascended Masters always) on this subject, even though it is not true. The person doing the channeling may really mean well and have extremely pure motives, however, they don't realize their beliefs are affecting the process. They also may be channeling an old thoughtform that once had truth but is no longer a truth. This is happening to a great extent in some of the Ashtar Command movements and in some of the Earth changes prophecies predictions which I do not mean as a criticism, but rather as a point of spiritual discernment.

Another filtering process is the fact that all channeling comes through one's information banks. The Masters cannot bring through information that is not to a certain extent already programmed into the subconscious mind from this life or past lives. The past life information banks are also harder to access than this life's. If you are not consciously proficient at astrology then you are not going to be able to do channelings on astrology in 99.9% of all cases in this regard, for example. Do you see, my beloved readers, how enormously this limits the channeling process and again how dangerous it would be to give your power to an external channel. I am not against lightworkers receiving external channelings; as a matter of fact I think it can be very helpful as long as the lightworkers have the proper understanding of how the process of channelings and psychic readings actually work.

Another example of how this process of channeling works is that if the person channeling is very childlike and self abusive then they will magnetize and attract an entity that is very fatherly and critical. These are the laws of energy.

Another filter and lens that affects the channeling process is the chakra or chakras that the person is most identified with. If the person giving the channeling is a heart chakra type of person then their channeling will come through the heart chakra and be very loving in nature and less informational. If they are a third chakra type of person their channeling may be very power centered. If they're throat chakra centered the channelings will be very communicative in nature. If they are third eye centered their channelings will be more informational. See the point, my beloved readers.

Another filter are the rays. If the person's monad and soul is on the first ray, their Ascended Master channelings might again be more power centered and even political. If their monad/soul personality is more second ray, then their channelings will be more spiritually educational. If they are fourth ray, the channelings will be more poetic and artistic and focus on harmony. If they're fifth ray, the channelings will be more scientific. If they are sixth ray, their channelings will be more devotional. My beloved readers, are you beginning to see how affected channelings are by each person's psychological and spiritual construction.

Integrated Ascension

All channelings and psychic readings will reflect the philosophy that the person giving the channeling holds even if they are channeling the Ascended Masters who believe in something else. Channeling and psychic information comes in energy impulses that must be interpreted by the receiver's monad, oversoul, personality, mind, emotions, and subconscious mind. Most channels and psychics don't even realize this. They believe they are receiving things directly and don't even realize how many filters are in operation. I am not saying that all channels and psychics fall into this category, I am just saying that there are a great many that do, and this book is written to help support all the channels and psychics and help clarify this issue of filters which is not discussed in almost any book dealing with the process of psychic and channeling development.

Another filter that can greatly color the channeling and psychic process is the issue of what archetype or archetypes the person doing the channeling is identified with. For example, let's say they are over identified with the teacher or wisdom archetype. They may hence feel compelled because of this imbalanced archetype to give answers to questions that they are not really qualified to answer. This could also take the form of being a "know it all." Another example of an overidentification of an archetype might be The Warrior. This person who is channeling will be inclined to channel guidance telling their clients to "…enter the fray of battle no matter what the cost." This could push the client out of their appropriate Tao, resulting in unnecessary hardship and great karmic repercussions. My beloved readers, these are just two classic examples of literally thousands of different imbalanced permutations that can take place if the twelve major archetypes are not integrated properly.

Another example of a filter might be whether one is more femininely or masculinely identified. The idea is obviously balance. If the person who is doing the channeling is more feminine then the channelings will obviously come through in a more feminine manner. If they are more masculine then the channelings will come through in a more masculine manner.

If a person has strong religious beliefs then the channelings will come through reflecting those beliefs. The process of channeling can be seen through the metaphor of the lenses of a prism. Most people channel through just one or a small number of lenses of the full prism. The problem stems not from this fact but from the belief the person has that they are channeling from the full prism, and from the belief that the person getting the channeling from this person has that this is a full prism channeling. I love channeling and I love all the psychic senses. I just want lightworkers to be aware of the filters that govern the process. This is not a judgment it is just a proper understanding of how the whole process works. The key to being a good channel and psychic is to achieve integrated ascension, then the information that will come through you will be clearer, more full prism and less colored by your personal programming. There is no one on the planet who does channeling and psychic work who does not color the information that is coming through them. The challenge is to be an integrated Ascended Master channel in whatever form it is your puzzle piece to do it.

Another place the channeling process can become tainted is if the person doing the channeling is not in their right puzzle piece. Let's say, for example, they are trying to do voice channeling for a living but their true puzzle piece is really to be a nurse. The glamour of channeling has gotten them misaligned and this will obviously affect the channeling and psychic work.

The number one biggest factor in causing contaminated channeling in psychic work is how much the person doing the work is out of their negative ego. This is one of the most least understood concepts on the planet and enormously effects the channeling and psychic process as well as everything else in their lives. If a person is run by their negative ego this may show up in their channeling and psychic work as self aggrandizement, power hungry, fame hungry, money hungry, seeking approval, telling clients what they want to hear, using the Ascended Masters as a weapon to support their beliefs, to name just a few of the ways this can happen.

The blind spots you have in your personality, information banks and character development will manifest as blind spots in your channeling. This is not a judgment, this is just a realistic statement of how the channeling process is intimately connected with the development of one's consciousness.

Another very interesting filter that I have seen in the New Age Movement is what I call the filter of being caught in a past time line. For example if a person is into Edgar Cayce and believes that he is the only valid channel on the planet then your consciousness will be caught on the timeline of 1940 and your channeling will reflect that time line. The same is true of the Alice Bailey books or the I Am Discourses of St. Germain or any fixed philosophical belief that someone gets caught in. This is meant as no criticism to Edgar Cayce, Alice Bailey or the I Am discourses, for I personally happen to love all three of these informational dispensations. The key is to not get locked in an egotistical or close-minded manner. Everything keeps evolving and changing and people must be open to this. These past dispensations are wonderful and extremely helpful in present time. The ideal is to take and utilize the best from the past, bring it into the present and be open to the new information Edgar Cayce, Djwhal Khul, and St. Germain, for example, are continuing to bring forth. In essence people get stuck in the 1940 version and are therefore not open to the present time and future time version.

Another filter that can often get in the way of the channeling process is the person's subconscious mind and sub-personalities. Often a person sincerely thinks they're channeling the Ascended Masters or some higher being when in truth they're channeling a sub-personality of their own subconscious mind. This is much more common than people realize. What also happens sometimes is that a person is

Integrated Ascension

channeling the Ascended Masters sometimes but slips out of the attunement to the Ascended Master and then begins channeling their conception of the Ascended Master rather than the real Ascended Master, however, they don't realize it. This would be like doing a make-believe role play but you are channeling and it might sound really excellent, however, it is not the real thing. There is nothing wrong with role playing, however, one shouldn't say they're channeling when they're not.

Another filter is what I call the integrity factor filter. Often someone asks a question to the channel that has been asked before. The person doing the channeling answers it from their conscious mind without telling the person that is receiving the channeling. This is not right.

Another filter interference in the channeling process that creates a great deal of static and breach of attunement are the negative extraterrestrial implants and negative elementals that the person hasn't cleared. This creates great disruption in the attunement and hence the informational receiving process.

Another filter and danger in the channeling process is interference from astral entities. Astral entities sometimes will parade as Ascended Masters just to have a soapbox, so to speak. If the person doing the channeling is very run by their emotional body, astral desire, inner child and/or negative ego, this can be a definite danger. Another way this can manifest on the astral level is in the form of glamour. We see in the New Age movement many channels who turn the channeling process into this glamorous process which is not really the way the Ascended Masters want to be presented, however undiscerning lightworkers often buy into this glamour.

Another way the negative ego often contaminates channels is through the issue of control. The channeling and psychic work is used to control others and also used as a tool to gain allies. If a person has very Elizabethan values and is very conservative then this will be totally reflected in the channelings. Even something as simple as whether you are in a male or female vehicle will affect the channelings. Your educational background, profession, political views, and social status will all color what comes through your channel. Your channelings will also be colored by your needs, wants, desires, hopes, dreams, aspirations, and motives.

One other major filter that affects the channeling is your initiation level. The higher your level of initiation the higher the attunement. Let me say, however, no matter what level of initiation you are at if you haven't done your psychological homework your channeling and psychic work will be greatly contaminated and corrupted. Initiations have to do with how much light you hold, not with how psychologically clear you are. Some of the most corrupted channeling and psychic work I've ever come across has come through initiates I know who have taken their seventh initiation and beyond. This may be hard to believe for some of my readers, however I tell you as GOD is my witness it is the truth. I was stunned and shocked myself at first, and now I see how commonplace it is. This is why I am writing this book. Too many lightworkers are focusing all their energies on the spiritual level and not enough on the psychological level and are becoming imbalanced which is causing enormous contamination and corruption in the spiritual work they are doing. The tragic thing is that they don't realize it.

One thing that lightworkers must realize is that just because a person can channel the Ascended Masters it doesn't mean they are practicing what they preach or that their mental body is in tune with the Masters or that their emotional body is in tune with the Masters. I know this is hard to believe but I know many channels and high level initiates where this is the case.

Another filter and interfering factor in the channeling and psychic process is the psychic and psychological energy that the client is sending to the person who is doing the channeled and psychic reading. Let's say for example that the client is a disbeliever. This greatly effects the energetic flow in the process. Another example might be a person who is doing a channeling for a whole group of people who are at a very low level of consciousness. This makes it much harder for the channel or psychic to do their work. The exact opposite is true if it's a high level group or person.

Another filter and interfering factor in the channeling and psychic reading process is what is going on in the person's personal life. If they have a lot of stuff going on this can be a distraction and break attunement in the channeling and psychic process. For example, what if they just had a fight with their spouse, or a close family member is in the hospital, or their pet is ill. This obviously affects and colors the process.

Another factor is the person's overall mastery over their mental, emotional and physical bodies and their ability to concentrate and focus. Some are more developed in this area than others. This lack of mastery and/or concentration can cause breaks in attunement, which causes subconscious personality and environmental contamination.

Another filter that affects the channeling and psychic reading process is one's astrological horoscope. Certain astrological configurations or even the full moon can cause the channelings or psychic readings to move in certain directions as can the person's overall sun sign. My beloved readers, are you seeing more clearly now most people who are channeling and doing psychic readings are doing so from a very small lens in the full prism understanding.

On the astral level, any delusion is called glamour. On the mental level, any delusion is called illusion. On the etheric level, any delusion is called maya. All personal glamour, illusion, and maya will be reflected in your channelings. *You cannot channel separate from yourself!* A channel may be able to bring through some information, however ultimately your stuff seeps in and colors the process. The secret to rectifying this is to do your homework and clear as much glamour, illusion and maya as possible and become as integrated as you can possibly be, and achieve your higher levels of initiation. This way, in whatever form you do your channeling it will carry a much higher level of purity.

Integrated Ascension

Another factor to consider in the channeling process is what level and development is the entity being channeled. The entity being channeled may be an astral entity, mental plane entity, Buddhic plane entity, atmic plane entity, monadic plane entity, or ascended entity. I know thousands of people who have taken the seventh initiation and many of them I consider to be very disturbed people. Many of them are extremely run by their emotional bodies, negative egos, lower-self desire, inner child, and subconscious mind. I do not say this to be critical, it's just the truth. They are spiritually developed but not psychologically developed. So a person could be channeling an ascended being and look who you could be channeling. Just because a person is an ascended master doesn't mean they are developed in all areas. Spiritual discernment in this regard is ever important. In truth you could be infinitely more developed than the entity you are receiving guidance from. The comical thing about the New Age Movement, however, is that for a great many lightworkers, if you say it's channeled they will believe it, like channeling makes it true. If the same person told them the information from their conscious mind and not in a channeled manner, they would probably reject it. This is called the glamour of channeling.

Another very interesting filter and understanding in the channeling and psychic attunement process is something I mentioned earlier about the Master A, B, and C grids. Although a person is channeling the Ascended Masters, they may be doing it on totally different grids. The C grid being the lowest and the A grid being the highest on the planetary level. There are actually grids higher than this as we move into the cosmic realm so I think you can see here that when someone says they are channeling the Ascended Masters most lightworkers don't consider what grid they are doing this from.

Another extremely important understanding about the channeling process is that no information comes through from the Ascended Masters or any place else unless you ask the question. There are many people who are excellent channels, but they do not have the consciousness within themselves to ask the questions they need to ask to take advantage of this ability. This may sound baffling to some of my readers, however I cannot tell you how many people I know who fall into this category. They have an ability to communicate with the Masters, however, don't consult them personally and they don't consult them for information. A given person may be the finest channel on the planet, however, if they don't ask the right questions no information comes through personally or information wise. Being able to ask the right questions is a skill and ability in and of itself. One of the main reasons I am able to bring through the level of information I do in my books is that I know how to ask the right questions and hence pull through information that is normally not available.

Another extremely important point in the channeling process is that it is not only the clients that often give their power to the external channel and entity being channeled, but the person doing the channeling often gives their power to the inner plane Ascended Master. This is not good and this is not what the Ascended Masters want. They want respect and love, however, they also want to give this respect and love in return. They may be an elder brother or sister, however it is still an equal relationship. They do not want to be seen as gurus, fathers, or mothers. For example, there may be times when you disagree with the guidance. The Masters may suggest that you move to Illinois to set up a center. You may not want to move to Illinois. You would prefer to move to Oregon. It is not only your right but it is essential for your psychological and spiritual health to dialogue with the Masters.

We on Earth are Sons and Daughters of GOD ourselves, and a great many of us are Masters in our own right. I personally find the guidance of the Masters to be very accurate, however, I always dialogue with them and out of that dialogue often comes much clearer guidance, information, and often new ideas that would not have come forth had I not owned my personal power and love and engaged them as an equal. This is what the Masters want.

We on Earth are members of the Spiritual Hierarchy and are part of the externalization of the hierarchy. There really is no difference between us and them, except for the fact that we still retain physical vehicles and they don't. You wouldn't give your power to someone on Earth who was a spiritual teacher, workshop leader, psychologist, counselor, psychic, philosopher, so why would you give your power to the Ascended Masters? Respect yes, and an understanding of their greater wisdom, but "no" on giving your power away. GOD wants you to own your power and speak to Him from a place of personal power and love not out of weakness. As *A Course In Miracles* also says, never give awe to a brother or sister. "Awe" is only a quality for GOD. Respect is the appropriate quality for all brothers and sisters no matter what dimension they're living on. We are all sons and daughters of GOD ,and, in truth, GOD only has one Son and we are all part of that Sonship.

Another very interesting filter that most lightworkers don't consider in the channeling and psychic process is the level of development of the person's monad and higher self. What most lightworkers don't realize is that each person's higher self and monad is in a state of evolution and not all higher selves and monads are at the same level of development. The development of your higher self or oversoul will be determined by all your past lives and all the past lives of your eleven other soul extensions. The development of your monad is determined by the past lives of all your 144 soul extensions. Given that each soul extension could have had 200 past lives, you can see how each monad and oversoul will be unbelievably different. Some monads and oversouls are not that developed and this will be totally reflected in the level of information coming through in the person's channel.

Another fascinating and disturbing thing that often happens in the channeling process is that the person doing the channeling begins to identify with the Ascended Master being channeled to the point where

Integrated Ascension

they actually think that they are the Ascended Master they are channeling. This may sound very bizarre to my readers, however, I have come across this quite often. Another form that this glamour can take place in is that the person doing the channeling glamorizes the connection thinking of themselves as, let's say, the wife of one of the Ascended Masters. One other form this takes is that the person doing the channeling of, let's say, some cosmic being like Melchizedek or the Mahatma thinks that they are at that level of initiation. This, of course, is total illusion, for no one living on this planet (except for Sai Baba who is the only exception) will ever come even light years near the level of evolution of Melchizedek, or the Mahatma as even more of an extreme case. This, of course, is the glamour of self-aggrandizement.

One other way this psychological disturbance can take place, in the case of a spiritual teacher, is where the channel, either clairaudient or telepathic, becomes so identified with the source of their channeling that they begin speaking as that cosmic being even when they are not channeling. So, for example, they may be channeling Metatron in their work, however, they present themselves in their discourses with the public even when not channeling as a father figure to the public. This is the height of egotism. Beautiful words may come through but they are on a massive ego trip placing themselves above others by forming a father/son and daughter relationship with the public. Naïve, undiscerning lightworkers buy into this ego trip and project their power away. A classic example of non-integrated ascension and more common than most people realize. It can happen with a mother deity as well. Always check your motives and the motives of the people who promote themselves this way. In my opinion, 98% of the time there has been negative ego contamination. There are some occasional exceptions. Sai Baba would be an example again. Being a universal avatar holding three times as much light as Lord Maitreya the planetary Christ, Sai Baba forms guru devotee relationships that are spiritually 100% clear. He also attempts as one's guru to empower and to always remind his devotees that they are GOD as well.

One other very common archetypal pattern within many channels I have come across is that they have great mastery when on stage, teaching classes or when giving individual readings. However, when they leave the professional realm and return to their personal life they live out of the inner child. I cannot tell you, my beloved readers, how common this is. The reason for this is that they are more developed in their subconscious minds, senses, and spiritually in the superconscious realm, however they are not developed in the conscious mind. The lack of development in the conscious mind is related to the parental function intrapsychically. I share this, not as a criticism, but as a reminder to channels to make sure that they are parenting their inner child properly. If the inner child and, hence, emotional body is too much in control this will throw off the channeling and psychic work.

This is also an important insight for lightworkers to have who are receiving external channelings or psychic readings. Just because a person is able to bring through great wisdom or psychic information on a very profound level professionally doesn't mean that their own personal life and personality are together in the slightest. This is very common, not only among channels and psychics but also spiritual teachers, movie stars, professional athletes, just to give a few examples. It is common for people and lightworkers to project one highly developed ability onto their entire Beingness on all levels. It is extremely rare that you find this to be true. It will only be true if the person has achieved integrated ascension, and there are not that many lightworkers who have achieved this. It is quite amazing to see how someone could be such a master on stage and such a child and victim in their personal life.

My beloved readers, I know that you know people and/or lightworkers that fall into this archetypal pattern. This relates to the schism of being more the mystic or occultist. The ideal is to integrate and blend these two aspects of self. The truth of the matter is that the world really needs less channels and psychics and more spiritual counselors who understand the level of work that I speak of in this book, *Soul Psychology* and *How to Clear the Negative Ego*.

Another interfering factor in the channeling and psychic process has to do with planetary glamour, maya, and illusion as opposed to personal glamour, maya and illusion. Just as living in a big city we often are living in a sea of smog, living on Earth all people of the Earth are living in a sea of planetary psychic smog. This planetary smog on the astral plane is planetary glamour. On the mental plane, this planetary smog is planetary illusion. On the etheric plane, this planetary smog is called planetary maya. When looked at clairvoyantly, the planet is covered in not only physical pollution but all this psychic pollution. When doing channeling and psychic work this infiltrates and often contaminates and causes a type of interference. This is a lesson we all have to deal with and the only remedy is to try and be as clear as one can possibly be and to try to be a master at all times and not a victim. This filter is also connected to Carl Jung's concept of the collective unconscious and, in New Age circles, the concept of mass consciousness. The key question being how much are we affected by mass consciousness in our thoughts, words, deeds, channeling and psychic work.

Continuing this discussion of planetary influences that affect the channeling and psychic process is the planetary ray for Earth, which creates a certain focus for all of humanity. We also live in a second ray solar system, which has a certain focus for everyone on planet Earth. There is also the photon belt, that is in operation very extensively from 1997 to the year 2000, which is creating a great deal of static interference in the channeling process. In addition, sunspots and solar flares, which put forth enormous electromagnetic frequencies, affect the channeling and psychic process. Also affecting the channeling and psychic process is the enormous spiritual acceleration of the planet during this time of mass ascension. The beginning of the new millennium and the Aquarian Age, and the ending of the Mayan calendar, is bringing forth enormous cosmic spiritual currents which often totally physically wipe out many lightworkers for many days at a time. Lightworkers doing channeling and psychic work are much more sensitive to these energies and are often greatly affected by them. Channels and psychics are sometimes too sensitive to them, and this also totally affects the channeling and psychic process.

Another filter that greatly affects the channeling and psychic process is the concept of biorhythms. Each person has their own unique biorhythm. Some people are morning people, some people are night people, some people are nappers, some people can't stand napping. People go through certain high periods of energy and low periods of energy. If a person is giving a channeling and psychic reading during a low portion of their biorhythm, what effect do you think this will have on the type of information that comes through? This is not even taking into consideration the issue of fatigue or physical health lessons that are always going on in people's physical bodies. Let alone the emotional lessons and mental chatter of the mind, which I like to call self-talk. For women, their menstrual cycle greatly affects their channeling and psychic abilities at any given moment. The increased hormones and PMS causes a hypersensitivity and creates a kind of a feeling often of wanting to jump right out of your skin, or so I'm told. Would you want to get a channeled psychic reading at this time?

Another filter and common interference is the whole psychic and/or astral world that we also are immersed in. If the channel, psychic, and client have not spiritually transcended this level in an Ascended Master sense, then there is the danger of much contamination and lower entity interference.

One other very important point to consider is that if the channel or psychic is not psychologically sophisticated or psychologically trained (and usually they're not), then how can they possibly give adequate answers to your personal questions in these areas? The same applies on an esoteric level. If the channel and psychic has never studied ascension work, Ascended Master teachings, initiations, rays, light quotient, chakra anchoring, then how can they possibly answer your esoteric questions in this regard? Do you see, my beloved readers, that they can only give you adequate information if they are trained in that area.

Then there is the issue I have come across quite often in many channels in terms of there actually being pathologies in their psychological structure and makeup. One example would be that of a split personality. Kind of a Dr. Jekyll and Mr. Hyde. This type of person would do fantastic channeling and psychic work one part of the day and when they become triggered, the channeling and psychic work becomes completely corrupted. This is just one example of the infinite numbers of psychopathologies that are potentialities within the psyche of people on Earth.

The next filter and interference that can take place has to do with it being more difficult to channel at the twilight hour between light and physical darkness. I'm not sure why this is, but it is harder to keep the channel connection. Another interference of a similar but slightly different nature would just be channeling in a big city. There are enormous amounts of electromagnetic energy that is unique to a city as compared to channeling in nature. There are also often electromagnetic interference in one's own home from all the electrical equipment or just energetic negative vortexes that need to be cleared. With all such interferences at play, the more is the need for one to become a Master and keep one's consciousness steady in the Light, and the less they will be affected.

Another filter and interference or aid in the channeling and psychic work is a person's past life experiences. Edgar Cayce, for example, was able to do much of the work that he did because of past life development. At any given time, we, as lightworkers, may be processing a certain past life or a past life of one of our soul extensions and this can greatly color our psychic and channeling work. For example, if you are processing an Egyptian past life this may color the channeling and psychic work you are doing. On the negative side of the coin, if you are processing some kind of traumatic death from a past life this might bring up a lot of emotional stuff and certain physical body ailments that can greatly color and interfere with the channeling and psychic process.

Another filter for the channeling and psychic work is one's numerological horoscope, so to speak. When done properly, not as a parlor game, one can get a sense of the tendencies and influences that your numerological readout will cause you to focus through. The numerological influences will not be as strong as the astrological and as the ray structure but they do have their influence.

The last filter and lens which the channeling and psychic work works through is the level of subconscious clarity. This is a big one. In truth, I could also say conscious clarity. As I spoke of in a previous chapter, often the subconscious mind in its beliefs and emotional life is not consistent with the conscious mind's beliefs. This inconsistency between the subconscious, conscious and even superconscious or spiritual levels will greatly contaminate and color all channeling and psychic work. The more clear you are on a conscious level, subconscious level and superconscious level the better your channeling and psychic work will be.

In Summation

My beloved readers, in summation I want to say here that I love channeling and intuitive psychic work. My entire set of books has been channeled, and every single chapter in every single book is a first draft. The reason I'm able to do that is because I channel them. The only books I've read in the last twenty years are channeled material. I think developing the ability to channel in some form is one of the most important spiritual practices on the spiritual path. I think people seeing external channels and spiritual psychics dealing with Ascended Master level material is of enormous value and I would recommend my readers to take advantage of such services. I provide such services in an extremely comprehensive form at the Melchizedek Synthesis Light Academy.

So, I want you to understand that no one is more fond of channeling and psychic work and exploration than me. Because of my extensive spiritual and psychological training however, I have come to understand how these processes actually work. I have also seen how incredibly naive and spiritually undiscerning many lightworkers are within themselves and in relationship to external psychics and channels. The purpose of this last section has been to comprehensively point out the filters and lenses that color the flow of information through any one individual.

So, please most definitely do continue to practice channeling in all the varied forms. Please continue to develop your psychic abilities and inner senses on all levels within yourself. Please do continue to take advantage of external channels and spiritual psychics. However, after reading this chapter I think you will have a much better sense of how channeling and psychic readings work and you will be much more spiritually discerning and much less likely to give your power away because of a glamorized projection in regards to this whole subject.

The purpose of this chapter has been to completely break apart this glamorized projection many lightworkers have and bring true spiritual discernment and discrimination to this subject. The information in this chapter is as important to lightworkers receiving readings or reading channeled material as it is to trained channels and psychics who are doing this work. Trained channels and psychics doing this work need to understand all the psychological and spiritual filters so that they can have a full spectrum understanding of the whole process and so it doesn't become a glamour. I am not saying that it is for many of you. I am just saying the points I have made in this chapter are some of the areas to watch out for and to consider in becoming a "fully integrated Ascended Master channel and psychic." I hope my humble efforts to bring Light and clarity to this often confusing and most misunderstood subject has been useful.

Atmic Senses

Now, my beloved readers, let us return back to the chart where I began this chapter. In review we have already discussed the physical, astral, lower mental senses, higher mental senses and Buddhic senses. Now we will discuss the five atmic senses. The five atmic senses on the atmic plane are: all knowledge, perfection, realization, active service, and beatitude. Let us begin with beatitude. The inner sense of beatitude deals with the sublime and refined sense or manifestation of beauty. It is beauty as it carries the essence of GOD. Jesus Christ in his ministry exemplified beatitude. The same could be said of Quan Yin and Lord Buddha. This could be seen in the way they moved, flowed, in their carriage and in their presence. The inner sense of active service has to do with the practicing and demonstrating of the presence of GOD in daily life. The sense of Realization on the atmic level has to do with fully merging into the monad or I Am Presence. It has to do with the individual fully realizing their unity with the All and feeling, intuiting, knowing and demonstrating this on all levels as a reality of their being. Thus a Master may proclaim, "I am a Realized being."

The next sense is perfection. This deals with the relative perfection of GOD, which is actually a very high state of Beingness. Perfection at this level demonstrates all the qualities that lightworkers strive to attain in their pursuit of excellence or perfection. It is the pursuit of a flawless character filled with Christ/Buddha attributes and a state of mind that transcends most negative ego qualities. The sense of all knowledge at the atmic level deals with the ability to tap into all available knowledge at that level and to ascertain truth behind any situation. A true knowingness, both on the higher and/or inner levels of being, as in knowing the wisdom of GOD and many details and workings of the cosmos. It is the knowledge of what is transpiring at the core essence of manifestation. It is the sense and ability to know the true motivation behind of all things.

Monadic Senses

The five monadic senses are: monadic group consciousness, full monadic merger, monadic comprehension, monadic vision and monadic realization. Monadic group consciousness deals with a greater feeling of unity with one's eleven other soul extensions from one's oversoul and 144 soul extensions from one's monad. It is also a greater sense of one's unity with the Spiritual Hierarchy and the New Group of World Servers on Earth. Full monadic merger is the realization of achieving one's ascension, which is the same thing as saying one has merged with their monad. Monadic comprehension is the sense of being able to comprehend things from the consciousness of the monad, no longer the higher self. Monadic vision deals with the sense of being able to see through the eyes of the monad and no longer through the eyes of the personality, the oversoul, negative ego, or lower-self desire. Monadic realization is the total feeling, intuition, and knowingness that you are the Mighty I Am Presence living in a physical body on Earth.

Logoic Senses

The six logoic senses are: synthesis, seeing with the eye of GOD, Divine plan comprehension, full attunement with the logos of the planet, logoic realization and logoic comprehension. Synthesis is the sense to be able to see and function through a full spectrum prism rather than functioning through a fragmented lens of that prism. The sense of synthesis fits into every level for that is the nature of synthesis. The higher up the circular or spiral ladder one goes on the ladder of evolution the more one has the ability, and the more necessary it is to incorporate, synthesis. Once the monadic level is reached, synthesis must be fully embraced upon the logoic level; it must be fully established and demonstrated as one is then a full representative of the planetary logos. At the cosmic level, synthesis must become part of the core essence of one's being in order that they demonstrate this in all the work that they do and in what they are. The higher or fuller or more inclusively one travels up the ladder of cosmic evolution, the more one embraces and becomes the synthesis of GOD as it is built into the individualized essence. Upon the cosmic levels, all must be approached from the platform or truth of synthesis.

Seeing with the eye of GOD has to do with having planetary vision, which extends into solar and cosmic realms as well. Divine plan comprehension is the sense to be able to comprehend the Divine plan of the planetary logos, Lord Buddha, as he intends it to be manifested upon all levels of our planetary system. Full attunement with the logos has to do with not only the completion of your seven levels of initiation but also with complete merger at the 99% level with your monad and with the logos of our planet Lord Buddha, who is the president and key guide of all planetary evolvement. Logoic realization has to do with the sense of full realization of the seventh plane of consciousness and the achievement of liberation from the physical wheel of rebirth. Logoic comprehension involves a higher level of comprehension than that which has been spoken of before. It is a level of comprehension that contains within it all seven planes of consciousness and a level of comprehension where full planetary mastery is bestowed upon the initiate.

The Cosmic Senses

The eleven cosmic senses are: cosmic synthesis, cosmic knowledge, cosmic perfection, cosmic realization, cosmic service, cosmic beatitude, cosmic idealism, cosmic vision, cosmic comprehension, cosmic healing, cosmic intuition. These eleven senses are the cosmic equivalents of the 38 planetary senses I have described in this chapter. Their meaning can be understood in the statement of Hermes when he said, "As within so without, as above so below." The planetary senses are realized in the first inch of a ten-inch ruler, so to speak. Cosmic ascension and the cosmic levels of consciousness deal with the other nine-tenths of the ruler. The planetary senses were developed within the movement of the first seven levels of initiation. The cosmic senses are developed within the 352 levels of initiation moving up the cosmic scale. One can begin to tap into these cosmic senses but not fully realize them until one realizes these cosmic levels as their experience in the initiatory process.

Final Conclusion

My beloved readers, we have now moved through the 38 planetary inner senses and the eleven cosmic inner senses. As you can clearly see GOD has built into us extra sensory apparatus far beyond anything we once realized. Some of these higher senses in the Buddhic, Atmic, Monadic, and Logoic realms are far more refined than the standard extra sensory perception that most people think about when they use that term. Please remember, those of you who are not clairaudient voice channels or clairvoyants, that although you may not have these spiritual gifts you may have a great many of these other spiritual senses and gifts that the clairvoyants and channels may not have. Certain of these senses are often given to mystics and certain other ones GOD has given to those of a more occult nature. Many lightworkers would like to be channels and clairvoyants, however, this may not be your destiny. What I want you to realize is that you probably have already inner senses that are just as profound that you have not acknowledged to yourself for no one has ever laid them out in easy to understand theoretical form.

Mystics need occultists, and occultists need mystics. Psychics need psychologists, and psychologists need psychics. People who are right-brain need left-brain people, and people who are left-brain need right-brain people. Intuitive emotional types need intuitive mental

Integrated Ascension

types, and vice versa. A great many of the inner senses are more occult inner senses. Other ones are more mystic inner senses. Occultists often want to be mystics. Mystics, in truth however, inwardly would like to be occultists because they do not have the intuition, telepathy, psychological clarity, mental abilities, and inner senses that occultists have. Mystic senses are not better than occult senses and occult senses are not better than mystic senses; they are just different.

Occultists have not been as aware of the advanced inner senses they are tapped into and this is one of my reasons for writing this chapter. Very often occultists are tapping a much higher level than the mystics who are channeling and doing psychic clairvoyant work. This may be a surprise to my readers but it's true. It is time now for all lightworkers, both mystic and occultist in nature, to fully honor, recognize, and integrate the full spectrum of sensory apparatus that GOD has built into us. Mystics tend to be a little more feminine in nature, while occultists tend to be a little more masculine in nature. Because of this, certain inner senses are uniquely available to each group. The mystics are more consciously aware of the inner senses they are utilizing than are occultists. Again, it is my hope that this chapter will clarify this most important point to occultists. The ideal is to integrate the mystic and the occultist senses and abilities within one's self, and again, this is referred to as "Integrated Ascension."

The last point I want to make here in concluding this chapter is that the foundation of all thirty-eight inner senses is one's psychological clarity and one's level of Integrated Ascension as I have spoken of it throughout this book. If Integrated Ascension and full spectrum prism consciousness has not been achieved then all the inner senses, both mystic and occult in nature, will be skewed, colored and in extreme cases corrupted and contaminated. I have focused a great deal of my discussion in this chapter on channeling and psychic readings in discussing all the different filters and lenses that color this process. I have purposely done this because this is where the focus was needed and is

Integrated Ascension

needed. I say again however in this moment that it is not just the mystic inner senses that will be skewed, corrupted and contaminated if psychological clarity and integrated ascension is not achieved. "It is all thirty-eight inner senses that will be skewed, colored and contaminated if your psychological homework is not done." This is not a judgment just a simple loving firm spiritual truth.

The single most important relationship in your life is *not* your relationship to GOD, the Cosmic Masters, Planetary Ascended Masters, Angels, Extraterrestrials, your Mighty I Am Presence, your Higher Self and/or Oversoul, your spouse, your child, your friends, your parents, your family, your spiritual teacher or guru. The single most important relationship in your life, bar none, is your relationship to your *self*. If you are not right with self, every single relationship in your life will be off-kilter and out of balance. This, my beloved readers, is the golden key and the secret of true success. When you develop a right relationship to self, every other relationship in your life will become right. You will develop the Midas Touch and everything you think, say, and do will turn to gold.

This entire chapter has been for the purpose of showing you, my beloved readers, how not having a right relationship to self can skew, color and contaminate the channeling, psychic reading and inner senses process of accessing information and knowledge. Again it is my humble prayer that this point was given forth sufficiently to firmly and lovingly make this point for this is the key to achieving inner peace, happiness, joy, success, Self-Realization, GOD-Realization and Integrated Ascension.

9

A More Expansive Look at the Dangers of Non-Integrated Channeling, Clairaudience, and Clairvoyance

"...And They Shall Draw Neigh Unto You"

The ability to attune to the higher dimensional frequencies and thereby receive messages and guidance from the inner plane hierarchy of Masters is rapidly growing. More and more people are developing the facility to hear or sense the guiding wisdom that the Masters are seeking to impart in order to assist humanity with its evolution. Through the development of the intuition, the third eye and crown chakra, we are enabled to tune into those upon the celestial realms whose work consists of assisting us in this fashion. Great numbers of inner plane Ascended Masters, beings from the Angelic and Archangelic realms, as well as the positive Extraterrestrials who seek to guide us through the light of their own expanded wisdom, are reaching into the minds and hearts of all who are open to hear, see or intuit their love and transmissions.

Integrated Ascension

This, my beloved readers, has obviously been an enormous help to so many of us. It has enabled lightworkers both to understand and to expand into areas that have never been available before. Where once the Masters' teachings were shrouded in great mystery and secrecy, revealed only to special initiates and confined within the boundaries of hidden secret mystery schools, vast amounts of such information now fill the bookshelves of the ever growing number of spiritual and metaphysical bookstores. Most lightworkers are themselves channels to one degree or another, even if as yet beneath the threshold of awareness.

There is, however, a danger within this wonderful process of acceleration and communion that the Masters are growing increasingly concerned about, and which they have specifically asked me to address in this book. Their primary concern is the lack of knowledge that most of us have concerning the channeling process, accompanied with the lack of discrimination that seems to go hand in hand with this fact. The channeling process, as well as the process that involves any sort of clairaudience, clairvoyance and certainly psychic impressions is much more intricate and complex than many tend to realize. While it is true that the Masters and all of the Celestial Hierarchy want to continue this process, it is likewise true that they want to *clarify* much regarding this process as well. I will therefore share with you, my beloved readers, that which has been shared with me, and then request that your final discernment is between you, your Higher Self and your own Mighty I Am Presence, for that is where your true relationship with GOD is fully established!

Filtering and Coloring of the Individual Channel

What first must be understood utterly and completely is that there is a distinctive filtering process by which any channeled information is brought through any individual channel. The clearer and more integrated the channel is, the clearer and more accurate the information

Integrated Ascension

will be. That is why it is so vital that we proceed upon the path of our initiations in as integrated a fashion and manner as possible. The more out of the way our negative ego personal agenda is, the more we are focused in Christ consciousness, the more every cell and level of our twelve-body system is vibrating to the harmonics of GOD, the purer we will be able to intuit, see, hear, sense and so forth, all that the Masters seek to reveal. Before we even investigate this process of purification and integration with regards to channeling, we must understand that no matter how pure the channel is the information and essence of what is being brought through will be somewhat colored by that individual. This is not something that needs to, nor can be corrected. This is something that merely needs to be understood. Each of us is unique, and as such we are composed of various ray configurations, astrological configurations, have a unique ascension lineage, environmental imprints, and chakras through which we predominantly function and so forth. We each have our own color and tone, which, if you are clairvoyant or clairaudient, you will actually be able to see and/or hear. We simply are who we are by virtue of our Monad, oversoul, soul family, soul, and the myriad rounds of births we have undergone. This is our individuality and we are not meant to try and deny this, for we simply could not!

What we do need to understand is that all of these factors cannot help but to color our channelings to one degree or another. Our own personal imprint is stamped upon them and they funnel through all the above mentioned individual characteristics, as well as our four lower bodies. You must realize, my beloved readers, that all inner visions, channeling and intuitions must also run through our mental/emotional body, which forms our unique psychology, our psychoepistemology or lens by which we view the world, our belief system, our etheric body and physical body. By the time the message is made manifest it has been filtered and colored by the unavoidable influence of our personal Beingness.

Integrated Ascension

The fact remains, however, that we are fortunate to have living in our world today some highly integrated initiates who are able to channel information at a profoundly accurate level. This does not preclude the fact that it will be colored by their own unique individuality. Yet, please bear in mind that the individuals who uphold this level of clarity are extremely well-balanced and integrated within themselves. In that regard, their personal stamp serves to enhance the revelations through their own purity and graciousness. Rather than distort the flow of guidance or revelation that the Master or Masters seek to impart, they simply flavor it with their own coloring and place their own individual tone upon it. The toned resonance of such a clear channel will be in utter harmony with that of the Celestial Being for whom they are channeling. We must, however, be extremely and diligently selective, discerning and discriminating in our search for these special individuals. They are, beloved readers, few and far between!

Do realize that if you are fortunate enough to come upon the teachings of a channel of this high caliber, you likewise understand that their work bears the distinctive imprint of their individual embodiments and configuration. This is important to be aware of, as you will find that some of you will resonate more harmoniously with one channel than with another. Even if two channels are of equal integration and share the same high caliber, one might be far more attuned to your own personal resonance, tones, and colorings than another. You will both more than likely have a common ascension lineage and perhaps even a shared or dovetailing puzzle piece! When you are clear enough to ask and the channel is clear, you will hear your Master's voice!

It is always of paramount importance that you use your highest level of discernment and discrimination at all times. In these days where there is a psychic at every corner and a channel every couple of blocks, it lies within each of us to discern the clarity, purity, motive, intent, and integration level of any and every one that we consult with in this manner. This likewise includes any written material that pertains to channeled messages and so forth. It must become your top priority to only allow those of the highest caliber into your auric field. By the same token, the more you balance, cleanse, purify and integrate all levels of initiation and all of the eight major quotients, the clearer and purer channel you yourself will become.

Clear Channeling

Before going into an in-depth study of the many pitfalls and danger points to look out for in regards to the channeling process, let me first give you a picture of a high level channel. This person, for one thing, would never presume to order you about. Truth, as it came through them, would be presented to you in a clear and concise manner. Any guidance would be put before you as suggestions, not commandments. No person has the right to control another person, and no true channel who is connected to GOD and the Masters would ever even hint at interfering with your own freedom of choice. They would leave you with the feeling of unconditional love and support. This does not mean that they would not present truth as it appeared to them and offer you guidance and suggestions, but that is as far as it would go. If they even made the slightest attempt to offend your right of free will, then that should signal to you that this is not a channel of the caliber of which I am speaking, and you would be wise to remove yourself from their attempted sphere of control.

A pure channel is a person of high integrity within themselves. They seek to align with GOD and the Masters and uphold the higher principles within their own lives. This helps them to maintain the level of frequency, clarity, and purity that is necessary for hearing, sensing, seeing or feeling the truth as it is revealed. They are clean flutes, so to speak, through which Krishna can play his melodies.

A person who is clear and aligned with their own Higher Self would never impose their channeling upon you. They would not invade your privacy by snooping about your aura and then offering unsolicited advice. There may be rare instances of exception to this rule, such as if a dear friend or loved one senses a specific danger or can offer you a genuine insight that will truly serve to benefit you, but even that should be done with all due respect. Generally speaking, most channels of a high caliber will wait to be invited to speak their truth or share their inner guidance. They will not storm through the gates of your private self, looking for psychic garbage to dump in your face. This may sound a bit harsh or over the top, but I can tell you that I have personally been subjected to this type of activity, and it is much like walking into what you think is the privacy of your own home to find an intruder who proceeds to tell you what they think is wrong about how you run your household and what exactly it is you should do about it. They are not invited guests, but rather complete strangers, and haven't a clue as to what you are trying to effectuate, nevertheless they presume to tell you how to do it better!. This, my beloved readers, is not a clear channel.

If you stay true to your own intuition and are not blown away simply by the fact that someone has honed their channeling or psychic abilities to a greater degree then you have, you will find that you do indeed have the ability to discriminate between the various levels of channelings and channelers. A clear channel works for GOD and the Masters. They work for the benefit of humankind, which may, for the moment, be you!. They do not, however, have any other agenda than to be of service.

This does not mean that they should not charge a fee. Some may not choose to, but most will. It has taken them lifetimes to perfect their skills. If we do not have a problem paying a car mechanic, computer expert or physician for a skill that it has probably only taken one or two lifetimes to perfect, why should we have a problem with one who has cultivated the precious art of channeling? We should not. If they are honest and aboveboard about their fee, then that should be no problem. If it is completely off the graph, you will know. What is of utmost importance is their centeredness of Being, their attitude of unconditional love, their desire to be of service, and their own personal integration and psychological clarity. They do not have to be a professional psychologist to do this work, nor do they even have to be at as high a level of initiation as yourself. They have a specialized skill and that is the gift that they have to offer, that is their puzzle piece and that is their field of service.

Know them by their level of light and love, by the way they present their wisdom, by their heartfelt caring and by their balanced integrity and integration. They have much to offer. Remember that even the best of channels will by the very nature of the channeling process somewhat color the information with their own individuality. That is all right and is to be expected. You are advised most urgently to pay utmost attention in regards to their motivation, and to discriminate until you are clear as to what that is! Are they there to serve you, GOD and the Masters, or are they there to glamorize themselves? Are they there to control you, or to help **you** gain control over your own life? These are key points to be aware of, my beloved readers. In knowing the answers to these questions you will know the level of those whom you are letting into your field. Seek only from the pure and wise and loving of heart, and then the counsel you receive will help you reach your own highest potential!

When looking for a clear channel, or indeed setting your intent on becoming a clear and pure channel yourself, the absolute top and bottom line of it is that *all importance be placed upon the work being done and NOT upon the personality doing the work!* What is of importance is only the information brought through and *not* the ego and personality of the one who is bringing that information into awareness. It does not matter if the individual is using voice or written channeling, is clairvoyant, clairaudient, psychic, telepathic or intuitive. The content, which must always be of service to either the individual who is seeking counsel or to the greater spectrum of planetary and cosmic revelation, is of importance, nothing else! The enveloping and overlighting presence of GOD must also be present, along with the

Integrated Ascension

incoming information from one or other of the Ascended Masters, Angels or Space Brothers and Sisters.

If you sense that in your own work you are making yourself more important than the process of bringing through information, please know that you as yet have much clearing and psychological adjustments to make. If you sense that any given channel is making themselves out to be more important than the work that they are doing, than I strongly suggest you look elsewhere. Any type of channeling or clairvoyant experience that is superseded by *self*-importance, cannot help but to be tainted to a large degree by that self or personality. Pure channeling has nothing to do with personality, unless it is in the interest of helping a person to more fully integrate their personality with their spiritual self. If it falls short of that high ideal by any degree, than this is not the channeling that you are looking for!

A feeling of unconditional love, compassion, unity, purity and sanctity must be present in anyone whom you seek guidance from in such a manner. If you are learning how to be a channel, or if the clairaudient, clairvoyant, intuitive senses are opening within yourself, you must be extra vigilant within your own intent of purity. The gifts that the Masters seek to bring through are most definitely not for the glorification of any personality, no matter how high an initiation level that person may be working from. In truth, the higher the level of "Integrated Initiation" and "Integrated Ascension," the *less* the individual will focus upon themselves at all. In the process of channeling, the less the focus on the individual performing the service, the more focus on GOD and His/Her Divine Grace! I ask you with utter sincerity to "Ponder on this," beloved readers, and to heed your own intuition. Channeling is not about personalities; it is about truth and about GOD!

Integrated Ascension

The Unwanted Astral Belt

Let us now proceed to explore some of the pitfalls that racing up the path in an unintegrated, unbalanced manner can present to us. The more we explore these potential dangers, the greater our ability will be to avoid them. We will attain the necessary clarity to make the adjustments that we need in order to safely and cohesively explore every aspect and level of GOD's Kingdom as balanced, integrated, and whole individuals. We will likewise know what to avoid in other people who have not done the necessary work, and we will have the wisdom not to seek their counsel. We will learn to avoid the illusions, the glamours, the delusions, and the manipulations of others who may have less than our best interest in mind. We will learn how to be truly integrated ascended Masters, so that when we cultivate the inner senses we will see and hear with the clarity of Spirit!

All of us are aware that there is much going on in the astral realm that is of a very low caliber of evolution. This is not to judge anyone who is working out their lessons upon the lower regions, but it is extremely important that we are aware that this is indeed a very active realm. It is one that untrained psychics will inadvertently allow into their fields without even being aware that they are doing so. It is vital that we do not allow ourselves to fall into this category. Just as we should not go on automatic pilot upon the physical realm, we must certainly be vigilant in keeping our focus upon the absolute highest when venturing into the inner realms.

The astral realm, as you know, is associated with desire and strong emotions. There are unfortunately many astral entities who literally feed off of the emotional bodies of others. This is not so very different than the incarnated personality who seeks to create or foster inappropriate excitement of the astral elemental or vehicle in others in order to feed off of the stimulation that is produced by the other person, and in many cases, to engage the willingness of the other party to share in the continued expansion of great emotions. An excellent example of this can be seen in "mob consciousness." In such a situation as this, what you have are many astral bodies exciting many other astral bodies to the point of pure hysteria. The mind cannot freely function, as the emotional body has assumed total control. People even become impervious to physical pain in such situations, as they are so focused within their emotional vehicle to the exclusion of all other bodies. It is not until later that they even feel the blow to the head or solar plexus. This is an extreme example, but a very tangible one, for we have all at least seen it at play on the news and have adequate reference to what I am speaking about here.

When we take this example and realize that these very emotions are what constitute the astral realm itself, we hopefully realize that we must be on full guard when opening ourselves up to the inner planes. Now, just as a point of interest, the astral realm as a whole is not as dark or unevolved as it was in humanity's earlier stage of evolution. The race as a whole has come far from that of so called "savage man" and has moved to higher realms within the astral sphere. That is not to say, however, that these spheres are not of themselves filled with much untamed astral energies, elementals and negativities. It is also not to imply that these are regions to be any less wary of now than in the past. It is simply to point out that all planes within this planetary sphere are themselves upraising due to the higher influx of light and the greater spiritual stimulation being sent into all levels of our atmosphere.

This being the case, however, the astral realms that we often find ourselves dealing with contain a greater glamour of sophistication, if I may use that term in the context of that which we are discussing. This glamour plays itself out in far more subtle forms than it was able to do at more primitive states of humanity's development, and therefore requires keener observation and discernment!

While it is true that one can encounter the lower elementals, most channels are operating from a spiritual intent and would not knowingly grant access or accommodation to these obviously ill intentioned forms. They can, however, find points of entry if one enters that world unguarded or with gaping holes in their auras. They do still present somewhat of a problem, which is why I suggest that all serious students of ascension and initiation do get clearings from all negative elementals, implants, energies and the like.

What I seek to draw your attention to here, however, is something that is not so obvious and which often holds many an otherwise sincere lightworker within its illusionary grasp. What I am speaking of here are the glamours and deceptions that come to and through anyone who either consciously or subconsciously seeks glory, glamour, fame, power, even spiritual prestige and recognition for themselves. It is here where we are at our most vulnerable, beloved readers, for we are often not in touch with these fragments of our lower nature that still hold sway over our egos, and form great blockages to our true spiritual motivations and intentions!

It is cosmic law that like will seek like. The possibilities and permutations within the astral or desire belt that surrounds each of us and our planet as a whole are infinite! The only way to avoid the influence of these glamours, as I shall refer to them from this point forward, is to rid them from our own personal auric fields. In that way there will be nothing within us as individuals in which these glamours or negative influences can find a point of resonance, and will therefore have no power or sway over us. That is, in truth, what Integrated Ascension is all about. A level must be worked with and cleansed, cleared and purified so that, to quote the Bible, "…when we are tried we are not found wanting"! There will be no desire for glamour within us through which the forces of glamour can attach. Unfortunately, this is not the predominant trend, even among the most sincere and well-meaning channelers and students alike. The negative ego still wants to get a "kick" out of being the best, the highest, having the "siddhis" (yogic powers), and this is an open invitation to all manner of glamour, illusion and deception.

Integrated Ascension

What frequently happens is that if this trend is very active within ourselves, the channel or spiritual clairvoyant we will be drawn to will be one who has much to work out in this regard. We will come to them looking for food for our negative egos, and all too often they will supply it. They will, in most cases, by no means do this intentionally. They will just be coloring their information with their own desire and linking that up with yours. The net result will be quite exciting, yet often far from the mark.

When the astral body is invested in the information it is receiving, rather than using it to quiet itself and move away from glamour of all sorts, it will excite itself and glamorize the process of channeling, clairvoyance, clairaudience, etc. This is something that we must all guard against more vigilantly, by first and foremost attending to the stilling of the astral vehicle through mediation and purification, and being forearmed with the knowledge that GOD and the Masters are not the least bit interested in glorifying the personality, negative ego or lower self of anyone, including our spiritual teachers. Remember the frequently quoted statement given forth by beloved Master Jesus, "He who is first among you, let him be last, for he who is last now will be first later." If you hold these words of wisdom within your heart, you will know what to guard against when seeking to either give or receive counsel from the inner planes.

I will conclude this segment on the astral planes by sharing with you a bit of information that is well worth having. Just as on the Earth plane, where one can don a costume complete with mask, or have fake licenses drawn up, phony credit cards and so forth, there are beings in the astral realms who will take on the garb of one or other of the Masters to play with you, so to speak. This is not something to be frightened of, for on the inner planes the senses are much more adept and it is not by their form but by their essence you shall know them! If anyone comes to you in an attempt to help you glorify the lower self or negative ego, please be aware that this is a deception. No true Master would ever do this, for their only interest is to bring you deeper and deeper within the heart and light of GOD that you may glorify the divinity within you and not the negative ego. This does not mean that they, the true Masters, will not offer much in support of who you are while in embodiment, for they honor every single level of your being. This is a subtlety many are likewise unaware of. The Masters take the whole being of each of us into account and embrace us fully, and that means who we are upon any and every plane that we are manifesting upon.

What I am specifically referring to here is not the honoring of one's various bodies, including the emotional in proper proportion, but the glorification of the separate self rather than the "Divine whole." Sometimes, and I have personally experienced this, the true Master will stand by to see how you respond to the accolades of a false Master and if you buy into the glorification of the separate self. This reveals much to them. They, the true Master, will never judge you for your own error in judgment, however, they will be easily able to gauge where your work lies! If you are ever in doubt, challenge them in the name of Christ three times. A Master who is not a Master cannot withstand this challenge when given forth in such a manner, and their reality will immediately be revealed.

Since the astral world is very related to the emotional and heart center, the best way to pass easily and gently through any of its traps, glamours, illusions, or delusions, is to stay focused within your heart. Align your heart with the Heart of GOD. Align your feeling center with the feelings of Divine and unconditional love, compassion and mercy. These energies will carry you to the higher aspect of the astral world, which is, in truth, a corollary of it, found upon the Buddhic (devachanic realm). It is all really quite simple, as it all boils down to selflessness, egolessness, love and compassion. It does not, as I have already told you, dishonor the feeling self. It does, however, raise the feeling self to levels of inclusiveness, and love that has nothing whatsoever to do with the glamours of the negative ego.

Integrated Ascension

If you follow the advice of beloved Master Jesus, who combined his energy with that of Lord Maitreya, and "...first take the beam out of your own eye," then I promise you, "You shall see clearly enough to take the speck out of your brother's/sister's eye!" Work on cleansing your own astral field to the point where the Divine attributes of feeling reign supreme. Then, whether you yourself are guided to channel or to consult with a channel, you will have the ability of discernment. This, my beloved readers, will give you the freedom to traverse the astral realms unfettered and with a clarity that will serve yourself and anyone who seeks your services. This will be your demonstration of Integrated Ascension, and your true liberation for any and all astral mishaps!

Channeled Manipulations

Anyone who is channeling through a non-integrated state of being can easily delude both themselves and their client, friend or student by subconsciously coloring the channeling to the point where it falls into the category of manipulation. There are many degrees, as well as many types of this type of channeling, and we must be on guard against all of them. More often then not, the channeler is completely unaware that this is taking place. It is vital that you become aware of this, for as you proceed upon your own path and certain psychic, channeling, clairaudient, clairvoyant, intuitive and telepathic abilities begin to open and blossom within you, you will want to be as pure and clear in your work as possible. This requires deep cleansing of the subconscious mind and the creating of a vehicle that will serve nothing less than the highest truth and the highest good for all concerned.

This becomes quite subtle, for as I have said; the conscious mind is not generally involved in this process. The best safeguard against this is to, first, approach your entire path of ascension and initiation in an integrated manner. Second, it is highly recommended that you begin each channeling session with a prayer to your own Mighty I Am

Presence, To GOD and the Masters, that only truth come through, if you are the channeler, and that only truth be received, if you are the client. In fact, a prayer for absolute truth to GOD Almighty would be the best way to begin each session whether you are the channeler or the receiver of information. By doing this, you are setting the intent, and therefore the frequencies, to allow in only that which is of the highest caliber. It then remains with you, beloved readers, to exercise your own discernment. Discernment is one of your most precious tools and one that you would be wise to incorporate into every stage and aspect of your journey. More about that later.

The way channeling manipulation works is two-fold. First and most commonly, it is operative on the part of the channeler. It comes into play when there is an underlying self-motive or interest at stake. The channeling will then take on certain phases, twists, turns, or even complete inaccuracies in order that these ends are met. In cases such as this, the subconscious mind, the negative ego, the inner child and the astral elemental are very active. The message is therefore distorted to one degree or another in order to satisfy this lower intent. The Master might be actually trying to give forth accurate and clear guidance and information, but the person channeling is coloring it so that it meets their own hidden agenda.

This type of channeling manipulation and ego boosting may take the form of actually boosting the negative ego of the client or recipient of the channeling, this, in turn, raises the esteem of the channeler in the recipients mind, as they have been given the information which their own negative ego wanted to hear, and a certain flattery and glamour is brought into play. In either case, what is *not* being given forth is clear and accurate information that will help the soul upon their true journey of evolution. We must all become aware of this subtle yet devious form of channeling, so that we may proceed as either the transmitter of guidance and information or the receiver of guidance in a clear, untainted way. If we allow ourselves to be manipulated by channeling, no matter what our role in it is, we will more than likely be guided from our higher path rather than toward it, and this would be most unfortunate, to say the least!

Check with your own intuition about whether or not you feel that anyone you are seeking either spiritual or psychological guidance from may have a hidden agenda that they seek to put into play. Even if it does not seem to apply to you in particular, I would advise you to quickly end any communications from that person even before they have begun! For example, if what they are seeking is to establish their own base of personal power, not from within themselves but rather based on fame, public recognition, money, and/or self-aggrandizement, they may simply seek to please you so that you are, in turn, pleased with them and hold them in high esteem.

An example of this may be in assuring you that you have reached a certain level of initiation, so that you feel good about yourself, and even better about they who give forth this knowledge! They may then proceed to tell you that any further advancements may require you following them in one form or another, even if all that means is getting channelings from them on a continuous basis. This helps to build up their agenda of self-importance. This may or may not even involve money. Sometimes the lower self is very concerned about having large sums of money from its followers. Sometimes it is much more concerned with the fame, glamour, and glory that simply go hand in hand with having the followers. Usually the two go together, but this is not at all necessarily the case.

What is true, and what shall be continued to be explored in regard to channeled manipulations may very well apply to spiritual or psychological teachers who are not channelers per say. They, as well as clairvoyants, clairaudients and so forth may be in the business of building their own self esteem by the number of people that they can claim as students. Whenever the lower or separative self manipulates in order to further its own ends you can be sure that the information received will be less then accurate.

Integrated Ascension

If there is a hidden agenda, beloved readers, that agenda is not working for your highest good, nor for GOD, nor for truth. It is working to fulfill the ego desires of someone who seeks power over others rather than power within themselves. Be very careful in this regard. Remember, beloved friends, GOD and the Masters are available to you personally at all times. If you are ever in doubt, seek within. That is where all true and lasting answers will eventually come from anyway and that is where you shall surely meet with GOD!

The Masters advise, suggest, and offer counsel. They do not order, and that is a fact! In the rare instance where they choose to be emphatic about a given issue, this will usually come through your own channel directly. Even in these cases they will strongly *advise*, perhaps even be adamant, but they will not order you about. If it reaches an extreme case, then you will definitely hear from them directly, either in vision, a lucid dream, or through you own inner senses. They cannot nor will not infringe upon human free will. This is law!

If any channeler ever orders you to behave in any fashion, I caution you to know for a fact that their channeling is being colored far beyond the unavoidable colorings that are inherent in the process itself. The right for humanity's free will stands as a given inalienable right. Never, beloved readers, let another person try to take that away from you, no matter whose voice they tell you they are speaking with. This is a GOD given right that no Master would ever directly interfere with. If interference does come, please be assured it is not from the true Master!

If a person delves into channeling from an unintegrated state of being, and their own negative ego wishes to assert itself, you may notice a trend in which the advice given forth moves from that of simple suggestions to that of giving out and out orders! If you are the channeler and you notice that your channelings are tending to head in this direction, then it is time for you to stop. Go back to some of your basic cleansing, clearing, and purifying practices and eliminate this negative ego pattern of destruction! What I am saying here applies both

Integrated Ascension

to channeler and to those of you receiving the guidance given forth. No matter what our particular role of the moment may be, we all ultimately need to strive to be as balanced, clear and integrated as possible. The only control that is to be asserted is that of your conscious mind and Will in service of your Higher Self and Mighty I Am Presence to deny the negative ego and to reaffirm Christ/Buddhic thinking. The attempt to control or override anyone else's free will is a Divine felony!

You will know your channeling is turning manipulative or that you are receiving manipulative channeling if frustration begins to make its presence felt. Personal frustration or any negative emotions are a sure sign that the negative ego is involved. If frustration or negative emotions begin to build into any form of anger or negativity whatsoever, then you will know beyond the shadow of a doubt that the channeling is off track. All that comes from GOD and the Masters comes with unconditional love and unattachment. Where there are negative emotions, my friends, there is attachment!

Do be open to becoming your own channel, to listening to that still small voice within, for that is the purest and safest road to Source. Ultimately, we each must travel the inner path to GOD anyway. This being so, I would also suggest being open to those who do strike you as being pure channels, for their gifts are of enormous benefit, particularly at this juncture in time. The fundamental truth of the matter is that unless you are integrated within yourself, you can manipulate yourself through your own inner channeling just as easily as another person can. So, it all circles back again to balance, clarity and integration!

I therefore repeat that if it is the highest truth you are after, voice that both inwardly add outwardly. Tell it to the GOD within you and the GOD within whoever is doing channeling or other clairvoyant or clairaudient work for you. We are all being given a piece of the puzzle, and even as channels, we each have gifts that are specific and unique to just ourselves. It would be a big mistake to cut ourselves off from this wisdom and the vision given to and through each other for fear of being manipulated.

All that I suggest is that you watch out for the signs of negative ego manipulation. They are the same signs in regard to the channeling process as they are in regard to anything else. If the focus is on the personal self, if there is anger, judgment, inducement of guilt, shame, fear, then there is manipulation. If there is truth, it shines in a halo of unconditional love and light, and is bereft of all judgment and any other aspect of the negative ego's personal agenda, or lower self. It is then a pure piece of the cosmic puzzle of GOD being revealed by one who has the ability and gifts to reveal it. When used purely and with no manipulation of personal self, then channeling and all of the other higher senses are simply one more step of the Kingdom of GOD being made manifest upon the Earth!

I trust that I have said enough on the subject of channeled manipulations to help you keep a watchful eye on the matter. I do not want to go on and on, lest you become a "doubting Thomas," and "throw the baby out with the bathwater"! We are all smart enough, if we just allow ourselves to be honest enough to know whether or not someone is trying to manipulate us. I have shared the major signs of manipulation with you and that should be more than enough to go on. I do want to reiterate two vital points. The first is that these signs of manipulation apply as much to an external channel as they do to information you are getting from within. The negative ego is just as happy to manipulate the body it inhabits as well as someone else's, so you must be ever vigilant in this regard. The second is the incredible asset that pure, integrated, balanced and clear channeling can be. When it is of the Spirit and non-manipulative, it becomes a wonderful venture into group consciousness and the revelations of the new millennium have many vessels through which to pour forth golden insights.

Integrated Ascension

Group Thought Forms

There is little doubt that as a race as a whole, and as lightworkers in particular, we are growing in our abilities of telepathy. This can be seen to manifest in several different ways. First, as was already addressed, this increased ability allows for a far greater, deeper and clearer connection with the Hierarchy of Inner Plane Ascended Masters. Secondly, this puts us in rapport with our fellow lightworkers and aligns us in our work and mission, even if we are not quite consciously aware that this is occurring. Thirdly, this brings us into ever deepening rapport with the heart of humanity, allowing us to sense the many levels from which the human race as a whole are functioning. The ultimate goal of this ability is that we may be of greater service to the needs of our brothers and sisters. The danger is that there is so much astral and mental miasma that this requires a very strong will and the invocation of protection against all negative influences coming from "the race of man."

This increased telepathic ability likewise is putting us in touch with members of the Confederation of Planets, so that we may gain from the wisdom and guidance that these incredible beings offer from their unique perspective. Lastly, but certainly not least, this facility enables us to attune to our higher self, Monad, and the very heart of GOD. We are, in greater and greater degrees, becoming open to the varying frequencies of the Most High, and attuning to the greater vision and the Divine plan. This will allow us to co-create with GOD and to help anchor the new millennium upon the Earth!

You can therefore see that quite a lot is happening concurrently. Many levels of awareness are operating through the increase of our telepathic faculties. We must work most diligently; however, to find the proper balance within ourselves to maximize our spiritual missions and to keep a watchful eye over any potential dangers that can arise due to this emergence. We have the increased ability to tap into various levels of energies, from those of the lower astral regions to that of the Heart of

Integrated Ascension

GOD Itself. We must therefore learn how to be extremely adept in deciphering from what level of frequency a particular impression is coming, so that we may deal with it accordingly.

Obviously, we all want to attune to our Higher Self, our own Mighty I Am Presence, the Inner Plane group of Planetary and Cosmic Ascended Masters and to GOD. There is also much service work that some of us will be called to do in helping others to deal with and overcome some of their own lower tendencies and imbalances. We must, beloved readers, wear the cloak of Divine protection, discrimination, and discernment at all times. In this manner, we will be able to use these abilities to help heal both ourselves and our brothers and sisters within the various kingdoms of evolution and the planet as a whole.

The overlighting theme remains that with Integrated Ascension, the more fully balanced and integrated we each become, the more clearly will we be able to accurately read the various levels of frequency, know from precisely what sphere they are originating, and how best to assist in the balancing of them. Clarity with self is of utmost importance in order that our own inner vision is not blocked by the many distractions and potential deceptions that can arise from accessing the various etheric, astral and mental thoughtforms of humanity. We also must build the antakarana to utter perfection so that we have a direct line to GOD, and can pass free and clear and at a moment's notice to the serene pastures of our own Mighty I Am Presence and to the Divine Heart of GOD in the Great Central Sun. It is there where we are truly given the nourishment, rest and guidance that we need in order to go forth and continue our work.

Let us now explore some of the potential confusion that can result as a by-product of our growing telepathic abilities. Be aware, however, that the more integrated, balanced and clear we each become within our selves, the more easily we will walk through any and every one of these danger zones. Keep in mind that it is our own integrated love-light that will shine upon all potential areas of confusion and enable us to be servers in the truest sense of the word. The clearer we become in the vision of that which is true and of GOD, the clearer will we be able to discern that which is illusion and distortions of truth.

To begin with, as we attune to humanity and grow more and more sensitive to the various frequencies of energies that surround us, we pick up the fields of the whole of humanity and of the individuals with whom we share proximity. What this in actuality means, is that their auric fields, which includes both astral and mental miasma, fog, hopes, dreams, desires, imaginings, fears and so forth are perceived by us, even if that perception is happening at a level that does not immediately register consciously.

The very first thing that we must do is to put up our protective shields, so to speak. This does not mean, however, that we necessarily must engage in defensive posturing. Rather that we pull into our own fields as much light, love and power as we are able, and seek to live within that presence on a moment to moment basis. Once we are firmly rooted in this type of Divine protective aura or encasement, we will then be much better able to function as the observer of these various frequency bands. We will not take on the world's confusion, but rather take note of it.

There is a vast difference between the two, beloved readers. As an observer who is living in the sacredness of their own GOD-Self, you will be able to see, feel, hear, intuit the group thoughtform of humanity and the individual, and to help uplift it. If you go on automatic pilot and allow yourself to be unprotected by your own love, light, and power, then you will buy into mass thoughtforms, and take them on. Therefore, you may find yourself irritable, fearful, angry, and so forth, without knowing why. In fact, there would be no personal reason why, other than that you have allowed yourself to stay open and indiscriminate within the fog of the masses.

In order to be able to assist humanity out of their mass confusion and help all who are able to make the transition into the next millennium, then you must disengage yourself from the group thoughtforms that humanity as a whole cultivated. You must therefore do all the necessary clearing work, to which I have alluded to and written about so often, so that there is nothing left within yourself in which thoughtforms that are less than the highest can take hold of. As most people are operating out of the negative ego consciousness, you must work upon the clearing of the Negative Ego Quotient and the building of your Christ Consciousness Quotient on a consistent basis if you truly want to walk through the present fog that surrounds our world and see clearly and truly by the light of GOD alone. In this regard, beloved readers, please do consider working diligently on all the eight major quotients that were given forth at the beginning of this book.

Stay ever centered, aware, and alert as to what is your "stuff" and what is not your "stuff." As I said, there are so many thoughtforms, both those based upon reality and possible realities, fears, dreams, wishes, etc. that it is easy to get clouded if you are not vigilant. Remember that you are a son or daughter of GOD, and ask yourself when you sense a particular fear, thought, concern, desire invading either your consciousness or your aura, whether or not it has anything whatsoever to do with you at all. More than likely you will find that it does not even belong to you, it is not even your "stuff" awaiting cleansing. It is simply the winding fog of mass confusion that has invaded your sacred space.

Keeping your inner space "your own" is your true job. In order to do this, however, you must first clear it out to as great a degree as possible. Even when you have done this, however, unless you are living out in the country and away from the hub-bub of any sort of city life or outer stimulation, you are bound to "bump" into other peoples' thoughtforms. Learn to discriminate and toss out what is not of the highest frequency.

For those of us working upon the inner planes, this becomes even more vital, and likewise takes on an extremely subtle quality. As we attune to our group of fellow lightworkers, we hook up with their own

Integrated Ascension

thought world as well. Our goal is, of course, to align our Higher Self and Monad with theirs. Since we are in embodiment and working within the sphere of the four lower worlds, we are just as likely to connect with their auric emanations upon the emotional and mental levels of their Being as well. This is actually by Divine design since it is often quite beneficial to be in telepathic rapport from mind to mind in regards to specific projects that we are working on with each other. What we don't want, however, is to be unprotected from their own personal dramas, issues and self-created thoughtforms.

One of the tools I personally use in regard to this is to ask Melchizedek, Metatron and the Mahatma to put up an etheric wall of protection against any lower energies that could potentially come through from any of the lightworkers I am working with. This wall is made out of a semi-permeable substance, and is constructed in a manner that will allow only that of the highest good on any and every level to flow back and forth. It works to protect both or all parties concerned once it is installed, and therefore keeps the energy exchange always functioning at the highest possible level. It is a good idea to request this in your work, even among yourselves, so that no one inadvertently passes on or takes on someone else's lesson. Lord Melchizedek, the Mahatma and Lord Metatron will be more than happy to put this in place for you by invoking a simple request. I highly recommend this, as it is a wonderful preventative and helps to keep all interactions clear and of the highest and purest caliber. Be sure to request that this be put permanently around you, not just in a particular situation.

The work that we as lightworkers can produce via our telepathic links with one another is vast. As you are all quite aware, "thoughts are things," and when a certain thoughtform is concentrated upon in group formation for the highest good of the Divine plan we can facilitate its manifestation a thousand-fold. It is almost as if we can literally think a thing into being. Of course, as the thrust of this Aquarian cycle is to bring Heaven upon Earth and to make our works a manifested reality, we will be required to do a certain amount of work upon the physical plane as well. This is part of the lesson of spiritualizing the material. The speed at which these works can be brought forth when using concentrated mental effort and thoughtform building, however, far exceeds the laborious process involved when relying on outward communication alone. This is indeed a time of awakening grace and abilities, and we should make the utmost of them.

Just as I have suggested the ascension buddy system to help in your ascension work, I now suggest a "project buddy system" to work on a joint puzzle piece in order to attune with those with whom you are working in a specific way to bring about an outer manifestation at stated and specific time periods. Begin by establishing a telepathic report. Ask that your ideas flow from your individual monad into your individual mind and then back and forth between the group mind. Have your goal clearly and specifically written out and ask that all insights and communications and thoughtform building be established for the sole purpose of manifesting the Divine blue print. Then see what happens. I guarantee you that as you work deliberately, consciously and in a protected fashion with your project, the results you see will astound and uplift you. Remember, "Naught is achieved but what Man/Woman/GOD can conceive!" The power of this type of work can help to make the Kingdom of GOD a reality upon Earth and at the same time help you to play an active part in the manifestation of the greater plan as truly conscious co-creators with GOD!

When dealing in the realm of thoughtforms, it is imperative that no one use the power of thoughtform building to exert control or to try and influence anyone else. This applies to members working on a joint project, to other lightworkers, or to humanity in general. Each person's inner thought world is their own sanctified territory and no one has the right to try and invade it through any form of manipulation whatsoever!

Integrated Ascension

Upon the outer world, many an unscrupulous scientist, usually in collusion with even more unscrupulous governmental matters, are experimenting with the use of thought or mind control. This is being done by artificial means, such as the use of mind-altering drugs, brain stimulation, and programming. All this, beloved readers, is just the tip of the iceberg. The power of the mind is vast, and I mention the above so that you can see that it is recognized to be so by those who are negative ego based as well as those who are functioning from the Christ consciousness.

It is vital that we become integrated within our own mental sphere and centered within our own Christ consciousness so that we eventually become impervious to any sort of thought manipulation whatsoever. The hype that we are given through media in general: television, radio, magazines, billboards, are all in actuality attempts at controlling our own thoughtforms by superimposing the thoughtform of another vision over our own. We must be clear as to our own intent at all times. We must learn how to mentally not buy what others are trying to sell if it is not for our highest good. This applies to all walks of life and to every possible arena of activity that you can think of!

Beloved Master Djwhal Khul gives us the best formula on how to do this in his writing through Alice A. Bailey when he simply states, "Hold the mind steady in the light." In these few words is the mystery of thoughtform projection utterly revealed! These words, beloved readers, were not given forth lightly, nor are they to be lost amidst their simple poetic imagery. They truly contain a formula, which, if vigilantly adhered to will keep all of us safe against the myriad of thought formations bombarding us daily and enable us to function freely within the realm of mind and to do the work that we came here to do.

This is why I so adamantly stress the importance of Integrated Ascension. This, of course, includes the full integration of the psychological self, for it is here where we are most vulnerable to the lower aspects of ourselves and others, unless we have done the necessary work. I ask you to do that work, beloved readers, that it may be said of you that you are one who upholds Christ consciousness at all times, and walks safely and empowered amidst the miasma of the world of thoughtforms, and there stands forth an integrated Master in service to GOD and the Divine plan!

Lower Psychisim

One of the pitfalls of non-integrated development and unintegrated ascension is that of lower psychisim. This is the experience of opening exclusively to the astral realms and pulling through information that may or may not be accurate. The information will, however, always stay below the threshold of the Higher Self, and even that of the mental realm, and so it will be very jumbled impressions that arise from the pool of emotional confusion.

Some of these readings may be more or less accurate, particularly when there is a very close emotional tie between two people, such as that between parent and child, or two lovers. If one is in danger, or in harm's way of any kind, the other person might very well sense this. For the less evolved masses, this will be sensed via the solar plexus region and is quite appropriate. Initiates should try to raise their frequencies to that of the heart, the heart/mind, the oversoul, and ultimately the Mighty I Am Presence. It all depends where one is upon the ladder of evolution.

The center where lower psychisim is activated, that of the solar plexus, is more or less instinctive in nature. Animals have been known to demonstrate this type of awareness at times. A well-loved animal member of a household can often sense when its human "parent" or "sibling" is in jeopardy. There have been many recorded instances of this type of "sensing" as the animal will act upon this knowing to the point of even saving the person's life. With regard to the animal involved, this marks a great stride in the animal's evolution, for it is demonstrating a deep and profound sense of love, loyalty, and bonding.

When we as lightworkers operate out of the solar plexus or instinctive nature, however, the inverse is true. We should ideally be bonded with one another in the feeling world through the heart chakra, which is based upon the spiritualization and deeper meaning of love. This is not to say that our emotions should not come into play. As I have stated elsewhere in this book, all levels of our being deserve the appropriate attention and expression. What I am saying is that our highest bonding should be from the heart center, and this center should ideally be the emotional base from which we operate. This raises us into the realm of intuition, which is where we as lightworkers belong, and helps us to avoid the rampant confusion that is often experienced when lower psychisim is in operation.

In bringing to your attention the dangers of an unintegrated approach to clairvoyance, clairaudience and channeling, lower psychisim cannot be overlooked, as it is itself a by-product of fragmented integration. Unless all the chakras, centers, initiations and eight major quotients as a whole are brought into alignment and balance, one can fall victim to functioning out of an inappropriate center for their point in evolution. This, my beloved readers, is the primary danger involved with lower psychisim.

Since this type of sense stems from the solar plexus, it indicates that one has not integrated their other centers and initiation levels. This then leaves the person open to all sorts of emotional impressions that they would not be open to if rightly functioning in an integrated manner, with the heart and head centers holding their appropriate place. The solar plexus and pure animal instinct does not know how to decipher truth from fiction, or fear from love. All it knows how to do is to simply react based upon the basest instinctual emotions, which are often fears that have no fact whatsoever in reality. These fears are felt, experienced, and acted upon nonetheless. They may even be believed in to such a strong degree that our very thought/feeling world will find a way to manifest them.

I know a case where a person went to consult with a psychic who made some sort of dire prediction. This prediction was simply based upon the psychic tapping into a primal fear of the person involved. This obviously made quite an impression upon that individual, as they literally breathed, ate, drank, and slept with that fear. When the psychic voiced it, that proved to be the ultimate confirmation! The specific case I am referring to has to do with a certain individual dying before a certain birthday. For whatever reason, the individual involved did not think he deserved to grace this planet past a certain age. The psychic picked this up via the solar plexus. When the astral body of the psychic and that of their client merged within this version of reality, something within the person made an inner commitment to make this a literal fact.

The truth of the matter is this was not at all founded in fact, but in fear. For several years the person cultivated and lived with this fear. Physical symptoms worsened as the predicted year of his demise encroached upon him. In this case, it was quite fortunate that the spouse of the individual had no belief in this "spiritual babble" whatsoever. They would not help to feed it to their mate, although their mate did an excellent job of feeding it to his own sub-conscious mind. He did, in fact, grow very weak as the hour of his impending doom grew closer! The spouse, however, had other ideas. What she did, in this specific case, was to create a very large diversion that lasted through the night of her mates' supposed last day on Earth! This centered around a major marital difficulty, all made up, that their daughter was going through. I am happy to report that it worked. When the hour of death came and went and the person was still alive, he knew a freedom and joy that he had not know for ten solid years following the psychic's prediction. His health rapidly restored itself to normal, and his life from that point on was conducted in a normal and liberated manner.

Integrated Ascension

The havoc that was wrecked upon this individual due to the words spoken by someone, who, in truth, had no business speaking those words to them, cannot be denied. The years of joy wasted were truly a tragedy! This, my beloved readers, is one of the most disturbing cases of autosuggestion and lower psychisim that I have personally encountered. This occurred back when I was a teenager and not so well aware of all the implications involved. I do, however, recall most vividly the torture that this poor man lived with for ten years, as well as his liberation when he passed through the jaws of death unscathed! It was enough to make a lasting impression upon me, and likewise serves to highlight the dangers involved in partial understanding of matters involving spirit and the absolute danger of fragmented ascension.

This bears witness to the responsibilities we each hold as lightworkers to live up to the highest standard possible. We are here to help people, and where we are not 100% clear that we are able to guide them in the right direction, then we had best keep silent. If we have not fully integrated all the various aspects of our own initiations and higher quotients within the totality of our Being, then that is what we should attend to. As beloved Paramahansa Yogananda says, "The path to GOD is not a circus." The realm of lower psychisim can be quite a circus, complete with lions and tigers and bears, and anything else that the human mind or emotions can conjure up. This is a realm to be avoided at all costs.

Beloved readers, it is really a very simple matter to avoid this realm, and that is by being focused within the heart, mind, and spirit! When you are operating out of the heart/mind/spirit center, then you are operating from the place where truth stands revealed. There is actually an eye within the awakened heart and a heart within the awakened inner eye. If you therefore stay focused in the heart, you will also be able to truly see beyond the psychic confusion of jumbled emotions. You will be able to tell the real from the imagined and to guide people in the healthiest directions.

Integrated Ascension

If you ever do have a premonition of impending doom, check that impression out within the heart, or higher intuitive body. The heart will check it out with the awakened eye. Lift the feeling into the oversoul and Monad and see what you get from your own GOD Source. Talk to the Masters. Under no circumstances blurt out anything of a negative nature as a *fait accompli*. "All prophesy, whether of a personal or planetary nature are given us so that we can change it!" There is so much mass confusion in regards to the New Age in general, not to mention the part each of us is called to individually fulfill within the bringing forth of the new millennium. We certainly do not want to add to this!

The Many, Many Prophesies!

The truth is that we are indeed living in times of mass transformation and change. We are all experiencing this individually and our planet is itself demonstrating this. Just how exactly this will manifest however, is not written in stone. Possibilities of how this might manifest are indeed carved within certain stones of antiquity, but the eventual outcome is a reality that shifts with each of us each and every day. We are the manifestation of prophesy, beloved readers, and the direction that transformation will ultimately take is based upon the road we individually and collectively walk!

There is obviously a momentous shift that is occurring, and we are all part of that shift. The movement into the seventh golden age is a great movement, and it is one that involves every single level of our many bodies, as well as the many bodies that comprise the various realms of our world. For this reason, this shift could literally be seen centuries ago. It likewise could be mathematically read, astrologically read and most certainly occultly envisioned. To the sages and prophets of antiquity, the coming of this new millennium has been no great secret, nor have the potential problems, shifts, and reconfigurations arising out of it. We are therefore able to consult with literature of centuries ago and see much of our present and future stand revealed. We do not, and I repeat, we do not, however, have the entire picture, for that is fluid and predicated upon what we have done and continue to do with the knowledge that we have from the past and the wisdom that is available to us on a daily basis. That is where you and I come in, for we are the future and shall create revelation according to how aligned we become with the Divine plan and how well we each fulfill our individual puzzle pieces and accept our highest calling.

It is true that certain events have been set in motion that will ultimately produce certain outcomes. Cause and effect is an exacting science, yet it is also a science that can be worked with. For example, if we know a certain cause will absolutely bring about a certain effect, there is still the power of prayer and invocation that can counter that effect, even after it has been set in motion. We can pray to learn by Grace rather than karma, and do all that we possibly can to alter any given effect by the power of prayer and the benediction of its ensuing Grace. I try to live my life in this manner, and to move through it moment by moment.

If we "transmute" the old by the power of Love, Light, Grace, and Divine intervention, Shiva may have little do to! "Why worry when you can pray." Why be idle when you can work to reconstruct and rebuild through Divine alchemy? Why be a doomsday junky when you can be a lightworker and a bridge to the next millennium?

It must also be continuously born in mind that books of prophecy are written on many levels simultaneously. They are not to be read purely on a literal physical plane level. Much of what is spoken about that will occur, is occurring now upon the astral and mental realms! I again remind you to take all the various bodies, both individually and on a planetary level into account. Some of what is written deals directly with the physical realm, and that only potentially. Some of this material was true in the past but is now completely outdated and inaccurate. Some of what is written is meant to apply to realms other than the physical. The ancient texts on this subject are quite intricate. They are, in fact, encoded writings of a most esoteric nature, and must be deciphered. They are not meant to be read like a novel or a book of fact. They are rather to be read like tablets concealing hidden truths and mysteries that require a great spiritual insight and GOD attunement to even begin to understand.

I am not attempting to decipher these most in-depth revelations here in this book, but to simply tell you that you yourself are an integral part of the revelation of the next millennium, including how it will outpicture upon Earth.

The bottom line in this regard is the same as that which we have been discussing all along. When shifts occur, whether of an inner or outer nature, you and I have the same ultimate place of stability and security, and that is within our own GOD Self! The more centered and balanced we are within our center, the less concerned we will be about what is transpiring. We will know beyond a shadow of a doubt that all that needs to be cleansed, cleared, and purified is being taken care of. We will trust in our attunement and have the high levels within the eight major quotients that will see us through anything.

The truth is that we will also have the ability to attune to the Tao of our own beings, and will find that we are in exactly the right place at the right time. Since we are here to help usher in the New Age, the place we find ourselves will be both for our own individual highest good and that which enables us to best serve the Divine Plan. So, rather than allow confusion to reign supreme in regard to the many various prophesies concurrent with this next millennium, let us focus upon doing the work of the moment.

Each step rightly taken along the way cannot but help to lead us down the pathway of our first best destiny. That path, my beloved readers, will serve us well! It will also keep us in the Divine flow so that we may each fulfill our part of the plan to our highest potential, which is all that is ever truly asked of us. Where there is surrender and attunement to the Tao, there is no conflict, only joy, light, love, harmony, and the freedom to serve!

The Need to Hold On To Your Own "Personal Power"

There is one point that cannot be overstated enough, and that is to never give your power away to any external channel! I don't care how highly evolved they are, what level of initiation they are at, or even how integrated they are in the process. Your personal power should remain under your own control at all times. That is one of GOD's precious gifts to you, and along with Love and Light form the three major aspects by which we each can most fully express our own GOD-Beingness.

There is something vital for each of your to understand, and that is that the Higher Self, Monad, the Hierarchy of Inner Plane Planetary and Cosmic Ascended Beings and the voice of GOD Itself speaks uniquely to and through each and every one of us. No matter how aligned we may be with one another, we each have our own stamp of individuality. This individual essence has its own distinctive way of perceiving that which is true, its own way of hearing, sensing, feeling, seeing and knowing.

As I said before, we each have our own unique frequencies, sound, our own unique tone, and our own specialized coloring. This is based upon the many and varied influences that make us up, which have been addressed in great detail elsewhere. It therefore follows, that when GOD or the Masters seek to commune with us, it will come through each and every one of us in line with our own frequency and vibrational range, tone and unique colors of the spectrum. It could not be otherwise, as this is the lens through which we see, and the vehicle by which we hear and contribute to the great cosmic symphony. As Source wants us to know truth directly, it makes perfect sense that it will commune with us in our own sacred language.

Integrated Ascension

If, in the process of obtaining information from an external channel, clairaudient or clairvoyant, you do not hold on to your own sense of personal power, you are in truth giving up your ability to take that information and commune with your own Higher Self and Monad about it. This can be quite dangerous for several reasons. First, the one thing that I advise most adamantly, is to never ever simply believe or buy into a statement just because that statement is coming from a clairvoyant, telepath, book, article, channel, teacher, etc., that you may respect. I advise this with my own books and teachings as well. I ask that you consider all that is given forth with an open mind, especially if you are consulting with someone you do in fact respect. Ultimately, however, the information has to resonate as correct and in harmony with your own Divine Self. If you simply believe it because someone has said it is channeled, or such and such a Master is telling you this and you do not attune to whether it is right and correct for you, then you are giving away your personal power and opening yourself up to be controlled by someone else.

Please do not do this, beloved readers, for you deserve much more! You deserve your own right of discernment, free will and integrity. You also deserve the right to hear GOD speak in your own voice and to commune with you in a direct manner. Even if you are at the stage where that communion is a simple feeling of "yes" or "no" to what is being said to you through an external medium, it is your Divine birthright to claim that communion. I ask you to do this, because no one can speak to you more clearly or intimately than your own Higher Self and Mighty I Am Presence! Do not give that power or right away to anyone outside of self. That is yours and yours alone!

Secondarily, if you do want to embrace your path of initiation in a balanced and integrated manner, it is vital that you own and cultivate your personal power. Personal power is an integral part of integration, for without this aspect under your own control, you will not have the force, will and strength necessary to hold all aspects of your ascension

Integrated Ascension

within the field of integration. In fact, this is one of the primary functions that personal power has to play within your evolution as a whole. With the deluge of channels and other clairvoyants, as well as the abundance of information that is now coming through via tapes. literature, lectures, and so forth, this gives you the perfect opportunity to practice holding firm to your personal power and center.

As I said before, it does not exclude in any way, shape or form being open to the wonderful and revelatory information that is being brought through by GOD-attuned channels. It does, however, ultimately throw you back upon yourself to discern what is and what is not in harmony with your own inner guidance. You must ultimately commune with self, for even if what is being given forth rings absolutely true, it is via your own GOD-attunement that you will ultimately be enabled to fully assimilate it within the totality of your own unique individuality.

The importance of personal power, however, cannot be over emphasized. I therefore caution you to proceed from that center of self, correcting yourself the moment you get off course. When you move outward from that center of personal power, you will know clarity and a strength that you have never known before!

As you begin to operate more and more from your own sense of personal power, your ability to commune with GOD and the Masters will likewise grow. Each of us has different puzzle pieces, so please don't assume that you will channel or be clairvoyant if that is not your particular mission. You will, however, develop your own unique telepathic and intuitive rapport with the Masters, Angelic Hierarchies, your Higher Self, your Mighty I Am Presence and GOD, and that is, in truth, what we are seeking.

It might very well be that your particular puzzle piece is in the realm of the visual arts. Your abilities will then flourish in that regard and you will find that you are painting or sculpting that which is representative of the higher realms. You may do it through musical composition or song. You might just as easily find that you tap into the essence of El

Integrated Ascension

Morya, and find yourself in the political arena, acting as a beacon of love, light, and wisdom within this most delicate and difficult aspect of civilization. The permutations of how you will express your own attunement with Source are endless. The one thing that remains a constant is that the attunement will ultimately be a direct hook-up and link between you, the Masters, and Source. This is only possible when you fully claim and hold on to your sacred place of personal power!

I have written much on the subject of personal power, and therefore am seeking here to simply help you become aware that it plays a distinctive and vital role in Integrated Ascension. It likewise serves as a protection against lack of discrimination when exploring in the teaching of others. There are a great number of wonderful resources for new insights, revelations, guidance, information, and introspection out there that we all can benefit from greatly. The essential point that I am making within this context is to do this without relinquishing your own personal power. This is essential. In fact, the arena of spiritual exploration can provide you with excellent opportunities to learn from others while at the same time strengthen your own inner source of power.

This, my beloved readers, would be the best approach to take, for you would be growing on two levels simultaneously. The first would be that of the wisdom gained through your spiritual exploration and the second would be the wisdom and strength garnered by claiming your personal power. I would recommend this highly, for in truth you would be growing by leaps and bounds, while at the same time learning how to integrate all within the sacredness of self! This would make for a wonderful journey through the world of the inner senses and take you straight into the heart of self-mastery! Go for it, with joy!

10

Dr. Lorphan's Healing Academy on Sirius

My beloved readers, it brings me great joy to begin this particular chapter. It is a common belief among many lightworkers not to value the physical body as much as the emotional, mental and spiritual bodies. It is very important for lightworkers to understand that the physical body is one of GOD's bodies as well. Everyone on the spiritual path has to deal with health lessons in one form or another. No one escapes this. Some people's physical bodies may be weaker than others, however, other people may have weaker emotional bodies, mental bodies, spiritual bodies or psychological selves. Everyone who is on an accelerated spiritual path will have physical health lessons to contend with. This is not necessarily from being sick or ill or from doing anything wrong, but from the accelerated speed of growth in the spiritual vehicle, mental vehicle, emotional vehicle, and the etheric vehicle. Every time these bodies take a leap in spiritual evolution, the physical body must catch up in vibration. I'm reminded of an incident at one of the Wesak Celebrations where Sai Baba and the Ascended Masters were giving a shaktipat through me as I touched people's third eye with Sai Baba's amrita or Divine nectar. I did this for three or four hundred people, which served to increase their vibrational frequencies. A couple of hours later, one woman reported that after she received the shaktipat from Sai Baba that she lost the vision in one of her eyes, partially. This again was just a quantum leap in the octave of light she was holding, which the physical vehicle was trying to catch up with. I called in the Ascended Masters to help in the situation, her physical eye lesson quickly recovered, and she was fine. I share this story to only point out how even people in perfect health on a physical level are going to have health lessons from accelerated spiritual growth. When planetary spiritual energies are pouring in, many lightworkers get wiped out for many days. This would be another example.

Other lightworkers might have physical health problems from doing too much meditation, or too many ascension activations. Other lightworkers develop physical health problems because of emotional lessons that are going on in their subconscious mind. Other lightworkers may develop health lessons from doing too much mental or spiritual work. Other lightworkers still develop health lessons from being too heavenly and hence not being physically grounded enough. One of the main points I'm making here is that physical health lessons are not bad. They are part and parcel of the spiritual path. Often lightworkers are very judgmental and self righteous when dealing with people who have health lessons often making the person feel bad by intonating that the person is doing something wrong and that they should figure out the cause immediately.

I'm here to tell you, my beloved readers, that their physical health lessons may be a sign that they're doing something right. It just may be a sign that they are growing spiritually at a very accelerated rate. It may also be a sign that they are doing a cleansing to reach a more purified level of GOD Realization. If they weren't focused on their spiritual life this may not even be happening. They also might be cleansing planetary karma as an act of service on some level. It might be a past life cleansing or cleansing an integration of a soul extension from one's Oversoul and Monad.

Integrated Ascension

Other lightworkers may be given health lessons by GOD to balance certain past karma and it is not because they are doing anything wrong in this lifetime. So, my friends, the possibilities are endless and there is not one of us on the planet that does not live by the axiom "But by the Grace of GOD go I." We all need to be much more compassionate and understanding with our fellow brothers and sisters who are dealing with physical health lessons.

As we evolve spiritually, we also take on spiritual leadership and much greater responsibility. We also take on great responsibility for many students and clients. All these things can take a toll on the physical vehicle no matter how evolved you are. The physical vehicle reflects every thought we think, every emotion we feel, every energy we channel, the food we eat, and every action we take. The more evolved we become the quicker our karma. The more evolved we become the more refined and sensitive our vehicles become.

Living in a dense, unrefined world doing service work will put stress on the physical vehicle no matter what level of initiation. I have just been speaking here of all the spiritual reasons why the physical body has ailments. I have not even begun to get into all the physical reasons why the physical body breaks down such as diet, accidents, pollution, lack of physical exercise, bacteria, viruses, poor sleep habits, job stress, relationship stress, weakened physical immune systems, digestive problems, and genetic inherited weakness. The list is endless.

Let me end this section by saying again that we all be very compassionate to others and ourselves. When we are going through health lessons it is common for lightworkers to think that we are the only ones. I am here to tell you that is not true. All lightworkers have to confront physical health lessons for it is just the nature of living in this planetary mystery school called Earth and inhabiting physical vehicles. Let us also remember the Biblical quotation, "After pride cometh the fall." I can't help but remember a channeling that Edgar Cayce gave to a gentleman who I believe was paralyzed. In the reading he was told that his physical ailment stemmed from a past life where he had an Adonis type of physical body and he used to criticize others for not being as healthy and handsome as he was. This should give us all pause to think and to ignite the compassion of Lord Buddha and Quan Yin.

Personal Sharing

My beloved readers, I have had my share of health lessons as well and because the traditional medical establishment I found to be a waste of time for me personally I explored the more holistic, naturopathic, homeopathic, New Age forms of physical healing as I'm sure all of you have as well. I want to be clear here that I'm not putting down traditional medicine, for it definitely has its place. I am just saying for me, personally, and the very subtle subclinical and spiritually induced physical lessons I was dealing with, traditional medicine was a total waste of time and money. It all depends on what kind of physical health lessons you're dealing with. My entire four-body system being so refined and purified that the taking of any drugs or invasive tests would be totally poisonous to me. As one medical doctor said to me, "You slipped through the cracks of Western medicine." I was dealing with such a level of spiritual subtlety that they didn't have a clue what to do with my particular health lessons at the time.

I found the entire holistic, naturopathic, homeopathic and New Age forms of healing and medicine to be fascinating and spent many years of my life cleansing residual toxins of the most refined nature. Things such as mercury fillings, vaccines, past antibiotics, metals, chemicals, parasites, vaccines, fungus, environmental toxins, past drugs used for healing, any mind altering drugs, disease toxins on a subclinical level (tuberculosis, cancer, Epstein-Barr, hepatitis are a few examples), caffeine, nicotine, lead (from paint), aluminum toxicity (from aluminum cookware), copper toxicity (copper pipes), radiation (too close to color T.V. and microwave), low grade electromagnetic disturbances (from all the electrical equipment in the home), alcohol, preservatives and toxins from poor diet, and/or junk food to name a few. What I would recommend is finding a good New Age homeopathic practitioner and bring in this list and tell him or her that you want to cleanse all these things from your system. If you can't afford to do this, or you can't find one, then go to your nearest homeopathic pharmacy and they can recommend certain generic homeopathics that help cleanse these residual toxins from the organs, glands, and blood.

Doing this cleansing of these residual toxins will do wonders for upgrading your immune system and increasing your vitality and overall health and energy. I also recommend taking homeopathics specifically for immune system building and organ cleansing. For greater emotional balance, I would recommend exploring Bach Flower Remedies taken in homeopathic form. For more information on this, I would recommend reading my book *How to Clear the Negative Ego*. Just as one wants to remove the mental toxin of negative ego from the mental body, one also wants to remove emotional toxins in the form of negative emotions from the emotional vehicle. One also wants to remove energetic toxins from the etheric vehicle. One also wants to remove physical toxins from the physical vehicle.

There are many New Age cutting-edge technologies for detecting these subtle toxins that have remained lodged in our organs and cells since childhood. The cleansing of all these residual toxins using homeopathics and herbs was a very spiritual experience for I felt like I was spiritualizing my physical vehicle to a very great extent. This also went along with eating an extremely pure diet. I do not recommend that people become fanatical on this level, however, for me personally, because of my unique lessons and path, it was essential that I be very disciplined in this area. The combination of removing all the residual toxins and eating such a pure diet has kept my immune system working at a very good level. Taking the time to spiritualize the physical vehicle in this manner is well worth one's time, energy, and even financial investment.

Integrated Ascension

One thing I have learned in my life is that if the physical vehicle is not supporting me, it is very difficult to do all the spiritual and service work that I love to do. So, again, it is important to pay one's "rent" to GOD on all levels (physical, etheric, emotional, mental and spiritual). The physical body is as much GOD as is the spiritual body. All faces of GOD must be honored and sanctified.

The Continuing Journey

As time went on in my evolutionary journey of initiation and ascension I began moving more and more away from physical forms of healing, and physical cures and began relying much more on Spirit and energetic cures. Now I want to say here that I am not recommending my particular path to you, my beloved readers. I feel the best path for most people is the balanced, integrated path. There is a time for Western medicine, a time for holistic New Age medicine, and there is a time to rely on Spirit and the Ascended Masters for help. Because of my incredibly refined and purified nature, system and mission, and incredibly subtle health lessons that were more energetic and electrical in nature, at one point in my life I stopped even taking herbs, homeopathics, vitamins and going to traditional medical and holistic New Age practitioners completely. I was so purified on those levels that it was a waste of time and my body no longer wanted to take any kind of physical substance of that kind. Again I emphasize I am not recommending this to other people, but for me personally it was the 100% right path.

I began relying much more on radionics which is the science of sending energy to my self from those substances such as homeopathics and herbs rather than taking the physical form itself. For me personally this worked much better and I found it to be much more effective. I went through a phase of getting laying on of hands treatments which for a period of my life was extremely helpful but eventually even that level became too gross for me. Now, my beloved readers, this whole process worked in conjunction with my initiation process. The higher I went in my initiation process and the more light I was carrying electrically, the more I relied on Spirit for all my physical healing. This process also correlated with eating less and less amounts of food. At this stage of my life, I still eat food in small amounts; however, in truth I am 90% now living on light. The amount of food I eat is so minute no third dimensional person would think that one could survive. Again, I do not recommend this to my readers except in extremely rare cases for I think it is much better that people be balanced on all levels and eat normally. For me personally, because of my unique health lessons and mission this was the 100% right path for me to follow. I also have done this very slowly over many years and have waited to live on light predominately until almost my twelfth initiation. So I do not recommend stopping eating 'cold turkey' for there are a handful of people on this planet that this is their destiny and not eating very physical food and living mostly on light seems to be my destiny. To be honest this is not something that I necessarily want to do it is just something that just progressed in this direction because of my unique health lessons, mission and destiny. I will say here that I feel stronger physically on this path than I did eating a normal diet and that is why I'm on this path. I also asked Melchizedek, the Mahatma, and Metatron to program my twelve-body system through certain fire letters, sacred geometries, and geometrical codes so I wouldn't lose weight. Although I still do eat some food and plan to continue this small amount of eating the rest of this incarnation, I am not losing weight. The light is somehow being transformed into physical mass.

The Healing Academy of Dr. Lorphan

At this stage of my life, having taken the twelfth initiation, I completely rely on Spirit, Melchizedek, the Mahatma, Metatron, Dr.

Integrated Ascension

Lorphan, the Galactic Healers, Sai Baba, Archangel Raphael, the Platinum Angels, Sananda, Djwhal Khul, a group of Masters called the Core 7, the Lord of Arcturus, my Monad or Mighty I Am Presence, the Divine Mother and Lady Masters, the 7 Chohans and the Core 21 for all my healing needs.

    Let me begin by introducing Dr. Lorphan, who is my doctor. So, my beloved readers, I still have a doctor and the humorous thing about it is that he doesn't live on Earth, he lives in the Great White Lodge on Sirius. He is the finest doctor in the entire galaxy and he is the director and head trainer of all the healers in the Great White Lodge on Sirius. This is not the physical planet of Sirius but rather the etheric spiritual capitol of our planet, which Shamballa is an outpost for. Masters travel throughout the galaxy to train with him and his wonderful staff of galactic healers. My beloved readers, I am introducing him and his staff to you now so he may become your doctor as well. I recommend that you keep your traditional earthly physician, and New Age holistic practitioners, and now add Dr. Lorphan and his team of galactic healers to your team healing approach. Although I only rely on Spirit, I want you, my beloved readers, to take advantage of all levels of healing support that are available to you. This is important in the concept of Integrated Ascension and synthesis, which my work is totally based upon. My unique mission to rely completely on Spirit allows me to bring this level of physical healing to you, my beloved readers, in a most unique and creative fashion. Because I rely so completely on Spirit for my physical health I am uniquely qualified to bring through this information for it is my personal experience. Maybe GOD has chosen this path for me for just this purpose. Most lightworkers don't realize the amount of help Spirit can provide even dealing with the dense physical vehicle. Remember that everything in the universe is just energy at different octaves of density. A dense ice cube when placed on the hot pavement melts into water and then steam. Spirit is like steam and the physical body is like the ice cube. All are just energy. The inner plane Ascended Masters are masters of energy transformation.

Healing Tools of Dr. Lorphan and His Healing Team

Let me begin by saying that Dr. Lorphan has asked me to write this chapter to let each of you know personally that he and his staff are willing to help any sincere lightworker with any and all physical health lessons that you are dealing with. The same offer applies to all the Ascended Masters who are also incredible healers themselves. I personally use both Dr. Lorphan and his healing staff and many of the Ascended Masters who you are familiar with. I also call on the Archangels and Angels as well and certain extraterrestrial groups who have certain advanced technologies in this regard. On this note let me begin by describing some of the spiritual healing tools I use which I share for the sole purpose of making them available to you, my beloved readers. I am purposely describing these tools in a very succinct and concise manner to make them easy to access and apply. In the following chapter, I will take more time to elaborate in more detail upon some of the more important ones. The purpose of this chapter is to just make them available to you in the most efficient, concise, practical way possible. On this note, I will now unfold the revelation of these most Divine spiritual healing tools.

The first tool I use is actually one of Melchizedek's, the Mahatma's, and Metatron's. It is called the Golden and/or Platinum Net. It is a net that you can call forth from Spirit that filters and strains out any imbalanced or negative energy. I would recommend that you request this at least twice a day. I would also recommend that you ask that the Platinum Net be placed in all the doorways and archways in your home on a permanent basis. This way every time you walk through an archway or a doorway you are automatically cleansed. Ask for this for your family in terms of the Platinum and Golden Net and your pets. It will also serve to clear negative implants and elementals. Also ask the 3 M's to bring forth the Platinum Net four times a day (morning, noon, early evening and before bed) every day without even having to ask. These beloved Masters will do this for you if you ask them to. Their love and compassion is unfathomable, as is their dedication to service.

Whenever you are sick or someone in your family is sick ask for a screen of protection so that their bacteria or virus cannot enter your field.

Whenever you sense any kind of bacteria on a subclinical or clinical level enter any of your subtle bodies call the three M's (Melchizedek, the Mahatma and Metatron) and Dr. Lorphan and his healing staff and call forth the Cosmic Bacterial Vacuum. These Masters will actually suck the bacteria out of your field like a vacuum cleaner.

Whenever you sense viral energy in your subtle or physical vehicle on a subclinical or clinical level call forth from the 3 M's, Dr. Lorphan and his healing staff to bring forth the Cosmic Viral Vacuum. This again will suck out the viral energy like a vacuum. Trust me, my beloved readers, it really does work. You still must be obedient to the other levels of Divinity and GOD's laws on those levels, however this process will lend tremendous support.

Call to the etheric healers for help in repairing your etheric vehicle. The etheric body can be damaged from past lives and/or past trauma in this life. Your etheric body is your blueprint body that your physical body works off of. If it is damaged, your physical body will never recover. This is easily remedied by asking the etheric healers to repair it.

Call to the Ascended Masters of your choice, and also ask that your monadic blueprint body be permanently anchored into your field as well as your mayavarupa body which are your higher perfect blueprint bodies. This will greatly accelerate physical healing.

Call to the 3 M's or any other Cosmic Masters of your choice to permanently anchor their energy through you 24 hours a day, 7 days a week, 365 days a year. This is what I have done with the 3 M's and this

Integrated Ascension

is the food that sustains my physical vehicle to a large extent. It can be yours as well for the asking. The law of the universe is you must ask, for these great and noble Masters are not allowed to give you these blessings without your request for they are not allowed to interfere with your free choice. My job, my beloved readers, is to humbly guide you what to ask for and the blessings of the cosmos shall be yours as long as you are sincere in your efforts to serve GOD and your brothers and sisters in Christ.

I have also asked the 3 M's to provide vitamins and minerals in the 3 M's cosmic light that they are constantly downpouring. I think this is part of the reason why I feel so sustained by the light. The color of the energy from Melchizedek is the highest purity of gold. The color of the energy from Metatron is platinum. The color of the energy from the Mahatma is rainbow white light. My beloved readers, do you see all the vitamins and minerals in this energy?

I've also asked the 3 M's to program my gematrian body and entire twelve body system with the fire letters, key codes and sacred geometries to partially live on light. So, the ideal here is to live on food but also to live on light.

If you want to gain weight, request to the 3 M's and Dr. Lorphan to program those fire letters, key codes and sacred geometries. If you want to lose weight, make the same prayer except in reverse.

If you have an area in your physical and etheric body that is especially weak call to Metatron and the Platinum Angels or Golden Angels to 24 hours a day, 7 days a week, 365 days a year live in that area. For example, I often get strained vocal chords from all the talking, counseling, lecturing, and phone calls. The Platinum Angels live in my vocal chords and throat lining to keep it soothed and also to keep any negative bacteria out for any place there is a weakness in the body bacteria and viruses tend to take hold. This can be easily remedied with this spiritual healing tool. I have the Platinum Angels now also living in my digestive system and have invited them into my entire body. The color of platinum is the highest frequency color available to Earth. The only frequency higher is the energy of GOD at the 352nd level of Divinity, which has no color.

For really tough health lessons, I would recommend calling forth the inner plane acupuncture team under the directorship of Dr. Lorphan. Share with them your physical health concern and they will place etheric needles in your etheric body which you will not even be aware of which will greatly activate the chi in your system in those areas needed.

When you feel your whole system being energetically clogged or just having too much cloudy astral, etheric and mental energy call forth the prana wind clearing device from the Lord of Arcturus. This beloved Master will anchor this etheric fan into your third chakra, which will blow out all the energy through all your nadis, meridians, veins, and arteries. Try it, it will do you wonders.

When you are fatigued, I recommend calling forth to the Lord of Arcturus who will use the advanced technology on his mother ship to revitalize and energize your system if you ask him to. It is better than a cup of coffee and you don't fill your physical vehicle with the two hundred known toxins that coffee contains. Try not to rely on artificial stimulants. Why use artificial stimulants when GOD and the GOD Force can be your source of energy?

When you are overworked and your energies are all out of balance and too top heavy I like to call the Lord of Arcturus and the Arcturian temple workers to balance my meridians. You will feel an immediate rush of energy through your meridian system.

Another wonderful Master to call on that specializes in healing is Archangel Raphael and his Healing Angels. Certain angels are given certain assignments in GOD's Kingdom. Archangel Raphael was created by GOD to do physical healing. Call on him and his Healing Angels whatever the health lesson.

Two other Masters that are incredibly proficient in healing are His Holiness the Lord Sai Baba and Sananda. Sai Baba, being an incarnated

Integrated Ascension

universal avatar, has enormous shakti and being omnipotent, omniscient and omnipresent can help with any problem you have, including physical ones. Sananda I have found to be an extremely effective healer as well. Sometimes I like to call on other Masters for healing just as a change of pace and to also merge and attune with their energies. These two Masters would definitely reside in this category.

One of the most effective healers of all which lightworkers forget to call on is their own Monad and/or Mighty I Am Presence. Who knows your body better than your own Monad, and who has more motivation to help heal it than your Monad who is your true self? Call on your Monad for help in this area and you will be amazed at the energetic support that it can provide.

Call to the 3 M's, Dr. Lorphan and the Galactic Healers once a week for an implant and negative elemental removal of all these imbalanced energies from all your subtle bodies. It is really as simple as just asking.

Clairvoyantly and/or intuitively I have often sensed certain crystallization developing in some of my joints on a very subclinical, etheric level. This sometimes develops from too much time spent doing office work, typing, computer work, and the like. I have asked my dear friend the Lord of Arcturus to keep this crystallization removed from my system at night while I sleep whenever I need it. He has graciously agreed to perform this service for me.

Whenever you are feeling out of balance emotionally and even mentally call to Dr. Lorphan and the Galactic Healers to rebalance your emotional and mental bodies which will also aid in the healing of your physical body.

Before starting your work each day be it counseling, typing, computer work, desk work, driving a truck, piloting a plane, administering to patients, call in the 3 M's and/or the inner plane Ascended Masters of your choice to run their energies through you throughout the day. I do this religiously and I find my stamina and energy level is literally increased one hundred fold and I find that my physical vehicle has a hundred times more durability. The idea is to run GOD and the GOD Force's energy while you work and not your own. Why use your battery when you can use GOD's battery?

When you have very serious or stubborn health lessons, sometimes one Master is not enough. At these times, I call on a whole group of Masters to work on me simultaneously. This might be, in my case, the entire Core 21, which are the council of Masters I work with. A subgroup of this is the Core 7. Another sub-group is the Divine Mother and the Lady Masters, who are wonderful healers and bring forth a feminine healing that is so often needed. I also call on the 7 Chohans who work extremely effectively as a unit. Try this particular spiritual healing tool when your health lessons are very stubborn.

In certain rare instances when great planetary world service is involved and I haven't been feeling well physically the 3 M's have actually completely stepped in and taken over my body in a way that I can only describe as how Lazarus must have felt when Jesus and Lord Maitreya raised him from the dead. In certain instances of great spiritual planetary importance, I have been amazed by the incredible healing abilities that they have at their disposal. From not feeling well, I felt instantly healed to do the planetary world service work that I needed to do.

For those of you who have a special attunement to Djwhal Khul as I do, Djwhal can be very helpful at times with certain health lessons. What I do is ask him to hook me up to his holographic computer in his office in his Ashram on the inner plane and through this most advanced holographic computer he can make very minute and finite energy corrections to balance the energy fields.

Another request I often make in a similar vein to Dr. Lorphan and the Galactic Healers and to the Lord of Arcturus and his Arcturian helpers is a request to just rebalance my energy fields.

I also take advantage of all the services of these most wonderful healers at night while I sleep. If there is an area in my physical etheric body that is a little electrically weak, I request before bed that for example the Lord of Arcturus run his Arcturian mother ship computerized energy all night long to strengthen that area. I find this to be extremely effective. The Arcturians have said that there is no physical health problem that they could not help to heal over time.

One other Arcturian tool for physical healing is to ask to be taken to the mechanism chamber in one's soul body at night while one sleeps in a bi-location type of sense. The mechanism chamber is specially constructed to work on physical health lessons.

Another very important spiritual healing tool is to call to Dr. Lorphan and the Galactic Healers to heal up any leaks, spots, tears, and/or irritations in the aura and in all five bodies (physical, etheric, astral, mental and spiritual). This tool is extremely important because any tears or holes in the aura will cause a leakage of energy almost like bleeding in a physical body, but this type of bleeding can occur on a etheric, astral and mental level.

Another preventative tool which probably is worth while to everyone to use every once in a while is to have Dr. Lorphan, the Lord of Arcturus and the Galactic Healers remove any cancerous energy that is starting to develop in any of the subtle bodies or in the physical body. These energies always begin in the subtle bodies and then move to the physical. This type of prayer request nips this in the bud.

Another very helpful spiritual healing tool for keeping the physical body in good working order is to request each day for Dr. Lorphan and the Galactic Healers to balance your chakras. This will keep your glandular system functioning properly as well as your organs.

If ever you are physically sick with some kind of immune system process, call to Dr. Lorphan and the Galactic Healers to give you etheric vitamin C shots. Remember, my friends and beloved readers, everything is just energy.

One other extremely important healing tool is to call forth to the 3 M's and Dr. Lorphan to clear your genetic line of all imbalanced energies. My beloved readers, we do not have to be a victim of anything in life and that includes our genetic heritage.

Call to Dr. Lorphan and the healing group to clear from your four-body system all etheric disease, astral disease, mental disease, spiritual disease and lastly physical disease. "Ask and you shall receive, knock and the door shall be opened."

Call to the Ascended Masters of your choosing as well as to Dr. Lorphan and his healing group to bring forth the Core Fear Matrix Removal Program and to pull out of your subconscious mind all thoughtforms, images and negative feelings connected with poor health. After letting the Masters work on you for 15 to 20 minutes with this process then request that they place into your subconscious mind thoughtforms, feelings, images and attributes of perfect health in every aspect of your physical body.

Another extremely helpful spiritual healing tool if you have a weak organ or area of your body, is to request from the 3 M's or any Cosmic Master of your choosing, to place a permanent energy beam from them to the particular spot in your physical body that is weak. Once this area of your body is healed and strengthened this energy beam can be removed or placed in a different area of your body.

One other very unique spiritual healing tool is to call to one of the Masters you are most connected with and request that he or she imprint their etheric body onto your physical body in a type of energetic telepathic battery hook up. I did this with Sai Baba at a time when I had a weakness in certain areas of my physical vehicle. My sense was this definitely gave me added energy and power source to those slightly weakened areas.

Earlier I suggested calling to the etheric team to repair the etheric body. Also, call to Dr. Lorphan and the Galactic Healers to repair any damage from past lives or this life to your astral and mental bodies. This will greatly strengthen your etheric physical vehicle as well.

Integrated Ascension

If you are aware of any residual physical toxins in your body that need cleansing you can call to the Lord of Arcturus and his Arcturian helpers to cleanse those toxins with help from the Arcturian technology. An example of this that I used one time was I was eating a lot of vegetables, however the vegetables I had bought were not organic and I could tell there were a lot of pesticides on them. I asked the Masters about the pesticide level in my body and they said it was too high. I asked the Lord of Arcturus about bringing that level down and about cleansing those particular toxins. He graciously agreed to help me do this. I also facilitated this process by putting a particular homeopathic on my radionics machine that also helped. I would also recommend to you, my beloved readers, to take homeopathics or herbs specifically designed for this purpose. Go to your neighborhood homeopathic pharmacy and they can guide you to what homeopathic is best for that. Again working on both levels, spiritual and earthly, is the most effective method in all these tools. I use the example here of pesticides but you could apply the same concept and principle to removing mercury from your system from leaking mercury fillings, or even smog from living in a city. Be creative.

One other very effective spiritual healing tool for physical healing is to call to the Lord of Arcturus to anchor and activate his liquid crystals which serves to deactivate any imbalanced energy going on in the five body system (physical, etheric, astral, mental and spiritual). I personally find this tool to be extremely effective.

Call to the 3 M's and the Ascended Masters of your choice to make sure you are not taking on any physical health karma from your eleven other soul extensions from your Oversoul. Also, request that you not take on any physical health karma from the 144 soul extensions from your twelve Oversouls and/or Monad. Part of this process is also to affirm this in your own mind that you are not going to allow this to happen. This must be done on both levels to be effective.

The possibilities of requesting help from Dr. Lorphan, the Galactic Healers, Raphael, the Platinum and Golden Angels, the Lord of Arcturus and the Ascended Masters is infinite. The most important thing is to remember to pray and ask for help and to ask these Masters very specifically as to your health concerns. If you do not get the results you desire, keep asking. In my personal experience, I find each of these different Masters I talk about do healing in a different way. I call on different Masters for different physical symptoms for in the process of trial and error certain Masters are more effective than others in regards to certain health problems. If it's a very serious health crisis you must be realistic and not expect to be instantly cured. This can happen, however it is not the norm. Keep rotating and trying out different Masters and groups of Masters to see which ones are most effective for you. Your intuition will guide you in this process.

One of the nicest things about working with Dr. Lorphan, the Galactic Healers, the Ascended Masters, Angels, and Extraterrestrials for healing is that they are available 24 hours a day, seven days a week, 365 days a year. You do not have to make an appointment in advance and they don't charge any money. It is their honor to serve.

Short Cut

One of the short cuts in this process that I have worked out with the Masters is first to give them all a blank check open invitation to work on me 24 hours a day, 7 days a week, 365 days a year without me having to ask each time. I want to be clear about this that I still ask all the time, however they are constantly working on me without me having to ask as well which I really appreciate.

I've also worked out some codes with them, which I will share with you, my beloved readers, to make this process even easier. I don't like having to go through these long-winded prayers each time I want them to come in. So, I worked out a deal with each of the individual Masters

Integrated Ascension

for a short code word that calls them forth. For example, my code for the Lord of Arcturus is "Call Arc," then I state the place in my body that needs work. So, this would be "Call Arc vocal chords." So with all the Masters I just say the words call and then their name and then the body part and they instantly come in and begin working on it. To have a code like this is helpful, for sometimes I am standing in line at the bank or in the market or at a workshop and I just telepathically or whisper to myself saying those three words of the Masters name and the body part, and it's quick, easy and efficient. If you want to set this up with them, just tell them you want to set up a similar system to what Joshua has and they will happily oblige.

Summation

In conclusion I am sure you, my beloved readers, can feel the power and profundity of these spiritual healing tools for enhanced physical health. Again you must be obedient to GOD's laws on all levels and you can't expect to eat a terrible diet, get no exercise, allow your negative ego to run rampant and be filled with negative emotions and expect the Ascended Masters to keep you physically healthy. These spiritual healing tools only support the good works you are doing on these other levels. If you will do your part, GOD and the Masters will do theirs. These spiritual healing tools are available to everyone regardless of your level of initiation. Everyone is deserving no matter what you are doing on your spiritual path. All that is requested by the Masters is that you are consciously moving forward on your spiritual path to the best of your abilities. Mistakes are O.K. Take advantage of this Divine dispensation of health from Dr. Lorphan, the Galactic Healers, the 3 M's, the Ascended Masters, the Arcturians, and the Angels. They are there to help you not only physically, but on all other levels as well. It is their joy to serve and help and they but await your call and invocation!

11

A Deeper & More Detailed Look at Some of the Major Healing Tools

Often even advanced lightworkers feel utterly bereft and devoid of spiritual connection when the physical vehicle falls into disharmony and disease. Their feelings can swoop down like some giant hammer out of nowhere and plunge one into a world of fear and pain, that seems to slice through any spiritual connection like a sharpened blade. That is why, beloved readers, I am writing in more detail of some of the Divine healing tools that at all times are available to be integrated into the physical being. I have explored some of these tools in this chapter, but new revelations keep coming in. It is my intent to add and expand upon these tools, so that you will have the opportunity to anchor them directly into your physical/etheric and even emotional/mental vehicles as you reach within towards an integrated understanding of the Ascension process.

No matter what your problem is, be it physical or with another of the four lower bodies, there is at the very least the immediate solution of the love, grace and benediction that comes from simply calling upon the names of the celestial beings who guard and guide us at every step of our journey from their wondrous spheres. Their Divine presence is itself a healing balm of utmost gentleness. There are likewise numerous

Integrated Ascension

tools that they are now in the process of revealing to us that we may apply just for the asking, and anchor into the physical vehicle in order to facilitate all manner of healing.

This chapter is dedicated to the glorious beings whose specific work is to help us integrate the Divine within our physical beings, and to the tools that are presently being made available to each of us as we follow our path of Integrated Ascension. Some of these beings will be quite familiar to you and others are just now in the process of revealing themselves. The tools they offer are further proof of the interweaving and integration of all the various levels of our beings into one coherent "whole." The physical body is honored with as much love, tenderness and devotion as the spiritual body, and the Masters seek to make this clear to us. Likewise do they seek to unveil these tools to our conscious minds so that we may work along with them in helping to integrate our physical vehicles into the state of wholeness and well beingness that GOD would have us manifest.

As you proceed to read the following, it is hoped that you will get a heightened sense of how much we are cared for and looked after by the Hierarchy of inner plane Ascended Planetary and Cosmic Beings, on all levels of our existence. They are here with us at every turn, and as they seek to help us make GOD a manifested reality upon this Earth, they do so down to our very physical cellular structure. The tools for Ascension that they give to us, are not separate from the tools for healing our physical bodies, for, in truth, all is one. As "integrated ascension" is indeed the "key," it is well worth bearing in mind that we are not alone upon any level of our beings. In the Heart of Source all aspects of self are contained. As we rise higher and higher upon the ladder of evolution, the love and light become anchored and grounded ever more deeply into so called dense physical matter.

The following tools and suggestions are ways in which the Masters will help you to help yourselves anchor the highest healing energies into the core physical structure. Consequently, the physical will function at a greater level of well beingness and light. At the same time, we will, by practicing these techniques, be raising ourselves to ever greater heights. As the inner and outer worlds blend and merge, healing cannot help but be the ultimate result.

Please feel free to use any or every suggestion offered. Remember that the GOD force, or Spirit Itself, seeks to integrate in wholeness within our lower vehicles with as much intensity as it calls us upward into our higher vehicles. In truth, there is no separation, except for that which the mind conceives. By accessing these tools, the chasm between the lower worlds and the higher will be filled, and there will be a Divine interchange and flow of energies from one level of Beingness to another. In this love and light of unity are the following tools given forth and do the following beings stand forth, asking simply that you call upon them as you journey through the labyrinth of Integrated Ascension!

Angels of the Healing Arts

Upon the inner plane there are a group of angels whose specific function is to help us with our personal healing process. As with all of the Angelic Kingdom and the Masters in all their varying posts and duties, they await our call in order to respond. The Angels of the Healing Arts are overlighted by the great Archangels Raphael and Mary, and even such Cosmic Archangels as Metatron. In truth, they all work in conjunction with one another, and are ever ready to be of service through our prayers, requests, and invocations.

Most of us have had some experience that involves the grace and touch of the healing angels. They are generally known for the comfort that they bring, soothing both the body and soul of one who is going through either major or minor health lessons. This type of comfort and relief cannot be overly stated, for their blessed presence has the ability to transform even the most intense health lesson into a vehicle with which to connect with these glorious beings, as well as with GOD. When this occurs, a Divine Synthesis is established between those incredible angelic beings who abide in the spiritual radiance of love and light, and we who are in need within the very essence of our physical embodiment.

Recently, however, I have discovered that there is a very definite science with which they work. When I tap into this aspect of their grace, not only do I experience the simple joy of their presence and the benefit of their healing refinements upon my physical vehicle, but I also tap into the radiance and wisdom of the more specific methods used. In this manner, their heavenly science is anchored directly into the physical, until there is no distinction between that which is of spirit and that which is of flesh, but simply "healing science" implemented at the level where it is most needed!

Metatron and His Platinum Healing Angels

Before discussing the Platinum Angels and their work, which is a relatively recent and quite amazing discovery, I would first like to discuss the Great Archangel, Lord Metatron himself, who is very seldom discussed under the banner of "Healing." Metatron, as you know, is the creator of the electron and all outer light within the Universe. He stands at the top of the Tree of Life, and therefore radiates his divine light and Beingness within all other branches. This being so, it logically follows that he would permeate his presence into the realm of healing.

This wondrous role as Healer that Metatron plays is, however, fairly newly discovered, even by one such as myself. Despite the fact that a great deal of who I am and what I do is to be the "Sherlock Holmes of the Cosmos" and seek out undiscovered or "hidden truths," it was not until I was shown vividly in a dream how much of a part Metatron plays within the healing force that I came to understand this now obvious fact.

As Lord Metatron works with light, and we are in our truest essence beings of light, who would be better suited to work with this healing force than Metatron! I was literally taken upon an inner plane journey with him, into the light and electronic structure of a person's limb. There I was shown how He uses his light to work within the living light of that which forms the physical vehicle, in order to infuse it with his own and to restructure the very electronic cell matrix for healing. I do not claim to fully grasp the science that this magnificent Archangel used, but I do share with you that I now know beyond the shadow of a doubt that He is one of the most advanced and proficient healers with whom each of us may work, if we so choose. One simple call will guarantee a response. He will then set about to work on extremely subtle frequencies to adjust the flow of light, eliminate obstructions, and, within karmic limits, eradicate disease. He works within the matrix of the electron itself, which is very profound. Once invoked, I suggest you just relax and, holding an attitude of faith, let him go to work. His method of healing is as I have stated, very subtle, but it will work its way into the physical vehicle in miraculous ways. His presence Itself cannot but help to heal the soul. I cannot encourage you strongly enough to call upon his divine intervention in the healing needs of any of your four bodies.

The Platinum Angels

There are a group of Angels whom I spoke of that assist Metatron in specific healing work, know as the Platinum Angels. After working directly with Metatron for a time, he sent these Angels to work with me in quite specific ways. When they first came into my aura, I was blessed to see their most resplendent and magnificent forms. I must tell you, they look quite unlike any angelic form I have ever encountered before. They told me that this was due to the specificity of the work that they, in mass, have undertaken to do.

Integrated Ascension

They are, as you must have already concluded, platinum in color. Their size, however, varies from that of great magnitude to about a quarter of an inch, or even the size of a pinpoint. In general, they assume the smaller size, for they work in group formation to control the growths of viruses and bacteria, as well as any other invasive substances. The work that I am most familiar with is in the process of keeping potential subclinical bacteria and viruses at bay. For example, if I have been in close contact with someone with a strong viral or bacterial infection and I want to insure that it does not lodge or take hold within myself, I will call them into an area that tends to be more vulnerable than others. I can actually see them cauterize any subclinical infections and then cover the area with an etheric platinum coating. I have absolutely no doubt that many a potential immune system deficiency has been avoided through the invocation and work of these angelic beings! I strongly suggest to each and every one of you to invite these most adept and unique healers into your own field and ask them to help you to either ward off an infection or to promote a healing.

This hierarchy of angels is the most efficient and barely known, if indeed, they are known at all. They have and will continue to aid humanity without your knowledge, but they are quite limited when working under such conditions. As with all of the great beings, they must be invoked or called forth in order to intervene, and so their healing is generally on a more abstract and global nature. When personally invoked they come right into the physical vehicle, and more specifically into the area that needs their touch. Please do give them a try. The healing work that they can do is monumental. The time in which we are living and the heightened frequencies have called forth their presence. Let us all make use of the gift of healing that these wondrous beings seek to bring forth. They truly wish to be of service, as it is through their service that they themselves evolve. It is also simply their nature to serve. Personally, I find it a great comfort to know that as I take all outer precautions with regard to my heath, these wonderful platinum beings are working away on the inner realms. I truly believe that as a race as a whole, we should use every means of healing available to us. Beloved readers, these angels are one of the greatest means of healing and preventative health that I have encountered. They await your call!

Running the Energies of Melchizedek, the Mahatma and Metatron

Before continuing, I must tell you that running the combined energies of Lord Melchizedek, the Mahatma, and Metatron have the most stimulating and healing effect that I have ever experienced! Together they form a healing frequency that is unlike any other I have experienced. As a unit, they do not heal in the conventional spiritual manner, such as directing healing energies to a specific diseased area. That type of healing falls more under the auspices of certain of the Archangels and Angels, as well as Divine inner plane healers such as Dr. Lorphan and his team of Galactic Healers, who I have already discussed in detail, as well as specific extraterrestrial beings such as the Arcturians. This combined energy force, however, is most healing and exhilarating.

The joint energy flow of His Holiness Lord Melchizedek, the Mahatma, and Lord Metatron, serves as a stimulating and elevating current that, by its very nature, helps to direct one's energy flow in a the proficient and healing manner possible. These high frequencies will lift you up, so to speak, beyond your physical ailments, so that you literally bypass the energies of discord within the four lower vehicles, and function at an accelerated vibratory level altogether. This enables the receiver of these cosmic currents to do their service work without being hampered by the denser frequencies that would normally slow us down and weigh us down to the denser realms within ourselves. Try calling upon them as a cosmic healing trinity, and ask them to run their combined energies through your vehicles as you set about to do your daily tasks and service work. The natural high that you will receive is beyond words. This energy will by its very nature serve to transform certain ills, as well as to enormously accelerate your ascension, or spiritual process.

The Platinum Net

One very specific way that Melchizedek, the Mahatma and Lord Metatron help to assist us in our healing, cleansing and purifying is through the use of the "Platinum Net," which I have referred to earlier. The "Platinum Net," when invoked, has the ability to sweep over large areas in order to cleanse and heal. For example, this can be done for a person's vehicles, as well as for their entire home. By use of this net, a more direct healing can be invoked from the combined energies of these magnificent beings than that which comes into play through the running of their energies, although the benefits of this are enormous in their own right. The "Platinum Net," like the Platinum Angels, has the power to cauterize and neutralize all sorts of viruses and bacteria, as well as to sweep the etheric, astral, mental and even spiritual fields clean of all obstructions. I often invoke the "Platinum Net" into the Melchizedek Synthesis Light Ashram, Academy and home. It serves to keep the atmosphere cleansed on a perpetual basis.

On the physical level I will light good quality incense, use a burning pot and run my radionics to concurrently purify the psychic, psychological, physical and etheric space. Another recent discovery regarding the 'Platinum Net' is that it works on all these levels, and even sweeps through the higher spiritual bodies to help create an alignment there. It is very refined and extremely effective.

The "Platinum Net" is a tool I would most highly recommend for the promotion of both individual and group health. If you work in an office or any kind of group situation, request that this net be swept over your environment three times daily. Certainly ask for one to be placed at the doorways in your home. Your guests will get an unexpected spiritual cleansing and healing. Using the "Platinum Net" is like taking your vitamins on a daily basis, but on a very refined and inclusive level. Why not give it a try and see how you feel? In truth, it is a wonderful gift given forth by the divine healing grace of Melchizedek, the Mahatma, and Metatron. It is one of the lesser know inner plane tools for healing and general well-being that I have come across, and it brings me great joy to share it with you.

The Viral Vacuum

I know that the name of the above mentioned inner plane tool for healing is not one of the more beatific or soul-stirring ones you will come across upon your spiritual pilgrimage. It does, nevertheless, work wonderfully, and has proven to be one of the most beneficial tools for vacuuming up viruses that I have yet to come upon. As many people carry within their auras viruses that are either overt or on a subclinical level, we are all exposed to them on a daily basis. The more balanced and healthy our physical and psychological diets are, the less susceptible we are to having any sort of virus finding access within our own fields. In all honesty, however, many lightworkers at various stages of spiritual development still have health lessons and/or are involved in a cleansing and clearing process. The more protected we are at every level, the less likely we are to pick this up, either from someone else or from our own cleansing process. To keep as clear from these microbes as possible, there is no better tool than the Viral Vacuum!

Simply request that the Masters use the Viral Vacuum to suck out any viral activity that may be building up within you. If you feel a bit tired and fatigued, or if you have been, or need to be, in close proximity with someone with a sore throat, cold, or who contains any viral activity whatsoever, you will generally be more vulnerable to viruses. The Masters will be more than happy to help keep you clear of this energy by sucking it up through their etheric viral vacuum. They will then transmute it into a more positive energy form, which in turn will serve to purify the entire energy field from one of disease to one of ease and positivity.

If you find that you are in the mist of a cold, flu or virus of any sort, it is not too late! The Viral Vacuum works equally well upon active and non-active or subclinical viruses. Take time to rest and relax. Allow yourself some moments to visualize this etheric vacuum sucking up all viral germs from your entire auric field. Call upon the assistance of the Archangels and angels of healing. Certainly give the physical body all the rest, liquids, vitamins and minerals, homeopathics, and herbs that you feel you require. Also, call upon the Viral Vacuum to work in conjunction with these physical methods. While using all tools, techniques and healing methods available and harmonious to you upon the physical plane, I urge you to not neglect the use of this etheric vacuum. I generally use it as a preventative, whenever I am in contact with a person who is carrying viral energy. I actually feel it at work and have had just about 100% success in preventing any virus from taking hold. It is certainly worth experimenting with!

Dr. Lorphan

Until very recently, Dr. Lorphan worked in anonymity, and through the healers that he himself trained. These healers are themselves Galactic in scope, and are some of the highest ranking healers that come to the aid of humanity from such great heights within the inner realms. As of late, Dr. Lorphan has stepped forward to make himself both known and available to all who are in need of deep Divine Healing. In his love, grace, scientific knowledge and skill, he asked me to be one of his channels of revelation, so that more and more of humanity can come to know him and avail themselves of his healing talents and techniques.

Integrated Ascension

I cannot, in truth, presume to say what Dr. Lorphan's healing methods are. I can say, however, that he works in areas that are still a total bafflement to the scientific and medical community of Earth. He uses tools that the medical people of our world have not even begun to dream of. I do know that these tools are within realms of light and function through the regulation and adjustments of vibrational frequencies in order to create a healing environment that will ultimately produce the desired healing. He, as do all the Masters and Angels, works within the karmic field of flexibility within each one of us, and by invitation only. He assures me, however, that there is overall, far more room within karmic limits to work with than we would suppose, and that he and his healers eagerly await our invocations.

Just as there are the many and varied positions within the Hierarchy that we are familiar with, such as those of the seven Chohans who themselves work within different spiritual departments, so there is a specialized department for healing. Beloved Dr. Lorphan heads this department and its many and varied branches. Some of his "students," who are Master Healers in their own right, specialize in healing through sound. Some work more directly with light. Others actually work with spiritual and etheric acupuncture. Others specialize in dentistry, while others are devoted to inner and outer plane sight. In this way, they really are the prototype for all of Earth's healers!

For all that call upon their aid, healing will be facilitated to an enormous, often miraculous extent. Dr. Lorphan and his staff of Master Healers will generally work directly with the individuals who request aid. Both himself and his healers will use their refined and divine healing methods to help correct disease in whatever body it is manifesting. The level or intensity of the illness is in no way is a hindrance to their work. The director and healers who work from within the great White Lodge in Sirius are not hampered in their services in the least by any disease, or combination thereof, that the human form can manifest. They also have access to all the levels and bodies that the disease is manifesting on. Being Galactic in scope, they work from the point of the disease's cause, and therefore work upon all vehicles concurrently.

They likewise work to overlight physical plane healers who work in either the third, fourth, or fifth dimensions. When called upon to do so, these Galactic Healers are equally willing and adept in overlighting a surgeon in his or her work as they are in overlighting an auric healer! From our perspective, Dr. Lorphan and his group of Galactic Healers are limitless in the help, care, and healing that they can and do effectuate. Dr. Lorphan has communicated to me that it is now perfect timing for those of us in earthly embodiment who seek to integrate divine healing into our lives to call upon him and his group freely and with no hesitation. They now step forward from the great halls of Sirius to offer healing and assistance to all that request it. He asks that I ask on his behalf for all to put forth this request. Beloved readers, as one who has been graced, touched and blessed by the miraculous healing hands of Dr. Lorphan, it is my honor and joy to do this on behalf of him and his staff of Galactic Healers!

The Lord of Arcturus and the Arcturian Technologies

I have spoken in the previous chapter about the healing technologies with which the Lord of Arcturus and the Arcturians have so lovingly made available to humanity. At this juncture, however, it bears mentioning again, as well as exploring in greater depth. Aboard the Mothership upon which the Lord of Arcturus dwells, along with a vast number of Arcturians, there are several healing devices that they have made available to those of humanity who request their aid. As they are an extremely advanced extraterrestrial civilization who are working for the upliftment of all of us who dwell upon the Earth, they seek to help us spiritually, mentally, emotionally, as well as etheric/physically. One of

Integrated Ascension

the key ways they seek to help us is by the healing of our physical bodies, although in truth, they seek to help us heal all of our bodies.

When considering just the physical/etheric nature, they have instruments of diagnosis that supersedes even the most imaginative minds that exist in the field of medical research today. These devices can literally transport the etheric form of any of us onto their vehicle in order that the manifested area of disease can be read and diagnosed accurately with their instruments upon the etheric vehicle. As they work very much with the holographic image, this process is completely painless. They also work very much with the etheric vehicle which reveals all the patterns, attributes, blueprints and level of health that manifests within the physical body, but is unattached to the nervous system by which we feel pain, discomfort, etc. Once this diagnosis is read from our etheric vehicle, it is then reintegrated into the body. This is done during sleep or meditation.

Also during the time frame that this body is on the Arcturian craft, the adjustments are set into motion within the etheric form based upon a certain specific holographic diagnosis. The necessary healing process is put into action. When this vehicle realigns with the physical, the healing radiances then seep through the etheric into the actual dense physical body. This is a most advanced technology, and yet for them, quite a simple procedure. For most of us who request their aid they will initiate this healing process, which we are then left to fully integrate into our physical lives and forms, not by any conscious knowledge of how to do this, but by trusting their work and being willing to work with the root cause of our disease. This is because they ultimately wish us to achieve healing upon all levels and to grow into the light beings that it is within our destiny and potential to grow. Their physical assistance, however, is available for all that request it.

Sometimes they will even create a spontaneous and seemingly miraculous healing, if they feel that by this grace we will learn and continue to grow. By whatever means they choose to deal with your particular ailment, please do call upon them, for their assistance is guaranteed! As the Arcturians work from the spiritual level, they are also equally available to assist with the healing of the emotional, mental and psychological vehicles. They do this by downloading adjustments into these vehicles, by revealing via dream or spontaneous insight where the root cause of a difficulty is, or by bringing the astral or mental body aboard their ship in the hours of sleep and using what I can only refer to as an advanced form of radionics to install the needed harmonious frequencies into those bodies.

They most definitely work on directly helping to accelerate the light and love quotient of the higher or spiritual bodies. The Arcturians are incredible spiritual beings themselves, and their intent in coming into such close rapport with us is to heal and uplift us in every and any way possible. Do not hesitate to ask them for their help in any area that you are struggling with, for it is their supreme joy to serve!

Insights into Djwhal Khul's Holographic Computer

As I have already written much concerning the use of Djwhal Khul's holographic computer as a vehicle for healing, I will not repeat here what I have previously written about. What I will tell you is that the holographic image, when used upon the higher dimensions, works much like an X-ray or radionics machine, but at a far, far higher frequency level. The holographic image is also able to reveal the "whole" within the reading of our basic cellular structure. I am not completely sure how this works exactly, except that it is a bit like getting a total read on a person's structure through a single sample of DNA. The word holographic itself contains the root word, "whole." Although I do not understand the process fully, cloning is itself based upon this principle which essentially manifests in a manner in which one singular part reveals the "whole." Therefore, the x-ray at this level would reveal not a singular difficulty but any obstructions within the entirety of the being involved. The holographic image of the higher dimensions also acts as a conduit of healing directly to the form that it stands in representation of. I tell you this to help clarify why I have so adamantly stressed calling upon Master Djwhal Khul in order to receive the healing that he is able to effectuate via these means.

To further clarify, this computer, much like the Arcturian technologies, works upon the physical/etheric, emotional and mental bodies simultaneously. As you already know, all four lower bodies are interconnected, or integrated, in a very direct manner. For a true and lasting healing to take place, all the bodies must simultaneously be cleansed, purified, aligned and, ultimately, healed. In cases where an illness or disease has taken strong physical hold, it is not unusual for a Master healer, such as those whom we have been discussing, to go directly into the etheric/physical body in order to promptly alleviate suffering.

The ultimate goal, however, is to adjust all of the bodies to reveal and help balance the individual at their core level. This will necessitate a process of healing that will ultimately involve all four lower bodies and the bringing of them into alignment with soul and spirit. I therefore take the liberty to again encourage you to call upon beloved Master Djwhal Khul and to ask for his assistance in your healing process. Request the holographic computer and be specific regarding the healing you feel most in need of.

Ask for Assistance in General

By virtue of their spiritual Mastery and integration, all of the healers will ultimately work on your total being, but they do appreciate it when you are as specific as possible about your health concerns. This serves well in three capacities. First, it gives them a point of immediate focus in which to begin their healing work. Second, it clues them into your particular need of the moment, which in turn reveals much about what you need to focus on and what needs healing in general. It therefore gets straight to the point concerning your immediate need and gives them an access point to the greater picture of your entire four-body system. Third, as was previously mentioned, there are specific inner plane healers—specialists, if you will—much the same way that there are specialists upon the Earth plane. Sometimes you may go to a General Practitioner, or a Cardiologist, who will, in turn, refer you to a thyroid specialist. This occurs when inner plane healing is involved as well.

For example, Djwhal Khul's holographic computer might reveal a certain imbalance that one of the 'specialists' who work with Dr. Lorphan from the Great White Lodge in Sirius is best qualified to attend to. Djwhal will then take it upon himself to consult with Dr. Lorphan in order to engage the services of that particular specialist. If this is deemed the best method of healing, you can be assured that the appropriate group of specialists will be sent forth to attend to you. Remember there is no competition upon the inner planes, for healers from on high do not charge fees, seek acclaim, etc. The welfare of each of us is their only concern, and in order to effectuate that, they work ultimately as a group body, even if they initially come from varying and differing sources. It is, however, up to each of us to invoke these wonderful healers in order to establish a light/love flow of healing from the inner planes into the outer form. It rests with each of us to take the first step and to make the call.

What is interesting to note is that we will most likely have more of an affinity with one group of healers than with others. This is due to the esoteric fact that our frequencies are more in resonant harmony with certain beings than with others. Many of us are extremely connected to the Angelic Hierarchies and will therefore be prompted to call upon their assistance first. Others have a particular connection with one or other of the Masters, and will therefore be inclined to either call upon them directly or to call to the group whose frequencies and vibrational flow is most in harmony with them. It is a good idea to follow these impulses. It is likewise a good idea to realize that all is connected upon the inner higher realms, and that we will ultimately be guided to those that are best suited to meet a specific need at a specific time.

A Word About the Masters Themselves

One point that needs to be clearly stated is that each of the seven Masters or Chohans of the seven rays are healers in their own right. They may not be specialists, and there will always be a group within their specific ray that focuses upon the art of healing with more of a direct specificity than they themselves do, as each of their jobs entails so much. Nevertheless, do not ever hesitate to call upon the healing currents of your own blessed Masters, for they can and will be of incredible assistance to you. It is important in this regard to remember that Sananda, who is best known for his incarnation as Jesus, is a Master healer. Sananda still functions in this capacity, so why not call upon beloved Master Jesus/Sananda? Help will be immediate. Sai Baba, who graces our planet in physical form embodying the Cosmic Christ, is himself primarily a divine healer. The miracles of healing that he has performed are openly spoken of in books, tapes and videos, as well as privately among his disciples. I urge you from the bottom of my heart and soul not to forget Sai Baba when invoking healing intervention. Sometimes, as in his case, you can find the most glorious gifts of heaven living right among us upon this Earth! I have written regarding my own miraculous healing experiences with Sai Baba, including an entire book devoted to His holiness the Lord Sai Baba Himself. He is one of the best vehicles for healing that I have ever known. We are all graced that he walks among us! Do call upon him. I promise you that you will be glad you did!

More Healing Tools

There are many tools which we often use for healing upon the physical plane, that are also available for use in a more refined energy field

Integrated Ascension

from the inner planes. There is generally a specific Master Healer who helps implement these various tools and who oversees the work being done with them in the etheric. Whenever you are unclear as to who on the inner plane is the actual "specialist" in regard to specific tools, it is a good idea to call upon Dr. Lorphan and his staff of inner plane Master healers. You can rest assured that the appropriate being will work with the specific tools and energies invoked.

Crystal healing is one tool and method of healing that is growing in ever increasing popularity. Synchronistically, we are being given greater and greater access to crystals that reside upon the inner plane realms. Depending upon the desired effect, the perfect crystal will be chosen by your inner plane healer to help facilitate your process of health on whatever level of your being that you are requesting healing work be done.

If, for example, you are specifically concerned with physical body healing, the crystals that will be used will usually be anchored from the etheric. As the physical vehicle and the etheric vehicle are so closely tied together, this is the most direct avenue of accessibility to the physical body itself. When requesting healing of this form, it is a good idea to get in as comfortable a position as possible, lying down being the most beneficial to this process providing that your particular ailment does not either prevent this or cause any undue stress or strain. Being as still and quiet as possible is also a good idea. If you prefer, soothing spiritual music can aid in the process of this type of relaxation, as well as tuning into the sounds of bird-song, the ocean, wind, or of course, the beatific sound of the silence itself.

Ask Dr. Lorphan and his inner plane staff of specialists for the type of healing that you feel most in need of. If you prefer or feel guided to, call upon the Angelic Kingdom or any of the Masters. The 'right' being or beings will attend to your needs. By invoking those with whom you feel most aligned, you will be assured of their assistance during your healing session. Be very specific with them. This will help them to immediately tune into your problem area, and likewise tune your own consciousness in to the point where the healing work is to be done. In this way you will be able to consciously contribute to the activation and activity of the crystals used.

One aspect of this type of crystal healing that is well worth noting is that certain crystals, when activated, will be used to stimulate core cell activity, increase energy flow and work overall as a stimulant. An example of this would be when an etheric crystal is placed in the thyroid of an individual who is suffering from hypo-thyroidism (an under-active thyroid). The emanations of the crystal would be geared towards stimulating and moving the energies to a faster, more normal pace. In the case of an individual who is suffering from hyper-thyroidism, where the thyroid is already way over active, the energies of the crystal will emit a soothing frequency in order to effectuate a calming of the thyroid. In both cases, specific crystals dealing with the thyroid will be placed within the etheric thyroid, but their functions will be totally opposite. One will activate and stimulate, while the other will calm and soothe. If you have a sense of the type of work being done, you are able to aid in the process by your visualizations. The key, however, is in knowing the invocations you can make, both to the Healers and in the invocations of some of the specific tools.

The healing crystals are available for a variety of applications, and in truth they exist in one form of another upon all the various realms within the 352 levels of Cosmos. For the purposes of keeping our discussion geared towards healing, we will confine our discussion to the realms of the four lower bodies as much as possible. You must realize, however, that as each of the planes intersects with the one above it and the one below it, causing all of the various planes and bodies to be interconnected, there will be overlaps within our discussion. We will, however, keep focused upon those that we are most conscious of on a daily basis.

Integrated Ascension

The emotional (astral or feeling body) is in need of healing and adjustment for almost the entire population. Most people neglect this fact unless they are so troubled by it that they seek out counseling or psychiatric intervention, or they are spiritually attuned enough to have taken it upon themselves to seek either a qualified spiritual counselor or are consciously working at quieting and controlling the emotional body, and/or calling forth a type of healing—such as those we are now discussing. If you are reading this book then I am under the assumption that you are using every means possible to properly balance this particular body and to align it correctly within your four-body system. The use of inner plane healing crystals in this regard is enormously helpful. What I shall describe in the following is equally applicable to the mental body or concrete mind.

Again, as in all healing work, place yourself in a relaxed and comfortable position. When having work done upon the emotional or mental vehicles, a meditative position works extremely well. If, however, reclining makes you feel more relaxed, then by all means continue to relax in that manner. Request the healing crystals to be installed within your emotional/astral body or your mental body. You might even ask for them to be installed simultaneously in both of these bodies, since they quite often function as a unit. Often when one feels severely emotionally misaligned and out of balance, one feels this mentally as well. The option is yours, however, as to how you wish to be treated. It may be the case that the root of your discomfort is clearly emotional. Speak that to your inner healers and request that for a particular healing, or group of healings, that the crystals be focused solely upon the emotional body. They will meet your request.

Where the emotions are concerned, the crystals that are used most often emit soothing, quieting and calming frequencies. The difficulties arising from the astral body are almost 100% due to overstimulation. Each of these frequencies has with it an accompanying color and tone. The colors and sounds of the crystals installed into the emotional/astral

Integrated Ascension

body vary according to the individual and the need, but will always be a color that is calming, most often in the bluish or blue/green family. If, however, there is a need for greater self-love, then the crystals will be in the pink family. You can ask that the color of the crystal your healer is working with be shown to you, so that you can have it to visualize. You can even ask to hear the tone or frequency that it is emitting. More people can generally see colors then hear specific tones, however, if your clairaudience is opened to a good extent then you might well be gifted with the tone of your healing crystal!

When dealing with the mental realm and mental body, the crystals will be geared towards one of several areas. They might be installed to quiet the mind and work in a very similar vein to the crystals used in the feeling body. They may likewise be used to stimulate brain activity in order to help one open up to the greater wisdoms in a more concrete fashion. They may be used to activate and stimulate certain functions of the mind, such as activating more of the yin/right brain mental functions or the yang/left brain mental functions. Several crystals can be installed at once in order to stimulate certain areas of the mind while quieting others. Again, be as specific as you can when making your request, but know that you are in the healing hands of a specialist from the inner realms, who will ultimately determine what is needed in order to bring about the highest level of equilibrium, balance, health, and harmony for any of the four lower bodies.

The uses of the inner plane healing crystals are numerous. Their effectiveness is incredible. In some instances, they may be installed for any given length of time, so that an individual receives their benefit on an on-going basis. I recommend that you ask for the experience of this wonderful healing process when you make your healing requests to your inner physicians. If you have worked with, and/or are currently working with third dimensional crystals, then know that you already have an attunement for this type of healing work. Also, know that you can request that the inner plane crystals work in conjunction with your outer plane crystals. Ask for a harmonic link between the two to be set up. The force of both will then be increased exponentially. I find this a most helpful tool, and the type of healing that automatically invokes a very beautiful and harmonious meditation.

Healings of Attunements

Earlier we discussed how you could request the Lord of Arcturus to etherically take you onboard the great Arcturian spacecraft in order to be directly healed through advanced Arcturian technologies. In a similar fashion, several mystical and sacred power points exist within Earth's body itself that can have amazing effects in the promoting of the healing process. Some of these exist within the Great Pyramid of Giza and other smaller pyramids in Egypt, as well as the Sphinx. There is, of course, the sacred river of Lourdes, in France, as well as several other sacred sites that the Blessed Virgin Mary has graced with her healing radiance. There is the vortex in India where His Holiness the Lord Sai Baba resides, previously known as the little village of Puttaparti. There is the great vortex to Atlantis in Bimini, Calvery, as well as several sacred points in Jerusalem, Mt. Sinai, Glastonberry and the Mountain of Mount Shasta, to name but a few. Although the benefits of actual physical pilgrimage to these sacred vortexes, grid points, temples and so forth, do increase the efficacy of the healing process, much can be accomplished through making an etheric pilgrimage and hook-up with these incredible healing sites.

What I am speaking of here, specifically deals with creating such a strong attunement to a healing point upon our planet, that we actually free our etheric vehicle to journey there. We often associate this process with visiting other dimensions, planets, star systems, or realms. I want you to realize that what I now call your attention to involves the etheric process of bilocation to specific places upon our planet that we might perhaps like to visit in our physical form, but are unable to do so at the present moment. We can, however, go there etherically and gain enormous benefit and healing.

If there is a particular place you feel attuned to or connected to, then cultivate that attunement. Allow yourself to go there in meditation. Request the guidance of a Master or Angelic Being, as well as the presence of a Master healer who works using the specific energies within the vortex or field you wish to visit. Allow yourself to relax and attune. Ask that the particular Master healer who works with the healing energies of your chosen location tend to your specific needs. Remember that the etheric bears the imprint of the physical and vice versa. Ask that as much healing as possible is integrated into your etheric form and that this healing manifests fully and completely upon the physical form. Enjoy the joy that visiting your place of holiness brings, and keep inviting ever deeper healings.

This may or may not involve the use of the emotional and mental vehicles. The truth of the matter is, however, that the more of yourself you put into this process of attunement, the more you will get out of it. Therefore, I suggest rather than simply using the mind to make your request, allow it to journey with you. The same goes for your feeling body. This will not only allow for a greater imprinting of the experience but will also allow the healing current to flow directly into the emotional and mental aura and fields. I suggest you give this one a try. It is certainly well worth the price of the airfare and motel!

The Grid Balancing Program

There is a form of healing and balancing known as the "Grid Balancing Program," which is most amazing. As you know, within our planet and within each one of us are certain very definite grid-like patterns. These patterns, among other things, are anchors for the flow of energy. When a particular grid pattern is perfectly aligned, the energy will flow perfectly and all will be in proper harmony and balance. When the grid patterns are not properly aligned, the result varies from slight to massive imbalance.

Calling upon the grid balancing beam will automatically activate the grid balancing program. Activating this program in a particular area will begin a shifting of the basic grid structure of the area until it settles upon the point of maximum balance. The greater the balance, the greater the harmony, as the energies of that particular area are brought into perfect alignment, which will eradicate all discordant energy patterns and put the field into one that radiates only health. This will occur as all patterns that act as an obstruction to health are thrown off, being replaced instead by perfect grid balancing.

This is a program and a process. It is not instantaneous, but once put into proper balance is quite miraculous. With the help of Master Hilarion, the Grid Balancing Program can be activated by any that so choose. This program can be worked to varying degrees and at various levels. It can be worked specifically or generally. For example, one who wishes to set in motion healing frequencies to even a small area such as the eye, can activate the grids that deal directly with that specific area. All that you need to do is to make the request and then give it fifteen or so minutes to begin the process of restructuring. This should not be done more than once a day at the beginning, then only twice a day at maximum in half-hour sessions. More is not necessarily better, as this is a very delicate and specific scientific process that needs time to work.

As you know, the physical body is the "effect" of higher or subtler causes, and being such, is the last to be impacted and takes the longest to heal. Do not be in a hurry. Simply work at calling forth the establishing of right grid patterns, and let the Master Healers do the rest. The call will ultimately compel the answer, although the results will first manifest upon the mental, emotional, etheric and finally the physical plane. That is why this is specifically referred to as a "program." It is a process to place yourself on, and trust that the outpicturing upon the physical will happen in the appropriate hour!

Integrated Ascension

The Grid Balancing Program can be used in a much broader capacity as well. It can be invoked as a generalized sweep over the entire four lower bodies, or even the twelve-body system, so that all psychic and subtle energies begin to flow in harmony and balance. In this way, it serves in a similar fashion to the axiatonal alignment.

This program can be used to directly deal with the balancing of the emotional body or the balancing of the mental body. In cases such as these, what you would need to do is to invoke the balancing grid to sweep across your entire emotional field, if that were your point of maximum and concentrated concern. As most of humanity struggles with the emotional body on a moment to moment basis, I would recommend that everyone implement the Grid Balancing Program in this capacity. As I said, more is not necessarily better, for the alignments being created and put into play through this process are extremely specific and scientific. I would, however, recommend that everyone do this on a daily basis for a five to ten minute period per day. Visualize all inappropriate emotional energies being pushed out of the system as the grid slowly and accurately aligns the emotional atmosphere to flow in a manner that is reflective of Christ Love and Divine feelings. Allow this time to be restful and relaxing, and know that in your invocation of this program you are helping to fully integrate and accelerate your ascension process.

In a similar fashion, you can do this with the mental body. You can work to align and balance the physical body as a whole, or work with specific organs, like the eye, or areas, like the entire chest region. You can use the Grid Balancing Program for the alignment of energies in any and every possible way. This is a wonderful program just recently revealed by the Masters. Master Hilarion, Archangel Metatron, Vywamus, and St. Germain are very involved in this program, as is Master Djwhal Khul. Call upon them, particularly Hilarion and Metatron for assistance.

Integrated Ascension

The major points that they wish to communicate about this program are that, first; it is one that slowly refines in accuracy as it is worked with over time. Second, they wish everyone to use this on the emotional vehicle, as what they are focusing upon now is a more integrated ascension than that which we have been experiencing. They also feel that as a race in general, our emotional bodies are lagging the farthest behind and are in dire need of alignment and proper balance. I therefore pass on their request to you, my beloved readers, and encourage you to take as much advantage of this program in any and every area of your lives as possible!

Geometric Probes and Repatterning

A new technique of healing that the Masters revealed to me quite recently was once based upon geometric repatterning. I am not sure exactly how this works, other than it is by the use of an etheric geometric probe that certain patterns of disease are detected. The Master Healer will then send forth the "proper" geometric configuration in order to etherically correct the diseased cell structure. This is generally used as a preventative tool and measure, whereby disease matrixes are diagnosed while still within the etheric form and eradicated there before they have a chance to materialize upon the physical.

Archangelic Intonation

Each of the Archangels carries within their aura a particular tone. Using focus of will, they can direct and increase that tone, until it surrounds an individual's entire electromagnetic field. Although some Archangels, particularly Mother Mary and Raphael, are know to function specifically within the healing arts, each of the Archangels is in truth a Divine and proficient healer.

When in physical, etheric, emotional or mental distress, feel free to call upon any of the Archangels. Ask them to grace you with the inner sound of their divine intonation. Their sound currents will bathe you in the frequencies that you need and create an inner plane vortex of sound atmosphere that will encourage the healing process. It does not matter to which Archangel you call. In fact, it is best to simply invoke Archangelic intervention for the purpose of healing through tone. The Archangel whose radiance and frequencies most align with your own specific need will be the one to answer your call. The most immediate and wondrous benefit of this process is the feeling of extreme peace that is felt within their blessed presence.

In Conclusion

The tools for healing that are available upon the inner planes are many and varied. Some individuals are more suited to certain of these healings and other individuals will be drawn to use different tools, techniques, and processes. This is natural. The same is true on the level of medicine that is more conventional and healing. As Hermes so eloquently puts it in his famous axiom, "As within so without, as above so below."

I simply encourage you to give the tools in this and the previous chapter that are most appealing to you a try, and see how you feel when doing a specific process, invocation, or calling upon a metaphysical physician in the truest sense of the word. Perhaps you might find that in calling upon the Archangels the feeling of peace creates an all-embracing calm so that all concerns leave you and your problems just fall away. The only way that you will know the effect is to experience the cause, which in this case is by putting some of these healing tools into practical application. I truly hope that you do, for I have found some of the divine effects to be most amazing, uplifting, and profoundly healing!

12

Twilight Masters, Cults, and Non-Integrated Ascension Groups

Shades of Gray

In terms of frequency, that which is said to be "of the light" conveys that it is of the Spirit, of GOD, of Source. That which is said to be "of the darkness" conveys the message of that which is clearly working against the higher Will of GOD, of Spirit, of Source. When we speak of the Great White Lodge, or the Great White Brotherhood, we are referring to those who are aligned with the Divine purpose, plan, love, and intent of the Highest. When we speak of the Black Lodge, we are referring to those who have chosen to align themselves in opposition to the Divine purpose, plan, love, and intent of the Highest. Between these two extremes fall the various shades of gray!

In the past, individuals, groups, or occultists were seen to be either on the path of light or the path of darkness, users of white magic or manipulators of the black arts. While these two extremes clearly do exist, there is a third category, which must be brought forward at this time of heightened energy and rapid transformation. Within this category are many varying degrees from that of the lightest shade of gray to that which is almost the utter embodiment of darkness. This, my beloved readers, is the realm of the "Twilight Masters," who are not completely aligned with either the plan of GOD or Light, or the manipulations of those who work *against* the forces of evolution, and are therefore the forces of darkness. This is the realm that spans the various spectrums and frequencies of the gray scale, and the one that is most confusing to lightworkers. It springs forth out of the womb of non-integration and is responsible for leading the majority of confused lightworkers from the path of their highest good.

What makes this realm a most insidious one is the fact that it and the teachers who embody it often contain much of the light within them. The more light they hold, the less distortion is given forth. The less light they hold, the deeper the gray, and therefore the more the distortion of the teachings. In any regard, however, there is enough light to attract light seekers and lightworkers, and enough darkness to lead them from that which they truly seek—the pure untainted light and love of the Most High. It is therefore essential that you become familiar with this realm and learn to recognize the many signals and signs, however subtle they may be, so that you do not succumb to the manipulations of anyone who dwells within the shadows of the gray zone!

Temptation of the Light

You must understand right off, that any teacher who wishes to win you over, to make you a student or even a follower of their particular way, will at first unveil to you that which is truly of the light. They will call to you with the truths of GOD that you know to be accurate and in alignment with Higher Intent. They will not come forth to you with shades of gray, for they know, either on a conscious or subconscious level, that if they were to do so they would not be able to attract any lightworker to them. They therefore begin on a platform of light and truth. This calls out to you for it is indeed in harmony with your Higher Self.

Integrated Ascension

I don't care how clear a teacher, teaching or a path may seem, you must always hold tightly and firmly to your own personal power, keep your discernment and discrimination ever active, and never go on automatic pilot. I am not saying this to scare you off, or in any way, shape or form, steer you away from the exploration of various spiritual paths. Many wonderful teachers, teachings, paths, groups, and centers are in full integrity and completely 100% devoted to the light. My main purpose in devoting a chapter to this subject is to help you discern for yourself that which is of the pure light, or striving to be so, and that which embodies shades of gray and therefore seeks to manipulate and control you.

If a teaching or a teacher calls you by their light, go forward in joy to explore that light. The chances are great that they will truly be connected to Source to their highest capacity and will offer you much. I myself have done this with various teachings and books, most of which I have written about in my other books. I have also come across those, who after a very brief time, began to manifest subtle discoloration within their teachings. It is from those teachers and groups that the Ascended Masters coined the term "Twilight Master," for they manifest both qualities of light and darkness within their auras. Often their teachings are based on some form of truth, however, their negative egos controlled their motives and over time began to color the teachings. We have all heard the saying "A little truth is often a dangerous thing."

Remember always, that no matter how bright anyone else's light shines, it is your own light that you need to cultivate. No matter how filled with love anyone else may be, it is truly our own job to connect our heart chakra to the Heart of GOD and thereby manifest and demonstrate that love. No matter how empowered even the greatest teacher you may encounter is, you must always seek to develop you own personal power and stay clear and centered within it. In this way, you will become invulnerable to anyone's teaching that might begin in light and clarity and slowly emerge to reveal shades of gray. As long as you are right with self, at whatever level you are at, then no one but you, your Higher Self and your own Mighty I Am Presence can influence your actions or alignments. This is why integration and synthesis is the true teaching of this next millennium. When you are integrated and right with self, you cannot help but to be centered in your own light of discernment.

Twilight Masters will indeed try to tempt you with the lighted part of themselves and their teachings. They will do this for two very distinct reasons. First, they know that you would not be in the least bit interested in them if they did not reveal the sacred part of their Being in the first place. If they came to you all cloudy and murky, no sincere lightworker would have anything whatsoever to do with them.

Secondly, many of them, on a conscious level, truly do want to be aligned with the light. They are themselves victims of their own fragmentation and negative ego manipulations. Due to this fact, the majority of those who work in the more subtle tones of gray and even many who work within the heavier gray tones are doing this unconsciously. What they seek from you is simple validation. They are basically off track and have let themselves be taken over by the negative ego and its separative motivations and manipulations. Because of this, they need your support. They need you to validate them, to feed their own depleted energy and to feel that they are worthwhile. The majority of people I have come across who fall into this category would be shocked if they truly had a good look at themselves, for as I stated before, it is not their conscious intention but their subconscious or unconscious unclarity and negative ego that has allowed the clouds of illusion and delusion to enter their own fields. They often are brilliant and charismatic in a certain area of growth potential, however if looked at clearly from GOD's eyes they are not operating fully from their Higher Self and Mighty I Am Presence. It may be a psychological brilliance or a certain sliver of truth which they brilliantly understand and demonstrate, but again, power, fame, money, sex, vanity, and self-interest is their god.

Integrated Ascension

Once you are aware of who they or their teachings are, you can simply walk away. You do not need them; it is they who need you. The more integrated you become, the less you will need anyone else's validation to continue your own true spiritual work. You will therefore be free to either inwardly and/or outwardly say no thank you, and to move on. The more aware you are of the existence of the Twilight Master, the more quickly will you be able to recognize them. You will then simply and easily move on to follow your own highest path, to connect up with those who are your true spiritual family and with those whom you can share the pure untainted light of your own beautiful GOD-Self!

Mixed Messages

The danger of the Twilight Master, their teachings, and their groups is in the mixed messages that they are giving out. They present half-truths, distortions of truths and even pure truth that is geared towards selfish purposes. Because of this, their power lies in getting their students so utterly confused that what generally occurs is that the student no longer trusts their own inner knowing. The mixed bag of truth, love, and insights, along with many false promises made, lead the student to become more and more dependent upon them. This can occur to the extreme in Cults. It likewise can occur within a looser group body or simply between individuals who are seeking counsel for themselves directly from a particular Twilight Master. The scenario varies, but in all cases, the individual is left with a bag of mixed messages and a mass of confusion to try and sort out.

If the light and the dark were not mixed together to form these various shades of gray, there would not be such rampant confusion. However, because there is always enough light and enough truth to any of the teachings being presented, the student who is not already 100% clear, fully integrated and firmly established within their own personal power cannot help but get somewhat, if not temporarily, lost in the

Integrated Ascension

miasma. When doubts do arise for the student, they can always call forth the good, the beautiful and the true that is contained within the messages and teaching of they who walk in twilight. This then enables the student to justify their connection with the teacher, teaching, or group, and to continue.

Those who are truly full-fledged Twilight Masters, under the domination of the negative ego and opened enough to the forces of darkness to create a very deep and intense gray zone, are generally masters at giving out mixed messages. This is because they are not simply a bit lost and operating out of the subconscious mind, but are consciously and willingly aligning themselves with impure motive. Once this is done, they will do anything and everything in their power to keep their students or 'followers' under their spell. Giving forth mixed messages becomes their greatest tool, both in attracting the student to them and in keeping the ones that they have!

When taken to the extreme they may go so far as to tell their students that what they must do for them is to literally offer up their physical life. The student or disciple is literally required to die for the sake of fulfilling the teacher's totally negative intention. This obviously applies to the most extreme cases, which the media has brought to our attention. This order then is interlaced with the truth that what will happen is that their students will merely leave their body and take on their subtler body on the inner plane. This is quite extreme, and most of you would have the needed discrimination to walk out of such a situation. What you must realize, however, is that by the time such a message is given forth there have been countless other messages filled with numerous shades of gray. Truths have been merged and laced with untruths in such a clever manner that it is hard for the student to tell the light from the darkness. Their utter devotion to the highest would lay all at the alter of sacrifice, even their physical existence. In the most extreme and severe cases that we see manifesting in some of the modern day cults no sacrifice is deemed too great, if only a mere kernel of truth can be obtained.

Integrated Ascension

In the less extreme cases, which are far, far more common, what we generally find are the more subtler shades of gray and the less obvious manifestations of mixed messages. There is still great power within this type of mixed message, and it still leaves the student confused and at least somewhat alienated from self and GOD. In truth, of course, one cannot alienate from GOD, for GOD embraces the All, the Eternal Whole. By the same token, one can consciously alienate from their personal attunement to that Whole or GOD, and it is in this alienation that the Twilight Master gains their power and control.

Just because a person is run by their negative ego to a certain extent doesn't mean they are a Twilight Master. The Twilight Master is the next step, so to speak, in the wrong direction and develops when they actually are manipulating people in a negative sense to serve their lower self. In this sense, they are taking people away from GOD. I repeat again, these are people who are often physically attractive and have enormous charisma and even brilliance in a certain spiritual or psychological teaching. This is where lightworkers are most susceptible to getting sucked in. Sometimes it is the glamour of psychic abilities that sucks lightworkers in. Sometimes it is magician-like psychological abilities or hypnotic-like abilities that pull people in. Other times still it is profound spiritual teachings, even of the Ascended Masters or other ancient truths that the Twilight Master uses to snag impressionable and undiscerning lightworkers.

Sometimes their Twilight Master activity is extremely subtle and covert and this may be the most dangerous Twilight Master of all. Twilight Masters may have profound spiritual knowledge and even psychological and spiritual abilities, however at their core, if you have the eyes to see and the ears to hear, they worship false gods and idols in a metaphysical sense. They may be high level initiates and may be representing themselves as representatives of great spiritual Masters, gurus, yogis, and even the Ascended Masters. This is what makes them often hard to discern at first, for their initial front may have a lot of light and truth. My beloved readers, look deeply and do not be fooled by wolves in sheep's clothing.

Self-Aggrandizement

By effectuating the students' alienation from self and GOD, the student then seeks to bond with their teacher. Unfortunately, in cases such as these, the Master that the student seeks to bond with is a Twilight Master. As such, the Master, or teacher seeks their own self-aggrandizement, rather than the glorification of GOD and the liberation of the student. This is one of the greatest themes that runs through all levels of Twilight Masters and through all the gradations of they who embody shades of gray.

I must point out here that both Twilight Master and student can be at an extremely high level of initiation and degree of fame and public recognition. This is a fact often overlooked. All of us at all times must hold steadfast to our vigilance to be of service to GOD and to embody the highest, purest and clearest frequencies. At any point, anyone of us can become victims of our own negative ego and thus falter. That is why the eight quotients that I have given you at the start of this book are so extremely important. It must always be the Christ consciousness that we manifest, the love, the light, the total control over the negative ego that we exhibit. We must remember that the true path of Godliness has nothing whatsoever to do with glorification of the personal self, and everything to do with glorification of GOD and the manifestation of the GOD within each of us. If ever you notice that your own personal self, your lower self, is seeking the glory, the fame, the adulation, please become immediately aware that you have momentarily stepped off your path and get right back on it. GOD has nothing to do with the little games that the negative ego can become engaged in!

Often it is when spiritual teachers, channels, healers and psychics come into their completion of their planetary initiations, power, fame, financial abundance and have a great many students under their tutelage that they are most susceptible and vulnerable to the seduction of the negative ego and Twilight Master characteristics and attunements. In my personal experience and observation of the New Age movement and the earthly world in general, this is where I see it happening the most.

Pay very close attention, beloved readers, to whether or not the person, teachings, or spiritual group you are involved with are focused even minutely on their own self-aggrandizement or self-importance. This is a sure sign that they are not focused upon GOD. No matter how much light or how beautiful some of the teachings coming through this person or group of people are, if it is geared in any way toward the glorification of that person or group then you can be sure it falls within the gray zone.

That which is purely of the light seeks only to glorify that light. It seeks the pure love of GOD as well, and its teachings are aimed at sharing that light and love with humanity and the planet as a whole. The focus is inward, only in the sense of inner attunement to GOD, the Mighty I Am Presence, the inner light and love, and the inner plane Hierarchy of Ascended Planetary and Cosmic Masters. It is never inwardly centered on the negative ego or personality. If you find that this is so, then you have likewise found a Twilight Master.

The energy of self-aggrandizement can be very subtle. It can also take the form of extending outward to glorify and build up the negative ego of the student or group of students. One of the ways that this can happen, and indeed is happening, is where the teacher sets themselves apart as the highest, the most advanced, the "only one able to access this or that," and then proceeds to either initiate their followers into this privilege or to tell them that by being part of this specific group that they too are the highest, the most advanced, the privileged few. This again runs the gamut from a teacher with a small group of followers to and including a cult leader with a very large group of totally devoted followers.

Integrated Ascension

The student or students are lead to believe that they are privy to the highest, that they alone have access to keys to the kingdom that no other individual or group has access to. This is obviously very separative in nature, but somehow it does not get perceived in that light. Instead it is interpreted through the lens that GOD has singled their teacher and their group out to be the absolute official voice of the highest truth, and that any other voice is of a lesser quality and therefore offers nothing in comparison with that which they have to say or what they have to offer.

Can you not, beloved readers, see how absolutely and utterly egotistical that is? I am sure you can. Yet, when you find yourself within such a situation it is not so very apparent at all. Remember that this is a process that has developed in stages. First, you were offered truth as it truly stands. You were given real validation for the light with which you shine. Slowly the shades of gray are brought in and slowly the focus is shifted from GOD to lower self. That is why the path of the Twilight Master is a very tricky one and often goes unnoticed until one finds themselves so deep within it that they need all their strength and personal power to climb out of the fog into the clear light of day once more.

I urge you, therefore, at the first sign of self-aggrandizement, negative ego empowerment, and personal glorification to immediately choose the road of Selflessness, Service, Christ consciousness, and light, and to immediately leave. While it is true that all aspects of self, including the four lower bodies, must be fully and totally integrated within your ascension process, they are never meant to steal the show or seek the glory or the glamour! All glory belongs to GOD alone! I tell you sincerely and with no compunction whatsoever, where there is self glorification there is negative ego and where there is negative ego the light of GOD is dim and shrouded in gray, if it shines at all. If you truly choose GOD you will not choose the negative ego, nor they who themselves choose the negative ego. If you want the Light then cling to the Light, glorify the Light, and serve only the Light. Do not accept anything less than the clearest Light of GOD and your path will remain ever pure.

Twilight Masters again often have very high levels of initiation and a wealth of pure and true spiritual information to draw on, which is part of their attractiveness. The problem is that they are psychologically unclear and have not worked out their personality stuff. They may be master spiritual teachers, channels, healers and psychics, however even though this is the case, they have allowed the negative ego to infiltrate their program and consciousness which has led them to serve two masters—the negative ego darkness and the Christ Light! They may have all the outer accouterments and knowledge to be master spiritual teachers and channels and even be world famous, however this does not mean they have any understanding in the slightest of what negative ego is and how it can corrupt. These, my friends, are the most dangerous Twilight Masters of all, and this is why every lightworker must become incredibly psychologically sophisticated as to the workings of the negative ego and the Christ mind within your selves, otherwise you will not be able to see it in others.

Recognizing the Light

Beloved readers, I feel it is imperative that I pause here to point out that there are unique situations wherein a true Master is so imbued, stabilized and centered in the light that they themselves do in fact stand as embodiments of the light. These rare and most magnificent beings are most definitely **not** whom I am addressing in this chapter on Twilight Masters. Although they reveal Glory through and within their individualized embodiments, it is the Glory of GOD that they embody and not the glory of the negative ego or indeed any glory lesser than that of GOD Itself. A perfect example of this in the past would be the embodiment of Lord Maitreya through Jesus/Sananda. A perfect example of this currently is His Holiness the Lord Sai Baba, the Cosmic Christ and an avatar in the truest sense of the word! When a Being such as Sai Baba stands forth in all his radiant glory, he is clearly recognized

Integrated Ascension

as an embodiment of and for the Glory of GOD. It is extremely vital here that there is no misunderstanding. It is as important to recognize the light as it is to recognize the twilight and the darkness. It is imperative that you discern through you own light when a great Master embodies as a manifestation of GOD and when a Twilight Master seeks to glorify their negative ego through the personal self. The difference is so vast and the gulf between the two so great that words could not begin to express it. This understanding must come from within! Through your own light you will surely be able to see and recognize a being who is so pure that the light they shine forth is the light of GOD alone. I trust that you all will do this and not misinterpret anything that I am saying in regards to Twilight Masters, cults and non-integrated ascension groups with They who have come forth out of the Light of GOD Itself to bring untold blessings upon us and our world!

"...I Am. We are. The Only Way."

To return to our discussion of Twilight Masters, cults, and non-integrated ascension groups, another key way in which they can be recognized is by the putting forth that they and they alone are the way to GOD. Their purpose is to separate you from all other paths, teachers, Masters, teachings and often even friends and relatives so that you come to rely solely upon them. They guide you away from any other helpful input, be it literature, workshops, teachings or teachers, in an attempt to put you in a state of isolation wherein you are dependent only upon them. They convince you to be so by playing up the superiority of what they have to offer and the inferiority of any other teachings. What they are doing, in truth, is simply building up the superiority of their own negative egos!

This is quite damaging in a number of areas. The first and most apparent is that it separates you from your very self. As I keep saying, if you are not right with self, you cannot be right with GOD, or anyone else. If you are cut off from self, then you literally have nowhere to turn, as you have been guided away from that part of you which is necessary and vital for you to seek truth with in the first place! Separating self from self, or even creating doubts between self and self, or self and GOD, is by far the greatest tool of the Twilight Master, or even the black magicians themselves. This is your most precious gift and birthright. Your relationship to self and to GOD and the Masters is literally the "gift of light" by which you see! Do not, under any circumstances, let any other person get hold of that. Nothing outside of self is the "only way." As beloved Master Jesus said, "The Kingdom of GOD is within you."

It is vital that you realize that when Jesus/Sananda spoke the words, "I Am the Way and the Truth and the Light," he was referring to the Christ Presence that resides in each and every one of us. He was *not* referring to himself as a person or a religion. The Christian religion didn't even exist when he spoke those words. They were spoken only to guide you to your own Christed Beingness, so that you may know your own path to GOD. When a Twilight Master, cult or even a non-integrated ascension group tries to tell you that they alone have the answer, run for the hills! Beloved readers, you, your relationship to self, to GOD, to the inner plane Hierarchy of Planetary and Cosmic Ascended Masters, and the Angelic Beings are your only true path. Do not let anyone try to convince you otherwise, for it just is not so!

Remember also that we each have our own system of chakras, petals to unfold, and wheels to turn within the chakra system. This is the etheric manifestation of our unique pathway to GOD, enlightenment, liberation, and ascension. While we are in embodiment, the chakras likewise have their physical manifestation within the specific glands that they are connected to. If you ever find yourself doubting that you are indeed your own path to the Godhead, simply have a good look at how you are etherically and physically constituted. This speaks for itself regarding this issue.

Integrated Ascension

It is vital that you recognize that when someone is trying to build a group of followers for the sake of their own personal worship, they cannot possibly be representing the God of which they are so glibly speaking. Light calls light unto itself by its own Divine radiance, just as love does. Light and love that is reflective of Source seeks to empower each and every individual to find their own first best destiny, ascension mission and puzzle piece within the whole.

Truth does not seek to create bondage by instilling fear that separates anyone from their own connection or calling, but seeks rather to activate each person's personal power. Know this, and you will avoid the pitfalls and dangers of anyone who tries to convince you otherwise. Light speaks the Language of Light and communicates to the lighted part of each of us. It does not ever seek to convince only to radiate, and be that which it is.

Be ever on guard against any person or group of people who use the tool of divisiveness in order to encourage you upon your path. That which is all inclusive can never be truly represented by that which seeks to exclude. You may find that a particular time in life calls you to a specific path, but again, that is the call of light unto light and not the manipulations of someone else trying to build up their own personal power of worship. You have the power of discernment.

As I said before, there are many quite wonderful paths you can travel upon. There are, however, no wonderful paths that are the one and only way. There are certainly no true paths that seek in any way, shape or form to disconnect you from self. Follow you own inner light and love, and be sure that when and if you do surrender to a particular path or teaching, that it is by your own free will and has within it an open door that you freely enter and can freely exit when and if Spirit calls you in another direction.

As long as the door remains open and you enter and exit by the power of your own free will and know that the path you are on is helping you to connect with self and GOD, then it can potentially be a wondrous experience. Use whatever path you are on to more deeply connect with self and GOD, and to learn how to become a more efficient server. Do not let any path attempt to, or by any means assume control over YOU! The only true path that is the only way is the path within. Never forget that and never fully surrender to anything less than your own GOD-Self!

The Lower Use of the Higher Self

Another point that you would do well to bear in mind, is that anyone who has traveled far enough along their path to be a master of any sort, even a Twilight Master, will have some use of the inner senses. This happens quite automatically as a by-product of evolution. This is likewise an area where extreme caution must be used, for there is much subtlety and many, many shades of gray within this area. In fact, it takes the skill of a truly trained and integrated mystic/occultist to be able to clearly discern what is going on within these realms and how to accurately read the astral, etheric and even mental forms surrounding a person, situation or the planet as a whole. Hang onto your own personal power in this area as well, for until you yourself have the full vision of discernment, or have found an individual who can accurately 'read' these inner realms, it is better to stay simple and focus upon self and GOD!

I will explain exactly what I mean here. Each of us has lots of various activity within each of the four lower bodies. The more fully integrated and the further along we are upon our path of ascension and initiation, the less stimulation is going on within these various bodies. Nevertheless, most, if not indeed all of us who are upon the Earth have certain activities in motion within our psychic and psychological structure. In truth, how could it be otherwise?

Much of what is in motion upon the emotional level is purely symbolic. We may dream of a spider's web in order to symbolically communicate to

Integrated Ascension

ourselves that we are trapped in something that we need to get out of. This 'something' could be of an astral/emotional nature, or it could be of a mental nature, such as a certain faulty belief system. Nevertheless, it appears within our aura, simply as a spider's web.

Beloved readers, it takes a truly clear and integrated Master of a very high order to be able to discern what in fact the webbing is symbolic of. This Master may have the ability to read it accurately themselves, or to get an accurate and clear reading while working with you and the messages of various chakras, along with helping you to decipher both your subconscious and conscious thought. They will do this in order to help you achieve your maximum freedom through their ability to assist you in unveiling the hidden meaning of your own personal symbolism.

A Master who works within the twilight or darker realms will not do this. First, if a person is caught upon the twilight path they themselves will not have the power of discernment they need in order to help you see clearly and accurately through the swirling forms that surround you on many levels. For example, they will not be able to tell what is coming from your wish life, dream life or from your conscious choices. All will appear to be one mass of indiscernible energy. This, most likely, however, will not stop their tongues from offering you their most definite advice based upon the vision that they are in truth, unable to read for themselves, let alone you!

Secondly, depending upon how much they need to feed their own negative ego needs and desires, they will "use" the information that your energy field supplies in order to manipulate you with fear. For instance, if we return to our example of the spider's web, they will most likely sense that you are caught in "something." They will not know what that "something" is or to seek to free you from it. Instead, they are quite capable of using that knowledge to induce fear and surrender to them by telling you enough about yourself for you to believe in their powers. Once your belief pattern has been established, they can then proceed to build upon it.

Integrated Ascension

They might, and again this is only a potential example, confirm for you that you feel trapped or caught. This will feel right and true and you will then validate this for them. Once you have done this, a certain link between you is established. They can then go on and build upon it in any way that serves their purpose for the moment. In most instances, the result will be you giving your power away to them. They will appear to be the only way out of that which you feel trapped by.

True cult leaders are quite adept at this process. They have spent much time in observing human nature in general and in developing their psychic and even higher senses to this end. They may be quite adept at reading thoughtforms as well, however, they may simply be your thoughtforms of worry, fears about the future, doubts, and concerns. They then will present themselves as the solution to these worries, concerns, doubts and so forth. They will do whatever they can in order to create a dependency upon them. This is, of course, the opposite of what a so-called White Magician or Master of the Light would do. Rather than leading you to GOD, they will be leading you to the altar of their own negative ego and helping to contaminate your own ego in the process!

As I said before, "A little knowledge is a dangerous thing." Nowhere is this truer than in the more occult realms and nowhere more dangerous than in the hands of a true full fledged Twilight Master, except of course, in the hands of one who has utterly devoted themselves to the darkness. The truth of the matter is, most of us are not very susceptible to the true black magician. As these beings do not give off any light at all, we are much more likely to stay away from them altogether. For us, the Twilight Master presents a much greater problem, because there is enough light within most of them to be drawn to them, and much good they can and do impart before revealing whatever level and shade of gray they are carrying.

We therefore often open up to them with little hesitation, and invite them into our auric fields. Beloved readers, we must be very, very careful who we invite into our holy temple of self! Our paths are truly between ourselves, GOD, and the highest grade of Master of Light and Angelic Presence. There are those who can be of great service along the way such as a sincere fellow lightworker. It is vital, however, that we do our own read upon them and/or get a referral from someone who has passed our own highest requirements before we allow anyone into our sacred temples.

Always bear in mind that it takes a high degree of training to be able to read through the etheric, astral and mental worlds that surround our fields. A true, highly integrated initiate will not mistake your field of hope or aspiration from your field of confusion. They will be able to read and interpret with accuracy. They will speak only truth that will propel you forward and never, ever say what they think you want to hear.

For example, if you want to hear that you have taken the seventh level of initiation, yet are truly at the fifth and require specific work in order to facilitate the actual taking of the seventh initiation of full and complete integrated ascension, what good does it serve if they tell you that you have already completed it? None! Not on your behalf anyway. What it does serve to do is to have you like them, bond with them, want to hear more from them; in short feed their negative ego by first feeding yours.

If you seek a spiritual consultation, which all of you who are my readers know I greatly encourage, be sure to be clear and ask for the highest truth only and find the right person. If you are in the process of becoming a channel and being able to do these readings for other people be sure to ask GOD and the Masters to help you see and state only that which serves the highest good of your client. The negative ego has absolutely no place whatsoever in this holy process! Speak only the clearest, purest truth as you can read it. Just because you pray for it doesn't mean you have it. The only way to truly have it is to do your psychological and spiritual homework and to be devastatingly honest with self.

Integrated Ascension

If you get unclear or cannot yet decipher certain patterns, be honest. Never allow yourself to fall into manipulation by abusing your higher abilities in any way and never allow anyone to do that to you! Seek and share only that which is accurate and for the highest purpose of Spiritual evolution, or else be *silent*. By the same token, ask for only that which will truly help you and not for that which you would like to hear. Again, I suggest that all of you seeking spiritual counseling run your own intuitive check on the channel. If you pick up any negative ego agendas, you have the right and responsibility to say, "No thank you." You also have the right and responsibility to get referrals from those whose work within the spiritual field you respect. Either or both these methods combined will serve you well. Please do make use of them. It is important in the process of truly being clear within self to be open to feedback from your dreams, own channel, friends, life, and spiritual teachers. Often people run by their negative ego and/or Twilight Masters are extremely defended and insulated and receive feedback only from a select few that have the same psychological imbalances they have.

I am happy to provide you with personal referrals myself, so please feel free to contact me at the number at the back of this book. I am sure many of you know of others whom you hold in high regard as trustworthy sources. Don't hesitate to ask for their recommendation, and never, ever forget to first and foremost consult with your own inner guidance.

Each of you has the ability of discernment. What is needed in regards to this specific subject, and in general, beloved readers, is your own personal cultivation of your faculty of discrimination and discernment! That is one of GOD's greatest gifts that each one of us should develop and use at all times and in all situations. Ultimately, it is by our own light and love that we shall recognize the light and love of GOD! Remember that it takes a great deal of inner and outer training in order to decipher the various frequencies that each center is emitting. It also takes the purest intent and GOD attunement to get an accurate reading. A Twilight Master will not bother about these points, for they will be too busy either consciously or unconsciously seeking to manipulate you with your own emotional and mental auric imprints. The goal, beloved readers, is to stay as far away from anyone who even dabbles amidst the shades of gray. This is just one area that we happen to be discussing now, for this particular area allows them to exert a specific type of control and influence.

Light goes to light, love to love and GOD intent goes to GOD Realization. Always follow your highest light and love, and steer clear of anything that feels the least bit murky. If you are even unclear about an individual's reading, simply ask yourself whether or not what they are saying is going to help you help yourself or help you to feed their own negative ego. Your answer to this one question will show you the truth and make your way clear.

All who want to serve GOD will want to serve their bothers and sisters own personal connection to GOD, or Source. All who are in anyway seeking to serve the negative ego will seek to create faulty dependence upon themselves, their group, their negative ego agenda. If they leave you feeling more self empowered and with a deeper connection to your own Higher Self and Monad, then they are truly doing GOD's work. If they leave you feeling confused, dependent upon them and cut off from your own Higher Self and/or Monad, then they are doing the work of the negative ego. It is that simple.

The other danger is that they leave you feeling self-inflated with guidance that is not based on truth. My beloved readers, the most important guidance I can give you in any of my books comes down to the following statement. Each and every moment of your life you must ask yourself in the deepest and most profound manner possible, "Do I want GOD or do I want my ego in this moment?" this is the question that Twilight Masters, borderline Twilight Masters and people who are run by the negative ego do not ask themselves. They may be Masters and brilliant on every other level, however if they do not remain "Vigilant for GOD and His Kingdom" on this point every moment of their life corruption and contamination will take place to varying degrees no matter how far the lightworker, spiritual teacher or channel has come. As the Bible says, "A man/woman cannot serve two Masters." He/She will both hate the one and love the other, or cling to the one and despise the other. Therefore, I say unto you, you cannot serve GOD and mammon (negative ego selfishness).

Confusions within Non-Integrated Ascension Groups

When individuals who have traversed the ascension path in an unintegrated manner come together and form ascension groups, the result is bound to be that of "group non-integration." In a situation such as this, the "whole" or non-integrated ascension group will inadvertently create a host of difficulties, deceptions, problems, and confusions within itself. There will be much to watch out for, much to avoid, and much to overcome. Such a group as this unwittingly falls into twilight, as this is the inevitable result of group clouding of the light. All this, we will explore together in a moment.

I would like to say, however, at the outset of this section, that there is one potential good to be garnered by this type of situation. This potential good is that each person who finds themselves in such a predicament can use each other person as a mirror of their own non-integration. In that way, lemonade can ultimately be made from the harsh and sour lemon of non-integration! It is important that we all remember that mistakes are only true mistakes if we fail to learn from them. As long as we keep open to the lesson that we need to master, our paths will always lead us out of any miasma into the pure, clear light of GOD!

People come together for many reasons on the spiritual path. One of the primary reasons is that of fellowship. The path of initiation is a path that is seemingly ultimately walked alone. The reason that I say

Integrated Ascension

"seemingly" is because, in truth, none of us are ever alone. We are guided and befriended by hosts of inner plane Ascended Masters, Archangels and our own personal Guardian Angel or Angels. We are likewise watched over by the Confederation of Planets, who are our brothers and sisters who help to guide us ever onward and upward upon the path of integrated initiations. Nevertheless, often for long periods of time we are left to work with our "stuff," to seemingly find our own way, with little or no apparent guidance from this multitude of inner plane beings with whom we, in truth, remain ever connected! Often our outer world seems as barren as the inner one. This, beloved readers, is one of the primary motivation factors for forming or joining spiritual groups.

The second biggest factor is that of spiritual fellowship. There is much truth and power within spiritual fellowship. It is my firm belief that there is no better outward aid to one's spiritual path than the ascension buddy system of which I have written extensively about, and made great use of upon my own journeys. Even beloved Master Jesus has said, "Whenever two or more of you are gathered in my name, there I will be also." So, what we are speaking of here is spiritual truth and spiritual law.

Lightworkers gathered together in groups are a very wonderful thing. Each person brings his or her own unique vision, talent, and puzzle piece. Inspiration and exploration of various teachings can be greatly facilitated. Feelings of isolation dissolve into feelings of love and unity of purpose. The problem arises when and if the individuals forming this group have themselves pursued their path of ascension and initiation in an unintegrated manner. The result of this is that you have one person's imbalance and confusion playing off of another person's imbalance and confusion. Negative egos are as likely to but heads as they are to be transmuted into Christ consciousness. In fact, they often fall deeply into modes of competition in such a situation. Therefore, this topic deserves an in-depth look, as many lightworkers are in this

Integrated Ascension

moment functioning within a non-integrated group body, and are therefore falling into glamours and illusions when they at heart, would rather be rising into light and love.

The first thing you need to do, if you are working within a group body, is to run a check on your own eight major quotients that were presented at the beginning of this book. See how you are doing with them for yourself first. Then, run the same type of check over the group body within which you are functioning. Take an honest reading and see if you, as an ascension group, are maintaining high levels of these most important quotients, or if, and to what degree, you are out of balance with them. Most likely, you will find yourself at a similar place personally as is the group as a whole. In some instances, your reading might reveal a great disparity, with you carrying high quotient readings and your group maintaining a low quotient reading. If this is the case, you will most likely have already been feeling out of harmony and at odds with your group. The reading that you take will give you tangible proof why that is so, and then it will become apparent that it is time for you to move on.

The main point to remember here is that no matter what is revealed, stay free and clear of judgment and in a place of unconditional love and compassion. Observe and discriminate what is and what is not appropriate. Do not judge, however, for that will immediately put you in tune with the negative ego and lower self, which I am sure is **not** where you want to be.

Currently many lightworkers are working within non-integrated ascension groups and do not even have the slightest clue about that fact. This is not altogether surprising, however, as many lightworkers are pursuing their own personal path of ascension in a most non-integrated fashion, and therefore the groups that develop out of this type of situation are bound to be reflective of the individuals involved. As you are becoming more and more aware of the need of your own

Integrated Ascension

personal integration, I feel that at this juncture of the book it is imperative to address non-integration in group formation.

The danger that exists within the un-integrated group is vast. When you have a body of individuals focusing their energies upon ascension in a non-integrated manner, you have mass confusion. Each person's negative ego is either feeding off of or battling with each other person's negative ego. This simple fact alone is indicative of a dysfunctioning individual and group. The light therefore, that both individual and group are trying to ignite is instead being "grayed out" by the joint force of the many battles that the lower self and negative ego are engaged in.

If you are reading this book as a group and feel there is truth to what I am saying here, then it is my humble privilege to offer you some pointers and suggestions. There are actually a few choices that may be made if you recognize this to be fact within your group and truly want to correct it.

The first is applicable to the situation where only one individual recognizes this as truth, and the others of the group feel as though they are functioning within right harmony. I addressed this earlier, but will restate it again for emphasis. If you, beloved reader, find that your own personal integrity and quotient levels are at a much higher standard than that of the group to which you form a part, the best choice for you is to lovingly and non-judgmentally take your leave of that group. A group situation can only be corrected if all within any given group seek to make correction. If you stand alone, than at all costs stand for your own personal light, love, and integrity!

It may be that the group is, in truth, only slightly off kilter from where you want to be, but that is enough. It is each person's responsibility to live up to the highest standard of his or her own GOD Self as possible. Move on, beloved one, and continue to work on your process of Integrated Ascension and to uphold you personal power, light, love, and the standard of your integrity. If you maintain the highest standards that are apparent to self, you will always remain on

Integrated Ascension

course! Most importantly however, make this choice and all choices from a state of consciousness and egolessness.

The second choice would be one possible solution to a group if the entire group did their own reading and found themselves to be both individually, and as a whole, functioning in an unintegrated manner. This would show up on personal readings based upon the eight major quotients and in the reading of the group as a whole in order to see where the unit or group body stood in relationship to the eight quotients. This would give a pretty accurate account of how integrated or unintegrated both individuals and the group were. If the reading did in fact reveal a low level in regards to the eight quotients and a high degree of non-integration, the group itself might opt to break up so that each individual member can get to work upon building these quotients for themselves. This is one of two possible solutions.

The advantage of this solution is that it would immediately break up the links that have been engendered and cultivated by functioning as a unit. The tendency for the negative ego of one person to feed off of the negative ego of another person would be brought to an immediate halt! Love and friendship of course would remain intact, but all telepathic hook-ups would be asked to be removed. This would allow each member to be freed of the pulls of the other members and to concentrate fully and completely upon their own process of balance and integration.

A little metaphor for this would be as if this group were functioning together in a communal room which they suddenly found to be an utter mess. Upon further investigation, they discovered that each of their own rooms was in the same state of disarray and confusion. Each person would return to their own room and clean it up! When the cleaning process was complete, and a certain number of cleaning skills were developed, the group would then come together once again in the community room and clean up their joint space. There would not need to be a permanent disbanding, but certainly a temporary one, as each

Integrated Ascension

person's 'mess' would be unique and require their undivided attention in order to attend to the work at hand. When that was completely successful they could again join forces, adding their newly developed skill and transform the community room into a place of splendor, light, love, true unity and Godliness.

There is always the chance and the choice that when the individuals involved become balanced and integrated within themselves that they will not rejoin with the group that they were originally working with. One of the key reasons for this would be that in cases where there is severe imbalance and negative ego issues, it would have been those imbalances which drew the specific group together in the first place. Once the members of the disbanded group are properly integrated, they will often, in cases such as this, find that there work lies elsewhere. The weaknesses that bound them together at a particular point of their journey is no longer prevalent and so the force of attraction becomes inappropriate. In this type of situation, the healthiest path is to let go of the past and to move forward via the coding of the integrated Christ mind, light, love, psychology, service and initiation quotients!

Another choice altogether would be to stay within the group and to work on individual and group integration concurrently. This choice would most likely occur when there is a deeply binding group karma, which most likely also involves a shared group mission and vision. This is not the easiest path, yet it can ultimately be the most effective. We have put much attention on the quote of beloved Master Jesus that tells us, "Whenever two or more are gathered in my name, there I am also." In this regard, the power of the Christ, flowing through Lord Maitreya, Kuthumi, and beloved Master Jesus/Sananda can be a most vital and healing force. When the intent is to walk through the darkness as one and to transform and transmute all lower and unintegrated energies into higher integrated energies, all the powers of the Cosmos will rise up to be of assistance.

Integrated Ascension

When this is the choice of any group, there must be equal attention given to the process of individual integration as to that of group integration. If the various individuals do not do their own personal work of integration, balance and the conquering of the negative ego and the replacement of it by Christ consciousness, there is no way that such a transformation can happen for the group. Each person's Saddna, or spiritual practice, is vital to the success of the whole.

The group, however, can function as windows of reflection, as each member and the group in mass mirrors back to the individual exactly where they are at. The tricky part of this is that both the group, its members and each individual seeking their own reflection within that structure, must be sure to do so in a state of utter clarity, purity, and forgiveness of self and forgiveness of the group and its members. In other words, each person is required to approach the process from their Christ consciousness, or immediately to raise up to that level of consciousness in order for this to work. If this is not done, the fragile negative ego will prevail, and all sorts of reactions, judgments, fears, recriminations, and the like will come to the fore.

The facets of the negative ego can themselves be a mirror of where the individual is at. The danger lurks within the fact that it is absolutely imperative that the Christ consciousness be summoned forth and that one does not indulge within the realm of the negative ego. If any member does not rise up to the level of the Christ consciousness, then they will fall to the level of the negative ego and endanger the group as a whole. Each member must be 100% committed to the process of individual and group integrated ascension, and to allow their negativity to rise to the surface only so that it can be seen and properly handled. No one can succumb to living out their negativity if the group as a whole, and they themselves, want to come to the appropriate place of balance and integration.

If, however, each one lives up to their highest standard, the force and power of the group to fulfill its highest calling will be exceptionally great. They will have demonstrated true unity of growth and evolvement, and remained clear to their greatest intent and vision. The group will stand as an example to all lightworkers of what is possible when the intention is pure and the highest standards are played out. Ultimately we all share in the group purpose of the planet as a whole. When a group demonstrates the overcoming of the lower through the invocation and application of the higher, they become a guiding light for the planet itself. This, however, cannot be forced, and will basically only work out when there is the deepest of bonds between the group members as well as a karma that binds them to the fulfillment of a particular ascension mission and collective puzzle piece!

The main point here is that however you choose to deal with a non-integrated ascension group, do make sure that you *do* deal with it. Just as its time for the blinders to come off personally and to take stock of your own ascension process and the levels of integration that you are exhibiting for yourself, it is time to do this in regards to groups. If you are already part of a group, do not be afraid to take a good and honest look and see exactly where this group is at. If you are looking to join in fellowship with a group body, make sure that their standards are up to your own caliber in terms of integration, balance, and integrity.

As I already stated, in truth we all form part of the group body of planet Earth. In another, more inclusive aspect we form part of the group body of the solar system. At still higher and more inclusive levels, we are part of the group body of the galaxy, universe, and Cosmos Itself. We are all ultimately part of the great unfathomable "whole" which we call GOD!

Groups are therefore not to be avoided but to be cultivated! We must all, however, come to terms with our own integrated approach to the ascension process, so that we can bring it to the group body of which we are a part. We must hold fast to our own personal integrity and not forsake that for any Earthly group that might try and convince us that we need them in order to complete our own ascension. What we need, beloved readers, is to be as balanced, whole and integrated within ourselves as possible, so that we can and do uplift the greater group body of planet Earth by virtue of our being here. This is the first and ultimate order of business, for out of who we are, out of the center of self, we radiate our energies into the greater whole.

The work of personal integration and balanced ascension that you do for yourself cannot help but to raise humankind in the process. Stay ever attuned to the highest vision, no matter what. I sincerely promise you that the entire Cosmos will come to your aid, for the Guardians of Light & Love are ever with you! You may feel alone, but that loneliness will last for only a moment of Divine time. In truth, you are never alone. The Masters and Angels ever walk with you, and you never were or shall be separate from GOD, the all embracing Source of all that is!

More on Twilight Masters, Cults, and Non-Integrated Ascension Groups

The best and most effective method of recognizing a Twilight Master, or indeed anyone who is carrying shades of gray within their field, is first and foremost by being as clear as you possibly can within your own self. The second thing you need to do is to be aware that Twilight Masters are indeed out there, and do seek to feed off of your own energy fields. It is very easy to become blinded by the light, so to speak, and to think that everyone who uses similar terms, language, expressions as you do is upon the path of ascension into the center of light, love and power of Source. Although that may be their ultimate destiny, be forewarned that there are many who have taken paths of divergence!

These individuals, cults or groups have allowed themselves to become enamored by the light, and have changed the focus of the light and love of GOD to the focus of the lesser light and love of the glorification and glamour of the lower self or personality. In order for these people to get what they are seeking, they need an appropriate audience

Integrated Ascension

for whom to perform the tricks of their lesser magic, and to provide the necessary energy through which they can work.

What must be understood is that the Masters will come to assist any and every one who sets their feet upon the path to GOD. They will guide, they will guard, and they will offer their love, light, wisdom, revelations, healing, and assistance on every level possible. They will be there, supporting and backing all their disciple's endeavors in order to facilitate the work of the Hierarchy upon Earth. If, however, an individual or group of individuals, no matter how far along the path they have gotten, turns their focus from that of GOD and service of humanity, to that of the negative ego and the manipulation of humanity, the Inner Plane Hierarchy of Ascended Planetary and Cosmic Masters will withdraw from those people. The individuals will then seek to maintain their own energy source. Rather then getting it from GOD and the Masters, they will seek to get it from anyone whom they can manipulate and control along the way. The greater a person's own frequency and light, the more the Twilight Master will be attracted to that person, as that person has more within their energy field to offer.

I am not telling you this to cause fear by any means. If you call upon GOD and the Masters you will always be protected and never have anything to fear. I am telling you this, however, in order that you may become aware of this fact so that you carefully choose who you will and will not consciously align with. The more integrated and free of the negative ego that you personally are, the clearer you will be able to see where another is coming from. While you are going through this process of self-integration, balancing and clearing, it is my intention to make you aware of certain tendencies within others to be on the look out for. In this way, the unbalanced choices that they made can in no way effect you. Your eyes will be fully opened, and you will be able to proceed upon your own path with gentleness and ease, unencumbered by anyone else's misaligned intentions.

Integrated Ascension

Beloved readers, the light and love that you have cultivated is sacred, holy and precious. It is GOD's gift to you, which you have earned by your own hard work. When you share it in loving service to the Divine Plan it becomes your gift back to GOD. It is like a self-contained, GOD ordained, perfectly functioning ecosystem.

When anyone, whoever they may be, tries to intrude upon your GOD-radiance, they are invading a sanctified and holy temple. They are doing this because they have temporarily lost their own alignment to GOD and the Masters, and so seek to access it through you. Since the Inner Plane Hierarchy of Ascended Planetary and Cosmic beings have withdrawn from such a person or group of individuals, they feel a void where once they felt an unending supply of light and love. In their own confusion and desperation they turn to you, to draw upon the light that the Masters are still making available to you, and also to the light and love that is radiating throughout your Being and essence.

They must be seen for who they are, and steadfastly refused. Their strongest weapon, as said very early in this chapter, is that there are yet aspects and qualities of the light that they have accessed and cultivated within them and within much of their teachings as well. Remember that we are not talking about someone who proudly presents themselves as Masters of Black Magic or Voodoo. These are beings that have worked, and often still continue to work, within the sphere of light. The problem is that they have allowed themselves to become so misaligned, fragmented, ruled by the negative ego, run by the inner child, run by lower-self desire, and often run by their emotions as well as being subject to glamour, that the Masters have had to put their Divine attention elsewhere. There is still much within these individuals to attract you, the lightworker. That is where their greatest potential for danger lies! That is also where the power of your ability to be truly discerning must come into play!

Do not judge them, however, do not align with them. When the negative ego, personality, and the need to control is in evidence, stay

Integrated Ascension

focused upon your own integrated ascension and you will be invulnerable. Do not let them seduce you through the offering of some glamorous project, or by believing they will initiate you into some secret teaching that they alone are privy to.

This type of talk is meant to stimulate any unbalanced energies that are still functioning within your own auric field, desire body, and lower mental body. It is given in the hopes that you will "follow them," and give your power over to them and their faulty thinking. If you do this they will have access to the higher frequencies of light and love that you, my friend, carry, and will use it to further their own ends, rather than to fulfill the Divine plan of GOD.

If you mistakenly allow this to occur, you will know that you have made the wrong choice by the unmistakable sensation that your own energy is being drained in the process. My advice then is to immediately get yourself out of that situation and to ask for the protection of Archangel Michael in the process. Know that the Masters have not deserted you, but you, in giving away your power, have temporarily deserted *yourself*! Note that I specifically say, "giving away your own power." A Twilight Master cannot take your energies from you, however, by aligning with them you are certainly free to offer your energies to them and to their misguided purposes. This is the reason, above and beyond any other, personal power is number one upon my list of qualities to cultivate, nurture, and claim!

Keep centered upon your own center, plan, and purpose. Learn from anyone who is truly filled with the light, but do not ever give your personal power away. GOD will not ask for it, for the energy that is GOD would have you radiant with power/will, light and love simultaneously! No true Master would ever ask for it. At certain phases of an initiate's training, particularly in the past and in certain Eastern disciplines, there is a surrendering that a Master may request. That surrendering, however, has nothing whatsoever to do with giving away your personal power. It is a surrendering process pertaining to the 'little' self, personality, egotistical self or negative ego, to that which is love and light in its purest form.

Never allow anyone to attempt to convince you otherwise. The type of surrendering that a Twilight Master or cult leader asks is disempowering. The type of surrendering asked for by GOD or those who in the past have acted as His/Her Divine representatives upon Earth is empowering. The chasm that exists between these two varied forms of surrender is wider than the ring-pass-not of your imagination! Do not, beloved readers, mistake the two!

Be aware that a Twilight Master literally gets their energy through zapping into the energy field of another who is firmly rooted within the continuous flow of light, love, power and wisdom. Depending upon how murky one has allowed themselves to become, is the degree to which they will enjoy this process. As most all of us are still in the process of fully integrating and balancing within ourselves, we will have a bit of murky coloring within our auric fields. The difference between ourselves and a Twilight Master in this case is that our intent is upon GOD and service. Their intent is no longer upon this. It is rather upon the manipulation of others for the building up of their own negative ego. They are not on the path of perfection, but have fallen prey to their own illusions and take varying degrees of pleasure in deception itself.

Recognize individuals for what they *are*, and not for what they *say* they are. See past promises of advanced initiations, the imparting of guarded secrets, or even the promise of furthering your wisdom and GOD connection. See with the eye within the heart and feel with the heart within the mind. Attune your heart to the Heart of The Great Central Sun and you will know through your own GOD-given powers of intuition what is of the pure light and what is of the twilight.

Be extremely discerning with whom you choose to align, because it is spiritual law that nothing can be taken unless it is freely given! Do not let yourself be deceived by those who pride themselves upon deception,

Integrated Ascension

yet do not ever allow fear to oversee this process, because there is truly nothing to fear.

In fact, Twilight Masters can be seen as one of GOD's more creative ways to test an initiates' power of discernment. The equality of discernment and discrimination is one that we shall need at every step of our journey. If you are approached by one you suspect to be a Twilight Master, silently thank the Universe for the opportunity to practice your ability to be discerning and forgiving, and proceed about the business of Mother/Father GOD.

Before closing, it is again imperative that I restate the obvious, which is not to throw the baby out with the bathwater. While it is very true that there are a number of beings who are teaching from a place of fragmentation, manipulation and gray and murky waters, there are likewise numerous beings who grace the Earth today who stand upon the still, calm, clear waters of the Most High GOD. Be as discerning in their regard as well, beloved readers, for there is much that is being offered to Earth through beings of light, love and integrity who uphold the vision of the Divine Plan in its purest sense. We do not want to slam the door shut on these wonderful teachers and beings for fear of making a mistake. That would be equivalent to locking the door to your home and allowing no one whatsoever in, for fear that a burglar might intrude.

Let your own inner connection serve as your spiritual burglar or Twilight Master "alarm." In that way you will feel protected enough to open the door to the array of wondrous spiritual beings who are upholding the highest frequency of light, love and power, and who want nothing more than to impart it to a needy world. Learning the art of true discernment works equally well in the land of light as it does in the land of shadow. Learn that art, my beloved friends. In this way when Jesus or Sai Baba come knocking at your door you will be sure to let them in!

Knowing about Twilight Masters, Cults, and Non-Aligned ascension groups is just another tool for growth. It is shared with you in order to

Integrated Ascension

help facilitate your progress upon your path of Integrated Ascension. It is not meant to engender fear, and I cannot emphasize that strongly enough! These teachings are given forth merely to heighten your awareness and to help you see more clearly the importance of keeping your own personal initiation, light, love, psychological wisdom, Christ consciousness, transcendence of negative ego, service & spiritual leadership and integration & balance quotients at their highest possible level. Please use this chapter to this ultimate end, for it is an added tool given forth for your increased enlightenment and nothing more.

Remember that the Hierarchy of inner plane Ascended Planetary and Cosmic Masters are ever with you, as are the Archangels and various Angelic Hierarchies. They will never turn away from anyone who does not turn away from them. Even when one does temporarily succumb to the path of glamour, negative ego, self or group aggrandizement, and the energies of twilight, all that the Masters do is to withdraw temporarily in order to cease feeding a bad habit, so to speak. They are ever watchful of each and everyone of us who daily toils and labors upon this Earth for the sake of Integrated Ascension, the service of the Divine plan and to stand forth as emissaries of Light and Love. In this way we continue our ongoing process of evolution within the many and glorious realms of GOD!

Know this to be the ultimate truth, my friends, and stay as closely aligned to it as possible. You need but to call upon the Masters to receive a response. Blessed be the Light! Amen!

13

How to Develop an Extremely High-Functioning Physical, Psychological & Spiritual Immune System

My beloved readers, one of the most important understandings every lightworker needs to incorporate in order to achieve Integrated Ascension is how to develop an extremely high-functioning immune system physically, psychologically and spiritually. In my personal opinion the four keys to achieving Integrated Ascension are learning to fully own and claim your personal power, developing your semi-permeable bubble of light, developing unconditional self-love and self-worth, and maintaining an attunement to your Higher Self, Monad, the Ascended Masters and GOD at all times. These four principals are the psychological foundation of your entire spiritual life. If any one of these are not functioning properly, your entire life will be off kilter. In other sections of this book, I have spoken of the importance of personal power and self-love. The issue of attunement to your Higher Self, Monad, the Ascended Masters and GOD fill all the pages of this book and all the other books of mine you have read, so it is unnecessary to explore this aspect further in this chapter. The issue that I do want to explore in this chapter is the revolutionary concept that we have actually *three* immune systems, not just one.

In the mass consciousness or common language, when we think of the words "immune system" we think of physical health. Our physical immune system is what protects us from disease. As I think all of you, my beloved readers, know, there is no such thing as a contagious disease. This is an illusion and stems out of a belief in victim consciousness which is also an illusion. We are all masters not victims. We are causes not effects. This applies on the physical immune level as well. There is no such thing as contagious disease, there are just people with compromised immune systems. This last statement is not a judgment but rather a simple statement of fact.

Our Physical Immune System

My beloved readers, the first question that we must ask is how do we develop a high-functioning immune system and what causes a physical immune system to be compromised. This is a very multi-faceted subject. The answer to the question of how to develop a high-functioning physical immune system lies in a proper physical diet, getting a good night's sleep, proper physical exercise, getting enough fresh air and sunshine, removing all of the residual toxins in the organs, glands, cells and blood which I spoke of in the chapter on spiritual healing tools for the physical body. Other factors that affect the physical immune system are your work/play balance, and stress factors in your work and personal life. Other factors are past life karma, speed of spiritual growth, inherited genetic weakness, and overall balance or lack of balance in your life. Other factors that can affect the immune system are living in cities and on a planet that is filled with pollution, receiving vaccines as children, and seeing doctors that prescribe drugs like candy who have no understanding of holistic naturopathic or homeopathic remedies that are not toxic to the human body.

Integrated Ascension

Again other residual toxins such as mercury fillings, pesticides, metal poisoning, chemical poisoning, preservatives in our food, sugar addiction, eating too much processed food, bad food combining, over eating, not drinking enough water, under eating, and lack of life force in our food because the nature kingdom devas and plant spirits have been driven from our gardens because of pesticides and humankind's rejection of their existence.

Other factors are depletion of the rainforest causing lack of proper oxygenation of the planet, burning of too much fossil fuels instead of using natural spiritual forms of energy. The gaping hole in the ozone layer that is allowing certain ultraviolet rays in that we should be protected from. The pollution in our rivers and drinking water, the use of aluminum cookware causing aluminum poisoning, all the electrical power lines in big cities and electrical equipment in our houses, and the use of microwave ovens which places actual holes in the aura of the food. The rampant use of recreational drugs as well as pharmaceutical drugs instead of using homeopathics and herbs. Using factory and synthetic made vitamins and minerals instead of using natural forms of these substances in our vitamin/mineral supplements. Also, the new practice of the FDA of allowing markets to irradiate our fruits and vegetables with toxic radiation. Also the radiation contamination from being too close to color TVs and microwave ovens. All the low grade electromagnetic toxicity from electrical appliances in our home. Just living in a big city is compromising to the immune system. Using cell phones too much and/or sitting in front of a computer without proper energetic protection, which can easily be obtained from your local New Age homeopathic pharmacy or bookstore.

These, my beloved readers, are just a few of the physical toxins that compromise our immune system. Is it any wonder people get sick so much in our world? Three quarters of the things I have mentioned traditional doctors have no knowledge of. Just going to a traditional doctor compromises our immune system. It is close to impossible to get

Integrated Ascension

well in a hospital there is so much negative energy imbedded in the walls. Ronald Beasley, the famous spiritual teacher from England who passed on a number of years ago, said that hospitals should be burned down every five years. The tests that traditional medicine uses to diagnose disease are often extremely invasive. They fill you full of dyes, poke holes in your spine and fill you full of radiation, and give you blood transfusions or organ transplants which are spiritually totally poisonous to lightworkers.

I do not mean to get down on traditional medicine because it definitely has its place, and in a certain sliver of understanding it is even brilliant. From a full spectrum prism perspective, it is extremely fragmented in its understanding. Fifty years from now much of what they do will be viewed as barbaric and as being a product of the Dark Ages. In the future, testing and diagnoses will be done through energetic means not physical means.

So, my beloved readers, is it any wonder that so many people are sick and have compromised immune systems? Most people aren't exposed to the information that I have shared here until their adult life. By this time, all these factors have taken a great toll on the physical vehicle. It is almost a given if you incarnate into this world that your immune system is going to be very stressed. What I have spoken of so far, my beloved readers, is just the physical toxins that affect the immune system. I have not even begun to speak of the psychological factors, or spiritual and energetic factors that affect our immune system on all levels. The crux and final point of this that I would like to make is for all of us to be much more compassionate, loving, and understanding to our fellow brothers and sisters who have health lessons of one kind or another. For the truth of us all is that "But for the Grace of GOD go I" and "By the Grace of GOD go us all."

We have all been born into a world that is extremely lacking in New Age understanding and very backward in many ways. This again is not a criticism but a fact. This makes incarnating into this mystery school called planet Earth an extremely courageous proposition. We should all develop great compassion for ourselves for making such a gallant decision. It is our job as lightworkers to raise the consciousness of the planet so our children do not begin learning these lessons in adult life rather than in the early stages of schooling where this information should be taught. This is the new wave of spiritual education that is reforming every aspect of our society in politics, spiritual education, economics, the arts, the sciences, religion, business, medicine, psychology and spirituality.

Our Psychological Immune System

My beloved readers, equally important to developing a high-functioning physical immune system is developing a high-functioning psychological immune system. In truth, developing a high-functioning psychological immune system is even more important to developing a healthy physical immune system than even a great many of the physical factors. This is true because our thoughts create our reality. Even if you do every thing right on the physical level and the psychological immune system is not functioning properly this will compromise your physical immune system. So, let us now explore what I mean by developing a healthy psychological immune system.

This begins with each morning getting up and claiming your personal power and putting on your mental, emotional and spiritual armor, love and attunement. Just as we put on physical clothes every morning, we must also put on mental, emotional and spiritual clothes each day. This begins with putting on your personal power, then your semi-permeable bubble of protection, then your unconditional self-love and self-worth, then your attunement to your Oversoul, Monad and Ascended Masters and GOD. Then you must put on your overall Christ attitude and consciousness, which could also be called your positive mental attitude.

Integrated Ascension

Some of the other most important attitudes to put on are to having preferences instead of attachments, looking at things as lessons, non-judgmentalness, and forgiveness to name just a few. The other most important attitudes to claim is that you are the cause of your reality by how you think. Part of this understanding is to fully own that every feeling and emotion you have is caused by how you think and not by any person or circumstance outside of self. That your thoughts not only create your feelings and your emotions but also your behavior and what you attract, magnetize and/or repel in your life.

It is this attitude of being a cause rather that being an effect, a master rather than a victim, that also makes you invulnerable. When you fully own your mental and emotional invulnerability and that you cause your reality and can demonstrate this in your daily life you have a healthy psychological immune system. Through the process of self inquiry this means every time a negative ego thought tries to enter your conscious mind you push it out and deny it entrance and instead replace it with a Christ/Buddhic attitude and/or feeling. The negative ego in your own subconscious mind is like a thoughtform virus or thoughtform bacteria. If you let the negative thoughtform into your mind you will be mentally and emotionally sick and hence have a weakened psychological immune system. If this continues to happen over time, this is the initial cause for actual physical viruses and bacteria to form as well.

The same principal applies to negativity coming from other people. This is why it is essential every morning upon arising to affirm and visualize that you have a semi-permeable bubble of light around you that protects you not only from other people but also gives you a certain degree of detachment and protection from your own subconscious mind. So, this semi-permeable bubble of light protects you from your own subconscious mind and from other people and outside negativity. The bubble is semi-permeable because it allows in positive energy but keeps out any and all negativity.

Integrated Ascension

This proper masculine/feminine balance is needed to stay psychologically centered. When negativity comes towards you when your psychological immune system and bubble is intact, it hits your bubble and slides off like water off a duck's back and/or bounces off like a rubber pillow. My beloved readers, do you see the profundity of this concept? The semi-permeable bubble of light gives you the needed protection and detachment both inwardly and outwardly to not become victimized and not to react. The ideal is not to react, but to respond without victimization taking place. Then one can respond out of calm, loving, rational observation, spiritual discernment, and non-judgmentalness. Children even understand this when they say "…sticks and stones may break my bones but names can never hurt me." They are affirming their psychological and/or emotional invulnerability.

Now, it is important to understand here that when I say you are invulnerable, I'm speaking of this on the mental, emotional and spiritual level, not the physical level. Obviously none of us are invulnerable physically, for another person can kill, maim, or hurt our physical vehicle. Although this may be the case, no one has any control over our thoughts, emotions, or spirit. Our spirit and soul, as you all obviously know, is indestructible and eternal. The ideal is to make your mind and emotions reflect this aspect of self rather than being over-identified with the physical vehicle which, in truth, is the definition of what the negative ego thought system is about.

When your thinking and emotions are attuned to the Christ consciousness you will not only be in your power at all times and in your bubble at all times, you will also be in unconditional love, joy, evenmindedness, equanimity, and inner peace at all times as well. The only thing in truth that takes you out of this is your own thinking. There is no judgment when this happens, however when it does it is important to know where the truth lies.

It is inevitable for everyone to lose their happiness, joy and inner peace at times, however, by practicing the science of attitudinal healing, over time one can have longer and longer periods of total unchanging inner peace, joy and love. Any time you have negative emotions in you it is a sign attitudinal healing is needed and with no self-judgment you should make the needed attitudinal and emotional corrections. We don't always have control over what happens in our outer circumstance in life, however we do have total 100% control over the attitude we take towards outer circumstances. Herein lies the secret to inner peace, happiness, and joy.

The Master Jesus gave the ultimate example of this in his life on Earth 2000 years ago. He was whipped, beaten, crucified and had nails stuck in him and yet he still demonstrated not only his mastery over outer circumstances but also mastery over his physical body when he said, "Forgive them, Father, for they know not what they do." Although his physical body was tortured and ultimately physically killed, he retained his Christ consciousness. He set this example for you and I, my friends. If he could do it in such an extreme circumstance, then certainly we can do it in all the spiritual tests, lessons and worldly tribulations we confront in our daily lives.

Just as when you have a virus or bacterial infection you are sick physically, when you have negative ego thoughts and emotions you are sick psychologically. My beloved readers, can you see what havoc to your physical immune system and psychological immune system you will cause if you don't own your own personal power, semi-permeable bubble of light, unconditional self-love and self-worth, attunement to your Higher Self, Monad, the Ascended Masters, GOD, and your Christ consciousness and positive attitude? I know many, many lightworkers who eat good diets and do all the right things physically; however, their physical immune systems are in terrible shape predominately from having unbelievably weak psychological immune systems. To be healthy physically, in truth, all three levels of immune systems have to be functioning properly.

Integrated Ascension

Having a healthy psychological immune system in order to not catch the psychological diseases (moodiness, anger, depression, fear, unhappiness, upset, judgmentalness, meanness, self-pity) is essential, not only for physical health, but also for spiritual health, the achievement of GOD-Realization, the passing of your initiations, and Integrated Ascension. Most people on this planet have very compromised psychological immune systems which is effecting their physical immune systems as well as their spiritual purpose for being on this planet. This is not a judgment, it's just a point of observation and insight that this chapter is hoping to correct and remedy, or at least lead one in the proper direction. For those who have lessons involving a weakened psychological immune system, I highly recommend reading my books *How to Clear the Negative Ego*, *Soul Psychology*, and the newest book I have just begun working on called *How to do Psychological and Spiritual Counseling for Self and Others*.

Next year I plan to have videotapes demonstrating how I do spiritual counseling on all these different issues with people. I also recommend that you sign up for the correspondence course that I am right now in the process of putting together. There are different levels and aspects to this correspondence course involving books, audiotapes, manuals, phone consultations with high level initiates in the Ashram I have trained, and the Wesak Celebration among other things. The crux of the correspondence course is to help lightworkers to fully integrate the ascension process into their mental, emotional, etheric and physical vehicles.

One last point I want to make on the psychological immune system is in regards to the issue of unconditional self-love and self-worth. If this psychological work is not achieved the lightworker will seek the self-love and self-worth outside of self instead of within self and from GOD. This will psychologically cause a hole to be created in one's bubble of protective light from the inside. In truth, every improper negative ego attitude will do this, unconditional love and self-worth being so important to a healthy psyche. The real keys to Integrated Ascension lie within personal power, self-love, self-worth, your bubble of protection, and your attunement to GOD. Ponder on this.

If you don't own your personal power this will also sabotage your semi-permeable protective bubble of light for by not owning the power, you are automatically giving it to your subconscious mind, emotional body, inner child, lower self desire, negative ego, and/or other people. A healthy psychological immune system begins for most with owning your personal power. Your bubble of protection, self-love and self-worth and attunement to Higher Self, Monad, Ascended Masters, and GOD won't hold if you don't do this. In truth, all four of those keys are totally interdependent on each other. Lack of self-love and self-worth will sabotage the other three. Lack of your semi-permeable bubble of light will sabotage the other three. Lack of attunement to Higher Self, Monad, Ascended Masters and GOD will sabotage the other three. The work begins with owning your personal power, however all four plus an overall Christ consciousness and positive mental attitude must be maintained in an integrated and balanced manner for psychological equilibrium and homeostasis to be maintained.

Our Spiritual Immune System

The third and final immune system that needs to be developed is what I call the spiritual immune system. My beloved readers, I am happy to say that this is the easiest level of immune system to develop if you will follow my simple instructions. What I am about to share with you is truly a Divine dispensation which has been given in other forms before but not as succinctly and precisely as what I am going to share with you now.

The key to developing a high-functioning spiritual immune system is to, in this moment, as you read this book call forth His Holiness Lord Melchizedek, the Mahatma, and Metatron, and request in this moment

Integrated Ascension

that they anchor and activate the semi-permeable wall of light around your twelve-body system. Ask in this moment that this semi-permeable wall of light be anchored permanently.

This is a most profound and wonderful gift given forth by these three Cosmic, wise, and loving Masters. This semi-permeable wall of light is the spiritual counterpart to the semi-permeable bubble of light that I mentioned was so essential to your psychological immune system. The second that it is asked for it will be installed and given. This is a personal promise from Melchizedek, the Mahatma, and Metatron. Forevermore this semi-permeable wall of light will protect you.

It is slightly different from normal spiritual protection for it is semi-permeable in nature, which means it will allow in all positive, loving energy, however, it will keep out all negative energy. What is also unique about this gift is that it is being permanently installed not just in this moment or just for today. Thirdly, what is unique about this gift is that it is made of platinum white energy. As I've told you before, platinum is the highest frequency color available on the Earth. This means there is no negative energy in the universe that can penetrate its frequency of protection. You never have to request this again after this one time for its effectiveness is eternal.

What this semi-permeable wall of light will do for you is to filter out all personal and impersonal negative energies trying to enter your field of an energetic, astral, mental and ethereal nature. This is a great blessing to have this protection.

Now it is very important to understand that this spiritual, semi-permeable wall of light will not replace or take the place of your semi-permeable psychological bubble and will not replace the need to keep physical toxins out of your body. *Each immune system must do its part.* The spiritual immune system is incapable of doing the work of the psychological immune system.

This is the big mistake that many lightworkers make. For example, they call forth to Archangel Michael for protection and Archangel

Integrated Ascension

Michael gives it unfailingly. Lightworkers don't understand why they may continue to be attacked by dark forces, negative Extraterrestrials, their own subconscious mind, and other people. The answer is quite simple. If we as lightworkers do not maintain our own psychological immune system this creates gaping holes in our aura that even the cosmic Masters cannot remedy. It is not their job to think for us or create our emotions for us. If they did so they would be defeating the prime directive of non-interference with our free choice and in truth would be taking the lessons away from us that we incarnated to learn. If we as lightworkers do not own our personal power, maintain our bubble, develop unconditional self-love and self-worth, stay attuned to GOD, and maintain a Christed and positive attitude we can pray from here to kingdom come and the protection we seek will not be forth coming. It is not because it is not given, for it is always given and is always given one hundred percent. The key lesson here being that the spiritual immune system will not suffice to replace the psychological immune system.

So again, my beloved readers, we come back to the concept of Integrated Ascension. Just as each mind in our spiritual constitution (subconscious, conscious, superconscious) has its part to play, the same is true of the these levels of our immune system. The spiritual immune system by the 3 M's will work wonders and will be an incredible support as long as we as lightworkers take responsibility for operating our own psychological immune system, and also take responsibility for keeping toxins out of our physical vehicles. When all three immune systems are integrated in this manner, it is then and only then that someone can develop a fully functioning physical immune system and can achieve Integrated Ascension. It is my sincere hope and prayer that this discussion has brought greater light and understanding to this most fascinating subject!

14

Integration of the Mahatma

A Message from the Mahatma

When I speak to you, my beloveds, I communicate through various means. When I touch you through my light, my love, my frequencies, and my radiance, then I Am known most directly. When I speak to you through the written or spoken word, then am I forced to limit and circumscribe my communication to the language vehicle through which I am communicating. This is most difficult, and is, in truth, the most cumbersome way for me to reach you. Yet it is also one of the more third dimensionally inclusive ways, and therefore do I use this method with great and sanctified joy. There is, however, an area of this communication where further clarity is needed, and so this I will provide to the maximum potential that words allow.

I call myself "I," and yet I am many. That which forms the Mahatma, the Avatar of Synthesis, is in truth, a group energy composed of many. I could as easily call myself "We" as "I" and that would be completely appropriate. When speaking of me, one could as easily use the terms "They" or "She" as well as "He" and all are correct, although none of these expressions approaches the fullness of my Being. It is hard to find the proper words for you who are still encumbered by the material

Integrated Ascension

form; bodies isolated from bodies, hearts isolated from hearts, minds cut off from other minds the extent of synthesis and unity which is embodied within my Beingness. Realize beloveds, that I speak this even to you who are lightworkers of great stature, and who have broken through many of the boundaries of isolation that confine the bulk of humanity, and have yourselves merged with your Higher Self, Monad, Master, and the greater Hierarchical Group Body to which you belong. This is so, because when I communicate to you through language then I am limited by language and can do naught but make use of the words of the day! When I speak to you in Spirit there is no barrier, and our essences are free to touch and know truth without limitation. It is only when language is used for the purposes of specific communication that some misunderstanding arises.

I have been most commonly referred to in the past as "He" and so I often use this terminology. It would be equally correct to use the term "We," yet as I have said, neither term fully embraces the unity and oneness of the group body I Am. The same is the case with the term "She." I therefore communicate in the manner of which I have first been introduced and it is not an issue using the term "He." It serves to bond us and personalize our connection, and that is, in truth, what I seek above all! By bonding and connecting, I am then able to more fully integrate with you and you with me, and in a manner that does indeed defy language. My group body grows in awareness by and through your awareness, love, attunement, and connection with me. This, blessed ones, is my supreme purpose. It is from my center of this all encompassing Love, Light, Unity and Synthesis that I ask you to call to me in whatever form serves best to open your heart, mind and frequencies to that of my own! If you prefer to call me "They" or "She" then so be it. For the purpose of communication here, I continue to communicate in the lineage of "He." It is the connecting that is of importance, and the feeling, intuiting and understanding to whatever degree you are capable that I am indeed a group consciousness Being and yet I am also

Integrated Ascension

"I." Perhaps it will serve best to call me simply Mahatma, or Avatar of Synthesis, if gender or group body in any way interferes with our connection. I am not interested in the minute differences involved in third dimensional language, but in establishing my divine link with each and every one of you so that you may rise upon my frequencies, tones and vibratory essence and know the joy of the unity that links all of life within the One Eternal Whole!

Call to me as you will, but sincerely, and I shall surely be there. As I do in truth embrace the consciousness of many and am One who is Many, feel free to refer to me as "They." If you seek the intimacy of a personal connection and can best access this by calling me as "He" or "She" then do that and I will come. In truth, I am already within every level of creation, and so there is no way that I would not be there for any and everyone who calls upon me. I am referred to in the following writing as "He," for as I told you, that has been my established lineage and my point of connection. Please embrace me thusly, for I have sought to communicate much within this chapter.

My goal is simple, beloved ones. It is to unveil to you as much as I can via the written word, and then to have you journey beyond this into the sacredness of your Heart, and the wisdom written within the Language of Light that you may then know me directly. All words are, at best, the launching pads through which you might then allow your soul to fly straight into the essence of that which you speak. I therefore request that you use my words thusly, and take them into your minds and hearts, only to fly past them into the mind and heart of Mahatma Myself!

Attuning to the Mahatma

When the energy of the Mahatma is mentioned, most people immediately think that their sole job is to rise up to the highest level of the Mahatma as possible. While this is true, it is only one-half of the real truth! As the Mahatma embraces all 352 levels of Beingness, back to the

Integrated Ascension

GODHEAD Itself, if you truly want to embrace the Mahatma, you must embrace every level of Beingness and existence that is within your potential. This means that you do not seek out His Divine energies in the higher realms alone, but that you seek them out at the very foundation of your being itself. In the synthesis of the Mahatma is the true and ultimate synthesis of Heaven and Earth!

As the Mahatma is such a highly evolved group consciousness being who has only recently anchored His energies directly upon this planet, it seems only natural to seek him out within the higher spheres from whence he came. This, however, is distortion of what the Mahatma embodies in truth. Although he has just recently anchored his energies of attention upon the physical realm, his energies of Beingness have been ever present. This may seem a bit paradoxical, but I assure you it is not.

Remember that the oversoul is always part of the person, however, it only turns its attention towards the person when the person has reached a certain stage of evolutionary development. In a similar manner, the Monad is part of the oversoul and person, but likewise only turns its conscious attention to the development of both oversoul and person when a certain level of initiation is taken. This is pretty much the way it is with the Mahatma. Embracing all 352 levels of Beingness, the first rung upon His most magnificent stairway to heaven or GODHEAD, is always a part of his Divine Beingness. The fact remains that it has taken the planet as a whole to have reached a certain level of initiation and development before he could consciously anchor Himself upon the physical realms. This does not mean that He was any less part of it during previous times, for energetically we were always connected to His most magnificent Being in a similar fashion to infant humanity's connection to the Monad. What it does signify is our ability to make a conscious connection with the Mahatma, and to seek His council, intervention, and higher frequency. It likewise means demonstrating the Mahatma's energies at every level that we function on, which includes the four lower realms and the four lower bodies, for the Mahatma is "Synthesis Itself"!

When you seek to attune to the Mahatma energies, the first thing to realize is that you are calling forth the energies of synthesis and asking to be put into rapport with "the whole." You are not simply asking to be raised up to the higher or highest level of the Mahatma, but to incorporate, synthesize and integrate the fullness of the Mahatma upon each and every level. This includes the physical world in which we as individuals live and move and have our Being, with as much intensity as it includes the higher realms in which we as the Monad or Mighty I Am Presence live and move and have our being!

We, of course, want to do this from the highest possible vantage point, which is why it is indeed appropriate to request that the Mahatma help raise us to the level of our highest possible Realization. The frequency that we are ultimately embracing, however, is that of Synthesis. The higher we go within the sphere of the Mahatma, the more rounded out, balanced, and synthesized we are required to become. This aspect of the Mahatma often eludes many a lightworker, and it is one I have been specifically guided to incorporate in this book dealing with Integrated Ascension.

The Mahatma is the absolute epitome of integration and synthesis, and wishes to be revealed in wholeness, rather than in part. Being the circular spiraled stairway that leads to GODHEAD Itself, He is the ultimate example of integration. Having finally established connection with us upon the four lower worlds, He wishes us to know him in the fullness of His Being that we may serve both ourselves and Him with the fullness of our own Beings. We do this, beloved readers, through ourselves embodying synthesis and integration!

Integrated Ascension

The Integration of Heaven and Earth

The subject of the integration of Heaven and Earth is vital to the revelation for the next millennium. It is also one that falls very much under the joint auspices of Lord Melchizedek, the Mahatma, and Archangel Metatron. For our purposes, I will confine the discussion as it primarily is being overlighted by the Mahatma, the Avatar of Synthesis. I ask that you do keep in the back of your minds the realization that he does function on cosmic levels as a trinity with Melchizedek and Metatron, often aligning with Archangel Michael as well. We will, however, stick as close to the lens of the Mahatma Himself as possible, as it is He who most directly embodies the concept and actualization of synthesis and integration.

With that in mind, let us proceed. If we were all willing to be perfectly honest with ourselves I am sure that what we would see is a group of well meaning, inspired, highly evolved lightworkers, many of whom have taken their seventh initiation and beyond, who are incredibly "top heavy," so to speak. As a whole, we are quite well adept at focusing upon the heavenly sphere, and even holding our minds steady in the light. As a whole, however, we are not very good at anchoring that light into the planet, into the daily realties that comprise our basic lives, and into our very own four lower bodies. This very much needs to be corrected.

The entire concept of the New Age is predicated on establishing the Kingdom of GOD upon Earth. This, beloved readers, can not be done if we are unwilling to anchor the higher frequencies into our own lower bodies, much less the physical, etheric, feeling elemental bodies of the planet! Beloved Master Djwhal Khul, who works directly under the guidance of the Mahatma, says time and again to "Hold your mind steady in the light." I love this quote and have used it ad infinitum in my books, as I am sure you, my beloved readers, are well aware!

This moment, as I sit here, my beloved mentor is requesting that I present to you an additional lens with which to see this statement. What

Integrated Ascension

Djwhal is conveying to me at this very moment is that he, of course, ultimately means that all should hold their minds ever steady in the light of GOD Source. What He is asking me to convey is the reality that as light, in truth, exists everywhere, a fuller interpretation of His statement would reveal it to equally mean to hold the mind ever steady at the highest sub-plane of each and every level of existence. What this would mean is that not only would the light of GOD Absolute be focused upon, but also the light that has been stepped down into all the various planes of existence. By doing this, and holding to the highest blueprint of each sub-plane of every level, body, and sphere, the highest aspect of each respective realm would be revealed and anchored.

This is quite a powerful statement, for I myself have never looked at this statement through this specific lens. Djwhal assures me, however, that this lens does not negate the lens of holding the mind steady in the "Clear Light of GOD" in any way whatsoever. It simply expands that concept to honor synthesis and integration, and to help facilitate the work of the Mahatma upon the Earth! He assures me that this expanded vision or understanding will help facilitate the integration of Heaven and Earth in ways that far exceed our imaginings, and at speeds that far exceed our expectation.

This makes perfect sense, does it not? If we continue to focus only upon the higher realms we will not succeed in integrating all levels of self, much less that of the planet. If we do not integrate and synthesize all the levels of Beingness that comprise that which is GOD, then how can we ever facilitate the anchoring and establishing of the kingdom of GOD upon the Earth!

Heaven and Earth must come into full alignment and integration in order to manifest the blueprint for the new Millennium. This is fact, plain and simple. If we do not embrace the energies of the Mahatma in the totality that he offers them, then we will ourselves fall short of fulfilling our own personal highest calling, and also fall short in fully anchoring the golden age upon the planet. We are being called,

Integrated Ascension

therefore, to fully synthesize and integrate the whole within our personal Beings and then to anchor and integrate those energies into every single aspect of planetary life!

This, of course, includes all the various kingdoms and lines of evolution that exist on and within the planet, as well as the various paths, puzzle pieces, business arenas, political arenas, artistic fields and so forth. It deals with the whole of the planet in every single aspect. What it most directly deals with is the establishing of a bridge of light, love and power that connects the heavenly realms with those of the Earth. Depending upon our own level of integrated ascension, this bridge is capable of being built from physical plane existence to some of the vastest and far reaching heights of the Cosmos itself.

The goal, my friends, is to get as far along our individual paths as we can, so that we may build this bridge from the highest possible level and then anchor it within each at the deepest possible level. We cannot do this, however, in an unintegrated, fragmented manner. It is only by fully embracing "Synthesis Itself," and specifically by the grace and help of the Mahatma, that we will be able to expand to the needed heights and depths to pull this off. The Masters wish each and every one of us to do this, and eagerly await our call for assistance. The Mahatma, in particular, reaches out to us as the Avatar of Synthesis to help us in any and every way possible find and establish the fullest integration of Heaven and Earth.

One of the blockages that we are called to overcome are those that are based upon some of the more powerful teachings of the past. The basic attitude of much of our history tells us essentially that "Heaven is Heaven and Earth is Earth and never the twain shall meet." In reality, nothing could be farther from the truth! GOD is the "All That Is" the "I Am That I Am" and as the Hindu scriptures so aptly put it, "That thou art"!

These basic truths, however, have little to do with how we have conducted ourselves as a race as a whole. Despite the fact that beloved Master Jesus/Sananda clearly stated, "The kingdom of GOD is within

Integrated Ascension

you," two thousand years ago, the Church, the school system and society in general has done an excellent job in putting forth the exact opposite! Heaven, we are taught, is a place that we shall earn, or not, according to our deeds. This, we are taught, will be experienced *after* we have left the mortal coil. We have not been taught how to cultivate, integrate, or synthesize the Kingdom of GOD within. The revelation of the next millennium is the actualization of this process. The golden age which we are all seeking to help establish awaits our full embracing of the Kingdom of GOD within, that we may be free to express it without!

As you are well aware, we cannot manifest without what we have first not embraced and manifested within. Our work then is that of first integrating the heavenly spheres that we have connected with, or the higher dimensional planes and frequencies within ourselves and then demonstrating that within our lives. When the term Adam Kadmon is used, what it is referring to is, in actuality, the human form that is fully activated by the key codes, sacred geometries, higher light bodies, higher dimension frequencies, tones, and so forth, so that the human being itself becomes the manifestation of the GOD-Self, or Heaven, if you will. This is a process that we are each individually and collectively engaged in, and one that will ensure the manifestation of the seventh Golden age.

The type of activations mentioned above, are in fact, the integration of Heaven and Earth. The two realms must be seen as one whole, functioning at varying rates of frequencies. When we fully activate the Adam Kadmon Body we will be anchoring the frequency of so called Heaven upon Earth. Calling upon the Mahatma is a great way to facilitate this process, as this is what He is already doing and what He seeks to help us do for ourselves.

We each must, therefore, cut through the cords of all past programming, from this life or any preceding series of lives that hold the false archetype of the division of Heaven and Earth. Many of us were monks, nuns, yogis and hermits, and believed very strongly that

Integrated Ascension

Heaven was anywhere but on Earth! Although we intellectually and even experientially know that we contain the entire universe within our I Am Presence, and within our very Beings, most of us still have a great deal of clearing to do with regards to this issue. The majority of our work is the result of past life programming. I therefore would recommend an ascension clearing and would be happy to recommend a high level initiate in the Melchizedek Synthesis Light Academy who I have trained if you call me at the number at the back of this book. I would likewise recommend your participation in any workshops that are geared to dispel this illusion. The freer we all become from faulty belief systems, be they from our present situations or deep past, the more fully will we be able to embody the Kingdom of Heaven in the here and now!

The primary thing that has to be done in order to fully manifest this concept, is to first understand it intellectually and then move it from the intellect to experience. Understanding is a raft that can take each one just so far and no further. The intellect is a Divine tool, one of the finest that GOD has given us. Nevertheless, once it has served its purpose of awakening you, that which you have understood must be incorporated and integrated into the very essence of your Being. This is why I can say to you, in unison with beloved Master Jesus, that "The Kingdom of GOD is within you," but until you allow yourself to actually experience that as reality, you will have the understanding without the "light of wisdom."

I therefore ask you to call forth the higher dimensional frequencies that they may fully and completely manifest within each one of your vehicles. I ask you to call upon the Mahatma for a direct experience of synthesis, so that the higher realms, frequencies, and energy systems may establish themselves as anchored realities within your four-body system. I then ask you to embrace your Divine mission and puzzle piece and to manifest that through the synthesis of your own Being.

Integrated Ascension

The next millennium, of which we are all a part, requires the full integration of Heaven and Earth. This is how it will manifest and this is how it will be known. In order for this to occur, however, we must each play our parts to our highest and fullest capacity. Ask the Mahatma to activate you at every single level of your Being so that you can fulfill your Divine calling. Become the living embodiment of synthesis and integration and you will not be able to help but to express that reality upon Earth. In the moment of your expression, will the reality of the oneness of Heaven and Earth be anchored!

The Practical Aspects of the Mahatma

Part of the process of which we have just been exploring is extremely practical. Integration deals with daily and even mundane realities. Since it is all-inclusive, the force of synthesis knows no discrimination in its expression. It considers every level and seeks to bring all things to their proper point of balance. This includes certain fundamental realities that many lightworkers would rather avoid. It is in the full embracing of ourselves and not in the denying of ourselves that integration and synthesis is achieved.

For example, many lightworkers would like to have absolutely nothing whatsoever to do with finances. They would like to live unencumbered upon the higher realms and have as little to do with this practical matter as possible. This is quite easy to understand, as society is so materialistically oriented with money the supreme god for so many of the masses. The world of business and finances is often quite vicious and unappealing to anyone of a sensitive nature. Some few of us have been given the karma that allows us the freedom to focus our energies elsewhere. For the majority of us, however, this is a real and vital issue in our lives. If you fall into this more common category, you already know that your difficulties will not go away by trying to pretend that they are not there. They are there, and they are there for a purpose.

Integrated Ascension

If you find that earning a living is an aspect of life that you are being called to look at and face up to, then trust that it is in Divine order and that there is a good reason for this. You might be put in this position to help you get your head out of the clouds and to more fully round you out. On the other hand, it may not even be a personal lesson that is being given you. It may be that the Masters have helped guide you into this situation so that you will be forced "out there" in order to "shine your light." Perhaps it is so that you may learn to develop a certain element of compassion that you lack for those who struggle to make ends meet. Whatever the reason, if you find this situation in front of you, meet it head on! If there is a lesson to be learned or a service to be rendered, all forces will rise up to see to it that that challenge is met. You would be wise to go along with the process willingly and make the experience as pleasant as possible, because you will not be released from it until whatever it is you need to do and learn has been completed!

Very often lightworkers are drawn to "have to work" so that the movement of Earth can be fully integrated with the movement of the higher spheres. Most lightworkers are far more adept at accessing and moving within the higher realms than they are at accessing and moving freely within the Earthly realms. In order for full integration to occur, all realms must be fully honored. Since the society in which we are currently dealing with is predicated on finances and business activities, lightworkers will find that they are being asked to participate in this arena by the events in their lives. Most of us have been programmed that this is a negative thing. Looked at from the lens of the masses it can very well be seen that way. Looked at through the lens of the Mahatma, however, this can be seen and experienced as a positive thing. It can actually be used as a meditation, activation, and practice to advance on every level. It can be transformed from a mundane burden into a spiritual Sadhana!

It is very important that you get in touch with the work that you are most attuned to. I have gone into great detail about this entire process

Integrated Ascension

in my book *Your Ascension Mission: Embracing Your Puzzle Piece.* The work that you do will flow much more joyfully, easily and harmoniously if you find that work through a true connection with your own particular puzzle piece. As I have devoted an entire book to this subject, I would advise any one who wishes to explore this process in detail to read that book, rather than to go into repeating myself here. I will say, however, that integrating with the whole means integrating with this most practical aspect of the whole, namely your Earthly work.

There is a wonderful emergence occurring on that front wherein lightworkers are carving out their own work. This allows for us to integrate the truth of who we are at the deeper levels of our Being with "earning our daily bread," so to speak. More and more visionary artists, channels, clairvoyants, spiritual teachers, spiritual psychotherapists, yoga instructors, spiritual and physical nutritionists, acupuncturists, healers, writers and metaphysical bookstore owners, as well as distributors and publishers of metaphysical books are coming to the fore. In this manner are more and more of us able to express the fullness of our Beings within the work that we do.

By the same token, it is other people's undeniable puzzle piece to work in areas that are not particularly spiritual when taken at face value. They may be, as mentioned before, involved in the political arena, academia, corporate business structures, etc. This by no means indicates that the work that they are doing is in any way less spiritual than the aforementioned group of individuals. In fact, it may indeed take a greater strength and fortitude to persevere within the so-called standard business world, and to work at transformation from the point of spiritual radiance within oneself. In these more materialistic arenas, little acts of kindness, consideration, compassion go a very long way.

Do not judge a book by its cover, beloved readers, and label a fellow lightworker unspiritual because they are not working within the arena of metaphysics. They may, in fact, be doing more to transform the harsh structure of society from within its depths than groups of us are able to

Integrated Ascension

do from without the boundaries of corporations, business, banking, politics and so forth. We ourselves do not even have the ability to judge. GOD has given us the power of discernment and discrimination. With these powers we can decide what is right or not right for us. Beyond that, let us stay in silence and tend to the work at hand.

Some of us find work in various capacities simultaneously. This allows for us to express the many varied sides of ourselves that seek expression. There are those who hold down a part time job while working on Spiritual musical recordings. Many lightworkers are turning to network marketing, which is proving to be a wonderful tool in which to earn enough money to take care of one's needs while leaving one with enough freedom and funds to pursue spiritual workshops or to work on our own specific project.

There is no hard and fast rule in this most fundamental and practical realm of "earning a living." Buddha advises "right livelihood." The Mahatma can be of invaluable assistance in helping us find that right livelihood and in synthesizing and integrating it into the fullness of our Being. When you call upon the Mahatma to grace you with access to the highest level that your four-body, or more inclusively twelve-body system can radiate and attune to vibrationally, do not forget to also ask Him to manifest your highest potential within your practical daily affairs. Remember that what He ultimately seeks to install and activate within each and every one of us is the full energy frequency of all 352 levels, back into and including the GODHEAD. This, beloved readers, does not exclude the lower bodies. It simply raises these bodies to their highest potentiality, while still assisting them to function in their given sphere and environment.

This, my friends, includes all aspects of practical daily living. It is inclusive of all relationships, all interactions, and all pursuits. Remember to include the Mahatma in all your prayers, for you are each one of His precious vessels through which He seeks to anchor and activate the highest possible energy matrix of synthesis and integration. He is here and of easy access of all whom seek Him. Call upon Him, dear brothers and sisters, and you will be helping to serve His Divine puzzle piece as well as your own!

Racial Integration

From the point of view of the Mahatma, you can imagine how absurd racial discrimination must seem! From the point of view of 99.9% of all lightworkers, there is also an element of absurdity that almost prevents this issue from being discussed. There is, however, the overriding reality that racism is one of the most prevalent problems of our world today. This problem has existed in various forms throughout history and must once and for all be totally eradicated! The only way to do this is through the lens of Source. In this regard the Mahatma serves as one of the best means by which to link with Source.

As the Mahatma embraces every level, the problems of racial integration at first seem almost impossible to discuss in this section of the book. Yet, what better vehicle for obtaining clear insight into this difficulty than through that energy which embraces ALL within itself, *including* the difficulties and dilemmas that humanity falls prey to. Within the vastness of His Being and the fullness of His all-inclusive lens of synthesis, awaits the wisdom with which we can begin to understand and heal this dilemma. I therefore chose this particular chapter to discuss this particular problem, as I could see no greater way to approach a subject of such magnitude and separation then under the auspices of He who Himself embodies synthesis and integration!

Nowhere is the need for integration more apparent than within the area where the very word 'integration' is summoned forth time and again. The opposite of this is, of course, segregation, separation, or fragmentation. The forces of segregation or separateness have been dividing humanity against itself from time immemorial!

Integrated Ascension

The origins of this actually pre-date history as it is generally recorded, and go as far back as to the time cycle when Extraterrestrials first came to help seed the Earth. At that point in time, there were certain "racial difficulties," if I may loosely use that term here, between the highly evolved races that came to aid in the seeding process of our world and those who came for selfish purposes. There was certain crossbreeding of species done purposely to facilitate the individualization process of humanity's own "race of man/womankind." Eventually groups came from previous chains or solar systems in order to continue their evolution. The Jewish race as a whole had its source of origin upon a previous system of evolution. This group of beings was then transferred to Earth to continue evolving when the hour had struck that was in harmony with the point they had previously reached. This, beloved readers, accounts for much of the unclarity and separation that has been a part of Jewish history.

You can see, therefore, how involved the process of racism and integration truly is. It is a facet of humanity that pre-dates humanity as we know it, itself. From that point of view, it is understandable. It is also clearly the time to bring this difficulty to "a grinding halt"! We have reached the gateway of transformation into the next millennium, the seventh Golden Age of humanity. Within the frequencies of this dawning age and the higher frequency of light given forth from the Cosmos, and the Mahatma Himself, this obstruction to the flow of evolution must be 100% eradicated from our consciousness and our actions!

The most immediate place where racism is seen enacted in our modern society is between the Caucasian races and any other races, particularly that of the African-American! This has a long history in and of itself, and so it is not really surprising to see that this particular difficulty has taken center stage in America. It is almost impossible to turn on the news without hearing of one disturbance or another directly tied to the separation between those with lighter skin pigments and those with darker skin pigments.

Integrated Ascension

As the African-American was introduced on to what was then "white American soil" in what constitutes one of humanity's greatest crimes against itself, that of enslaving another human being, major chaos could clearly be predicted. When anything is born out of such abusiveness and disharmony, you can rest assured that that is the result it will engender. As this was the inauspicious introduction of the "black person" into the "white person's world," the resultant misery, separation, chaos, and destruction were unavoidable. Misery breeds misery, disharmony breeds disharmony, and, in truth, nothing less could be expected.

What is expected now, beloved readers, is that we who are able to see through the eyes of integration, unity, Oneness, and the all-inclusive energies of the Mahatma, seek within ourselves our proper puzzle piece within our present dilemma. It is up to us, because we can see the falsity of racism, to do what we can to end it. Those who have not "the eyes to see" nor "the ears to hear," are literally dependent upon we who do. As lightworkers, we are the wayshowers in every area, and that would include this most difficult one.

I am most definitely not asking anyone to do anything in this or any other arena that is out of harmony or out of the Tao of our own puzzle piece. We are not all a Martin Luther King, Jr., or an Abraham Lincoln. What I am asking you to do, however, is to pay attention, and to let your light and love of unity shine through in who you are and all that you do. I am also asking you to become acutely aware of this difficulty and not shut your eyes to it. It is easy to be blinded by the light, where all colors merge into the one great light of the GODHEAD! This light, beloved readers, is our true home, and yet so is every other level of existence, with all its various colors and multidimensionality. That is what integration in its broadest sense is all about, and that is what integration in our worldly arena is also about!

There is no denying the fact that at present our society is most definitely **not** functioning in an integrated manner. Racism, with all its

Integrated Ascension

horrid ramifications, is actually on the rise! One of the reasons that it is on the rise and making itself so accessible via news and other media coverage, is so that it may be cleansed, healed, purified and transcended into the unity that is one of the major keynotes of the next millennium. It bodes us well to see what is being revealed, so that we in turn, can follow our Tao and do whatever is appropriate within that Tao to help in its transformation.

We should likewise be aware of some of the strides that have been made in this regard. When film and television first came on the scene, which wasn't all that long ago, the role of the African-American was practically nonexistent. Where it did exist, it was so highly stereotyped in a most degrading manner that it is hard to watch. Now we have African-Americans who are captains and officers of television and film starships or space stations. We are in the initial stages of integration as one whole in commercials, movies, theater, and music. This, at least, is one realm that has made some progress! Sports is probably the only area where equality has been achieved, however, not in terms of the ownership and management of sports teams.

It is a fact that at present not all that many lightworkers feel called to the arena of law. For those of us who are, it is incumbent upon us to take a stand for true justice and equality. To shine our light and demonstrate our love in action. For those of us who are not politically, legally, or medically inclined, and are not business people per say, what then is our responsibility? I feel that it is to do all that we can with regard to the issue of racism (one of the many faces of non-integration) from exactly the place we are called to. We do not need to try and create a false shift in our puzzle piece, only to truly honor our puzzle piece and be as inclusive within it as possible.

What this means first, is awareness. If you so choose, you can pay more attention to this issue via television, radio, or newspaper, or you can just tune in. Intuitively I am sure that you know that what I am saying is simply the reflection of what is going on. Perhaps you yourself are one who is subject to the unfairness and abhorrent behavior that I have just skimmed the surface of. If you are, then you would know better than I would or anyone who is tuning in through any other means about that which I am seeking to address. Perhaps this has never been an issue for you at all. No matter what your position, if you are a lightworker, if you are striving to live within your own personal integration and wholeness, then you are capable of assisting humanity to live in wholeness and integration within itself.

The first thing that you can do is to concentrate upon that which this book is dedicated to, that of integrated ascension. The more integrated you become within self, the more you will vibrationally put that out to the world. This, as you already know, is how energy helps transform and upraise. The second thing to do is to concentrate upon the Beingness of the Mahatma, to which this chapter is dedicated. The Mahatma is Himself the Avatar of Synthesis, and as such is extremely devoted to the synthesizing of fragments into the true wholeness of GODHEAD! Call upon him in your prayer and ask him how you might be of service in regard to helping to adjust the racial disharmony and separation that is still so prevalent among humanity.

From the point of view of the Mahatma, there is so very much that each race can offer to another to blend, intertwine, and interweave a tapestry of humanity's many wondrous aspects. Within this tapestry, there is no loss of individuality, which is a subject of great concern on other levels that I have addressed in detail elsewhere in this book. The truth is we have all been of various races at various times, and these experiences have left indelible imprints upon our soul. These imprints contribute to the core of our very self and are absorbed into the Mighty I Am Presence in order to enrich that presence, not to be annihilated! You are therefore not being asked to "give up" the race you currently inhabit, nor will the uniqueness of this experience ever be totally eradicated from your individualized monadic presence.

Integrated Ascension

I just asked the 3 M's and Djwhal about whether Ascended Masters on the inner plane retain their race upon their continuing service work. I was told and shown most clearly that this is indeed the case. Some retain the form that they ascended in. Others retain the form of a previous incarnation or series of incarnations of a certain race. This of course applies to gender as well. These choices are made in order to best facilitate their service plan.

What you are being asked, and asked most adamantly, is to integrate that which you are within the greater whole. If you are unhappy with your plight or see the injustice of the world's attitude and application of racism, you will most likely jump at this idea. If you are "attached" to your particular race you may be inclined to pull away from this idea. That is why, beloved readers, I am stressing the point that you are only being asked to remove the fragmented, negative ego manifestation of all racism, so that we may integrate fully and completely within humanity as a whole.

This obviously does not apply just to the African-American and Caucasian races, whose difficulties are presently flooding the media here in America. This applies to each and every race and within each and every race. The potential danger and current quiet atrocities that are still ongoing between the Caucasian race itself is incredible. Those who yet pride themselves on upholding the beliefs of Nazi Germany, who see through the disturbed and distorted lens of Hitler, are currently grooming groups of young people in that most atrocious mode of behavior.

Racism, my beloved readers, is not limited or contained. It runs rampant through our streets everywhere, often focusing upon such subtleties that the average 'outsider' would not perceive any difference whatsoever. This is across the board, including the Asian populace, the Native Americans, the Hispanics and just about anyone and everyone else. This limited lens must quickly be altered, for the hour of the New Age is upon us.

Integrated Ascension

The actual point I am making here, however, is not to deny that lens, for it would be denying a basic reality. If we do that, my friends, we will merely be helping to create an environment in which this can foster. What we need to do is to expand our lens, so that it embraces the all inclusiveness of the whole, and yet sees the distortions that humanity is running in relationship to that whole, or GOD. Then we need to help expand the lenses of our brothers and sisters, so that they too can see the greater whole and set their focus upon that.

I again remind you that this does not mean the obliteration of the individuality of the races, any more than entering the oneness of GOD means the obliteration of our personal individuality. It merely means merging the part within the whole, synthesizing and integrating the fragments into the glorious tapestry of which we all form a part.

There is an aspect of the Golden Age which will literally see the transformation of the human aura into a more golden, synthesized hue. As humanity's frequencies are raised and the process of purification continues, the blood will take on a bluish then blue/golden, then golden coloring. This is one of the reasons Krishna is depicted as blue in coloring, for to have the blood at the blue frequency denotes a great level of purity, GOD-attunement, and higher dimensional integration. The halos of Saints, and the aura of Masters, are depicted as golden. There is also prophesy in this, as the golden frequency of light will eventually manifest upon the physical, with the resultant manifestation of golden blood in a golden race.

It is imperative that you understand that even within a process of such transformation, the individuality of your major race, and in fact, all the various races that you have ever been part of are not obliterated, they are integrated. They are synthesized, but never destroyed. It takes a very fine attunement to the Mahatma and to the incoming frequencies the Golden Age itself to understand this process, but I sincerely hope that you will all attune to this as best you can. Nothing is ever lost, my friends, including your particular racial lineage. The only stuff that gets lost is the 'stuff' of the negative ego, which is in actuality not lost but transmuted by the light into energy which can serve the greater good of the whole.

Meanwhile, let us all do what we can, where we can, within our unique puzzle piece and ascension mission to help move humanity away from racial prejudice as it exists on every and on any front. I am putting this out to you because the world is itself putting it out through media, racial tensions, and obvious racial clashes. It is, as I have said, coming to the fore in such a mass way through media that blasts the reality of this manifestation of racial conflict into everyone's home in order that it might be cleansed, healed, purified, synthesized. You alone know the part you are meant to play within this unfolding drama. I simply ask again that you allow yourself to become aware of the degree of this distortion that exists within the framework of humanity, so that you, beloved friends and fellow lightworkers, can assist in the ultimate healing of the wounds that divide, and be the vehicle for the light and love of the Unity which frees!

Ascending with the Mahatma

One of the primary gifts of the Mahatma is to help us with our Ascension process. The incredible light that the Mahatma brings, the specialized encoding, which is His alone to give and release to each and every one of us who request it, as well as His all embracing love activates our process of ascension to a phenomenal degree. He also installs specific rods that are designed to match our individual frequency and to help that frequency increase and rise to ever-higher levels. Along with this, He brings a spectrum of tones that work in a similar fashion. Remember that light and sound are one, and are used conjointly upon the higher realms.

The Mahatma is available to us in each of the ways mentioned above and at far greater levels than the conscious mind can conceive. He

Integrated Ascension

comes forth as a unique Cosmic Being, who is in fact a group consciousness with many facets to it. He presents himself as One, however, and seeks to be addressed as either the Mahatma, or the Avatar of Synthesis. Having all these facets to him, however, he aids us in numerous ways. This is one of the reasons that various individuals tune into various aspects of him, and choose to focus more on one facet than another. He is so vast and inclusive that it is almost impossible for this different point of focus to not occur. All his work, however, helps facilitate our individual ascension process.

For me, I seem to focus mostly upon his essential embodiment as the Avatar of Synthesis. My beloved mentor Djwhal Khul works directly under His auspices in this regard, and therefore so do I. This is not to discount all the various ways in which the Mahatma can assist us. In fact, I call on Him for just about everything from healing to activation work. I do this, however, under the greater umbrella of synthesis per say. In that way I feel that I am at once accessing the highest energies and frequencies that I am able to absorb from the Mahatma, while keeping as balanced and synthesized as possible in the process. I personally believe that this is truly how he seeks to work. As he is Himself the Avatar of Synthesis, it feels correct to call upon him in that capacity and to work with Him under the guiding light of synthesis and integration!

When I visualize ascending with the Mahatma, or through the grace and aid of the Mahatma, I see it as a totally integrated, balanced and synthesized ascension. All levels are given their due, and honored to their highest degree. All levels are likewise cleansed, cleared, and purified and brought into balance and harmony within the greater whole. No stone is left unturned and no facet is overlooked. The process of ascension therefore automatically is that of integrated ascension! Under the auspices and guiding light of the Mahatma, all lesser lights are integrated, incorporated, balanced, and honored.

Now remember, the Mahatma has ultimately come to Earth to help us heal our separation with GOD. He seeks at this unique period of

Integrated Ascension

grace, to help us upraise our frequencies all the way back to the GOD-HEAD Itself. This includes the raising of the dense physical plane so that it can function at the highest sub-plane of physical matter and keep raising the planet to its next dimensional level of frequency. Until June of 1988, the Mahatma was not grounded physically upon the Earth. The shifts of vibration that the planet as a whole have gone through allows him to now work directly with us while in physical embodiment. In fact, he specifically requests that we each stay as open to him as possible in order that he may all the more fully anchor and ground his energies into the very core of Earth itself. In other words, He is here to help upraise and synthesize every single level of existence.

Integrated Ascension, my beloved readers, is in actuality ascending via the Mahatma. An all inclusive, all embracing process that will ultimately liberate us from all the chains that bind. We can call upon the Mahatma's energies to assist us in the transmutation of any level of energy that is not functioning at its highest rate of frequency.

For example, if we request that he assist us physically, then what we are really calling for is the healing of our physical vehicle, the heightening of its vibrations, alignment with our Higher Self and/or Monad, alignment with the Mahatma and full attunement to GOD. When we do this with utter sincerity of intent we will be able to demonstrate mastery over the physical vehicle. We are likewise automatically assisting to anchor the Mahatma's resonances firmly into the physical structure of the Earth. It is in this way that the Mahatma serves our greatest good, while we, in turn, work to help him serve the greater good of the planet.

The same basic principles apply to calling upon Him for assistance with our emotional body and astral elemental. As the Mahatma is now working fully and directly with all levels of the four lower bodies, he is as much available to us in regard to any of these as he has been in the past in regard to our higher bodies. We can therefore ask for his Divine intervention as we struggle to gain control of our astral elemental and achieve total mastery over our emotional selves. I again must mention

Integrated Ascension

that this does not mean that he seeks to eliminate all feeling from any of us. In fact, just the opposite is true. It is not his purpose, GOD's purpose, nor should it be our purpose to try and annihilate any part of self. What we must do, however, is to seek mastery over every aspect of self and likewise raise it to its highest possible frequency. In dealing with the emotional body our concern would therefore be to raise our feeling world to the level of heart and out of the lower or baser desires.

This, my beloved readers, does not mean that we in any way close down, shut out or stop up our feeling world. What it does mean is that through the Mahatma's assistance and our own efforts, we raise up our feeling body to receive the more refined and subtle frequencies of unconditional love, love of humanity, love of all sentient beings and love of GOD.

This is not meant to imply that we should seek to denounce our desire for human love in the process. If romantic love is part of our make-up and puzzle piece, and this is true for the majority of people, then intimate human love will still function freely between a couple. This will very often take the shape of including love of family and friends as well. The exchange of human love will, however, be raised to its highest possible frequency and be centered in the heart, yet at the same time it will have its full and normal range of expression that can exist on all levels, including that between romantic partners. Remember always that the energy of the Mahatma is integrated and all-inclusive. It does not seek to exclude anything within the range of normal healthy living, but simply to synthesize it within the highest possible radiance of being and to demonstrate it as such. That is all!

This would likewise include all aspects that pertain to the mental level as well. The Mahatma Himself, while not wanting to be limited to any mental concept, has revealed Himself to the minds of humanity. The truth is that no human mind could possibly contain the enormity of his Beingness or the light of his Divine wisdom. Nevertheless, he has accessed the human mind in order to make certain aspects of himself

Integrated Ascension

and his work known. That is one of the reasons I love him so much, and have dedicated a chapter to integrating the Mahatma. When we ascend through His Divine grace we ascend through all the various levels of our Being, and thus achieve the Integrated Ascension that we must ultimately achieve in order to be fully and completely free.

Meditating upon the Mahatma will stimulate the cells of the concrete mind, and those of the physical brain to the point where our capacity to receive wisdom is heightened and increased by leaps and bounds. Along with this will we access the ability to act as the Mighty I Am Presence and to be the Master in control of our mental vehicle! The mental vehicle that we will be masters of, will, however, be itself refined and stimulated by the light that the Mahatma brings. This is truly a win-win situation.

Every cell of all of our twelve-body system, as well as our subtle light bodies, will be reconstructed and recalibrated in order to fully receive the Divine outpouring of the Mahatma. They will also be fully synthesized within themselves as well as with our entire outer and inner plane structure in order to best reflect the energies of Synthesis itself. This process cannot help but to enhance our ability to take higher and higher initiations, and to do so in an integrated fashion. We will, by the help of the Mahatma, ascend in the wholeness and completeness that GOD has always intended us to. There will be no need to hang out on any plane pertaining to the four lower worlds, unless we choose to for the sake of service. For this reason, above and beyond all others, do I choose to take every opportunity that the Mahatma will provide to ascend within the sphere of His radiant Being.

I cannot suggest strongly enough that you accept the grace that he has to offer, and ask that you continue your path of ascension within His most radiant Self. As he is all inclusive, this does not exclude you from following the path you are on, following your heart felt calling or by any means removing yourself from your Divine lineage! All you will be doing is "adding" the energies of the Avatar of Synthesis into your process. This will help you facilitate a most Integrated Ascension and at the same time offer you a field of service, just by allowing him to work through you and grace you with his presence! I can't think of a better offer than this, my friends, and do hope that you sincerely consider availing yourself of the wondrous glory of the Avatar of Synthesis!

Pure Beingness: Existence, Consciousness, Bliss, and Service

When our path involves integrating with the Mahatma, we will find that not only do we approach our ascension process in a most integrated manner, as was just discussed, but that our consciousness itself undergoes great expansion. The type of consciousness that I am referring to here supersedes and yet includes that of the concrete mind that was previously discussed. It supersedes that of the subconscious and conscious mind as it is ordinarily discussed and takes us instead in to the heart of the superconscious mind and beyond!

I must point out, however, that I am not using the term superconscious as it is normally used, although it does pertain very much to the higher sphere of consciousness and is indicative of information received via the Higher Self and the Mighty I Am Presence. I am not limiting it to even these vast realms. I am speaking of it as a consciousness that surpasses all the various aspects of mind and consciousness as they have previously been discussed. The consciousness that I am addressing is that of *"pure awareness itself."* It is, in fact, the language of symbols, the language of liquid golden light, the language of pure frequency, tone, and energy!

You must realize, beloved readers, that as we are stimulated by an energy as vast as that of the Mahatma, who Himself works in unity with Melchizedek and Metatron, we are speaking of energies that defy language altogether. Yet language being the raft that we are using to take us to the far country of "Pure Beingness," I will, of course, attempt to voice the silence as it has unveiled itself to me through my attunement. If I

Integrated Ascension

had the ability to speak to you in pure frequency, what I seek to convey would be far more accurate. Yet I myself have received much of this information through word and imagery, and therefore it is appropriate that it is so conveyed. In fact, one of the most wondrous aspects of the Mahatma is that as he contains all levels within Himself, there is really no separation. This lack of separation allows that which is pure frequency and vibration to take the form of words that speak to the mind with little, if any, distortion. There are certain aspects obviously that must remain unsaid, as they have nothing to do with language as we presently use it. They await our discovery and direct experience. It is also quite true that the intensity of the type of consciousness that streams forth from Beingness itself, cannot be conveyed, although it most certainly can be inferred.

What I must make absolutely clear here, is that the full force of this information is given to me by the combined energies of the Mahatma, Lord Melchizedek and Archangel Metatron. They are a Cosmic trinity with whom I work very closely, and it is the joint energy of their combined Universal Synthesizing force and Divine light that have been conveyed to me.

What they are seeking to impart is the fact that consciousness itself is limitless. Most of us tend to limit it to the four minds or the subconscious, conscious, superconscious aspects of mind. The unenlightened see it as stemming from the brain, which is truly a limited lens, and one that slowly but surely is being replaced by the concept of mind per say. When we are speaking of consciousness, what we are speaking of in reality is the essence of GODHEAD itself. As I mentioned earlier in this book, the expression "Sat Chit Ananda" that is spoken of in the Hindu religion approaches most closely the heart and truth of what I am trying to convey. Translated into English, "Sat Chit Ananda" means existence, consciousness, bliss. This is a very close expression of the type of consciousness that becomes available at the higher stages of integrated ascension.

Integrated Ascension

The higher we go on our respective paths of initiation the more we embrace this state of consciousness of Beingness. When we reach the soul merge at the third initiation, we begin to get a glimpse of this. When we pass through the portal of our seventh sub-plane of the seventh initiation, and are literally functioning as the Monad, we certainly live within a stepped down version of this consciousness. When we begin to advance higher and higher upon the circular-spiraled ladder of evolution and receive the rod of power and the secret rods of consciousness from the joint energies of Melchizedek, the Mahatma, and Metatron, we begin to bathe in this language of light and Beingness, this consciousness that supersedes all limitation and to delve within the scared tone of "Sat Chit Ananda."

As we continue to receive the activations and benedictions that we summon forth through our sincere and heartfelt requests, the Mahatma, along with Melchizedek and Metatron will help bring us to higher and higher states of consciousness and pure awareness. The activations, the great brilliance of the light, and the frequencies that this holy Cosmic trinity wishes to impart to us necessitates that our bodies are capable of receiving these frequencies. In the process of fulfilling these requirements, the Mahatma, as I have stated in the last section, will be most helpful.

Once the bodies are brought into their proper alignment and integration, then we are brought deeper and deeper into pure consciousness itself. This is a state of pure Beingness that is truly beyond description. Almost all of us who get glimpses of this get but a fragment of a glimpse while in the waking state. Most all of us are brought into the higher resonances of this when we are out of the physical body during sleep. In fact, we are, in truth, out of and beyond the etheric, emotional and mental bodies as well, and travel to that high place via the Monad itself. The reason that it is so imperative for the lower vehicles to be functioning at such a high frequency is because, as the greater always includes the lesser, the vibration of *"Pure*

Integrated Ascension

Consciousness" will invariably leave its impression upon all the various bodies to which we are connected.

What is happening to those of us who have made the required degree of progress upon our ascension path is that we are indeed taken into aspects of the realm of pure consciousness, or "Sat Chit Ananda." There is no denying, my beloved readers, that bliss is as much a part of this realm of experience as is pure existence and pure consciousness.

What then is occurring, is that the installation of the sacred geometries, key codes, symbols and frequencies are being anchored into our twelve-body system, including the very physical body itself. As we continue on our journey of Integrated Ascension, these symbols are becoming more and more activated. The language of pure light is beginning to shine within us, generally just below the threshold of awareness. Certain mysteries are being revealed to our conscious minds, and ancient secret symbols are being decoded and understood.

This is very much the direct result of the combined "Rods of Light, Power, and Consciousness" that are being given to those who are ready to receive them by Melchizedek, the Mahatma, and Metatron. Inherent in the Rod of light is the Rod of love. You should be aware that from a higher perspective lens, the energies of love and light coexist as part of the same whole. This is the primary reason why I have put so much emphasis upon the development of the love quotient. Upon the outer planes, and even many of the inner planes, light and love hold a distinctive and separate frequency. The further into the Heart of GOD that we proceed the more the two become intertwined and interwoven. If you truly seek the bliss of pure consciousness and the Heart of GOD within the Great Central Sun, then you will not storm the gates of your seventh initiation without building up your love quotient to its maximum potential. If you do, you will only be held at that point until you fully integrate love into the very essence of your Being.

My beloved friends, pure consciousness awaits each and every one of us. It is from that absolute state of Beingness that all the worlds and we

Integrated Ascension

ourselves first sprung forth. It is to that state of Beingness that we all ultimately return. We go back to Source, to the GODHEAD, to existence, consciousness, Bliss, as we travel the path of Integrated Ascension. I know that what I have tapped into has been but a fragment of this awareness, as the fullness of it cannot be experienced until we have reached the 352nd level of the Mahatma and are in complete and total resonance with the GODHEAD Itself.

The primary reason that I call this to your attention is because each and every one of us is on our way there and as lightworkers have advanced far enough along the path to begin to have a sense of this realm. More importantly and more to the point is the fact that we have now made enough progress to have gained access to realms of pure consciousness that were heretofore denied. Within these realms we are slowly integrating the language of light and learning the meaning of the sacred symbols. We are venturing beyond intellect and mind, as we have known it in the past, to a great new expanse.

I want to re-emphasize the importance of synthesis and integration and the part that the Mahatma has to play in this new awakening. We are meant to be able to both access and then anchor into our outer minds and the very Earth itself, the mysteries that are now being revealed. In order to do this it is essential that we tend to the business at hand, and purify ourselves to the highest degree possible. We must do this for we have chosen to be the wayshowers of the New Age, and GOD in turn, has chosen us. This is a joint agreement that each of us has made. You can be certain that the Hierarchy of Inner Plane Planetary and Cosmic Ascended Masters are doing their part to help us keep this sanctified agreement and to fulfill our Divine destinies. It is incumbent upon each of us that we do our part and see to it that the vision becomes reality!

I also want to let you know that beyond the boundary of the mind as we normally define it, awaits the realm of pure consciousness for us to access. Although the deepest levels of this will be experienced when we have traversed all 352 levels of Being, there is much sweetness and enlightenment available to each of us right where we are in the moment. If we allow ourselves to get beyond the realm of concepts and expectation, we can call forth the energy of pure consciousness to resonate within our Beings even during our daily activities. This is the ultimate goal that the yogi has striven for throughout eons of time. We now, in mass, have greater and deeper access to this most glorious realm, if we but take the time to attune to it.

As the Mahatma includes all levels of Beingness within Himself, and yet supersede them all in the realm of GODHEAD, so we too can attend to that which is our mission to attend to, and yet likewise find a resting place of pure peace within "Sat Chit Ananda." This is available to each of us now, in this very moment. We just need to be aware of that fact and ask to be put into attunement with that state of Beingness. When we allow ourselves to live at the highest vibration of pure consciousness that we can reach, and yet stay focused and centered within our daily lives, we can say with utter bliss that we are indeed "…in the world but not of it." We will also then be accessing all that is needed in order to help establish and fully anchor the New Age upon this sphere.

Beloved readers, do not keep this state of consciousness from yourselves. GOD invites us all to partake of as much of this pure radiant frequency that we are capable. GOD also seeks for each of us to be vessels for which these frequencies are anchored and made manifest. The Mahatma has come forth from Cosmic spheres in order to help us do this. He seeks our help in the process, for it is we who physically walk the Earth and are the ones who can ground these frequencies into the Earth. I urge each and every one of you to integrate with the Mahatma to as great a degree as you possibly can. Call forth to him for his activations. Sincerely consider allowing him to walk within you to facilitate the needed and necessary grounding work. Ask to be taken as far as you can within the realm of pure consciousness, that you may experience the bliss that words cannot describe. The more deeply rooted you are in pure consciousness, the more deeply anchored you will be within GOD!

The Avatar of Synthesis holds the key to unlock these many doors, the many levels of Being that will make this a reality for us. Please do call upon him! As you seek to fulfill your mission and to ascend in an integrated manner, there is no one better qualified to help in this process than the Mahatma is. Let him into your life and I guarantee you, he will let you into his life. The secrets of the universe will become unveiled and the experience of pure existence, consciousness, and bliss will grow ever stronger within you. You will find that you are serving the planet by simply being upon it. This is His Divine gift to you and your Divine gift to Him!

15

The Power of the Spoken Word

Those who are able to see with "inner vision," would see as do the Masters, that words are far more than they seem to be, even by the standard of the occultist! Every single word has not only frequency of vibration but also, upon the etheric realm, literally has weight, shape, form, color and tone. Each and every word uttered is a power packed force of singular substance.

When we string words together in sentences, particularly when formatted with emotional and/or mental imagery, we, as human beings, harness and make manifest a great and dynamic powerhouse of force. This great, and substantial force is then flung forth via the movement of lips and tongue, much like a firm arrow is shot from a strong and steady bow. Whether it be the bow and arrow of the warrior that carries death in its thrust, or the arrow of the love-force of Cupid, lies within the intent, motive and construction of those who send it forth.

Most of humanity has little or no idea that they are the harbingers and executors of a force as powerful as that of the spoken word. This lack of knowledge inadvertently causes a maelstrom of destruction.

Those of heart who are indeed aware of the power of the word and who are attuned with the intent of Divine Will, construct words that are themselves healing temples. The status of those who use words with conscious awareness of the great strength, force, and substance inherent within such usage is as conscious co-creators of the Golden Age.

It is time for us all to be aware of the vital force and power of the spoken word, so this abundant energy is neither wasted in idleness, nor worse, used unthinkingly and unintentionally to do harm. The hour is upon us when we who call ourselves "The Workers of Light" are asked to use the light, form, substance and vibrational tone of the holy word in dedication to the healing and upliftment of the planet.

"In the beginning was the word and the word was with GOD and the word was GOD." This is the force we wield with every single utterance we make!

This truth is not meant to make any of us overly self-conscious or unduly preoccupied with our daily conversations. It is simply meant to shed light upon the enormous power available to each of us. Daily chitchat is generally of a harmless nature, as again, the intent behind such conversation is light and thus constructs lighter, more etherialized thought/word formations.

However, one must be exceedingly careful when the emotional and mental bodies are deeply engrossed in the process of forming statements, for these build weighty and powerful forms with deep vibrational frequency. Be extremely vigilant over these types of utterances and be fully cognizant of the fact that we can potentially be building a weapon that, in our heart of hearts, we would rather not send forth into the atmosphere. First and foremost, think before you speak.

Preceding even this, meditate and attune with your soul, Monad, and Mighty I Am Presence before you even think. This will align your motive and intent with that of GOD, which automatically puts you in the realm of world server and healer.

The thoughts that then enter your being will be of a higher order and the words that therefore follow these thoughts will be synchronistic with them. They will carry with them the shape, tone, color and frequency of that which, for you, is the highest and best expression of

Integrated Ascension

GOD. Your words then will be an upliftment, not only to humanity, but also to every kingdom and evolution that exists upon the planet.

We all know from direct experience the impact hurtful words from others have had upon ourselves. We likewise have seen the effect our own negative and deleterious words have had upon our fellow human beings. Most of us are aware of the enormous effect the "silent words" we speak to ourselves have on our physical, etheric, emotional and mental bodies. If we take but a moment to recall, observe and ponder upon this, little more needs even be said.

Words are indeed a force to be reckoned with, and are one of our most potent tools for good or ill. It is generally assumed that lightworkers would use their words for good. They need only be reminded of the incredible power they wield.

What is interesting to note, is that words, operating in the realm of frequency, tone and intent, have an incredibly powerful effect upon other kingdoms and evolutions that do not respond to the actual literal meaning of words the way the human kingdom does. An easy example of this can be seen when dealing with the Animal Kingdom.

Any pet owner will tell you that their animal brother or sister responds to the tone and energy expressed to him rather than the actual word. Although, in time domestic animals will learn more and more of what the resonance of certain words mean, we guarantee you, if you were to offer your dog a cookie in an angry and aggressive or accusatory manner he would react to your tone rather than the offering.

Inversely, there is so much power of calm within the tones of the dolphin and whale, that humanity has recorded their sounds and will happily spend money on the purchasing of these recordings. These beautiful tones are often used to soothe, heal, and induce tranquil and meditative states. When we commune with the nature kingdom, or the Angelic kingdom, it is our frequency and tone-color that warrants their response. Our words, however, are at their most powerful when both the words, the intent, and the tone-color are all in harmony with love, light, and the Divine Will of GOD.

This cycles us back to the origin of this article. Words are something we all participate in, not only on a daily or hourly basis, but often also on a moment to moment basis. In point of fact, as a race in general, we speak far too much and think about what we are saying far too little. Words, however, and thought on a more refined level, are part of our very make-up. As this is so, it is well worth our while to explore how to use this vital part of ourselves to help implement the plan of GOD, usher in the new millennium and establish the seventh Golden Age upon our planet.

As lightworkers, we have all taken on certain very definite assignments and missions. We each hold a very specific and vital piece of the unfolding puzzle of GOD upon Earth. As human beings we often fall a bit into the trap of thinking that our way is just a little bit better, more powerful, more aligned than the next person's. This is sometimes due to the faulty thinking of the negative ego and often due to the passion with which we embrace our particular puzzle piece.

In either event, this can lead to a subtle but insidious form of judgment. Some of us will fall into judgment of other people and slip into the modality of the critic. Others of us will succumb to self-judgment and belittle ourselves for not holding as grandiose or seemingly important puzzle piece as someone else.

This invariably leads to negative talk, be it outwardly or inwardly directed. This negative talk must cease! The harm it is doing to the mission we all share is great, if often unintentional. It is for this reason we call your attention to the power inherent within the word and ask you to please make the necessary adjustment to use words that uplift and heal and not ones that lash out or belittle.

Be ever mindful of that which we speak and that which we cultivate as thought. All of us are here for a common purpose, and purposely have we each been given distinct and individualized puzzle pieces and missions. We are asked to spend our time honoring our own work and endeavoring to bring that forth, rather than in critiquing the work of our brothers and sisters.

As beloved Master Jesus Christ put it, "First take the beam out of thine own eye, then thou shalt see clearly enough to take the speck out of thy brother's eye." In other words, we're requested to tend to our own work and seek to effectuate that to its highest potential. In doing that, we cannot help but raise up the work of our brothers and sisters. If we criticize, judge or speak harshly, we will not only bring harm to them, but we will be unleashing a destructive force that will ultimately hurt ourselves.

It has been rightly stated that "thoughts are things." If this be so, you can rest assured that words are much more substantial things. Use them wisely and in service, seeking to harm no one or no-thing in the process. We have the capacity and destiny to be Master builders. Words are one of the strongest and most influential tools of our trade, no matter what our particular profession happens to be. The wise and benevolent usage of words is instrumental to the healing of our planet and us.

16

World Service Meditations

Integrating the World into Our Ascension Service Work

Beloved readers, I have been guided to end this book by offering a number of suggested meditations specifically geared towards world service issues. The Masters tell me that it is in this way that all the work that is done on the level of personal integrated ascension can most efficiently and effectively be brought into "Integrated Planetary Ascension." As there will be a variety of meditations to choose from, it is suggested that you choose those that are closest to your heart, spiritual mission and puzzle piece. Do, however, rotate among them, as I am sure each of you will find that many of these areas touch your heart to one degree or another. On behalf of the inner plane Hierarchy of Planetary and Cosmic Ascended Masters, I thank you in advance for joining in this world service activity!

Planetary Axiatonal Alignment

As with all the following meditations, assume a comfortable position either sitting up or lying down, with your spine straight. Sitting up is preferable in these types of meditations, as you are generally more focused that way. Leaning against a wall if you are sitting on the floor, or upon the back of a chair is perfectly fine as long as the spine is held as straight as possible. Lying down is also all right, as long as you maintain your focus.

First, request a personal axiatonal alignment so that you yourself are as balanced as possible. Then request a full axiatonal alignment for the Earth Herself. Visualize the bodies of Earth on all the various levels, totally and completely aligned, with all energies of our planet as a whole fully aligned with Solar, Galactic, Universal, Multiuniversal and Cosmic Divine intent! Breathe slowly and relaxed, all the while holding the focus of a totally aligned, balanced and integrated Earth! Stay with this for as long as you feel comfortable, up to five minutes.

Platinum Net Sweep

Begin by asking for the platinum net to sweep over yourself and/or your group first, so that you can be cleared of your own misqualified energies. Then request that the same be done for the planet as a whole. Request this for the physical, etheric, astral and mental atmosphere of the Earth. In this way each of the four lower bodies of Earth Herself will receive one of the most potent cleansings, purifying, and healing tools being currently offered by the Cosmic Masters. You need not remain in meditation too long, just long enough for fully visualize a gigantic platinum net sweeping over the four bodies of the planet and cleansing these bodies of as much debris as possible. The more this is done, the healthier the planet will become.

Meditation for the Earth Mother

When seated comfortably in your meditation position, call first for the overlighting presence of your own Monad. Then from that place, invoke within all of the Masters who work with the physical, etheric, astral, and mental bodies of Earth Herself. Call specifically upon Lord Buddha, our Planetary Logos. Allow these wonderful healing energies to pour through you and fill your entire being. When you feel fully infused with these divine energies, anchor your own grounding cord deep into the Earth. Turn your palms upward on your lap, or even extend the arms upward for a time if you like. Ask that the healing currents of all the blessed Masters whose presence you have invoked flow through you and outward into the Earth.

First visualize and direct these energies into the very core heart of Mother Earth. Ask that there be a balancing and harmonizing within the very foundation of the planet itself. Pour forth Love that all that need healing may be healed, balanced and cleansed through grace rather than karma. Then put your attention upon the Earth's etheric body. Once again, ask all the Masters in attendance to help radiate through you their blessed healing energies. Do the same for the astral atmosphere and astral body of the Earth, that all negative emotions are brought to a quiet, peaceful, loving calm. Follow this with putting your attention upon the mental atmosphere or mental body of Earth. Send out only positive thoughtforms. Ask the Masters to again bless and heal through you, and to infuse the mental world with their divine and glorious vision of positivity. Ask them to fill the mental atmosphere with their own though outpicturing of the wondrous expression of the next millennium.

Let all these blessings come to harmony within yourself. Continue to meditate for as long as you feel comfortable, knowing that you are acting as a focal point for healing Mother Earth.

Political Hot Spots

There are very definite political "hot spots" around the planet. The Middle East is certainly a very key one at this time, and has been for a very long time. Bosnia is of course, another. Russia is undergoing enormous stress, change and transformation. In fact, these political hot spots are so pervasive that I leave it up to your discretion and personal attunement to select the ones that you personally key into. Once you have done this, invoke the Masters who you are most connected with on a personal level, as well as calling upon beloved Masters St. Germain and El Morya.

Ask to be fully surrounded and protected by your semi-permeable bubble of golden-white light, as well as the pure white light of the Christ. Then connect your third eye with your heart chakra. Then align all of your chakras while at the same time keeping special attention and focus upon the third eye and heart. Hold the particular political hot spot that you have chosen within your mind's eye, as well as within your heart. See all stresses and tensions melting away. Pray to the beloved Masters, Archangels, Angels, and Elohim to help co-create and co-build a peaceful and harmonious situation. Prayer is most powerful in this specific world service meditation, as we are dealing with very delicate issues and really want to be sure to invoke and invite the help of the Masters. Call also upon the particular angel of the country that you are concentrating with. It is not necessary to know the name of the angel, just ask that the angel of that particular country and even geographical area come to offer their assistance by virtue of your invitation and prayer. Ask also for the assistance of the Arcturians and the Ashtar Command, and they too will assist as far as their law of non-interference permits.

Hold to your positive meditation for as long as you like. When you conclude, do remember to thank the Masters for their help and remember also to hold to your positive imagery as you go about your day!

Social Issues

Each meditation that is done in regard for world service should first be applied to self. Before beginning your meditation for social issues, for example, ask that any disharmony within your personal social life be brought into a harmonious condition. A simple prayer such as this, beloved readers, helps to integrate you within the service work that you are doing for the world. You need not spend much time in this, just long enough to make the request. As each of us are part of the world for which we are praying, it makes perfect sense to ask for help in order to correct personal imbalances in ourselves that we are asking for the planet. Doing this both activates and demonstrates our own integration with the world. As I will not specifically stress this point again, please do remember to include this basic format in each of your world service mediations.

Once this is done and you are comfortably in meditation position, pick out one of the social issues to which you feel closely attuned. Examples of these might be the following: the integration of the races, children in need of greater protection, starving children, all starving people around the globe, elevating the consciousness of society's youths, the elimination of gang violence and the pervasive issue of homelessness. There are of course others that you might choose to focus upon, as there is no shortage in this department. Once again, call upon the Masters of your choosing. The Cosmic Avatar of Synthesis, the Mahatma, is an excellent being to call upon, as one of His prime functions is to integrate his high frequency energies into every level of existence. His power and presence is enormous, and yet filters down to the most basic level of life. Call him in, beloved readers, for he can serve through each of you who do so.

Fix your attention upon the particular social issue that you have selected as your world service meditation and begin to channel the Love, Light and Will-to-Good of GOD directly into the heart of that issue. See it transform within your inner vision from a situation of unfairness, disharmony, and discrimination, into a love infused, light infused expression of GOD. Feel the Healing Masters who work with these ideas pour their radiance through you. Feel the transformative and transmuting power of St. Germain as he graces the situation with the light fire of his violet transmuting flame. Feel the power of El Morya and Archangel Michael. Feel the immensity and enormity of the Mahatma, who through your willingness to serve, easily transmits his most glorious presence to the situation at hand, uplifting and transforming that all may come into the highest expression of GOD as possible, at any given time.

Stay within the healing and peace of your service meditation until you feel you are complete. Again, when you have concluded the meditation, always give thanks to the Celestial Hierarchy who has helped you. Give thanks to your own soul and Monad as well as to your self for entering into such a meditation. Remember to continue to hold a positive focus upon the issue you have prayed and meditated upon. If the news confronts you with negativity, if you even come face to face with the negativity that you are seeking to transmute and transform and heal, take note and then immediately shift gears to one of positive visualization, imagery and prayer. You are a healer in this regard, and just as does any good physician, you note the disease but concentrate and devote all your energies upon the cure!

Child Abuse and Spousal Abuse

Begin this meditation as you have been previously instructed. Ask for the proper protection and then ask that all abusive nature to "self" be transmuted. Surround yourself with a field of unconditional self-love. Then invoke your Masters, including beloved Mother Mary, Quan Yin and beloved Lord Maitreya.

This particular social issue has been singled out, as it is also a personal issue that many suffer with in silence. It is often well hidden from all except those that are most directly involved. By the power of this healing meditation, the required light and love will reach into those dark and hidden places. If there is a specific situation of this kind that you wish to focus on, then do so. Otherwise, ask that your meditation go outward to anyone and everyone in need. This would include the abuser as well as the abused. Ask for the unconditional love of Mother Mary, the all-pervasive and healing compassion and mercy of Quan Yin, the love/Wisdom of The Christ to infuse all abusive situations. Also, request the Violet Flame of St. Germain that all misqualified energies contributing to the situation be transmuted.

Visualize now this unconditional love, wisdom, mercy, compassion, and divine alchemy transforming these particular energies of abuse into energies of love. See and feel that which you have invoked entering into the field and hearts of all involved in this type of situation, quieting all storms and allowing wisdom and love to rule rather than uncontrolled anger. Focus this mostly upon the perpetrator, yet do not forget to ask for the compassion and mercy of Quan Yin to enter the heart and minds of those who have been abused. In order for a total healing to take place, all must ultimately be forgiven and brought to some form of harmony and peace. So, what we are trying to accomplish via the Masters' help is to help heal the entire situation in as complete a manner as possible. This is a most sensitive area that we have ventured into here, and we do our best work by means of prayer and requesting the divine intervention of the Masters as long as the higher selves of those involved agree. The most appropriate way to do this work is to allow the Masters to work through us.

These prayers are much needed, my beloved readers, and anyone who gives any service time by requesting to be conduits for this healing energy will surely be much blessed. At the conclusion of this meditation, be sure to ask to be cleared of any unwanted and extraneous emotional energies that you may have picked up.

Invocation to the Healing Angels

The healing angels are ever ready to be of service to anyone who is ill, in the hospital or to come to the aid of any and everybody involved in an accident, natural disaster, or harmed by any means. In truth, their

Integrated Ascension

divine presence can be seen and felt by those with inner vision in hospitals everywhere, and around the ill and wounded, however, their work and their numbers would exponentially increase by our simple prayers and invocations.

I again, take a moment to remind you to request their presence within your own life, and to help you with your own personal healing process. Then, focus your attention either on a particular individual who is ill, a specific hospital, hospitals in general, or upon any specific or generalized situation where their particular help is needed. Call upon the Mighty Archangels Raphael and Mother Mary to oversee this work. Then proceed to call upon the angels of healing in general and direct them to the area you have chosen upon. For the benefit of those of you leading meditations such as these, the following is an example of this particular meditation.

***

Close eyes.

Assume a comfortable meditative posture, either sitting up or lying down. We now invoke the pure white Light of the Christ and the semipermeable bubble of golden-white light for protection. Only that which is good and of GOD can pass through this bubble. Only that which is of GOD can pass outward to our fellow human beings and to the planet. We are protected and act as conduits and servers for the highest purposes only.

We now invoke the blessed presence of Archangel Raphael and Mother Mary, his divine counterpart, to overlight this meditation.

We now invoke the presence of all of the Angels of the Healing Arts.

We ask that any and every aspect of disharmony or disease within our own personal bodies be bathed and washed clean within your healing light.

We now direct our attention to all hospitals around the globe.

We ask for the overlighting presence of Archangels Raphael and Mother Mary to infuse these hospitals, that all may be bathed within your blessed healing love-light.

We now ask for as many healing angels that are needed in order to help effectuate healing on all levels of the four lower bodies to come and stand by the bedside of all who are suffering within the various hospitals everywhere.

We ask that you come in answer to our prayers and invocations, as long as the higher self of the individuals involved agree.

Please, oh blessed angels, pour forth all the divine and glorious healing force that you have into each and everyone in need of you this moment

Now let us be silent and allow the angels to work.

(Allow a few moments of silence)

Now let us add our own love and healing energies to these places and the people in need, as we ourselves are healed by the force of the healing energies flowing through us.

(Allow another few minutes of meditation)

Integrated Ascension

We give thanks to you, Raphael, and Mother Mary.

We give thanks to all the Angels of the Healing Arts who are answering our heartfelt prayers this very moment.

We ask that you stay as long as you are needed and that you continue to overlight any and all who are suffering.

Amen, Amen, Amen.

When you feel ready focus back into your bodies and open your eyes.

Carry this peace and healing radiance within you as you leave this meditation and resume your own work and go about your lives.

✶✶✶

Invocation for the Highest Light for Those Souls Making Their Transition

Beloved readers, I am being asked, even as I write this, to continue to present these meditations in specific guided form. As much has been explained to you regarding these world service meditations in the earlier ones, I will now lead you through the following meditations directly. For anyone using these to themselves guide a group or a class through mediation, please follow the format, as I am laying it out for you here. For those of you meditating alone, this will provide you with a basic outline to follow. Of course, make the appropriate changes for the particular situation, world issue, specific situation that you are addressing, as well as using these meditations to help heal a special or personal situation that falls within these categories.

Integrated Ascension

Close eyes.

Find your meditative position.

We now call for a semi-permeable golden-white bubble of protection and for the pure white Light of the Christ.

We ask that the little transitions that each one of us participating in this meditation is going though serves but to direct us to the highest light.

We call upon our Higher Self, Monad, the inner plane Hierarchy of Planetary and Cosmic Ascended Masters, all Archangels, Elohim and GOD.

We ask that anyone (or give specific name if you are praying for someone you know) who is now going through their transition called "death" seek only the highest Light.

We pray to their particular Masters and guardian angels to help direct them to this light.

We pray also that they move quickly, gently and easily though any Bardo experiences that they may be having.

We ask that they know themselves to be the light and love of GOD, and that they joyfully merge with the highest possible light of GOD radiance that presents itself to them.

We pray for their peace, joy, love and glory as they merge with the Light of GOD and know themselves to be a flame of the ever burning Fire of GOD.

May their lives on the inner plane be filled with the love and light that embraces them and calls them home.

Kodoish, Kodoish, Kodoish. Adonai Tsebayoth!

***

Invocation of Liberation For All Souls Who Are Earthbound and/or Are Trapped in The Astral Plane

Please note, since the beginnings of all meditations are the same, I am writing only the basics at this point. For greater detail, please study the previous.

Close eyes.

Assume your meditation position.

We now call forth for a semi-permeable bubble of golden-white light for protection.

We invoke the Hierarchy of inner plane Planetary and Cosmic Ascended Masters, the Archangels and Elohim.

In whatever way we each are personally bound to the Earth or trapped within the lower caverns of our astral nature, we now ask for the Divine assistance of the Masters to help to set us free!

On behalf of any of our brothers and sisters (specific trapped souls that you may have either encountered or know of can be named here in place of a more generalized prayer) that are trapped within the lower astral realms and are tied or held to the Earth in any unhealthy manner may immediately be assisted to make their full transition to the inner planes in order to continue their evolution.

We ask and invoke the Masters and angels aid to help awaken these earthbound souls to their situation that they may willingly and joyfully let go of all attachments that no longer serve, and seek the their rightful place within the Father's Mansions.

We pray that they accept the help being offered them this moment, and joyfully find their higher purpose within the light.

Amen.

We ask that any negativity or emotionalism that we may have unknowingly taken in be immediately removed by the Masters.

We give thanks and say, Amen.

(Sound three "Oms")

Come back into the room, into the body, open eyes.

***

Integration and Harmony between the Human, Elemental and Angelic Kingdoms

Close eyes.

Assume comfortable meditative position.

Integrated Ascension

We call forth our semi-permeable bubble of golden-white light for protection and ask to be surrounded by the pure white Light of the Christ.

The Light of Lord Buddha, His Holiness Sai Baba, Krishna, Babaji, and so forth can also be used. Again, this depends upon your particular connection and the tone of the particular group you are dealing with. Invoking the pure white Light of the Christ has been used for a long period of time and is found to be quite effective, so I am choosing to write the meditations in this format. Feel free to invoke or include any of the Masters that you wish.

We invoke the entire Hierarchy of inner plane Planetary and Cosmic Ascended Masters, all the Archangels and Elohim.

We each individually set our intention to work in harmony with the nature spirits, devas, elementals and all of the angels and lesser builders, as well as the Archangels and Elohim.

Within our inner vision and imagination we can see the elementals and nature spirits at work within the grasslands, meadows, gardens, forests, oceans, lakes, rivers, within the currents and streams of air, wind and the movement of the seasons. We see these beings dancing within the flames that heat our food and warm our bodies, and within the great fire of the Sun.

We breathe in unconditional love, from our own Mighty I am Presence.

We now breathe this love outward to the other streams of evolution, who share the work and the glory of establishing the Seventh Golden Age upon our world.

Integrated Ascension

We seek them to know us as beings of light and love and we likewise acknowledge them as such beings.

We call upon the Masters to help guide us that we may walk gently upon the soil and that our actions are in harmony with the purpose of the whole, which includes the Divine purpose of the nature spirits and elementals.

We ask to be guided and shown how to properly respect and honor them, and request the same from them that we may work in closer and closer cooperation.

We especially invoke the guidance and direction of the great Archangels and Elohim.

We now meditate upon the love, joy and peace of this Divine cooperation and integration.

(Allow some time for silent meditation)

We come back into our bodies, infusing each cell with the joy, love, peace and harmony that we have meditated upon.

We give thanks for the work of the nature spirits and elementals, for the lesser builders, the angels, the grace of the Archangels and the Elohim.

We establish our grounding cord within the Earth and in so doing make a deeper connection from Spirit to Earth.

We now open our eyes.

★★★

Core Fear Matrix Removal Program for the Earth Mother Herself and For All of Humanity

Close eyes.

Assume meditation position.

We invoke our bubble of protection.

We call forth the Hierarchy of inner plane Ascended Planetary and Cosmic Masters, all Archangels and Elohim.

We call forth the presence of Divine Mother and the Lady Masters.

We call forth Lord Buddha, Sanat Kumara, and Vywamus.

We ask that the Core Fear Matrix Removal Program be brought into effect for the collective body of humanity and include ourselves in this, and for the Earth Mother Herself.

We request that any and all fear within the four lower bodies of Earth Mother and the collective body of humanity be lifted, plucked out, and completely removed.

We watch with our inner eye as these black weeds are taken from the field of the Earth Mother and lifted directly into the center of the Violet Fire of Transmutation.

All that is of a fearful and negative nature within the bodies of the Earth Mother and the collective of humanity are transmuted into energy that shall be used only for positive purposes.

In place of the fear that has been removed, we now ask the Divine Mother and Lady Masters to fill with unconditional Divine Love.

As part of the Earth Mother and the collective of humanity, we feel this love filling our physical, etheric, emotional/astral and mental bodies.

We give thanks to the glorious beings that have assisted us in this work.

Amen, Amen, Amen.

Extend grounding cord deep within the Earth's core.

Send or channel love through that cord and feel the nectar of this Divine Love bathe you in its sanctified light.

Come back fully into the body.

Open eyes.

***

Bridging the Extraterrestrials with the Consciousness of Humanity to Prepare for More Open Dialogue

Close eyes.

Assume meditation position.

Invoke the bubble of protection, pure white Light of the Christ.

Call forth the Hierarchy of inner plane Cosmic and Planetary Ascended Masters, the Archangels and Elohim.

Integrated Ascension

We now open ourselves up to the Confederation of Planets that have come from other worlds in order to assist the Earth in its evolution.

We now visualize the most spiritually attuned political leaders being elected into office.

We ask the Hierarchy to intercede in whatever manner that they are able in order to place lightworkers in these key political positions. We specifically request the help of El Morya and St. Germain.

We now ask for the mass mind of humanity itself to begin to open to greater and greater awareness and acceptance of these benevolent beings who have come to aid us in our evolution

We also visualize all the lightworkers of the world becoming clearer in their attunements to the work of our Extraterrestrial brothers and sisters.

We now see, with our inner vision, the governments of the planet openly communicating with our space brethren for the purpose of the betterment of Earth and the cooperation of our planet with divine intent.

We visualize clearly that the masses of humanity are now aware and educated, through the intervention of governmental leaders taking a stand for 'truth' as to the reality and purpose of our space brothers and sisters.

We also see, with our inner vision, how the lightworkers of the planet are able to work openly and collectively upon their particular mission in mutual cooperation with the Confederation of Planets.

Integrated Ascension

We can feel the joy of all of humanity, as well as that of our space brethren, as together we participate in manifesting the plan of GOD, and bringing the Earth forward into ever higher frequencies of light, love, power and the Will-to-Good.

We take a few moments to now ourselves connect with any incoming transmissions from this aspect of the Celestial Command. We know that if we are not consciously hearing their intent, we are nevertheless receiving it through the Universal Language of Light.

We bathe in this wonderful outpouring of grace and connectedness.

(Allow some time for silence)

We now thank the Celestial Hierarchy from other worlds who are here on humanity's behalf.

As we prepare to leave this meditation we know that we will hold to the vision of lightworkers entering and being elected into the foreground of politics both in the United States and in all the countries of the world.

We feel the joy of transformation through the mutual cooperation of humanity and the civilization and beings who form the Confederation of Planets.

We establish our grounding cords, come back into our bodies, and open eyes.

***

Integrated Ascension

The Golden Cylinder over the Whole Planet

Close eyes.

Assume meditation posture.

Invoke the golden-white semi-permeable bubble of light for protection and the pure white Light of the Christ.

Call forth the Hierarchy of inner plane Ascended Planetary and Cosmic Masters, as well as the Archangels and the Elohim.

We now call forth the golden cylinder of light, to envelope ourselves within its cleansing and purifying radiance, that it may lift from within our personal auric fields any negative debris, negative elementals, thoughtforms, emotional currents or misqualified energy of any kind and remove it from our four lower bodies.

Now visualize within your mind's eye this golden cylinder growing larger and larger, merging with all the golden cylinders that each one of you have invoked.

The golden cylinder keeps growing in size until it encompasses the entire planet, enveloping within its radiant sphere the collective bodies of humanity as they exist on the physical, etheric, astral and mental levels.

Now watch, with the inner eye of visualization as the golden cylinder begins to draw all misqualified energy that has lodged within the dense physical vehicle of Earth herself upward, until it reaches unfathomable heights where it is broken apart into so many little fragments of dust. See this dust, bathed within the golden light itself, transformed into

Integrated Ascension

light patterns of energy. Know within your minds and hearts that this once misqualified and negative energy has now been transformed into pure light. Watch as it gently falls back upon the physical Earth as pure light substance, which acts as a stimulant for healing. Rejoice as you feel and see how that which was once toxic and misqualified energies has been changed by the golden cylinder into that which is a generator of light and healing.

Now see this process repeat itself as all etheric debris rises upward within the golden cylinder of light, to likewise be transformed into sparkles of light.

Watch and feel the transformation, as this new transmuted energy falls from the mysterious heights to which the golden cylinder has carried it, back into the planet's etheric body, to heal and regenerate.

Now see and deeply feel the impact of the same process as it repeats itself upon the astral plane. Watch as all negative emotional elementals that have been created from humanity's uncontrolled feeling vehicle rise upward within the golden light cylinder. Feel the joy of unconditional love, as these negative elementals return in a transmuted form, falling gently and sweetly back into the astral body of the planet as pink, white and golden hearts, tinged with the violet of transmutation. Take one of these hearts and place it within your own. Feel the impact of this most pure love. Taste the sweetness of transmutation, as you fully realize that it is within the co-creative power of you and the GOD-Force to transform all negative and misqualifed energies into pure love and light.

Watch as this process repeats one final time. The golden cylinder sweeps upward the mass of negative thoughtforms and lifts them beyond harms way, out of Earth's atmosphere entirely. These thoughtforms are then transmuted into minute particles of light, and gently rain down upon the Earth's mental body, cleansing, clearing, purifying, and helping to uplift and stimulate the minds of all.

Now the golden cylinder itself lifts up, getting smaller and smaller as it fades from sight. Sit for a few moments and bathe in the divinely rarefied air that now pervades the collective consciousness of Earth and all humanity.

Meditate upon the joy, love and lightness that at once pervades you and fills you.

(Allow for a few minutes of silence)

Ground yourself now fully into the physical body, extending your grounding cord within the Earth.

When you are ready, open your eyes, feeling refreshed and renewed!

***

Preservation of the Rain Forests

Close eyes.

Assume meditation posture.

Invoke the golden-white semi-permeable bubble of protection and the pure white Light of the Christ.

Call forth the inner plane Hierarchy of Ascended Planetary and Cosmic Masters, the Archangels and the Elohim.

Integrated Ascension

Silently and within yourself bless the rain forests and ask that the Masters and overlighting Devas of the rain forests carry your personal prayer into the collective consciousness of those who execute their power to render decisions upon the fate of the rain forests.

Now join with each other to form a group conscious prayer that links you with the group body of those who share the same concern over the preservation of the rain forests.

Call upon the Earth Mother to support you in this prayer. Call once again upon the Overlighting Deva of the Rain Forests. Ask them to assist you in building a group thoughtform that is strong enough to effect the thoughtforms of those who wish to destroy these sacred woodlands.

Ask that truth be revealed, and that all alike may see and intuit the preciousness of the hallowed ground, and know that it is in divine order that the rain forests be left to thrive.

Visualize these forests thriving healthily and functioning in wonderful harmony with humanity and all the various kingdoms of evolution upon this planet.

Feel the blessings of Lady Gaia and that of the overlighting Deva as they support this visualization and do all within their power to help you manifest your divine intention.

Allow yourself to smell the forest and to feel the gentle breezes of the woodland as they caress you in Love.

Meditate for a few moments upon the harmony of all nature.

(Allow time for silence)

Give thanks to all the various beings who help to maintain the growth of the rain forests and to the forests themselves.

When you feel ready, anchor your grounding cord fully into the Earth and send love and blessing through that cord into the very core structure of the Earth.

When you feel ready, open your eyes.

***

Endangered Species and The Tender Handling of the Animal Kingdom

Close eyes.

Assume meditation posture.

Invoke the golden-white semi-permeable bubble of light and the pure white Light of the Christ for personal protection.

Call forth the inner plane Hierarchy of Ascended Planetary and Cosmic Masters, all of the Angels, Archangels, and the Elohim.

Send a personal message of love and tenderness to yourself. Ask to be cleared of all blockages that is a potential danger for you to freely and lovingly express who you are within the divine plan of GOD.

Now call upon beloved Master Kuthumi, who as you know, in a past incarnation blessed this Earth as St. Francis. Call also upon gentle

Integrated Ascension

Jesus/Sananda, who holds within his Beingness the quality of pure devotion. Call also upon Quan Yin, Goddess of Mercy and Compassion.

Ask these wonderful beings to assist you in your meditation to protect the endangered species of our world, to help put a stop to animal abuse in any and every kind, and to help in its place promote the tender handling of the Animal Kingdom.

Visualize the animals of the wild roving freely about, following their natural instincts without interference by humanity. See the forests and jungles free and clear of any traps that could potentially harm these animals. Watch as they run wild and free.

Allow your visualization to expand and include tenderness to all animals. See alternatives being imprinted upon the mind of humanity, which will allow the knowledge that is currently sought through animal experimentation to utterly cease, being replaced instead by benign forms of study. Hear within the joy as all animals know that they are free to follow their own destiny without any harmful interference by man.

Now let your thoughts and feelings drift to divine harmony between humanity and our animal brothers and sisters. See the loved and cared for animal, living, learning, loving and evolving along with its human family.

Go deep within to that place where love alone abides and that time where the lion shall indeed lay down with the lamb.

Feel the utter joy that exists between the kingdom of humanity and the kingdom of animals.

Meditate upon this harmony.

(Allow time for silence)

Place your hands over your hearts that you may carry this love with you.

Anchor in your grounding cord, and when you are ready, open your eyes.

***

Mass Implant and Negative Elemental Removal for the Entire Planet

Close eyes.

Assume meditation posture.

Invoke the golden-white bubble of light and the pure white Light of the Christ for personal protection.

Call forth the inner plane Hierarchy of Planetary and Cosmic Ascended Masters, the Archangels and the Elohim.

Call upon Vywamus, Lenduce, Djwhal Khul, and St. Germain to assist you in neutralizing and eliminating all negative implants within your four lower bodies.

Thank these beloved Masters and ask them to remain in order to help to remove and deactivate all negative implants within all of humanity around the entire globe, as well as from within the fields of our pets.

Integrated Ascension

Call upon Archangels Michael & Faith for extra protection.

Call also upon the Lord of Arcturus for any assistance He and his fellow Arcturians can provide with their advanced technology.

Call also upon beloved Lord Buddha, our planetary Logos and upon Sanat Kumara.

See within you inner sense pure golden light flowing into the mental, emotional, etheric and even physical bodies of every single person around the globe.

Watch as this light neutralizes any and every implant within the four lower bodies.

See this light become the hands of Vywamus, Sanat Kumara, Lenduce and St. Germain as they lift these implants and elementals out of every aspect and area that they have been lodged.

The ones that are lifted by Vywamus, Lenduce and Sanat Kumara are transmuted by the touch of their golden light. The ones being lifted out by the hands of St. Germain are transmuted by his Violet Transmuting Flame that glows from within his hands. Djwhal Khul does this process through the use of his holographic computer.

Feel a lightness come over your entire being and let this light-ness flow across the globe as you visualize all implants and elementals of a negative nature being either removed altogether or turned totally inactive.

Ask beloved Archangels Michael and Faith for extra protection against any further negative implants being installed. Request this also from the Lord of Arcturus, so that he and the Arcturians may intervene.

Ask to be filled with the essence of pure love and radiant light and the infusion of the first ray of Will. Specifically request El Morya to assist you in strengthening your own will power and that of all humanity as the will of all merges with the Will of GOD.

Know within the core of your being that unconditional pure love, pure Light, and the Will-to-Good act as barriers against any outside interference.

Once again, invoke the added protection of Archangels Michael and Faith. Invoke them each and every night before you go to sleep, both for your further protection and for the protection of all humanity and the animals that reside within our dwelling.

Return into your newly cleansed bodies. Remind yourself to stay ever centered within light, love, and power, and build up an impenetrable force field of protection. Pray that all of humanity come to the understanding and application of Divine law.

Thank all the beloved beings of the Celestial Realms who have been of assistance during this meditation.

Anchor your grounding cord and open your eyes.

***

Mass Clearing of All Unwanted Astral Entities Interfering with Humanity's Free Will

Close eyes.

Prepare for meditation.

Integrated Ascension

Put on your semi-permeable bubble of golden-white light and invoke the pure white Light of the Christ for protection.

Call upon the entire inner plane Hierarchy of Ascended Planetary and Cosmic Masters, all Archangels and Elohim.

Attune to your specific lineage of Masters and to the Master that you are working most closely with.

Ask them to help remove all unwanted astral entities, elementals or thoughtforms that are clouding your own vision, intuition, judgment, or who may be directly trying to interfere with your own free will by clouding your perception.

Now ask the appropriate Masters to help in the clearing of the unwanted astral entities, elementals or thoughtforms that are clouding the feeling and perception of humanity as a whole.

Ask that any astral entities engaged in direct interference with anyone's free thinking, clarity of vision or free will be immediately escorted to the astral sphere which best matches their vibratory rate. Ask that a ring-pass-not be placed around them to hold them there in order that they may learn their appropriate lessons while at the same time being kept at a safe distance from meddling with humanity and our divine gift of free will.

See them being removed from both your personal sphere and the sphere of all of humanity while being held in unconditional love. It is not our place to judge them, but it is certainly our place, our right, and even our obligation to ask them to be removed from our personal and collective worlds.

Feel a new clarity of feeling, thought, vision and intuition fill both you and the world of incarnated souls.

Sit and meditate upon this feeling of freedom, clarity, and light.

(Allow time for silence)

Give thanks to your personal lineage of Masters and the Master or Masters who you have worked most closely with.

Thank all in the Celestial Hierarchy that has aided in this process for every single person upon Earth.

Anchor your grounding cord and open your eyes.

***

Healing any Auric Holes, Spots, Irritations, and Leakages in the Physical, Etheric, Astral, and Mental Body of Planet Earth

Close eyes.

Assume meditation posture.

Golden-white bubble of protection and pure white Light of Christ.

Call upon the entire inner plane Hierarchy of Ascended Planetary and Cosmic Masters, all Archangels and all Elohim.

Call upon Helios & Vesta, Lord Buddha, Sanat Kumara and the Chohans of each of the rays, as well as the Manu, the Christ and the

Integrated Ascension

Mahachohan. Ask them to send their healing radiance in order that any personal auric holes, leakages, spots and irritations within your four lower bodies be healed.

Now call upon the Divine Mother, Lord Melchizedek, the Mahatma, and Archangel Metatron. Request that they radiate their Cosmic healing energies, along with the other Masters who have been invoked, in order to plug up any leakages, auric holes, and to clear up all spots and irritations in the physical, etheric, astral and mental bodies of the planet as a whole.

Feel the divine aura surrounding and penetrating the entire planet as you make this invocation. Feel health and vitality returning to the Earth and all that dwell therein.

Sit and bathe in this most divine radiance and benediction as you feel this enormous healing and cleansing taking place.

Drink in the aura of divinity within all your four lower bodies and all your spiritual bodies as well.

Let us sit and meditate upon the divine healing that is now occurring for the Earth and each one of us who have prayed on Her behalf.

(Allow time for silence)

Anchor your grounding cord into the core of the Earth and radiate your own love and light into Her. Accept back her all encompassing love as it is radiated to you through the stream of light moving through your grounding cord.

Silently and deeply thank all of the Planetary and Cosmic Masters who have aided the Earth in this healing.

Fully anchor back into the body and open your eyes.

***

Cosmic Vacuum for Clearing up All Planetary Glamour, Maya and Illusion

Close eyes.

Assume meditation posture.

Put up your golden-white bubble for personal protection and call also to be clothed and protected in the pure white Light of the Christ.

Call upon the entire inner plane Hierarchy of Planetary and Cosmic Ascended Masters, the Archangels and Elohim.

First call upon your own personal Ascended Master lineage and request that all personal glamour, illusion, and maya be vacuumed up from the aura of your four lower bodies.

Now call forth the Mahatma, Melchizedek, and Metatron.

Request that they use their divine powers to vacuum up the mass consciousness of glamour, maya, and illusion that is effecting the planet as a whole.

Watch as glamour, illusion, and maya are lifted from the veil of delusion of the entire planet.

See the Earth stand crystal clean and pure, radiating only that which is true, holy, sanctified and of GOD.

As this process continues, bask in the glow of the radiance of these Cosmic Masters.

Feel the incredible blessing of love, light and synthesis as the entire planetary aura grows cleaner, clearer and ever more reflective of Source Itself.

Mediate in silence and stillness upon the pure Light and Love of GOD.

(Allow time for silence)

Feel yourself become a greater and greater reflection of pure Divine essence, even as this is happening for the planet as a whole.

Give thanks to His Holiness Lord Melchizedek, the Mahatma, and Metatron and to the group of Ascended Masters that you have called upon. Also, give thanks to all of the Masters that have participated in this clearing on behalf of each and every individual upon planet Earth.

Anchor your grounding cord, feel yourself back in the body and open eyes.

***

Ashtar Command and Lord of Arcturus: To Help Vacuum Up Physical Pollution in the Atmosphere and Help Repair The Ozone Layer

Close eyes.

Assume meditation posture.

Integrated Ascension

Put up your golden-white semi-permeable bubble for protection and call upon the pure white Light of the Christ.

Call upon the entire inner plane Hierarchy of Ascended Planetary and Cosmic Masters, all Archangels, and Elohim.

Invoke the presence of beloved Commander Ashtar and the entire Ashtar Command, as well as the beloved Lord of Arcturus and the Arcturians who serve with him.

Ask first that they use their advanced technology to vacuum up all negative energies, which form the personal pollutants in your own physical and etheric bodies. In this manner, will your own bodies be in a state of much increased purity, in order that you can serve as a better vessel for the service work that you are now engaging in.

Allow for a moment of silence as you visualize all negative energies within your aura being vacuumed up by these wonderful beings. See these energies lift from your four-body system upon a stream of light that serves as a highly developed etheric vacuum, to be taken from you and transmuted and neutralized into harmless energy upon their great ships. Trust in their advanced technology to do this work, and enjoy the feeling of lightness coming into your physical and etheric vehicles.

Now ask that they use their combined energies to sweep across the entire planet, and to vacuum up all physical pollution that has lodged itself within Earth's atmosphere on both a physical and etheric level.

Visualize their combined technologies creating a vacuum that spans the globe, and watch as all the pollutants that we have let loose within the physical/etheric atmosphere of our world are lifted up upon this energy stream, to be rendered neutral and harmless aboard their ships.

Integrated Ascension

Feel a wonderful sense of purity and cleanliness pervade the entire planet.

While still holding to this visualization, also ask them to use their advanced technologies to help repair the ozone layer all around the globe. Know in your heart that by making this request they will give all the help that they are able to. They cannot, however, act without being asked, so feel the joy within the making of these requests, for you are helping to create the world as GOD would have it be.

Sit in meditation for a while, feeling a lightness and purity and healing taking place both within your own physical vehicle and within the physical/etheric body of the Earth Herself.

Visualize all the pollutants being vacuumed out of Earth's atmosphere and feel the incredible love and compassion of these wonderful beings that are helping us according to our request.

Enjoy the feeling of increasing lightness, purity, and love which fills you and radiates around the globe at this time.

(Allow a few moments for silence)

Give thanks to the Lord of Arcturus and Commander Ashtar and all those who work beside them.

When you have done this, anchor your grounding cord, feel yourself fully in the body and upon the Earth, and open your eyes, feeling cleansed and refreshed.

***

Integrated Ascension

Anchoring the Monadic Blueprint Body for the Earth

Close eyes.

Assume meditation posture.

Put up your golden-white semi-permeable bubble of light and call upon the pure white Light of the Christ.

Call upon the entire inner plane Hierarchy of Ascended Planetary and Cosmic Masters, all Archangels and all Elohim.

Invoke the presence of beloved Melchior, Helios & Vesta, Sanat Kumara, and Lord Buddha.

Now call upon the particular Master or Masters with whom you work. Ask for a full and complete anchoring of your own personal Monadic Blueprint body.

Feel the activation, joy, love, and light as this is deeply installed within you.

Meditate for a moment upon this feeling. Feel also the tingling sensation as the Language of Light is activated within you through this process, and all key codes, sacred geometries and fire letters are fully installed and stimulated at this tine.

Now tune in once again to Melchior, Helios & Vesta, Sanat Kumara, and Lord Buddha. Ask that the Monadic Blueprint body be anchored into and around the entire globe.

Integrated Ascension

Call upon the help of beloved St. Germain to help in this process, as you again make this prayer request for the Divine Monadic Blueprint body to be anchored within Earth Herself for the full manifestation of the New Millennium!

Ask that all who are ready gain access to the Language of Light and that the highest activation possible of all key codes, sacred geometries and fire letters be given to those upon the planet who are able to receive them.

Sit now for a few minutes in silent mediation as you visualize this great down pouring of light, the anchoring of the Planetary Monadic Blueprint Body, and the installation and activation of the key codes, fire letters and sacred geometries around the globe.

(Allow a few short moments of silence)

Know that the Divine Celestial Masters will give the highest that each may personally receive and that your prayers and invocations are helping to safely accelerate the evolution of the globe and to more fully, quickly and completely anchor in the New Millennium.

Meditate and enjoy this feeling

(Allow time for silence)

Give thanks to all the Masters that have helped in this sacred process.

Feel yourself align with your own Monadic Blueprint body while at the same time fully integrate within your twelve-body system.

Establish and anchor yourself back into your mental, emotional, etheric and physical vehicles.

Anchor in your grounding cord

Open eyes.

***

Specialized Meditation for a Shower of Core Love and Core Light!

Close eyes.

Assume your meditation posture.

Put up your semi-permeable bubble of golden-white light for protection. Call also upon the great white Light of the Christ.

Call upon the entire inner plane Hierarchy of Ascended Planetary and Cosmic Masters, all Archangels and all Elohim.

Invoke the Presence of the Divine Mother and all the Lady Masters, focusing upon their glorious Heart Energy.

Call and invoke now the Divine Father and all the masculine energies, focusing upon their attribute of light.

Call specifically upon His Holiness the Lord Sai Baba, Melchizedek, the Mahatma and Metatron.

Integrated Ascension

Now connect your self with all your fellow brothers and sisters upon the planet.

See and feel your interconnectedness with the Earth Herself and with every single kingdom that is evolving upon her hallowed soil, within her waters, who ride upon the air and who dance within her fires.

In this state of blessed unity, call forth to all the Celestial Hierarchy for a shower of Core Love and Core Light to come forth from the very Heart/Mind of the GODHEAD.

Feel the divine outpouring of the purest essence of love that you have ever felt. Take this love deep into your heart. Infuse every cell, atom, and electron of your twelve-body system with it.

Feel the immensity and enormity of this Core Love as it pours forth into every being and aspect of creation upon the planet.

(Allow a few moments of silence)

Now feel and see the essence of Core Light as it streams forth from the eternal fire of GOD. Feel this light infuse every cell, atom, and electron within your twelve body system.

Feel the immensity and enormity of this Core Light as it streams forth into every being and aspect of creation upon the planet

Sit for a few minutes in silence and bask in the radiance of Core Love and Core Light as it blesses and graces both you and the entire world.

(Allow for five to ten minutes of silence)

Integrated Ascension

With deepest reverence give thanks to the Divine Mother and the Divine Father and all of the Celestial realms that have given of themselves in order to assist in this divine benediction.

Feel yourself coming fully into your mental, emotional, etheric and physical body.

Anchor your grounding cord within the love and light infused Earth.

Open eyes.

***

Beloved bothers and sisters who are participating in these service mediations, know that you are blessed a thousand fold from the Masters and all the Celestial Hierarchy. The Masters have guided me at this point, to give you a list of other world service issues that, if you would meditate and pray upon, would greatly help in their divine efforts of healing, uplifting and preparing humanity for the new millennium. Please follow the basic guidelines of all the preceding meditations, and then just create your own prayer and meditation upon any or all of the following issues that touch your heart. The list is as follows:

1. Help in finding a cure for those who are suffering from AIDS or who test HIV positive. Finding a preventative for AIDS and HIV positive individuals.

2. Support for those who want to stop smoking. Cigarette manufacturers and companies being honest in regard to the deleterious effects of second hand smoke.

3. End to political corruption, partisan politics, gridlocks, and political selfishness.

Integrated Ascension

4. Total revamping of the tax system so that it is spiritual and fair.

5. Proper money management in the governments of the world. The removal of the power and control of the power elite and trilateral commission. An end to the greed, selfishness and injustice of having only a small, select group which comprises the wealthiest families of the world, running the global economy.

6. Return of all POW's.

7. The establishment of true political spiritual party representatives.

8. The importance of spiritual education and spiritual values being integrated into the school system in a non-fundamentalist way.

9. Religious tolerance.

10. Health insurance for every single person, which includes coverage for alternative medical treatment as well.

11. The transformation of the criminal justice system from one of punishment to one of spiritual rehabilitation.

12. An end to the preoccupation of violence on television and in movies.

13. An end to the world's preoccupation of glamour and gossip.

14. Better care and respect for the elderly.

15. An end to unfair treatment and disregard to Veterans.

16. Free and high quality treatment to all Veterans who are ill due to germ warfare used in Vietnam and the Gulf War.

17. The resumption of peace talks between the PLO and Israelis.

18. The establishment of comprehensive peace in the Middle East with all countries involved.

19. An end to all illusory negative belief systems in religion and the New Age Movement involving the ending of the world and Armageddon.

20. Enough jobs for everyone who seeks work. Provisions for those who have been kicked out of welfare to be helped to get back on their feet financially and on all levels.

21. The ending of all wars.

22. Greater power and influence of the U.N.

23. An influx of the more highly evolved initiates into politics in order to revamp the system. An awareness on the part of all initiates whose puzzle piece this is to get in touch with it and to have the courage and fortitude to pursue their divine mission.

24. Greater world focus on service work and on volunteering.

25. More compassion for those who are suffering on all levels.

26. The stopping of Drug Cartels, and the psychic and physical poisoning of our children through drugs.

27. The necessary insight to put spirituality before materialism, technology and money.

28. An end to pornography and the over-identification and over-glorification of the physical vehicle.

29. An end to sexual harassment for both women and men.

30. An end to sport hunting, rodeos, bull fighting, wearing of furs and overall animal cruelty.

31. An end to all Cults.

32. A movement and integration of the more traditional medicine with holistic health and naturopathy.

33. An end to crime.

34. The admittance by the governments of the world as to the existence of UFO's.

35. The destruction of all nuclear weapons, biological weapons, and all weapons of mass destruction.

36. The ending of terrorism.

37. Anything that touches your heart that you choose to pray and meditate about.

Be creative! Namaste!

17

Ascension in the Many Kingdoms of GOD

Integrated Ascension and Evolution

I have noticed that there is still a great deal of confusion in the minds of many lightworkers in regards to the evolution of the Animal Kingdom and utter bafflement in regards to the various other Kingdoms in nature. One of the reasons for this is that it is a distinct and most specific science, one which greatly intertwines and blends within the complete understanding of our own human evolution and planetary ascension process. In truth, there was no understanding of this process ever given forth until the event of the Theosophical Movement and later the writings of Alice A. Bailey, who channeled Djwhal Khul. A great many lightworkers have not investigated this subject even within these writings. For those who did, the information was not fully fleshed out, since its main intent was to open the doorway to our basic understanding of it.

It is with great joy that I devote an entire chapter to the specificity of this little known matter, in hopes of clearing the many points of confusion that remain as gaps within the lightworker, or any interested individual's mind and heart. It must be understood at the outset that there is a definite overlapping of this process. Many aspects appearing contradictory in nature exist simultaneously. We are delving into depths which have long remained hidden due to the extreme overlapping, intertwining and interblending of many truths into one coherent whole.

To begin with, an aspect of each person's monad passes through all the various "lower" Kingdoms. It passes through the Mineral Kingdom, the Plant Kingdom, and the Animal Kingdom. Eventually it individualizes into our unique expressions as Sons and Daughters of GOD to finally transcend this phase, often after many incarnations, and joins the ranks of what is known as the fifth, or Spiritual Kingdom, where dwell the inner plane Ascended Planetary Masters. Then, as those of you who are sincere students of the occult and/or have read some of my more advanced material such as *Beyond Ascension* or *Cosmic Ascension* know our evolution continues into ever greater, deeper spheres within the realm of Cosmic evolution and Cosmic Ascension itself!

Before proceeding further, I share with you the fact that this process is interwoven with the truth that the birth of humanity as a species had much to do with direct intervention of certain extraterrestrial Beings! They came, in fact, to those who had achieved the rudimentary form of the human being and contained within their evolution the seed of mind. Through the assistance of these Extraterrestrials, the Logos, GOD powered forth the Divine flame of human individualization. This, my beloved readers, is the individualized human Monad, the Mighty I Am Presence, and the spark of the Great ever-burning Fire of GOD.

When one therefore states that we are Sons and Daughters of GOD, this is absolute truth. Our individuality was born of the birthing fire of Father/Mother GOD, which flows directly and ultimately from Source. This, however, is in utter harmony with an aspect, or outpouring of our basic monadic essence passing through each of the three lower Kingdoms of evolution! So an aspect of each person's Monad or Mighty

Integrated Ascension

I Am Presence prior to its hour of individuation as an incarnating Son or Daughter of GOD spends some evolutionary period of part of its consciousness evolving itself through the Mineral, Plant and Animal Kingdoms.

What's missing in even the most advanced animal is the full outpouring of the principle of "mind." So, it would *not* be accurate to say that each of us was a mineral, plant or animal in a past life. However, it would be accurate to say that an aspect of our monad, not all our monad, did experience those various phases of evolution.

What I'm sharing here is very profound. There are really two distinct points of individual creation by GOD. The first act of creation by GOD is the creation of the monad, which is an individual spark of GOD that first emerges as an outpouring of pure essence. The second act of individuation by GOD is the creation of soul extensions of Sons and Daughters of GOD (remember each monad has 144 soul extensions). This second act of individuation by GOD and the GOD Force comes *after* the monad has evolved part of its consciousness through the Mineral, Plant, and Animal Kingdoms. This is why it would not be accurate to say we had past lives in these kingdoms, for in truth, this was prior to our individuation or creation by the monad. It was, however, part of the monad's evolution to get to that point. Edgar Cayce stated that there is no such thing as transmigration of the soul, and this is true. There is, however, transmigration of a part of our monad prior to our second individuation. After our second individualized creation as Sons and Daughters of GOD, we never transmigrate *back* into a mineral, plant, or animal.

This type of confusion also exists within the understanding of the Devic/Angelic line of evolution. Many lightworkers who know the reality of the nature spirits, confuse the deva who is tending to a mineral, stone, plant, with the life of the specific mineral, stone, plant. Although intertwined, they are two separate and distinct entities.

Integrated Ascension

The Plant Kingdom, for example, has it's own evolutionary process, while the devas tending to the Plant Kingdom likewise have their own separate and unique line of evolution. To further complicate the issue, certain devas who are specifically known as the "building devas" and are, in truth, elementals and part of the Elohim lineage, create the outer form or bodies of this kingdom, as well as the other kingdoms. They do this out of their own essence, and the manipulation of the elemental energies that they both overlight and are composed of.

You can see, therefore, why an entire chapter is needed to even get a semblance of the true understanding of this multifaceted process. In addressing the subject of Integrated Ascension, it is clear to me that the integration of humanity's process must be seen within the greater scope of the various kingdoms of evolution that co-exist with us. In truth, we will not ultimately be able to fully integrate into the wholeness of our own Beings if we do not include the many faceted aspects of our planet, as well as our younger brothers and sisters of the less evolved kingdoms. We must likewise include the devic and angelic line of evolution in this process, for we are all a part of the same whole!

The Three Lines of Evolution

My beloved readers, what I want you to understand here, which is incredibly fascinating, is that there are three distinct lineages of evolution. There are the Sons & Daughters of GOD or the Adam Kadmon, which makes up almost all the physically incarnated beings on Earth. Then there is the second lineage, which is the Angelic Monadic lineage. Interestingly enough, there are Angelic Monadic lineage beings in physical embodiment at this particular time because of the unique phase of Earth's evolution. There are billions and billions of this Angelic/Monadic lineage currently incarnated on this planet in an etheric sense, which I will discuss in a moment. The third distinct line of evolution is the Elohim Monadic Essence. The Elohim, being the co-creator Gods and Goddesses and thought of as the attributes of GOD. I have already explained the creation process for the Sons and Daughters of GOD or the Adam Kadmon Monadic lineage. Now let us examine the Angelic Monadic line of evolution.

Angelic Line of Evolution

Just as a part of the monad of the Sons and Daughters of GOD evolves through the Mineral, Plant and Animal Kingdoms, the Monad of the Angelic Kingdom prior to individuation, go through a different stepped down process to prepare its essence for its second individuation. In the Angelic line, its monad evolves first through the beginning etheric stages of Earth's evolution as Brownies, fairies, devas, mineral devas, plant devas, animal devas and finally evolving to Overlighting Angels. Individuation in the second act of creation by GOD in this line of evolution is when they are created by their Cosmic Monad into individualized Angels of a higher order such as Cherubim, Seraphim, Archangels, Cosmic Angel Watchers and Protectors, to name just a few. So, Angels then eventually evolve into Archangels or what would be the equivalent of an Archangel, since there are different kinds of Angels. So, do you see, my beloved readers, that Angels evolve in a very similar way as do Sons and Daughters of GOD, but usually a little more etherically. However, they too begin at the bottom rung in their monadic essence, have two individuation processes, and eventually evolve through planetary, solar, galactic, universal, multi-universal, and GOD levels as well, in just a slightly different, but essentially similar manner.

The Angels are more feminine in nature as compared to the Elohim. They are nurturers and givers of Love and are more the feeling tones of GOD. For more information on the Angels, please read my book *Hidden Mysteries*.

Elohim Line of Evolution

The Elohim, or co-creator Gods and Goddesses, are the least understood of the three lines of evolution. The Masters have told me that their Monadic essence evolves in a very similar manner as do Sons and Daughters of GOD and Angels. They have Monads as well, who must evolve their consciousness after the first act of creation on a bottom rung of a ladder to prepare its Elohim Monadic essence for its full consciousness expansion. The Elohim's Monadic evolutionary process is more similar to the Angelic than the Adam Kadmon, and is more etheric and group conscious in nature. The Elohim go through this process differently than the Sons and Daughters of GOD and Angels, however there is an evolutionary process of waking up and developing that all Beings in GOD's Creation must go through.

The Elohim are more of what might be called the masculine side of GOD and the Angels the more feminine side of GOD. The Elohim line of evolution is focused upon the building of form. Where Angels evolve their consciousness at the bottom rung of Creation beginning with certain devas and nature fairies, the Elohim evolve their consciousness at the bottom rung of Creation through the work of the elementals and devas associated with the building of form. The Elohim and the Angelic lines of evolution have been confused and lumped together with most of the credit going to the Angels. The angelic line of evolution is not involved with the building of form, or the package, so to speak; it is involved with the nourishing and feeling tones of GOD's Creation.

As the elementals evolve as "mini-Elohim," so to speak, they take on larger and larger building responsibilities. This could range from the building of a tiny grain of sand, to a flower, solar system, galaxy, universe, multi-universe and finally back to the fully mature Elohim at the 352nd level of the GODHEAD who helps GOD create the infinite universe.

Integrated Ascension

From our perspective on Earth, as Sons and Daughters of GOD, it would seem that when GOD created the Elohim (Creator-Gods and Goddesses) and the Archangels, that these beings never had to evolve, that they were fully conscious, omnipotent, omniscient, and omnipresent. The Masters, specifically Archangel Metatron, has told us that this is not true. It **is** true from the perspective of this Cosmic Day or this Day of the Year of Brahma, however, even they, the Archangels and Elohim at this highest level, in a previous year or century of Brahma, had to go through some kind of evolutionary awakening process to get to the omnipotent, omniscient, and omnipresent positions they now hold. Being of the Angelic and/or Elohim lines of evolution, their evolutionary process is different than the Sons and Daughters of GOD because they have different functions in GOD's Creation. However, all three lines of evolution as you can see, manifesting as the elemental, deva, fairy or mineral, plant, animal, evolve from the bottom rung of evolution to the top of Creation.

Now again, in the Sons and Daughters of GOD lineage it is a part of our monad that does this, not individualized soul, so it would be inaccurate to say that we had past lives as a mineral, plant, or animal. The same is true of the Angelic and Elohim lines of evolution. Archangel Metatron or Archangel Michael in a past century of Brahma were *not* plant devas. The co-creator Elohim were not flower elementals. It is more like the "Cosmic Monad," which is their essential Self, incarnated an aspect of Self into the lower worlds for service experience and to raise its own consciousness.

Metatron and Djwhal have just told me that this process is similar to our creation as Sons and Daughters of GOD. The evolutionary process occurs prior to their individual creation as well. The Cosmic Monad is a higher level monad than that which I have spoken of in my other books. It is the monad that exists at the 352nd level of the GODHEAD and literally trillions of soul extensions, Oversouls, and individualized monads emanate from the core of its Being. In this sense Sons and

Integrated Ascension

Daughters of GOD, Archangels or Cosmic Angels and Elohim all emanate from a Cosmic Monad and eventually merge with that monad and in essence become that monad in the evolutionary process. The merging with the Cosmic Monad is that moment when they merge back with GOD in the highest sense of the term in *full consciousness*. The key here is the term "full consciousness," for all are one with GOD, however it takes the evolutionary process to integrate back into the Oneness in full consciousness.

The Archangels and Cosmic Angels and Elohim are different than Sons or Daughters of GOD in that their evolution is usually more etheric. There are, however, many angelic beings that are physically incarnate at this time. The Elohim do not incarnate and the Archangels don't incarnate, however, less evolved Angels do on occasion. On rare occasions an Archangel or, on an even rarer occasion, an Elohim, will incarnate an aspect of Self, but not the full consciousness. As our planet Earth evolves, the Adam Kadmon line and the Angelic line are merging more and more. The Angelic line of evolution is more involved with the Sons and Daughters of GOD than are the Elohim; although the smaller elementals and overlighting devas of form are very involved with Earth's evolution.

Ultimately, all three lines of evolution merge and become united at the 352nd level of the GODHEAD. So, my beloved readers, we can see very clearly now that every being in the infinite universe is connected to, and operates out of one of these three lines of evolution. No being is created totally Self-conscious and is exempt from the evolutionary process. All beings must evolve, however, depending upon the lineage that GOD created you upon will determine the form in which this evolutionary process will take. All three lines of evolution, in truth, work in perfect harmony and love together and one is not better than another, for each serves a different function in GOD's Divine Plan. Some Sons and Daughters of GOD have more attunement to Angels, some more attunement to the Elohim and some to both lines of evolution. There is no right or wrong, there is just how GOD created you and hence the puzzle piece it is your destiny to fulfill.

All three lines of evolution are involved in the initiation process, which is GOD's system of accounting of one's stage of evolution. The initiation process for all three lines of evolution is different for each lineage, yet similar in concept.

Archangel Metatron was also kind enough to answer another burning question of mine. I asked him after his individuation by his Cosmic Monad if he was just "born" into being an Archangel or if that was something he had to evolve into. He told me that in essence a "hundred million days of Brahma ago," he and all the Archangels were once Angels. Through a second sequence of evolution, he has evolved and all Archangels evolve back to full Cosmic Ascension. This, my beloved readers, is looking at the evolutionary process from an infinite perspective. From the perspective of how most lightworkers have looked at this process in the past, it would appear that the Archangels and the Elohim came right out of GOD in their present form. From one lens and/or the perspective of *this* Cosmic Day, this would appear to be true and rightly so, because by the time our Cosmic Day (4.1 billion years) began, the Archangels and Elohim had long ago achieved this level of evolution. When looked at from a full spectrum lens of "*ALL Cosmic Days*," and there are infinite numbers of them, there was a time in the ancient past where even the Archangels and Elohim were in a state of evolution as individual identities, not just as Cosmic Monads. It is my job, as the "Cosmic Sherlock Holmes" to track down such obscure facts. As Metatron just said rather humorously that the sub-title of this book is the "Revelation for the Next Millennium"!

One other fascinating Cosmic golden nugget insight that Metatron just confirmed for me is that, whereas the Elohim are more the masculine face of GOD and the Angels the more feminine face of GOD, the Sons and Daughters of GOD are more reflective of the face and lineage of GOD whose job it is to demonstrate feminine/masculine balance.

Again, my beloved readers, we can't seem to escape this concept of Integrated Ascension.

Now the Mahatma has just graciously told me upon another burning question that he, as the embodiment of the 352 levels of the GODHEAD, is the embodiment of all three lines of evolution, synthesized into one unified consciousness. This would explain why he is a Being referred to as a group conscious being.

Lord Melchizedek, our Universal Logos, is on the Sons and Daughters of GOD line of evolution, however he has just told me that as part of his training to become a Universal Logos he has taken initiations on both the Angelic and Elohim lines of evolution. Lord Buddha, our Planetary Logos, has just shared that he as well has had to go through similar training incorporating all three lines of evolution into his Being. What Melchizedek and Lord Buddha have just said is that on the higher spiritual planes of reality, these three distinct lines of evolution come together more in a synthesized fashion and as part of the Cosmic Integrated Ascension process.

Summation of this Section

My beloved readers, what I would like to share with you here are some personal thoughts and reflections of writing this last section. The writing and channeling of this last section has clarified and brought to light, like the completion of a puzzle, a certain understanding of the structure, synthesis and unity of GOD.

Consider first, my friends, that each of our monads was involved in the Animal, Plant, and Mineral Kingdoms. Knowing this, can you ever look at an animal, plant, and mineral in the same way? They are not only a spiritual part of you, but they are even physically part of your heritage. If people on Earth understood this, could they ever be cruel to an animal? Could they take an unsanctified attitude towards plants? Could they not appreciate the Mineral Kingdom? They are not just spiritually part of you in the abstract sense, they are physically part of your monadic heritage. This is very profound.

Also, please consider, my friends, that minerals evolve into plants, and plants evolve into animals and animals have the potential to ultimately move into the Human Kingdom and eventually become Ascended Masters. So animals, plants and minerals are not just our younger brothers and sisters in an abstract sense, but in a very, very literal and physical real sense. My beloved readers, can you ever look at life the same after knowing this truth?

Also, consider the profundity of this revelation that there are three lines of evolution. GOD's feminine nature being the Angelic line and GOD's masculine nature being the Elohim line of evolution. Sons and Daughters of GOD being the central pillar whose job it is to balance and integrate both sides equally. This is very profound. This understanding that the Elohim is a line of evolution is truly a revelation, for they have been merged and confused with the Angelic line of evolution.

The Elohim have always esoterically been considered these vast cosmic beings or co-creator Gods that have very little relationship to Sons and Daughters of GOD on Earth. This revelation reveals to us, however, that there are infinite numbers of mini-Elohim all around us. We even have infinite numbers of mini-Elohim living in our physical body as well as an overlighting Elohim that is sustaining our body elemental! Do you see, my beloved readers, that every physical structure on Earth and "Earth Herself" is sustained by varying ranks and grades of Elohim. The Angels obviously play a great part in this from another perspective of more the nourishing and radiating of energy, however, this has been more understood than the Elohim line of evolution. The point I am trying to make here is to show you, my beloved readers, how connected you are to the Elohim, not only spiritually as creator-Gods, but also in sustaining our physical bodies, creating the food we eat and the structure and form upon which we live. Again pointing out this spiritual and physical connection to the unity of all life.

Integrated Ascension

The same applies on the Angelic line of evolution. From the tiniest angelic deva and fairy upwards, they create our physical food, they sustain the physical Earth herself. They work with the elementals to nourish the form while the elementals build it. Each of us has at least one Guardian Angel that has been with us since our first incarnation. They guide us spiritually, they inspire, and they heal. They come to us in infinite ways that we do not even know about. Every time we pray to GOD, GOD does not come Himself, He sends His Angels. When Mohammed brought through his revelation of the Islamic faith, Archangel Gabriel was his guide and teacher. When the Virgin Mary was guided in her ministry, Archangel Gabriel, again, was overlighting her. When Moses spoke to GOD in the form of the burning bush, the Masters just told me yesterday that it was an Archangel who he was speaking to, which was a new revelation and understanding to me that I did not have before.

There are infinite numbers of Angels who help us everyday. We could literally not even live on Earth if it were not for the Angels and the Angelic line of evolution. So again, my friends, do you see that we are not just spiritually connected with the Angels, but are literally physically connected. There are many, many Angels literally incarnated in physical bodies, and many of you reading this book may fall into this category. There are many others who bounce back and forth between the Sons and Daughters of GOD line and the Angelic line. Again, I am sure many of you reading this book can relate to this. Others of you may have a greater attunement to the Elohim line, and still others, both lines. Ultimately all merge back into the Oneness of GOD.

The main point here is to fully realize your inter-connectedness with the Angelic and Elohimic lines of evolution, both spiritually and in the most tangible physical sense, as well as both etherically, astrally, and mentally. Knowing these things, can you ever look upon a (garden, the food you eat, the physical body you live in, or the Earth Herself) the same? All is literally a part of ourselves.

Integrated Ascension

The last point I want to make here is in regard to how even the Angels and Elohim in their original monadic essence must incarnate an aspect of self into the very lower rungs of evolution in an etheric sense. We as Sons and Daughters of GOD do it through an aspect of our monad through the Mineral, Plant, and Animal Kingdoms. The Angels through the devas and fairies, and the Elohim through the elementals and devic builders. So, do you see, my beloved readers, that all lines of creation are really going through the same evolutionary process in different forms yet in a similar manner? Do you see, my friends, that even the Archangels and the Elohim creator-Gods after their individuation and/or creation still have to evolve themselves as do their monads prior to their individuation. All of GOD's Creation which in truth is just One Being, are going through the same process as we are as Sons and Daughters of GOD! Do you see that the Archangels and Elohim are in truth very similar to ourselves? They are not separate from us or like icons that are so idealized that they cannot be related to. Their personal experience of having to go through the evolutionary process in their monads and in themselves is very similar to ours. They may have attained GOD Realization in the far distant past, however there was a point in the infinite unfolding of worlds where their personal experience was not that dissimilar to ours upon their own line of evolution. This revelatory understanding has a very profound, unifying, humbling and inclusive effect upon my consciousness and I hope upon yours. We are all the same. We are all going through the same process. We are all GOD incarnating at various levels of GOD, with different missions in GOD's Divine Plan, and all in the process now of returning back to GOD! As my beloved friend Metatron put it yesterday, "This is the dance of GOD!"

Exploring the Animal Kingdom

As the Animal Kingdom is the one humanity is most directly involved with on an emotional and psychological level, I have decided to begin with a discussion pertaining to this Kingdom in general, and the animals who are most evolved within it. The dog, cat, horse, and elephant are the basic group of animals who stand at the doorway of individualization. They have achieved the level of development that they have do to our direct emotional, and to a certain degree, even our mental interactions with them.

For those of you who are very bonded with a specific bird, I am not addressing them at this point only because they will take their next step of development along the line of the devic/Angelic pathway. There are certain bird species and individuals that fall into the same category as the aforementioned animals, however, they will find their point of individualization upon another lineage.

Let us then, turn our attention to our beloved pets. Many a devoted pet parent (I do not say owner because we cannot own another being) has been accused of anthropomorphizing their pets' emotions. Many people are not at all tuned into the Animal Kingdom, and therefore wear blinders in regard to the very specific and developed feeling bodies of the animals we love. There is, my beloved readers, even the germ of mental bodies which can be seen among the more evolved of the Animal Kingdom, however, you must be attuned to them to truly see what is going on.

It is true that some of us can get a bit carried away and impose emotions, feelings and attributes upon our animals that they do not hold personally. In fact, it is not uncommon for an individual to voice a feeling or a need that they themselves are afraid to give voice to by saying that such and such a dog or cat, etc., feels what, in truth, their caretaker feels. In these cases, one is most definitely anthropomorphizing. The fact that this does occur gives the non-animal oriented person all the

Integrated Ascension

ammunition that they need to continue looking at the true situation through their very limited lens.

In most cases, the animals that we live with will in fact pick up the feelings that their caretaker/parent has, and take the same feeling into their own auric fields and emotional bodies. Since it is the emotional body of our pets that is most developed, and since their very evolution corresponds to a great degree with the love, attention and interaction that we show to them, it is most appropriate and even logical that they will be empathic to our feeling world.

Although this is not always the case, it is generally the case that the behavior and feeling of any particular pet will reflect that which its caretaker or family exhibits most prominently. When you enter the home where the people within are of a quiet and meditative nature, the animal will usually exhibit a parallel behavior. When you enter a household that is filled with fanaticism, confusion, and hostility, the animal will most likely demonstrate this. Where a person or family is living in deep fear, the pet will appear fearful and skittish. This information is readily available to anyone who wishes to read basic studies of animal behavior and patterns in simple books, magazines or articles that address the basic care and training of a pet. This last paragraph is common knowledge to anyone who has ever given a little time to the exploration of animal behavior in order to understand their own pet. It does not therefore, fall under the category of hidden occult mysteries, but rather that of common knowledge.

Where this information transfers into the world of occult understanding is in the fact that the exchange of behavior between pet and family has a great bearing and influence upon the evolutionary process of the animal itself. The dog, cat, horse, and elephant do not simply experience emotions, they evolve through them. These emotions become more and more refined through each successive birth, and the seed of a mental body develops. The animal at this stage stands at the very doorway and brink of individualization. They await only the opening of that doorway during a future round (great cycle) of Earth, or may even receive the Divine spark from GOD and take individualization upon another planet. They would not "leave" before the full bond between them and their human family is completed upon the inner planes.

Preceding the individualization of the animal into the human kingdom, is a long series where they are not even individualized within their own kingdom. Many of you are familiar with the term "group soul" as it is used in reference to the Animal Kingdom. For the sake of those of you who are not, I will explain what that means in detail.

What I would like to make clear first, however, is that for those of you who are bonded deeply with your pet, you can rest assured that it has its own unique individuality. If it did not, if it were still a part of the basic group soul, there would not be the deep bonding that you feel. There would also not be the deep love and bonding that your animal feels towards you. You therefore do not have to worry whether or not you will meet your animal friend on the inner planes. If you feel such devotion towards them that you are even thinking of such a concept, I guarantee you that your pet will be awaiting you when you cross over. Remember, you have been an essential part of its evolutionary process, and the bonds run deep. No matter how high you go into the light, you will have access to your beloved friend and they to you.

The Group Soul of the Animal Kingdom

Before an animal reaches the stage where it begins to incarnate successively and individually within the Animal Kingdom, it cycles in and out of incarnation as part of a group soul, or group whole. The many and varied experiences that each animal has within embodiment is then brought back with them into this group soul. Depending upon the species of animal and how close it is to separating from the group soul there will be a specific time that it is guided to spend upon the astral realm. It will uphold its pattern of individuality during this period, after which it is reabsorbed into the group from which it originated. It will add to that group soul all that it has cultivated in terms of the emotional or feeling body during its time in incarnation. This is the process by which the group soul evolves as a whole to ultimately produce an animal that carries enough evolved energies to be separated from that group and to incarnate successively on its own.

The group soul to which an animal belongs holds within it the patterns and coded messages that form what we perceive as the basic instinct of any given group of animals. As each unique experience of the animals who belong to a given group soul are reabsorbed within the group, it colors the overall soul with that experience. This accounts for the timidness of deer, for instance, in regard to the Human Kingdom, as they are so often the victims of the hunter. The experience that an animal undergoes on its journey to the slaughterhouse, and the death that it experiences within, shoot like a missile of fear into the group body of those animals whom we call upon to function in that manner. The same is true in reverse. To those animals to which we express tenderness, love, and care, those emotions are likewise added into the group composite. The interactions that we as a species have with the Animal Kingdom in general contributes much to the manner in which they evolve as a whole.

The closer we draw to a certain species of animal, the more we help to contribute to its evolution. The more love we give, the more tenderness we exhibit, the more overall involvement, both emotionally and even mentally that we give to a given species, the more quickly will that species begin to individualize. Once the process of individualization for the animal within its own kingdom occurs, the animal is then on its way toward working to bring its evolution to the next stage of development, which would be that of a human being.

It must be clearly understood, and so reemphasized, that when an animal enters the Human Kingdom it is through both the process of evolution as well as the process of receiving a spark of individualized GOD essence. This spark is breathed out the mouth of GOD, or the Logos, at an extremely high level. An entire new being is born from this fire breath of GOD. This being, is then a true Son or Daughter of the Most High, as well as the product of its own evolution. Once the individualized I Am Presence is given forth from Monadic Source, the true GOD-man/woman is born.

A Look at How Humanity Can Aid the Animal Kingdom

In a moment we will move on to take a look at the process of evolution beginning with that most mysterious of all processes, involution. It would not feel right just to move on, however, before taking a quick look at how we might help to serve the Animal Kingdom, as well as to honor the many ways in which they are of service to us.

The first consideration is the fact that the Animal Kingdom en masse are our true younger brothers and sisters. They are not separate and apart from ourselves, but part of ourselves. They are worthy and deserving of the utmost of care and consideration right at the point they are at now, irregardless of whether they are individualized animal souls, part of a high order of group soul, such as the dog or cat, or animals in the wild, such as the bear, the tiger, lion, rhino or cheetah. This is an extremely important point for you to be clear about. All in the Animal Kingdom are our younger brethren. They are also part of ourselves, as GOD embraces the whole of Creation. It is not okay to set jungle traps and cause pain to any of these beings.

Even the less evolved animals have emotional bodies and sensations. They most certainly have physical sensations. The horrendous acts done to animals out of the misaligned need to fulfill the negative ego's desire is out and out wrong. Of course, the ultimate decision on how you choose to handle the information that is being imparted entirely rests with you. I do, however, ask that you strongly consider the points that are being presented here and check within your own emotional body and Christ Mind to see if they find resonance. I believe that they will!

As long as we are discussing this point, I ask you for a moment to consider the inhumane acts done to the dolphin and the whale. Most lightworkers know that these creatures are highly evolved beings of another order. In fact, they have come from the far reaches of space in order to help impregnate our struggling planet with "love." I do not suppose that anyone reading this book is involved in harming them in any way, shape or form. What I would like to suggest, however, is that if you feel a kindred spirit with them, take whale and dolphin tours. Talk to them. Offer them back the love that they are offering to us. Love breeds love, and this would be a wonderful service indeed.

In regard to those of you who have adopted a pet into your life, know that you and your pet are intimately connected on the emotional, and to a degree, even on the mental level. Think of that animal as part of your family, and not an adornment or an amusement. The animals that most of us take as "pets" are actually quite evolved, with extremely sensitive nervous systems and emotional bodies. We can help raise their frequency enormously by demonstrating to them actions that come forth from our own integrated hearts and Christed minds.

The way we interact with our adopted animal will contribute highly to the way in which they evolve. As was addressed earlier, they are literally mirrors of our own emotional nature. The more unconditional love, attention, care, interaction we demonstrate to them, the more these traits will be built into them. Certain pets have demonstrated a loyalty that can only be regarded as Christ consciousness activated to its full potential! Have you ever wondered and marveled that a pet would risk its own life, to seek out a member of its family in order to save that person from impending disaster? The animal that does this type of service is actually using that small germ of mind in order to make the choice to proceed in this course of action. It is not acting out of fear or out of obedience, since it was issued no command.

Integrated Ascension

Why then does it, of its own "free will," go out and put itself at risk in order to either jump into a freezing lake, climb up a hazardous mountain range, explore the depths of a cave, or suffer the dead of winter in order to rescue its caretaker? In a word, LOVE! It is truly the combination of great abiding love, loyalty, devotion, and the seed of mind. The little germ or seedling of mental ability is the last, highest and most developed ingredient, which when added to the whole, prompts the animal to be willing to sacrifice itself for the sake of its caretaker. There is much going on with the Animal Kingdom, my beloved readers, much we are receiving on a daily basis and much that we are taking for granted. Let us give them their due respect and fulfill Djwhal Khul's admonition through Alice Bailey that we all engage in the practice of "…the tender handling of the Animal Kingdom"!

A Brief Look at the Process of Involution

Before there is evolution, there is involution. It is not my intent to go into any great depth regarding this subject here, yet this process must be mentioned if you are to understand the occult intricacies of the process of evolution. Simply stated, involution is the process of energy manifesting from the higher, formless realms, into the denser and denser realms, until the realm of matter is reached. It is from that point that the process of evolution "back" to GOD proceeds. This also could be termed the inbreath and outbreath of GOD.

If you recall, the joint voice of Jesus/Sananda and Lord Maitreya spoke the words, "No one can return unto the Father unless they first came from the Father." This is one of the most powerful and truly occult statements ever uttered. It embraces truth on a most profound and multidimensional level. The obvious implication to lightworkers is that we are all Sons and Daughters of GOD, and by following the Christ essence within ourselves we will return from the Source that originated us. This is a statement of utmost truth.

Integrated Ascension

The far deeper understanding of these words has to do with the fact that before we even begin any process of evolution back to GODHEAD, we must realize that our basic core essence flowed from Source, down the many graded realms and levels, until it reached a stage in which the evolutionary forces began to signal back its return. This process is called "involution." It has to do with the downpouring of the most primal, essential essence. This essence goes through various transformative processes as it slowly descends from the level of Source downward.

Therefore, beloved readers, in this most basic and primal way do we descend the spiraling levels into form. At this point, we are dealing with basic elemental essence. I am not here referring to the elementals in the commonly used fashion, but as an illustration of the basic element of creation descending from itself in order that it may later ascend back into itself. The purpose of involution is ultimately evolution. The purpose of evolution is to add to and enrich the whole, the all pervading Eternal Source of Beingness Itself.

As this chapter is being written in order to explore the various complexities of evolution in the various kingdoms and how they integrate within the whole and interact with ourselves, little more is being given forth regarding involution. In truth, the Masters themselves have guided me away from further attunement to this process, as that is clearly not what they wish to be explored at this point. They have asked me to include the essence of this process, in order that you can have a sense of how vast, deep and layered the process of evolution is. The outbreath and the inbreath of GOD occurs simultaneously. Although there are definitely Days and Nights of Brahma, which I have discussed in detail in my books *The Complete Ascension Manual* and *Cosmic Ascension*, there is likewise the outbreath and inbreath of involution and evolution. Subsuming all the varied and various stages and details of these processes is the overlighting "whole" in which all is ultimately integrated and unified!

Integrated Ascension

Integration within the Mineral Kingdom

It is a fact that all of us upon the human line of evolution have at one time or other within an aspect of our monads been part of the Mineral Kingdom. It is equally true that if anyone came to me with a book entitled something like *My Life As A Rock*, I would know that they were entirely off-base. What must be understood is that it is not our individualized selves that were part of the Mineral Kingdom. If you recall the full birthing of our individuality did not occur until after an aspect of our monadic essence raised out of the confines of the Animal Kingdom. If we could not write a book accounting of our escapades as a cat, dog, cow or tiger with any truth or accuracy in it, surely we could not recount our passage through the Mineral Kingdom. And yet, an aspect of our essence did most definitely pass through the Mineral, Plant and Animal Kingdoms.

There are distinctive outpourings from Source in the process of individualization. These outpourings manifest through an aspect of our monad passing within the confines of the various kingdoms under discussion. We do this via group consciousness. This is obviously not the group consciousness that is enjoyed by the advanced initiate of the Ascended Master. The latter has individuality at its core and stems from the merger of fully awakened, enlightened monads, Mighty I Am Presences or Flames if you will, that burn within the eternal fire of GOD. The former is a most rudimentary form of group consciousness that is gathering experience on its way towards individualization. The chasm between the two is universes apart.

Yet, the bottom line fact is that both these types of group consciousness exist within the One Eternal Whole, and both types of consciousness are expressions of our monadic essence. The basest and most primal and rudimentary of these expressions are found within the group body or soul of the Mineral Kingdom. Although touching, and embracing but a fragment of what the monad will eventually become, it nevertheless is an experience that an aspect of our monad must undergo.

The consciousness within the Mineral Kingdom is obviously at an extremely low frequency. It is barely awake, yet it is not asleep. Through this kingdom, certain very basic yet vital experiences are engendered, which ultimately contribute to the process of evolution as it continues. The Mineral Kingdom has a very specific function within the scheme of things in general. There is also evolution within that kingdom itself, which you may or may not be aware of.

After an appropriate span of time, certain very basic minerals will themselves evolve into more refined ones. As this occurs, the group body that composes a particular segment of the Mineral Kingdom grows lighter, more responsive, more refined. This can be seen reflected in the handling of various minerals by humanity itself. The common stone is picked up and tossed casually into the riverbed. Diamonds and other precious gems are mined, often at the risk of one's life. People have gone into caverns and caves near collapse in search of finding even one precious gem. This illustrates the different levels of growth and evolution within the Mineral Kingdom, even as there is growth and evolution within the confines of the Animal Kingdom.

Many lightworkers confuse the rudimentary response of certain minerals with the powerful response that the deva of that mineral is apt to display. Again, we must clearly delineate the difference between the deva who has a particular mineral, flower or vegetable, in its care, from the consciousness of that mineral, flower or vegetable. We are dealing with two very distinct Beings here. The third line of evolution involved in the process is that of the elemental being who is in charge of building the actual form. We therefore are actually dealing with three distinct lines of evolution. Please be aware of this, for this has been a point of much confusion.

It is quite important that you bear in mind that as was previously alluded to, even the most basic of minerals holds an essential place within the whole of the Earth. In fact, the Mineral Kingdom itself forms the very crust and core structure of the planet, and without the humblest member of this kingdom, there would not be the foundation upon which any other of the kingdoms could evolve! In this last sentence, beloved readers, can be seen the very "essence" of integrated functioning throughout all the kingdoms. The "puzzle piece" of the Mineral Kingdom is vital indeed!

Bearing this in mind, let us return a moment to consider the devas in relation to the Mineral Kingdom. In truth, they function almost identically within the Plant Kingdom as well. There are certain core similarities within the higher kingdoms, but for the moment the basic patterning and the overall structure can best and most appropriately be demonstrated through the Mineral Kingdom.

To begin with, we are really dealing with three distinct consciousnesses. In no particular order, the first we will look at is the consciousness of the mineral itself, as it is the evolution of the mineral that we are discussing. This, as was stated, is a very basic and rudimentary consciousness. This consciousness, and in fact the form through which that consciousness is expressing is itself in a state of evolution. As the mineral evolves within its own kingdom it will take higher and higher forms, each one being more expressive of the type of refinement of consciousness that it is experiencing. This pretty much parallels humanity's evolution through the various rounds of birth and rebirth.

As each successive incarnation will manifest a form that is constructed in a manner which is reflective of the state of consciousness reached, more light, higher attunement of chakras, greater sensitivity and so forth, so too the mineral will move from that of a rock to that of a gemstone to that of a precious stone. As we are currently concerned with the consciousness of the mineral involved, let me clearly state that at each turn of the spiral the consciousness of the mineral is greatly expanded, relatively speaking of course.

Integrated Ascension

We can therefore see that the consciousness of the mineral is itself a distinct and separate entity, in the process of its own growth and expansion. Next we shall consider consciousness of the particular deva attending that mineral. This also forms a distinct Being that is itself evolving separate and apart from the consciousness of the mineral. The attending deva evolves through its service work and guardianship role to the mineral, and has its own set of feelings and motivations to contend with. The reaction of a deva to the cutting of a particular gemstone from its quarry may be great indeed. Many confuse the sharp reaction of the deva to be coming from the mineral. It is not. The mineral, although at a higher frequency than when it began its evolution, is still expressing a rudimentary consciousness. The deva is more actively expressive. It is important to clearly see that there is as much of a separation between the two as there is an interblending. The coexistence of the interblending and the separate evolutionary paths is what makes it so difficult to discern between the two. There is, however, a most distinct difference!

The third element to consider is that of the building devas which are the "builders of form." These particular devas are on the line of the Elohim and are elemental in nature. The devas referred to in the preceding paragraph are on the line of Angelic evolution. The interblending between the evolutions, my beloved readers, is extremely intricate at every level of evolvement. These devas have a very distinctive function, separate and apart from the mineral and the attending deva. These Beings are actually the great builders who construct the form that all consciousness inhabits. They work from elemental essence and are deeply involved in the process of evolution with regard to how it expresses in form. They then are the third component that is involved in the evolution of the mineral.

As what we are discussing here is the various stages that contribute to the eventual birth into individualization in the human kingdom, it is primarily the consciousness of the mineral itself that we need to focus on.

The mineral then, is one stage on the evolutionary path toward eventual individualization. The mineral is alive, evolving, and conscious. It holds within its sphere a particular quality or essence of GOD that will eventually move it into the vegetable, animal and finally the human kingdom. The human kingdom will see the birth of the true individualized human or GOD-man/woman. The human will eventually rejoin with its highest GOD-source, the Mighty I Am Presence or the Monad, and continue further expansion throughout the cosmos, traveling all 352 planes or levels back to GODHEAD or Source. It will then, as was stated, merge into the Whole without any loss of individuality.

The first stage of this process is when an aspect of our monadic essence passes through the Mineral Kingdom. Next time you haphazardly toss a stone into a lake or riverbed be aware that is your younger brother that you are tossing. Know that there is certainly no harm in doing this, however it might behoove you to hold that stone near your heart for a moment and honor it for what it is…a blessed link in the chain of humanity itself, an integrated part of that which is GOD!

Integration within the Plant Kingdom

The Plant Kingdom is the next stage of evolution for the Soul Group, or that aspect of our monadic essence evolving through the lower kingdoms. With regard to the Plant Kingdom, we can see many things occurring simultaneously. There is a similar pattern to that within the Mineral Kingdom, however, the consciousness involved has relatively much more feeling within its scope than that which is confined within the limits and boundaries of the Mineral Kingdom. There is actually the exchange of breath between the Human Kingdom and the Plant Kingdom, as the oxygen the plant omits is basic to the need for human survival. The Plant Kingdom serves as our best form of nourishment, and provides sustenance to the Animal Kingdom as well. The nature

Integrated Ascension

elementals play a keen role within the growing and care of the Plant Kingdom. At this point and cycle humanity is being called to work in cooperation both with these wondrous devas, as well as with the Plant Kingdom as a whole.

We can see within the manifestation of the various vegetables, shrubbery, forests, grasses, weeds, and so forth, a vast array and a formidable difference in manifestation. This is again reflective of the consciousness within the evolving Plant Kingdom. The weed that is crushed underfoot, or that grows in disorderly patches destroying in its wake the growth of the healthier, more refined vegetation is at one level of development. The roses that are tended to with love, properly cared for by humans, attended to in a peaceful environment by the overlighting deva fairy is at another stage of manifestation within its own kingdom.

As is the case with the Mineral Kingdom, various levels of expression manifesting physically reveal somewhat the level of development of consciousness within the kingdom itself. This is an important point to know, as many are not aware that evolution within the lower kingdoms is taking place. From the point of view of the conscious development, these various levels are of a minuscule nature. They nonetheless exist and play an important role in the ascension that ultimately leads from the confines of one kingdom into the kingdom next above it.

In the realization of this insight much is also revealed regarding the evolution of the attending devas. A building deva on the line of the Elohim would find their work within the building and maintaining of briarwood, weeds and underbrush. A more highly evolved deva along this line would be involved in the building of the outer form of the evolving lily and rose. Remember that this involves the work of two types of devas. The one type are they who are the builders and who fashion and build the actual flower of vegetation through their ability to manipulate and create the form out of elemental essence, of which they themselves direct and embody. The second group of devas, those that are aligned with the Angelic evolution, are the ones who help the specific flora and vegetation to grow. They tend to the needs of the plant. This type of deva would then minister to the care of the aforementioned lily or rose. All work together along separate, yet totally integrated and intertwined lines of evolution.

Understand that there are three types of consciousness we are dealing with here. One is that of the Angelic line who nourishes the plant. A fairy along this line may actually make a temporary home within a particular flower in order to do this work. So, for example, in this case we have a fairy who is inhabiting a certain flower in order to care for it, provide nourishment and tend to its needs through love in action. Then there is the building deva who creates and maintains the actual structure of the flower by holding to the thoughtform and building via its own elemental essence. There is then, the consciousness of the flower itself. All are intertwined and interconnected, yet all mentioned are individually evolving.

Towering above all these beings whom we have discussed is the God of the Nature Kingdom Himself, which, of course, is Pan who is on the Elohim line of evolution and overlights all the devas, elementals, and their world. He is of an extremely high order, and in a sense holds all of the aforementioned elementals, devas, flowers, and foliage within his auric field. He does this in a similar way as the Master of a ray holds all the evolving monads of that ray, each of us, within their own auric field. Looked at from one point of view, all of the nature kingdoms are finding their point of integration within the Beingness of Pan!

I hope that I am making it perfectly clear that as is the case of the Mineral Kingdom where we explored the difference between the consciousness of the attending deva and that which is the most rudimentary form of consciousness within the mineral form, so, too, are we dealing with very distinct states of awareness when dealing with the Plant Kingdom. This is very vital to understand. As more and more lightworkers develop their higher senses, they may mistakenly suppose the outrage of the attending deva is that of the plant itself. It is not, the consciousness of the plant, which we shall discuss in a moment, is very basic and subtle. Although it exists and should indeed be honored and attended to, it is the deva who is working with the plant who will have the greater response of the two. The devas take their work very seriously, and when humanity comes along and unthinkingly plucks a flower they are tending to, or mows down acre after acre of precious vegetation, grasslands, redwoods, etc., they will definitely show their displeasure in almost an alarming fashion.

In truth, humanity must wake up to both the needs of the Plant Kingdom in and of itself, and to the Angelic and Elemental Kingdoms who are tending to their growth. Within any given garden, the two are interwoven, interblended and intertwined. They are, my beloved readers, fully integrated. When humanity shows disrespect to the Plant Kingdom, we are likewise showing disrespect to the nature and Elemental Kingdoms that tends to their growth! It is our responsibility to realize our own integration within this process and to understand how connected humanity is to both the Elemental and Angelic line of evolution and to the evolving group soul and monad of the Plant Kingdom.

Remember that it is the Plant Kingdom that feeds us. We breathe our breath into them and they breathe their breath into us. There is such a deep integration between these two kingdoms that it is astounding that humanity has not yet realized this. Instead, our race as a whole causes mass destruction and utter devastation in some cases, to that kingdom which in a physical sense is our very life itself! In doing this, we are obviously not caring for the kingdom of flora and vegetation in its own right, and are in truth, acting out of negative ego consciousness rather than Christ consciousness in this regard.

We must approach our path in an integrated fashion. We must work at the development of our Christ consciousness, for it is by the light and love of the Christ self that we will be able to see and therefore act in accordance with the highest principles and integrity in every area of life! By not doing this we are creating further imbalance and cultivating an attitude of separation between the various kingdoms and lines of evolution, which in fact does not exist at all! Many lightworkers are already quite aware of the vast implication that our actions have upon both the Plant Kingdom and the devas who attend them. This is a wonderful place to begin to integrate and implement this knowledge!

One of the saddest results that comes out of mass ignorance of this pervading unity, is that the angelic devas themselves have had to withdraw from the overcrowded, uncaring world that humanity has created. In doing this they have literally abandoned many a woodland, garden, and tree in their retreat into the quietude of more harmonious environments. The growth of the average city plant, flower, vegetable is left pretty much up to the laws of nature themselves, and to the few rare human beings who seek to be of true assistance. The absence of the devas has manifested in poorer crops, or total crop failure, and an overall weakness in the growth of all vegetation from which their helpful and loving presence is absent!

It would greatly behoove each and every one of us to create an alignment with the Plant Kingdom, the nature spirits attending to this kingdom, as well as to the elementals. If we do not, we will surely reap the devastating results that continued separation engenders. We can begin by asking the forgiveness of the Plant Kingdom for the disrespect we have shown it through the use of pesticides and other harmful chemicals, neglect and abuse. We can likewise call upon Pan and ask his forgiveness as well as his Divine direction. We can maintain an integrated and balanced outlook and approach to life in general, which could not help but to reflect upon our treatment of this kingdom. When we truly follow the path of initiations in an integrated manner, then all of GOD's kingdoms will automatically find their own point of integration within our open hearts.

Integrated Ascension

There are a couple of little things that we can do which will likewise help heal the wounds of separation between these kingdoms and ourselves. When we pick a flower, hold its stem in your hand stroking it tenderly. Although the feeling level of a flower itself is quite minimal, it does nevertheless exist. It feels the wrenching when it is thoughtlessly plucked from a garden. The tender stroking that I have suggested can quiet this wrenching feeling. We can also give a bit of warning to both the flower and the attending deva about what we are about to do. The deva will then feel the love we have and willingly retreat, rather than react at our deed of unthinking harshness.

We can all make use of the guidance that has come forth from actual scientific experiments and talk to our plants, whether they are house plants or garden plants. The same holds true in regard to any vegetable that we may be growing. The playing of soothing music has been proven to aid in the growth of plants. The exposure to harsh music or grating loud noises is proven to have just the opposite effect. These are little ways in which we can help in the care and development of the Plant Kingdom without interfering in the natural flow of our own lives.

The inner plane Ascended Masters have asked me to expand just a little more on the process of evolution in the lower Kingdoms. It must be understood that just as human beings do not have past lives as animals, plants or minerals in a literal sense, neither do animals have past lives as plants or minerals in a literal sense. In both cases, it is a monadic aspect that has had experience in the previous Kingdoms.

Another essential point to understand in this process is that when a mineral evolves into the Plant Kingdom it is not a linear or singular movement, as in the case of human beings who have an individualized identity. Minerals evolve through their Kingdom and then merge back into a group monadic essence. It is a mixture of the evolution of the mineral with the group consciousness of all minerals in that monad and with the monad itself that allows for eventually a new outpouring from the Source Monad to move into the next Kingdom.

Integrated Ascension

The same is true in the Plant Kingdom. Again, it is not a singular or individualized movement. By this, I mean the tomato plant in your house is not going to be your pet cat in the next life. The plant will evolve within its Kingdom; for example, a rose is a more evolved plant than a weed in your front lawn. Just as in the Mineral Kingdom, a diamond is more evolved than lapis, which is more evolved than a rock you may find on a country road. Each has their place in GOD's plan, but it is important to understand that everything in GOD's creation is in a state of evolution. When a plant reaches its highest state of evolution it then, upon its Earthly death, merges its soul essence back into the group monadic consciousness from whence it came. When the group monadic consciousness of all plants involved reaches a certain point in evolution it mixes with its monad in some mysterious alchemical way, and the Source Monad then brings forth the new outpouring of GOD-essence to move that group plant consciousness into the beginning stage of the Animal Kingdom.

The newborn animal then begins its evolutionary process through its Kingdom. The dog, cat, horse, and elephant for example, are again more evolved than an insect, hyena, or rhinoceros. Now the Animal Kingdom is different than the Mineral and Plant Kingdoms because animals within the higher stages of evolution in that Kingdom for the first time can take on an individualized identity through their interaction with their human caretakers and people in general. Through the process of sharing love, serving and helping their human caretaker, and being given a name, their consciousness evolves. It is important to understand, however, that although they have an individualized identity in this latter stage of animal evolution, upon death there is not a direct linear movement to becoming a human being. The animal most often is not allowed to become a human until the end of the cycle or round our planet is currently in. This deals with what I spoke of in my book *The Complete Ascension Manual* regarding the completion of the seven root races, which deals with certain Cosmic cycles of evolution

Integrated Ascension

within the Solar System, Galaxy, and our own Universe. There are some exceptions to this Cosmic law, where some animals are allowed to pass through the portal of human evolution before the end of this Planetary or Solar round. I must say, however, that this is extremely rare. To all my beloved readers who want their pet to be this exception, please realize that, in truth, time does not really exist and that a round in GOD's time is less than a blink of an eye. So, since almost all pets do not immediately go into human evolution, the question is what do they do? They often keep reincarnating as animals, coming back into the lives of their past human caretakers to serve and share love. These animals, in essence, have achieved "animal liberation" or "animal ascension," and come back as "animal bodhisatvas," so to speak. Also often at this stage animals do not reincarnate and instead serve previous human caretakers from the Inner Plane as animal guides. Remember, my beloved readers, it is ever the Force of Love that binds and is the magnet that brings all sentient beings back together. Animals sometimes go to other planets on the etheric realm and/or other planets that will allow physical human rebirth to take place.

It must be understood here, however, that although the animal has an individual identity at this point, there is still not a direct linear singular evolutionary movement as in the Human Kingdom's movement into the Spiritual Kingdom. The animal at this stage before becoming human merges back with its monad and through some alchemical process, again of its own evolution and the overall evolution of the entire monad, the Source Monad then brings forth a new outpouring that allows the transformation from the Animal Kingdom to the Human Kingdom to take place. This is why the newly formed human will have no recollection of being an animal. Because, again, the animal's evolution is just an extremely small aspect of the monad's overall evolution. Much GOD essence substance of the monad is needed separate from the animal's evolution to allow this transformation to take place. This is why repeatedly in this chapter I have stated that humans do not have literal past lives as animals, animals do not have literal past lives as plants, and plants do not have literal past lives as minerals. It is an aspect of the monad in all these cases that has had past experience in these Kingdoms. This is not a linear relationship, as I think you can now see, my friends.

The newfound human being, will of course, have to evolve through the seven levels of initiation and achieve Integrated Ascension before full Planetary Ascended Master status is achieved. The next Kingdom to follow in this evolutionary chain is the Solar Kingdom, which is the beginning of Cosmic Ascension at the beginning of the 10th Initiation. The 11th Initiation begins the Galactic Kingdom. The 12th Initiation begins the Universal Kingdom. After that, we can look forward to 340 more initiations through the Cosmic realms to take us back to the GODHEAD. For more information on Cosmic Ascension, please read my book called *Cosmic Ascension*.

I want to emphasize here one more time that all beings in GOD's infinite universe go through this process or something similar to it, regardless of whether they are on the Sons and Daughters of GOD lineage, the Angelic lineage, or the Elohim lineage. I asked all the inner plane Ascended Masters and Cosmic Ascended Masters, including Melchizedek, Mahatma, Metatron, Archangel Michael, the Divine Mother, the Elohim, Sai Baba, and the Archangels, and every single one of them without exception said that they went through a similar process at some ancient time in their evolutionary process. No one escapes from this, nor should you want to. This is GOD's Divine Plan for all sentient beings and the manifestation and expression of Father/Mother GOD!

One last point I want to make here is, that in the Angelic and/or Elohim lineage this process of an aspect of one's monad incarnating in material/etheric existence still takes place, however, in the case of an Angel it will manifest as an aspect of the monad incarnating in the Bird Kingdom, and/or eventually working up through the graded ranks as Mineral, Plant, and Animal Devas and Nature Spirits. Prior to the Bird and/or Nature Spirit incarnations, these Angelic Line beings must themselves serve in some capacity in relationship to the Mineral and Plant Kingdoms. The exact science of how this works is a subject for a future book I will be writing called *Ascending with the Angels & Elohim*. All that is important here is that the Angelic Line must incarnate an aspect of its monad as well as those on the Human Line.

The Elohim Lineage again incarnates an aspect of their monad as Elementals who are the builders of all minerals', plants", animals', humans', and angels' physical/etheric form. So, even the Mighty Elohim and the Archangels go through this process in their evolution. There is just a slight difference in the three lineages in how this process takes place. It also obviously doesn't take place just on the Earth or just in this material universe, but in all planets, solar systems, galaxies, universes, and multiuniverses throughout the infinity of GOD's creation.

Starseeds and Angel Helpers

What I must state for clarity's sake is that, as alluded to earlier, there are those of us who have come to Earth specifically to serve the Divine plan. We are those referred to as the "Starseeds." This does not mean that this small group (less than 5% of Earth's population) who is specifically on the mission to raise Earth's frequencies are freed from all the laws pertaining to evolution, development, initiation and ascension. In fact, in order to acclimate ourselves to the planet of our chosen work, all must go through Her curriculum and reenact each of the initiations. We are required to cleanse and purify and raise our frequencies so that there are no hindrances between us and our Mighty I Am Presence and the work that we have set out to do. What is essential to understand in regard to this group, is that those of us belonging to it do not see ourselves as "better" than anyone else. In fact, just the opposite is true. It is our unique ability to see ourselves as utterly *equal* with all of humanity that is the true mark of a Starseed!

Integrated Ascension

I only mention this at this juncture as much detail has been given forth pertaining to the path of evolution and it feels essential to mention that there are those among us who have traveled this pathway eons ago and are simply here to reenact it in order to join in frequency and unity with Earth's vibratory essence. What is also interesting to note is that this group faces the same tests, follows the same basic path and is absolutely required to be free and clear of the negative ego. Whether or not you are a Starseed is not the point, for as I have said before, and I quote, "Before enlightenment we chop wood and carry water, and after enlightenment we chop wood and carry water."

I would be remiss, however, to not incorporate this group in the understanding of evolution and the process of initiation. They come to Earth with their joint missions already established, but must work at discovering it and manifesting it the same as anyone else. The only difference between the path of initiation and ascension previously outlined is that for the bulk of Earth humanity this is the first time this path is followed and for the Starseeds and Angelic Helpers in human form, this has been mastered at an earlier phase of linear time.

It is wise to remember, beloved readers, that they who see themselves as most equal among humanity are they who carry the greatest light! So again I present this understanding to you in order to be as complete as possible in my description of the evolutionary process and not to set you wondering if you are one of the Starseed, Star helpers or Earth Angels. If you are, you will "…be about the Father's business." If you are not, but are truly on the path of Integrated Ascension you will "…be about the Father's business."

Those of us who are bonded by our destinies, karma, mission will find one another so that the work can go forward as planned and the path of isolation transmuted. Therefore, I conclude this little extra piece of the puzzle regarding the process of evolution for no other purpose than to help your understanding be as complete as possible on this matter. Other than that, let us all continue to "…chop wood and carry water" in order that we may all the more quickly, gracefully, and joyously manifest the Kingdom of GOD upon the Earth!

The Care and Integration of the Earth Mother

Within the sphere of the Earth Mother, all the four lower bodies of humanity emit their individualized frequencies. She therefore embodies the totality of our physical, etheric, astral/emotional, and mental fields. In addition, she wears the Earth itself as her skin, thus embodying the emanations of the three lower kingdoms through which we grow and evolve, as well as the elemental and angelic forces that function within her sphere. The composite of our integrated physical/etheric selves, our emotional selves and our mental selves is the vastness she overlights. From one point of view, she embodies the Earth itself. In truth, she is the Divine Feminine of this planet, and wears it at once as a garment and as her very self!

If it is truly integration that we are seeking, there is no way that we can fully achieve this unless and until we acknowledge and act upon the fact that we are at one with she whom is Lady Gaia, Earth Mother, the overlighting feminine principle of our planet. The way in which civilization has evolved has been to treat this most holy of beings with dire disrespect. As you can see from all that we have discussed thus far, if we disrespect her, then we disrespect ourselves. If we do not elevate and integrate into our own higher state of GOD-Beingness, then we will continue to pollute the blessed Earth Mother. We will pour the contaminants of our misqualified energy into her physical, etheric, astral and mental bodies until she will be embodying a world filled with the miasma, confusion and psychic debris that we have been spewing forth!

The lightworkers of the world are finally waking up to their connection with the Earth Mother, the feminine spirit of the planet itself. It therefore falls upon those of us who are aware of the severity of

Integrated Ascension

the situation that we ourselves have created, to take the first steps in rectifying that situation. The ultimate way in which we can proceed with the purification of the Earth Mother and all the spheres that she inhabits, is to become fully integrated ascended beings ourselves. When we do this, we will be creating physical, etheric, emotional and mental bodies that are free of misqualified energy, psychic, emotional and mental debris. When we do this en masse, we will be transforming the greater Earth Body. We will be washing clean the many levels of Earth Mother!

Another tool that we have available to us is that of education. Although most people are somewhat aware of environmental and ecological issues, the so-called great leaders of our world have not yet banded together to help correct this situation. We need to educate the masses ourselves, my friends, and the best way to educate, by far, is through example!

Each of us must first and foremost attend to our own inner worlds. The many facets of this have been discussed throughout this book as well as all the books that comprise my series. The basic gist is in learning how to function through the Christ consciousness rather than the negative ego, manifesting the highest level of light, love, psychological integration, service and spiritual leadership and of course, integration and balance within our own twelve-body systems.

For those of us who are writers, we write about raising these quotients and becoming living examples of GOD upon Earth. For those of us who are artists, I encourage you to put forth that higher vision in your painting, in your music, in your dance. For those in the political, legal or business arenas certainly bring it forward as directly as possible. Unveil the light of truth that the shadow can be seen and done away with.

This would, of course, apply to any area of life. We are all capable of living up to the highest possible standards within our own home. We are capable of demonstrating the tender handling of the Animal

Integrated Ascension

Kingdom, proper care and feeding of the Plant Kingdom, and proper Christ consciousness in regard to the Mineral Kingdom—who literally forms the physical structure of Earth Mother and upon whose foundation all other kingdoms grow and thrive! We can recycle our newspapers, our cans, and our jars. We can keep our cars as clean as possible. We can turn off the television, radio, and lamps when we are not using them. We can do the maximum to help cleanse and purify our planet. We can do this simply by a minimum of effort that can show forth a maximum level of transformation by the process of demonstrating our awareness.

One does not need to attempt to return to the Stone Age in order to effectuate this process. We do not need to abandon our cars, throw out our televisions, or destroy our computers. We are well aware of the harmful radiation that they produce and are quite capable of minimizing the effects of this by making very subtle changes. We can see to it that our cars have the best and purest gas put into them, and that they are not emitting any unnecessary harmful fumes. We can turn off our televisions when we are not watching them. We should surely turn off our computers when they are not in use, as we ourselves are the immediate direct recipients of some of its more harmful emanations.

Here again, I ask you to pause and to consider that in healing the Earth Mother we are helping to heal ourselves, for we are indeed integrated, and are in essence functioning as 'one'. We can also learn directly from the Earth and what she herself has to teach us. The effects of the pollutants in our water and in our atmosphere are obvious. The chemicalized process by which we grow our crops has also been proven dangerous and potentially lethal over the years. Much disease stems from the by-products of certain chemicals and fertilizers, even science has told us this! In this regard, science is but speaking the words of the Earth Mother herself.

Nowhere has the Earth Mother cried out in her deepest agonies as when we have used nuclear warfare. A blind person can hear her voice

Integrated Ascension

when a nuclear disruption occurs, and a deaf person can see it. Anyone around it will feel it as does Mother Earth Herself, and as human beings they will be destroyed by it, and have been, as our history so painfully reveals. Listen, beloved readers, for the Earth Herself will speak her needs to you, and you will hear them, see them, and feel them. That is because, as I have already stated, you and I are bonded in oneness with her and share "one body," so to speak.

The Earth can speak to us in positive ways as well, and there has been much demonstrated in various cultures of the past that can be applied towards the emergence of the next millennium. The Native Americans thrived on listening to the teaching of Mother Earth. We, in term, should begin to listen ever more closely to the teachings of the Native American. There is much guidance on basic living within their history, which after all thrived not that long ago.

We can, and in fact, we are in the process of rediscovering Atlantis. Although there was much that was demonstrated in a negative vein toward her decline, there are also many advanced techniques on healing and the running of machinery that was exhibited that we have yet to re-access and use. The combination of Atlantean and ancient Egyptian methods of working with the very elements themselves in order to use them in a beneficial way holds much of the blueprint for the Golden Age. Ask for these secrets to be once again unveiled. Pay attention to the aspects of them that are, such as the work now being done with crystals, and put this to practical use. By combining both ancient and modern wisdom, and the listening to the voice of Mother Earth herself, will the way become clear.

So very much of the needed healing of the Earth Mother stands right before us, if only we would pay attention and heed her voice. This does not mean that we become extremists and tiptoe about, walking on eggshells afraid to fully participate in the modern world of which we form a part. What it does mean is that we do so in a balanced and integrated manner. We take the steps within our immediate environment to help clean, purify and transmute negativity of any kind. We do not have to run out and become activists. What we do need to do is to become actively involved in the world of which we are all a part, which is the very body and substance of the sacred Earth Mother!

Integrating the Goddess

It would certainly be inappropriate to leave this chapter without calling to your attention the dire need that we all have to fully integrate the Goddess energies, or the Divine Feminine within our lives. There has always been the evolution of the feminine energies upon our planet, and that of course includes the evolution of the Lady Masters. During various phases of our planet's history this evolution and lineage has been focused upon to the benefit of humanity as a whole. It is quite apparent that in more recent periods of history this energy has been severely neglected. The time has come 'round once again to integrate this wonderful aspect of life into the full spectrum prism of our perception, mode of being, and behavior alike.

Although the Goddess energy does not literally fall into the category of a separate kingdom of evolution, because we have so deeply alienated it from the scope of evolution in general we need to pause for a moment to simply recognize its place within the scheme of things. In truth, each of us upon our path of evolution and initiation do in fact evolve the goddess energy within. This has most commonly been referred to as the proper balancing of the masculine/feminine or the Yin/Yang energies, although in truth the Goddess energy supersedes this most important aspect. It is an unequivocal fact that as we progress upon our divine path, so does the Divine feminine energies that we embody! This has been out of balance, which is one of the main reasons that the emerging millennium is calling these energies forth, and why I have been guided to draw your attention to this aspect, if only briefly in this particular book. In order for the New Age to manifest according to the Will of GOD, the Goddess energies must be once again activated, demonstrated and brought forward to their full potential. As I said, they have already been brought forward to a certain degree, as we could not truly have made progress upon our path of evolution if they were in fact dormant. However, they have been functioning at a very low level of their potential, and are no longer content to do so. It is time for us all to appreciate and integrate this most important facet of our beings. It is time for the Lady Masters to assume their rightful acknowledgment for their work, and to work and to walk as openly among us as do the masculine Masters. This, my beloved readers, is in the process of occurring.

Looked at from one very important lens, the entire manifested universe of form is the energy of the Divine Mother or Divine Feminine Principle. The unmanifested essence of Spirit is that of the Divine Father, or Divine Masculine Principle. The two always work together, forming the ONE. As Hermes/Thoth says, "All is gender." This is Divine law. How then can we go onward and upward without balancing this whole, this Divine Oneness that springs forth out the fount of the Divine Masculine and Divine Feminine without acknowledging this most essential aspect of ourselves, and life as a whole? My beloved readers, we cannot. What I am saying here is of a very basic and rudimentary nature, however in a book about integration, the window into the world of the Goddess must at least be held slightly ajar. This entire subject is explored in a book which is devoted exclusively to it called *Empowerment and Integration through the Goddess*, thus giving full attention to all the intricacies that I have merely hinted at at this particular juncture. This book is now available in manuscript form from the Academy.

I leave you with this one thought. When you awake each morning and hear the bird-song, see the sunrise or feel the breath of the cool wind upon your face, know that it is the Goddess Herself that is greeting you. Know that all of manifestation, both seen and unseen sings Her praises and bears tribute to Her Beingness, even as the essential nature

Integrated Ascension

of Spirit itself, the Divine Masculine is the Source of all the worlds and every universe upon universe! In the perfect blending of the two is the Divine WHOLE! Think also upon this, "As above so below, as within so without." Each and every one of us is the microcosmic expression of the macrocosmic truth, and therefore we hold within us the Divine unity of Father/Mother GOD!

Integration with Lord Buddha—Our Planetary Logos

There is no way that we can discuss integrating with the various Kingdoms of GOD without addressing the Realm, the Kingdom, the ultimate service, and yes, sacrifice, of He who holds the position of the Planetary Logos. For 18.5 million years this position was held by Sanat Kumara. Within the sphere of His Divine radius all on Earth truly lived and moved and had their Being. This mantle of this truth and service is now upheld by beloved Lord Buddha.

Much confusion exists in the true understanding of the Planetary Logos for the subject is intricate and complex. For one thing, the Planetary Logos places a self imposed limitation of service by enfolding all aspects and planes of Earth's existence within his very own Being. Although He does this utterly and completely, He is likewise a separate being and Himself proceeding upon the pathway of His own evolution. We thus can pray to Buddha as the personal GOD of this planet.

The Planetary Logos is integrated into every phase of our existence. This includes all the various Kingdoms, lines of evolution—such as the Elemental/Angelic—as well as all of the inner plane realms. The more we acknowledge this unity and consciously participate in accelerating the Divine Plan as it exists within the mind of the Planetary Logos, the more fully integrated we become with the purpose and plan of GOD. In actuality it is within His Beingness that the Lords of each Ray uphold their position, for again, every aspect of planetary life is embraced by the Logos of our planet.

Integrated Ascension

The keynote of our particular planet is the fourth ray—that of harmony through conflict. It is therefore the quality, tone, and color of this ray that has planetary dominance, much as on a greater scale, the second ray of Love/Wisdom of the solar system overlights the fourth ray. While we are involved in the Earth's evolution, the fourth ray will hold the basic resonance infused within our evolutionary process. Although we move at some point out of the Earth's primary ray dominance, the essence of our experience within this sphere will be indelibly marked upon our soul and Spirit/Monad.

Part of the basic Divine structure and plan is that the conflict aspect of this ray is transmuted into Divine harmony. All forces are set in motion for this particular purpose, and to this end all within Earth's sphere are moving. Even those of us who have come from other worlds and other systems of worlds will be building this quality into our essential beings, just because we have put ourselves within this radiance.

Beloved readers, as we each work on a daily basis to further integrate within ourselves and with all upon the Earth, know that we are likewise drawing ever closer in consciousness to the Planetary Logos. Just as in when we consider the Mahatma and all 352 levels of Being which He embodies, we must consider the fact that Lord Buddha now holds the position of He who embodies all upon Earth. Attunement to Him is attunement to our immediate plan and purpose.

In advancing our awareness into the cosmic realms and levels of initiation, one danger exists. That danger, my friends, is in seeking to bypass the very intent, plan and purpose of our beloved Planetary Logos. In truth, we cannot do this, for each specific planet has a Divine attribute and quality to uphold and perfect. If we seek to bypass our Divine unity with the Will, plan and purpose of our own Planetary Logos, we will ultimately fall short of our purpose. This will result in certain karmic repercussions that will force us to attend to the full and total integration and participation within the sphere of the Buddha.

Integrated Ascension

This tendency to disregard the keynote of Earth Herself and the Planetary Logos who upholds all within Himself is much like the tendency to disregard certain basic quotients and developments, such as the Psychological and/or the Spiritual Leadership Quotient and so on. It is imperative that we fully integrate the intent of our Planetary Logos within ourselves so that we can consciously and joyously integrate that frequency into ever greater spheres, such as that of Solar Logoi who hold the entire solar system in Their sphere under the keynote of Love/Wisdom, or beloved Melchizedek, who as the Universal Logos holds all in this universe within His sphere under the keynote of Courage!

When Lord Buddha agreed to uphold the position of Planetary Logos in order to allow Sanat Kumara to move on in his greater cosmic evolution, he did so out of deep and abiding love. It is interesting to note that though there are, in actuality, many Kumaras involved in the Earth's evolution, some are fully awake and functioning consciously in actual physical incarnation while others are awakening to who they truly are, and others still are functioning outside of physical embodiment. Implicit in the term "Logos" is more than one, although the Planetary Logos heads the leadership and assumes the greatest responsibility. In the case of the Earth, it is seven Kumaras who have specifically functioned jointly in this capacity.

In order for a being to uphold this position, they have had to experience incarnation within the Human Kingdom. Although Source is their true essence and home—as indeed it is with each and every one of us—they must build into their total Monadic experience that of ascension through the process of human evolution. Lord Buddha, as did Sanat Kumara and beloved Sananda, all passed through this experience upon the planet of Love, Venus. Both Lord Buddha and Sananda recapitulated their process of initiation and ascension through definite periods of embodiment upon this planet. This was done, beloved readers, so that they could fully integrate within the essential matrix and structure inherent to the Earth body itself. If they did not do this, they would not be able to serve in the vast, yet specific capacity that these incredible beings have and continue to do.

What I want you to fully grasp is the fact that Lord Buddha and the six other Kumaras now working beside him as a unit both concurrently embody the entirety of realms and all forms and sentient beings within themselves and yet remain individualized beings. It is a similar situation as that which is occurring with the Earth Mother and indeed is duplicated by all these Great Ones who hold us within their auric Sphere. We are integrated parts of them, and must honor that completely. We must likewise honor our own individuality, which continues to expand within and into the ever-greater whole!

Summary and Conclusion

The more we each grow and evolve, the more in attunement to the greater whole we become. All or you reading this part are mentally aware of this fact. The mental knowledge of this, beloved readers, is not enough. The cycle of the new millennium demands that we embody and actualize this truth at every single level of our beings. It is the frequency of the cycle we are now entering that has called forth this book into manifestation. Integration must be complete and it must be demonstrated!

It is not enough any longer to merely know or sense that "Love makes the world go "round." We must move up that Love Quotient so high that we ourselves become love in action! What good is it to say "I love," yet walk away from a brother or sister in need, abuse or neglect the Animal Kingdom, poison our oceans, air, soil, with the destructive fire of hate and separation? In the same vein, so what if in the distant past you were a Kumara, an Angel, a high Priest or Priestess or famous past life prophet or Saint? This is meaningless if you are not demonstrating Godliness and egolessness now.

Integrated Ascension

Many lightworkers fall into the trap of glamorizing where they have come from or how highly evolved they were in a past life or ancient lineage. This may be true, however, it doesn't mean in the slightest that this person is psychologically and spiritually clear now. As I told you previously, a person can lose their attunement at even the highest levels of initiation in this life, let alone from a previous one. There are many that were egoless in past lives, but are totally run by their ego in this life. Each life the initiation process must be recapitulated and the nature of matter and living in a physical body makes you forget. Even incredibly advanced beings sometimes sleep through physical incarnations although they had high hopes to do great service work before coming in.

So, my beloved readers, do not get sucked into the glamour or ego of such information, for it is meaningless in the whole scheme of things. All that matters is what you are doing now, not what you did in the past. No matter how high a being you are or what level of initiation you are at, the negative ego can take over in an instant if you are not vigilant. Getting too caught up in the glamours of such information is a sign it already has. My beloved friends, please be ever watchful on this point, for there is much corruption and astral glamour going on in the New Age Movement in these matters as I'm sure you, my friends, have noticed as well.

When we clutter the mental body with negative thoughts, intents, or devious plans, we fill that which is the total mass of humanity's collective mental atmosphere with mental confusion and debris. This in turn creates an almost impenetrable wall between that which is the Divine Wisdom of the Higher Mind and the lower concrete mind. We then are unable to clearly bring through "truth" as the Masters would unveil it because of the density we have collectively built between pure abstract yet practical wisdom and the concrete mind and physical brain.

When we abuse the physical Earth, we are literally participating in the destruction of part of ourselves. As was addressed in this chapter, the Mineral and Plant Kingdoms, the devas who work with them, the

Integrated Ascension

beloved Earth Mother and the Planetary Logos itself, are all integrated within the structure and foundation of this planet. All of this integrates with the totality of the fourth or Human Kingdom, and the second or Animal Kingdom. Beloved readers, full and total integration between all that has been previously mentioned *must* become a manifested and demonstrated fact, totally and honestly embraced by every aspect of our Beings. The reason for this is because it *already exists as "fact" within spiritual reality,* and unless and until we bring this into manifestation, *we will not be able to express and demonstrate the energies of the next millennium!*

I ask you with full sincerity of heart to please consider all that has been stated and shared within this chapter. Although of an esoteric nature, it is also extremely practical. It shows the Earth "as it is" and pays homage to the sentient life which composes every aspect of our planet's existence. Do not simply read this and believe this because I have said it. Meditate upon it within the cave of your own heart. See it within the eyes and hearts of your animal brethren. Behold it within the lily of the field and the sacred crystal you use for healing!

In this way, my friends, it will utterly and completely become your own truth. It will well up in your heart as you meditate and not be simply something you have read in a book. That which is book knowledge is an extremely wonderful *tool* for growth and understanding; that which is direct essence within your own hearts and vision *is* growth, understanding, and wisdom. The subjects addressed throughout this book are too vital and important to simply "believe." This chapter is too personal and vital in its implications to be simply a part of your mental computer banks or to form a belief system upon. The truth I speak here begs to be known and known intimately by each and every one of you. I therefore again request that you meditate upon all that has been given forth in the sacredness of your own Being, that you might "know" for yourself the profundity of this information!

Integrated Ascension

Within this particular chapter are many keys that will unlock the door to the Age of Aquarius and provide entry into the glorious seventh Golden Age. Look within your own heart for therein lies the doorway through which you will find safe passage between your own heart/mind and the heart/mind within the Great Central Sun. I encourage you from the depths of my soul to use that key, beloved ones, for it will take you to the Source of your own GOD-Self and reveal your unique ascension mission and puzzle piece in the manifestation of the next millennium!

18

My Spiritual Mission and Purpose
by
Dr. Joshua David Stone

My Spiritual mission and purpose is a multifaceted process. Spirit and the inner plane Ascended Masters have asked myself and Wistancia (married since 1998), to anchor onto the Earth an inner plane Ashram and Spiritual/Psycho-logical/Physical/Earthly Teaching and Healing Academy! This Academy is called the Melchizedek Synthesis Light Academy! We are overlighted in this mission by Melchizedek, the Mahatma, Archangel Metatron, the Inner Plane Ascended Master Djwhal Khul, and a large group of Ascended Masters and Angels such as the Divine Mother, Archangel Michael, Archangel Gabriel, Sai Baba, Vywamus, the Lord of Arcturus, Lord Buddha, Lord Maitreya, Mother Mary, Quan Yin, El Morya, Kuthumi, Serapis Bey, Paul the Venetian, Master Hilarion, Sananda, Lady Portia and Saint Germain, and a great many others who we like to call the "Core Group"!

I have also been asked by the inner plane Ascended Master Djwhal Khul, who again wrote the Alice Bailey books, and was also involved in the Theosophical Movement, to take over his inner plane Ashram when he moves on to his next Cosmic Position, in the not too distant future.

Integrated Ascension

Djwhal holds Spiritual Leadership over what is called the inner plane Second Ray Synthesis Ashram. On the inner plane the Second Ray Department is a gigantic three story building complex with vast gardens.

The Ascended Master Djwhal Khul runs the first floor of the Second Ray Department in the Spiritual Hierarchy. Master Kuthumi, the Chohan of the Second Ray, runs the second floor. Lord Maitreya the Planetary Christ runs the third floor! When Djwhal Khul leaves for his next Cosmic Position, I will be taking over this first floor Department. The Second Ray Department is focused on the "Spiritual Education," of all lightworkers on Earth, and is the Planetary Ray of the Love/Wisdom of God. What is unique, however, about the Synthesis Ashram, is that it has a unique mission and purpose which is to help light-workers perfectly master and integrate all Twelve Planetary Rays which is one of the reasons I love this particular Spiritual leadership position and assignment so much! For this has been a great mission and focus of all my work!

Wistancia and my mission has been to anchor the Synthesis Ashram and Teaching Academy onto the physical Earth, which we have done and are continuing to do in an ever increasing manner on a global Level. Currently there are over 15 branches of the Academy that have also been set up around the world! The Academy actually first came into existence in 1996! This we have been guided to call the Melchizedek Synthesis Light Academy for the following reasons. It is called this because of the Overlighting Presence of Melchizedek (Our Universal Logos), The Mahatma (Avatar of Synthesis), and the Light which is the embodiment of Archangel Metatron, who created all outer light in our Universe and is the creator of the electron! These three beings, Djwhal Khul, and a very large Core Group of inner plane Planetary and Cosmic Masters help us in all this work.

I have also been asked by the inner plane Ascended Masters to be one of the main "High Priest Spokespersons for the Planetary Ascension Movement on Earth." I have been asked to do this because of the cutting edge, yet easy to understand nature of all my books and work, as well as certain Spiritual Leader-ship qualities I humbly possess. In this regard, I represent all the Masters, which works out perfectly given the Synthesis nature of my work. I function as kind of a "Point Man" for the Ascended Masters on Earth, as they have described it to me.

The Masters, under the guidance of Lord Buddha our Planetary Logos, have also guided us as part of our mission to bring Wesak to the West! So, for the last six years we have held a Global Festival and Conference in Mt Shasta, California for 2000 People. This, of course, honors the Wesak Festival, which is the holiest day of the year to the inner plane Ascended Masters, and the high point of incoming Spiritual energies to the Earth on the Taurus Full moon each year! We invite all lightworkers to join us each year from all over the world for this momentous Celebration, which is considered to be one of the premiere Spiritual Events in the New Age Movement!

The fourth part of my mission and purpose is the 30 Volume Easy to Read Encyclopedia of the Spiritual Path I have written. So far I have completed 27 volumes in this Ascension book series. The Ascended Master Djwhal Khul prophesized in the 1940's that there would be a third dispensation of Ascended Master teachings what would appear at the turn of the century. The first dispensation of Ascended Master teachings was the "Theosophical Movement," channeled by Madam Blavatsky. The second dispensation of Ascended Master teachings was the "Alice Bailey" books, channeled by Djwhal Khul, and the "I Am Discourses," channeled by Saint Germain. My 30 volume series of books is by the grace of GOD and the Masters, the third dispensation of Ascended Master teachings as prophesized by Djwhal Khul. These books are co-creative channeled writings of myself and the inner plane Ascended Masters. What is unique about my work is how easy to read and understand it is, how practical, comprehensive, cutting edge, as well as integrated and synthesized. Wistancia has added to this work with her wonderful book *Invocations to the Light*.

Integrated Ascension

The fifth aspect of our work and mission, which is extremely unique, is the emphasis of "Synthesis." My books and all my work integrate in a very beautiful way all religions, all Spiritual paths, all mystery schools, all Spiritual teachings, and all forms of psychology! Everyone feels at home in this work because of its incredible inclusive nature! This synthesis ideal is also seen at the Wesak Celebrations, for people come from all religions, Spiritual paths, mystery schools, and teachings. The Event is overlighted by over one million inner plane Ascended Masters, Archangels and Angels, Elohim Masters, and Christed Extraterrestrials. Wesak, the Books, the Academy and all our work, embody this synthesis principle. This is part of why I and we have been given Spiritual Leadership of the Synthesis Ashram on earth, and soon on the Inner Plane as well. This also explains our unique relationship to Melchizedek who holds responsibility for the "synthesis development," of all beings in our Universe. Our connection to the Mahatma is explained by the fact that the Mahatma is the Cosmic embodiment of "Synthesis" in the infinite Universe. This is also why the Mahatma also goes by the name, "The Avatar of Synthesis." Archangel Metatron who holds the position in the Cosmic Tree of Life of Kether, or the Crown, hence has a "Synthesis Overview," of all of the Sephiroth or Centers of the Cosmic Tree of Life! Djwhal Khul holds Spiritual leadership of the "Synthesis Ashram" on the Planetary, Solar, and Galactic levels for the earth! The Core Group of Masters that overlight our mission are, again, the embodiment of the synthesis understanding!

The unique thing about our work is that it teaches some of the most cutting edge co-created channeled work on the planet, in the realm of Ascension and Ascended Master Teachings. This can be seen in my books *The Complete Ascension Manual, Beyond Ascension, Cosmic Ascension, Revelations of a Melchizedek Initiate,* and *How To Teach Ascension Classes.* Because of my back ground as a professional Psychologist and Licensed Marriage Family Child Counselor, I also specialize in some of the most advanced cutting edge work on the planet in the field of Spiritual psychology. In this regard, I would guide you to my books, *Soul Psychology, Integrated Ascension, How To Clear the Negative Ego,* and *Ascension and Romantic Relationships*! Thirdly, I also have humbly brought forth some extremely cutting edge work on the physical/earthly level in the field of healing, Spirituality and society, politics, social issues, Extraterrestrials, Spiritual leadership, Spirituality and business, Goddess work with Wistancia, and of course the annual Wesak Celebrations. This can be found in my books: *The Golden Keys to Ascension and Healing, Hidden Mysteries, Manual for Planetary Leadership, Your Ascension Mission: Embracing Your Puzzle Piece, How to be Successful in your Business from a Spiritual and Financial Perspective,* and *Empowerment and Integration of The Goddess*—written by Wistancia and myself.

Adding to this, the eleven new books I have just completed and am completing. *The Golden Book of Melchizedek: How to Become an Integrated Christ/Buddha in this Lifetime, How to Release Fear-Based Thinking and Feeling: An In-depth Study of Spiritual Psychology, The Little Flame and Big Flame* (my first children's book), *Letters of Guidance to Students and Friends, Ascension Names and Terms Glossary, Ascension Activation Meditations of the Spiritual Hierarchy, The Divine Blue Print for the Seventh Golden Age, How to do Psychological and Spiritual Counseling for Self and Others, God and His Team of Super Heroes* (my second children's book) and *How to Achieve Perfect Radiant Health from the Soul's Perspective*!

Currently I have completed 27 Volumes in my Ascension Book Series. Fourteen of these books are published by Light Technology Publishers. A new version of Soul Psychology has just been published by Ballantine Publishers, owned by Random House, which I am quite excited about as well! The other books are in manuscript form and I am currently negotiating with various publishers for publishing rights! My books have also been translated and published in Germany, Brazil, Japan, Holland, Israel and this process continues to expand.

Integrated Ascension

Spirit and the inner plane Ascended Masters have told me that because of this unique focus, that what I have actually done in a co-creative way and manner with them, is open a new Portal to God. This new portal opening stems out of all the cutting-edge Ascension Activations and Ascended Master Teachings, the totally cutting-edge Spiritual Psychology work because of my background as a Psychologist and Licensed Marriage, Family, and Child Counselor, and the unique ability to ground all the work into the physical/earthly world in a balanced and integrated manner. Spirit and the Masters have told me that this new Portal to God is on an inner and outer plane level, and continues to be built in a co-creative way with Spirit, the Masters, myself, and certain other Masters and High Level Initiates who are helping me on the inner and outer planes! I have Spiritual leadership, however, in spearheading this project, and is one of the most exciting projects I am involved in.

In terms of my Spiritual initiation process as I have spoken of in my books, I have currently now taken my 14th major initiation. These are not the minor initiations that some groups work with, but are the major initiations that embody all the minor initiations within them. The Seventh Initiation is the achieving of Liberation and Ascension. The Tenth Initiation is the completion of Planetary Ascension and the beginning of Solar Initiation. The Eleventh Initiation, being the first Galactic Initiation. The Twelfth Initiation, being the first Universal Initiation from an Earthly perspective. Having taken my 14th initiation, what is most important to me is that these initiations have been taken in an "integrated manner," for, in truth, the Masters told me that they are not really into Ascension, which may surprise a great many lightworkers. The Masters are into "Integrated Ascension"! There are many lightworkers taking initiations, but many are not doing so in an integrated and balanced manner! They are taking them on a Spiritual level, but they are not being properly integrated into the mental and emotional bodies or psychological level properly. They are also not transcending negative ego fear-based thinking and feeling and properly balancing their four-body system. They are also not integrating their initiations fully into the physical/earthly level, addressing such things as: Healing, Grounding their Missions, Finding their Puzzle Piece Mission and Purpose, Prosperity Consciousness and Financial and Earthly Success, Integrating the God/Goddess, Embracing the Earth Mother and the Nature Kingdom, Properly Integrating into Third Dimensional Society and Civilization in terms of the focus of their Service Mission. This is just mentioned as a very loving reminder of the importance of an integrated and balanced approach to one's Spiritual Path. The grace to have been able to take these 14 major initiations and be able to have completed my Planetary Ascension process and to have moved deeply into my Cosmic Ascension process, I give to GOD, Christ, the Holy Spirit, Melchizedek, the Mahatma, Archangel Metatron, and the Core Group of Masters I work with. I have dedicated myself and my life to GOD and the Masters' service, and I have humbly attempted to share everything I know, have used, and have done in my Spiritual path and Ascension process with all of you, my Beloved Readers!

Melchizedek, the Universal Logos, has also inwardly told me, that because of the Cosmic work I am involved with, that I have taken on the Spiritual assignment of being one of the "Twelve Prophets of Melchizedek on Earth." I am very humbled to serve in this capacity. For Melchizedek is the Universal Logos, who is like the President of our entire Universe. In truth, all Religions and Spiritual teachings have their source in Melchizedek and in the Great Ancient Order of Melchizedek. It is my great honor and privilege to serve GOD and Melchizedek in this capacity. This is something I have never spoken of before, although I have known of this for many, many years. I have been guided after all this time to share a little more deeply about my Spiritual mission on Earth at this time.

The Academy Website is one of the most profound Spiritual Web sites you will ever explore, because it embodies this "synthesis nature,"

Integrated Ascension

and is an ever-expanding living easy to read Spiritual encyclopedia that fully integrates all 12 Rays in design and creation! This is also embodied in the free 140 page information packet that we send out to all who ask who wish to get involved and know more about our work! The information in the information packet is also available by just exploring the Academy Website!

We have also set up a wonderful Ministers Ordination and Training Program, which we invite all interested to read about. I am also very excited about a relatively recent book I have written called *How to Teach Ascension Classes*. Because I have become so busy with my Spiritual leadership and global world service work, I really do not have the time to teach weekly classes, as I have in the past. I firmly believe in the motto "Why give a person a fish, when you can teach them to fish!" In this vein, the Masters guided me to write a book on how to teach people to teach Ascension classes based on my work. I humbly suggest it is a most wonderful channeled book that can teach you in the easiest way and manner on every level to teach Ascension classes in your home or on a larger level if you choose. These classes are springing up now all over the globe and have been successful beyond my wildest dreams and expectations. When I wrote the book I was so involved with the process of writing it, I never fully envisioned the tremendous success it would have on a planetary and global level. Using this book and my other books, I have really done the initial homework for you, which can and will allow you to immediately begin teaching Ascension classes yourself. I humbly suggest that you look into the possibility of doing this yourself if you are so guided!

One other very interesting aspect of our Spiritual mission is something the Masters have been speaking to us about for over ten years which is what they described as being "Ambassadors for the Christed Extraterrestrials"! We have always known this to be true! This was part of the reason I wrote the book *Hidden Mysteries*, which I humbly suggest is one of the best overviews and an easy to read and understand manner, of the entire extraterrestrial movement, as it has affected our planet. If you have not read this book, I highly recommend that you do so. It is truly fascinating reading! My strongest personal connection to the Extraterrestrials is with the Arcturians! The Arcturians are the most advanced Christed Extraterrestrial race in our galaxy. They hold the future blueprint for the unfoldment of this planet. The Arcturians are like our future planet and future selves on a collective level. Part of my work, along with the Ascended Master Teachings I have been asked to bring through, has been to bring through a more conscious and personal connection to the Arcturians, the Ashtar Command, and other such Christed Extraterrestrial races. This year's Platinum Wesak, because of being the year 2001, will have a special connection to these Christed Extraterrestrials, and we invite you all to attend for this reason and many others! I also encourage you to read my book "Beyond Ascension" where I explore some of my personal experiences with the Arcturians, and how you may do so as well!

Currently, behind the scenes, we are working on some further expansions of this aspect of our mission, which we will share at a later time! Wistancia has also been involved with White Time Healing, which is another most wonderful extraterrestrial healing modality that she offers to the public!

One other aspect of our mission deals with having developed with help from the inner plane Ascended Masters, some of the most advanced Ascension activation processes to accelerate Spiritual evolution that has ever been brought forth to this planet. In this co-creative process with the Masters, we have discovered the "keys to how to accelerate Spiritual evolution at a rate of speed that in past years and centuries would have been unimaginable! This is why I call working with the Ascended Masters "The Rocketship to GOD Method of Spiritual Growth." There is no faster path to God Realization than working with the Ascended Masters, Archangels and Angels, Elohim Masters and Christed Extraterrestrials! What is wonderful about this

Integrated Ascension

process is that you do not have to leave your current Spiritual practice, religion, or Spiritual path. Stay on the path you are and just integrate this work into what you are currently doing! All paths as you know, lead to GOD, my friends! This is the profundity of following an eclectic path, and path of synthesis! I humbly suggest I have found some short cuts! I share this with all lightworkers on earth, for I love GOD with all my heart and soul and mind and might, and I recognize that we are all incarnations of GOD, and Sons and Daughters of this same GOD, regardless of what religion, Spiritual path, or mystery school we are on. We are all, in truth, the Eternal Self and are all God! There is in truth only GOD, so what I share with you, I share with you, GOD, and myself for in the highest sense we are all one! What we each hold back from each other, we hold back from ourselves and from GOD. This is why I give freely all that I am, have learned and have, to you, my Beloved Readers, giving everything and holding back nothing! In my books and audiotapes, I have literally shared every single one of these ideas, tools, and Ascension activation methods for accelerating evolution that I have used and come to understand. My Beloved Readers, these tools and methods found in my books and on the audiotapes will "blow your mind as to their effectiveness," in terms of how profound, and easy to use they are! I would highly recommend that all lightworkers obtain the 13 Ascension Activation Meditation tapes I have put together for this purpose. Most of them were taped at the Wesak Celebrations with 1500 to 2000 people in attendance, with over one million inner plane Ascended Masters, Archangels and Angels, Elohim Masters, and Christed Extraterrestrials in attendance, under the Wesak full moon and the mountain of Mt Shasta. You can only imagine the power, love, and effectiveness of these Ascension activation audiotapes. I recommend getting all 13 tapes and working with one tape every day or every other day! I personally guarantee you that these tapes will accelerate your Spiritual evolution a thousand-fold! You can find them in the information packets and on our Website. They are only available

Integrated Ascension

from the Academy! Trust me on this, the combination of reading my books, Wistancia's book, and working with these audio ascension activation tapes, will accelerate your Spiritual evolution beyond your wildest dreams and imagination!

One other extremely important part of my mission, which is a tremendous Spiritual passion of mine, is the training of lightworkers on earth in the area of Spiritual/Christ/Buddha thinking and negative ego/separative/fear-based thinking! These are the only two ways of thinking in the world, and each person thinks with one, the other, or a combination of both. If a person does not learn how to transcend negative ego thinking and feeling, it will end up, over time, corrupting every aspect of their lives including all channeling work, Spiritual teaching, and even healing work! One cannot be wrong with self and right with GOD. This is because our thoughts create our reality, as we all know! I cannot recommend more highly that every person reading this, read my books *Soul Psychology, The Golden Book of Melchizedek: How to Become an Integrated Christ/Buddha in this Lifetime,* and *How to Release Fear-Based Thinking and Feeling: An In-depth Study of Spiritual Psychology*! I humbly suggest that these three books will be three of the most extraordinary self-help books in the area of mastering this psychological area of life. They are extremely easy to read, very practical and filled with tools that will help you in untold ways. The last two books I have mentioned are only available through the Academy. Being a channel for the Ascended Masters and being uniquely trained as a Spiritual Psychologist and Marriage, Family, and Child Counselor, as well as being raised in a family of psychologists, has given me an extraordinary ability to teach this material through my books in a most effective manner. The combination of my books on Ascension, and these books on Spiritual Psychology, along with Wistancia's book on the art of invocation will literally revolutionize your consciousness in the comfort of your own home! The most extraordinary thing about all this work is how incredibly easy to read, and easy to understand it is. It is

Integrated Ascension

also incredibly comprehensive, completely cutting-edge, and totally integrated, balanced, and synthesized. It contains the best of all schools of thought in the past, present, and channeled cutting edge future understanding that is available now! I humbly ask you to trust me in this regard and just read one of these books and you will immediately want to buy the others!

One other aspect of our work and mission is our involvement with the "Water of Life" and the Perfect Science products for the healing of our own physical bodies and the physical body of Mother Earth of all pollution, in the air, water and Earth. This is the miracle Mother Earth has been waiting for to bring her back to her "original edenic state" after so much abuse. This is not the time or the place to get into this subject in detail; however, I invite you to check out the "Water of Life" and the Perfect Science Information in the Information Packet and on the Academy Website! It is truly the miracle we have all been waiting for to help heal the earth!

One other aspect of our work and mission is a project that the Ascended Masters have asked us to put together on behalf of lightworkers and people around the globe. It is called the "Interdimensional Prayer Altar Program"! that the Masters have guided us to set up in the Academy in Agoura Hills, California on the property we live on. We have set up a "Physical Interdimensional Prayer Altar" where people can send in their prayers on any subject and we will place them on this Altar. In consultation with the Masters, Archangels and Angels, Elohim Masters, and Christed Extraterrestrials, we have set up an arrangement with them that all physical letters placed upon this Altar will be immediately worked upon by these Masters. We have been guided by the inner plane Ascended Masters to create 15 Prayer Altar Programs in different areas of life that people can sign up for. For example, there is one for health and one for financial help in your Spiritual mission. Two-thirds of these programs are totally free. There are five or six that are more advanced Spiritual acceleration programs where written material is sent to you to work with

Integrated Ascension

in conjunction with these programs so as to accelerate Spiritual growth. All letters we receive by e-mail, fax, or letter, are placed on the Altar by myself or my personal assistant. It is kept 100% confidential and is an extremely special service provided by the inner plane Ascended Masters and Angels to help all lightworkers and people on earth with immediate help for whatever they need, should they desire assistance. Other examples of Prayer Altars are: Building your Higher Light Body, Extra Protection, Relationship Help, World Service Prayers, Help for your Animals, Prayer Altar for the Children, Integrating the Goddess, Integrating your Archetypes, Integrating the Seven Rays and working with the Seven Inner Plane Ashrams of the Christ, Integrating the Mantle of the Christ, Ascension Seat Integration, and Light, Love, and Power Body Building Program! These Prayer Altar Programs have been co-created with the inner plane Ascended Masters as another tool for not only helping all lightworkers with whatever they need help with, but also as another cutting-edge tool to accelerate Spiritual evolution!

In a similar regard, the Masters have guided us to set up a Melchizedek Synthesis Light Academy Membership Program which is based on three levels of involvement. Stage One, Stage Two, and Stage Three! Stage One and Stage Three are totally free. Stage Two costs only $20 for a Lifetime Membership with no other fees required. You also receive free large colored pictures of Melchizedek, the Mahatma, Archangel Metatron, and Djwhal Khul for joining. It is not necessary to join to get involved in the work; however, it has been set up by the inner plane Ascended Masters as another service and tool of the Academy to help lightworkers accelerate their Spiritual evolution! When joining the different Stages, the Masters take you under their wing, so to speak, and accelerate your evolution by working with you much more closely on the inner plane while you sleep at night and during your conscious waking hours. The joining is nothing more than a process that gives them the permission to work with you in this more intensive fashion! Again, it is not necessary to join to get involved in the work, and is really just another one of the many fantastic tools and services the Academy has made available to you to accelerate your Spiritual, psychological, and earthly/physical evolution in an integrated and balanced manner!

I had a dream shortly after just about completing my two new books, *The Golden Book of Melchizedek: How To Become an Integrated Christ/Buddha in This Lifetime,* and my book *How To Release Fear-Based Thinking and Feeling: An In-depth Study of Spiritual Psychology*. In the dream, I was being shown the different Spiritual missions people had. My Spiritual mission was the embodiment of the Holy Spirit. I clearly was shown how other people within GOD, Christ, and the Holy Spirit had missions of being more detached off-shoots of the Holy Spirit, and continuing outward from there, had all kinds of different Spiritual missions. However, mine was the embodiment of the Holy Spirit on earth.

My Beloved Readers, I want to be very clear here that in sharing this I am in no way, shape, or form claiming to be the Holy Spirit. There is enough glamour in the New Age Movement and I am not interested in adding any more to it. What I am sharing here in this chapter, which is being given to more clearly and precisely share my Spiritual mission and purpose, is to share that which I am here to strive to embody and demonstrate. The Holy Spirit is the third aspect of the Trinity of GOD. I have always greatly loved the Holy Spirit, for the Holy Spirit is like the "Voice of GOD"! It is the "Still, Small Voice Within"! When one prays to GOD, it is the Holy Spirit who answers for GOD. The Holy Spirit is the answer to all questions, challenges, and problems. The Holy Spirit speaks for the Atonement or the At-one-ment! It teaches the Sons and Daughters of GOD how to recognize their true identity as God, Christ, the Buddha, and the Eternal Self! In truth, there are only two voices in life! There is the voice of the negative ego and the "Voice of the Holy Spirit"! There is the voice of negative ego/fear-based/separative thinking and feeling, and there is the Voice of God/Spiritual/Christ/Buddha thinking and feeling! There is the "Voice of Love" and the voice of fear! There is the "Voice of Oneness" and the voice of separation!

I was given this dream after completing these two books because, I humbly suggest, this is the energy I was embodying in writing them and that I am striving to embody at all times in my Spiritual mission and purpose on Earth. This is not surprising in the sense that this has always been my Spiritual ideal and the dream was just an inward confirmation in that moment that I was embodying and demonstrating that Spiritual Ideal in the energy flow I was in. This is what I strive to do in all my work, be it my Ascension Book Series, Wesak Celebrations, Teaching, Counseling, Videotapes, Audiotapes, and all my work, which is to strive to be the embodiment of a "Voice for God"! By the grace of GOD, Christ, the Holy Spirit, and the Masters, I provide a lot of the "answers" people and lightworkers are seeking! I teach people how to "undo" negative ego/fear-based/separative thinking and feeling, and show then how to fully realize God/Christ/Buddha thinking and feeling! I show them how to release and undo glamour, illusion, and maya, and instead seek "Truth, as GOD, Christ, the Holy Spirit, and the Masters would have you seek it!"

My real purpose, however, is not to just be the embodiment of the Holy Spirit on Earth, for I would not be embodying the Voice and Vision of the Holy Spirit if I just focused on this. The Voice and Vision of GOD, Christ, the Holy Spirit, and Melchizedek is that of synthesis! This is the other thing I feel in the deepest part of my heart and soul that I am here to embody! So my "truest and highest Spiritual ideal" that I am here to strive to embody, is GOD, Christ, the Holy Spirit, the inner plane Ascended Masters, the Archangels and Angels of the Light of GOD, the Elohim Councils of the Light of GOD, and the Christed Extraterrestrials of the Light of GOD. I feel in the deepest part of my heart and soul, and what I try to embody every moment of my life is "All that is of GOD and the Godforce on earth!" In this regard, it is my Spiritual mission and purpose to strive to be the embodiment of the

Integrated Ascension

"synthesis nature of God on Earth!" This is why I have been given Spiritual leadership of the Synthesis Ashram and Academy on earth and future leadership of the inner plane Synthesis Ashram that governs our Planet

The other thing I strive to do in my Spiritual mission is to embody Spiritual mastery on a Spiritual, psychological, and physical/earthly level. What most people and lightworkers do not realize is that there are three distinct levels to God Realization. There is a Spiritual level, a psychological level, and a physical/earthly level! To achieve true God Realization, all three levels must be equally mastered! Another way of saying this is that there are "Four Faces of GOD"! There is a Spiritual Face, a Mental Face, an Emotional Face, and a Material Face! To truly realize God, all four must be equally mastered, loved, honored, sanctified, integrated, and balanced! The "Mental and Emotional Faces of GOD" make up the psychological level of GOD. So, my Spiritual mission and purpose is to fully embody Spiritual mastery and unconditional love on all three of these levels and in all Four Faces of GOD! In a similar vein, my Spiritual mission and purpose is to embody self-mastery and proper integration of all "Seven Rays of GOD," not just one or a few. For the "Seven Rays of GOD" are, in truth, the true "Personality of GOD"! My Spiritual mission and purpose is to not only strive to embody all levels of GOD, but to also try and develop all my God-given abilities and Spiritual gifts, on a Spiritual, Psychological, and Physical/Earthly level, and in all Four Faces of GOD!

My Beloved Readers, all these things that I have written about in this chapter are what I strive to fully embody and demonstrate on the earth every moment of my life, and is what I strive with all my heart and soul and mind and might to teach others to do as well!

As the Founder and Director of the Melchizedek Synthesis Light Academy along with Wistancia, with great humbleness and humility, it has been my great honor and privilege to share "my Spiritual mission and purpose" in a deeper and more profound manner at this time. I do so in the hopes that all who feel a resonance and attunement with this work will get involved with the "Academy's Teachings" and all that it has to offer. I also share this so that all who choose to get involved might join this vast group of lightworkers around the globe, to help spread the teachings and work of the inner plane Ascended Masters. The inner plane Ascended Masters and I, along with the Archangels and Angels, Elohim Councils, and Christed Extraterrestrials, put forth the Clarion Call to lightworkers around the world to first explore this work, then integrate this work, and then become Ambassadors of the Ascended Masters, so we may at this time in Beloved Earth's history bring in fully now the Seventh Golden Age in all its Glory!

About the Author

Dr. Joshua David Stone has a Ph.D. in Transpersonal Psychology and is a Licensed Marriage, Family, and Child Counselor, in Agoura Hills, California. On a Spiritual level, he anchors *The Melchizedek Synthesis Light Academy and Ashram*, which is an integrated inner and outer plane ashram that seeks to represent all paths to God! He serves as one of the leading spokespersons for the Planetary Ascension Movement. Through his books, tapes, workshops, lectures, and annual Wesak Celebrations, Dr. Stone is known as one of the leading Spiritual Teachers and Channels in the world on the teachings of the Ascended Masters, Spiritual Psychology, and Ascension! He has currently written over 27 volumes in his "Ascension Book Series," which he also likes to call "The Easy to Read Encyclopedia of the Spiritual Path!"

For a free information packet of all Dr. Stone's workshops, books, audiotapes, Academy membership program, and global outreach program, please call or write to the following address:

Dr. Joshua David Stone
Melchizedek Synthesis Light Academy
28951 Malibu Rancho Rd
Agoura Hills, CA 91301

Integrated Ascension

Phone: 818-706-8458
Fax: 818-706-8540
e-mail: drstone@best.com

Please come visit my new Website at:
http://www.drjoshuadavidstone.com